On Being Different

Also Available from McGraw-Hill by Conrad Phillip Kottak

Anthropology: The Exploration of Human Diversity, 9th ed. (2002)

Cultural Anthropology, 9th ed. (2002)

Mirror for Humanity: A Concise Introduction to Cultural Anthropology, 3rd ed. (2003)

Assault on Paradise: Social Changes in a Brazilian Village, 3rd ed. (1999)

The Teaching of Anthropology: Problems, Issues, and Decisions, edited by Conrad Phillip Kottak, Jane White, Richard Furlow, and Patricia Rice (1997)

On Being Different:

Diversity and Multiculturalism in the North American Mainstream

SECOND EDITION

Conrad Phillip Kottak
University of Michigan

Kathryn A. Kozaitis
Georgia State University

Mc Graw Hill

Boston   Burr Ridge, IL   Dubuque, IA   Madison, WI   New York
San Francisco   St. Louis   Bangkok   Bogotá   Caracas   Kuala Lumpur
Lisbon   London   Madrid   Mexico City   Milan   Montreal   New Delhi
Santiago   Seoul   Singapore   Sydney   Taipei   Toronto

McGraw-Hill Higher Education

A Division of The McGraw-Hill Companies

ON BEING DIFFERENT:
DIVERSITY AND MULTICULTURALISM IN THE NORTH AMERICAN MAINSTREAM
Published by McGraw-Hill, a business unit of The McGraw-Hill Companies, Inc., 1221
Avenue of the Americas, New York, NY, 10020. Copyright © 2003, 1999 by The McGraw-Hill
Companies, Inc. All rights reserved. No part of this publication may be reproduced or
distributed in any form or by any means, or stored in a database or retrieval system, without
the prior written permission of The McGraw-Hill Companies, Inc., including, but not limited
to, in any network or other electronic storage or transmission, or broadcast for distance
learning.

Some ancillaries, including electronic and print components, may not be available to
customers outside the United States.
This book is printed on acid-free paper.

2 3 4 5 6 7 8 9 0 QWF/QWF 0 9 8 7 6 5 4 3

ISBN 0-07-241716-1

Editorial director: *Phillip A. Butcher*
Sponsoring editor: *Kevin Witt*
Developmental editor: *Pamela Gordon*
Senior marketing manager: *Daniel M. Loch*
Project manager: *Diane M. Folliard*
Production supervisor: *Carol A. Bielski*
Photo research coordinator: *Judy Kausal*
Photo researcher: *Barbara Salz*
Senior supplement producer: *Marc Mattson*
Cover design: *Mary E. Kazak*
Cover photo: © *LWA–Dann Tardif/corbisstock.com*
Typeface: *10/12 New Aster*
Compositor: *GAC Indianapolis*
Printer: *Quebecor World/Fairfield*

Library of Congress Cataloging-in-Publication Data
Kottak, Conrad Phillip.
    On being different : diversity and multiculturalism in the North American mainstream /
    Conrad Phillip Kottak, Kathryn A. Kozaitis.—2nd ed.
        p. cm.
    Includes bibliographical references and index.
    ISBN 0-07-241716-1 (softcover : alk. paper)
        1. Ethnology—North America. 2. Multiculturalism—North America. 3. Ethnicity—North
America. 4. Minorities—North America. 5. Social structure—North America. 6. North
America—Race relations. 7. North America—Social conditions. I. Kozaitis, Kathryn A.
II. Title.
GN550 .K67 2003
305.8'0097--dc21   2002075380

www.mhhe.com

To our students, who teach us about the struggles and privileges of being citizens of the world and architects of our multicultural society.

Contents in Brief

Contents

List of Boxes

About the Authors

CONRAD PHILLIP KOTTAK (A.B. Columbia College, 1963; Ph.D. Columbia University, 1966) is a professor and chair of the Department of Anthropology at the University of Michigan, where he has taught since 1968. In 1991 he was honored for his teaching by the University of Michigan and the state of Michigan. In 1992 he received an excellence in teaching award from the College of Literature, Science, and the Arts of the University of Michigan. And in 1999 the American Anthropological Association (AAA) awarded Professor Kottak the AAA/Mayfield Award for Excellence in the Undergraduate Teaching of Anthropology.

Professor Kottak has done ethnographic field work in Brazil (since 1962), Madagascar (since 1966), and the United States. His general interests are in the processes by which local cultures are incorporated—and resist incorporation—into larger systems. These interests link his earlier work on ecology and state formation in Africa and Madagascar to his more recent research on global change, national and international culture, and the mass media.

The third edition of Kottak's case study *Assault on Paradise: Social Change in a Brazilian Village,* based on his field work in Arembepe, Bahia, Brazil, was published in 1999 by McGraw-Hill. In "Television's Behavioral Effects in Brazil," a research project conducted during the 1980s, Kottak blended ethnography and survey research. This research is the basis of Kottak's book *Prime-Time Society: An Anthropological Analysis of Television and Culture* (Wadsworth 1990)—a comparative study of the nature and impact of television in Brazil and the United States.

Kottak's other books include *The Past in the Present: History, Ecology and Cultural Variation in Highland Madagascar* (1980), *Researching American Culture: A Guide for Student Anthropologists* (1982) (both University of Michigan Press), as well as *Madagascar: Society and History* (1986) (Carolina Academic Press). The most recent editions (ninth) of his texts *Anthropology:*

The Exploration of Human Diversity and *Cultural Anthropology* were published by McGraw-Hill in 2002. He is also the author of *Mirror for Humanity: A Concise Introduction to Cultural Anthropology*, whose third edition was published by McGraw-Hill in 2003.

Conrad Kottak's articles have appeared in academic journals including *American Anthropologist, Journal of Anthropological Research, American Ethnologist, Ethnology, Human Organization,* and *Luso-Brazilian Review.* He has also written for more popular journals, including *Transaction/SOCIETY, Natural History, Psychology Today,* and *General Anthropology.*

In recent research projects, Kottak and his colleagues have investigated the emergence of ecological awareness in Brazil, the social context of deforestation in Madagascar, and popular participation in economic development planning in northeastern Brazil. Since 1999 Professor Kottak has been active in the University of Michigan's Center for the Ethnography of Everyday Life, supported by the Alfred P. Sloan Foundation. In that capacity, for a research project entitled "Media, Family, and Work in a Middle-Class Midwestern Town," Kottak is now investigating how middle-class families draw on various media in planning, managing, and evaluating their choices and solutions with respect to competing demands of work and family.

Conrad Kottak appreciates comments about his books from professors and students. He can be readily reached by e-mail at ckottak@umich.edu.

KATHRYN A. KOZAITIS is an associate professor of anthropology and chair of the Department of Anthropology and Geography at Georgia State University. She is also the director of the Center for Hellenic Studies in the College of Arts and Sciences of Georgia State University. Dr. Kozaitis serves as adjunct faculty in the Department of Anthropology at Emory University in Atlanta, Georgia, and in 2002 she was a visiting assistant professor in the Department of Anthropology at the University of Michigan, in Ann Arbor. Dr. Kozaitis received her Ph.D. in social work and anthropology at the University of Michigan in 1993.

Her key interests are the relationship between global transformations and local adaptations, particularly the processes by which economically, politically, and socially subordinated collectivities use culture to construct community, identity, and meaning. Her work with Gypsies in Greece and Greeks in the United States has focused on ethnicity, cultural change, identity, and conscious adaptation to social marginality. In addition to her writings on these topics, Kozaitis has published articles on anthropological praxis, systemic change, and educational anthropology.

As an urban applied anthropologist she specializes in social intervention theory and method, community development, and educational reform. Presently she is conducting participatory action research on sustainable systemic reform in a predominantly African-American school district in Atlanta, Georgia. She is also engaged in a study on cultural competence in social service delivery to socioculturally diverse client populations.

Professor Kozaitis has taught popular courses on contemporary American society and culture; race, racism, and ethnicity; anthropological theory and praxis; complex societies; ethnographic analysis; and qualitative research methods. She has been recognized repeatedly for excellence in teaching by the Phi Beta Kappa Society and the College of Arts and Sciences at Georgia State University. She is the recipient of several grants from the National Science Foundation for her applied research, and the 2001 Praxis Award for outstanding achievement in applied anthropology. Her commitment to anthropological praxis finds expression in her many public seminars on the *cultural imperative* to health, education, and welfare reform.

Preface

OVERVIEW/APPROACH

We live and work in a rapidly changing society. In less than 50 years our economy has changed from the production of industrial goods to a proliferation of services—elite, highly skilled professions, and low-status skilled and unskilled service jobs. Our labor force is more diversified than ever. Women, people of color, sexual minorities, first-generation college graduates, and migrants from different parts of the world live and work with descendants of the conventional dominant class. Exposure to cultural diversity has never been greater. The need to appreciate human unity has never been more urgent.

An information age shapes images, experiences, emotions, and beliefs that unify us as a species. Communication technology intensifies contact between colleagues and friends across the globe and between members of families separated by choice or necessity. Global political and economic elites integrate societies and nations, albeit without the conscious consent of most citizens. But globalization does not a village make. People, caught in a global web of relations, are compelled to reconstruct a local web of relationships.

Global village is a contradiction in terms. Globalization generates villages, not a village. A social map of contemporary North America reveals countless culturally and politically identified human groups, with fluid, permeable boundaries and interlocked statuses. Distinct cultures, or affinity groups, which are becoming increasingly visible, struggle for security, power, legitimacy, and meaning in the face of a state in decline, and a society too large to protect all its citizens. Systems of classification and stratification, including race, ethnicity, religion, sexual orientation, and age, offer people a basis on which to build community and to claim human rights. Institutions, households, and affective relationships accommodate diversity and multiculturalism.

Today, a proper education is a multicultural education. In most colleges and universities, the systematic study of humanity through a liberal arts

curriculum requires attention to multiple histories, traditions, and symbols
that represent different peoples, places, and voices. Professional schools,
such as business, education, medicine, and social work schools, seek to prepare graduates for careers in serving a culturally diverse population of customers, students, patients, and clients.

**This book responds to a national call to understand, manage, and
live resourcefully within our multicultural society.** We address a wide
and continuing concern with sociocultural unrest in the daily life of North
Americans, particularly as this is affected by current demographic trends, a
global market, and geopolitical transformations. **We have written this
book in the belief that anthropology, the study of humanity, must be
central to curricula that emphasize cultural diversity.** Cultural diversity
is the hallmark of anthropology. More and more colleges and universities offer courses on human diversity and multiculturalism as electives or as graduation requirements. This book is intended to be used in diversity courses
in anthropology, sociology, social work, and education, or in a general college course designed to satisfy a diversity requirement.

Anthropology focuses increasingly on contemporary issues and societies, including those in the United States and Canada. Because of its focus
on human nature and culture, across time and space, anthropology contributes critically to discussions of diversity involving **culture, race, ethnicity, gender, sexual orientation, age, and other factors that make us
different**. Our increasing focus on problems and issues related to multiculturalism in North America adds value to the field within today's colleges and
universities, which have increasingly diverse student bodies and faculties.
**Teachers of courses on cultural diversity, including the "diversity re-
quirement" (sometimes called a race and ethnicity course), will benefit from a comprehensive, cross-cultural, and interdisciplinary
treatment of cultural diversity, identity politics, human rights movements, and multiculturalism.**

OUTLINE AND ORGANIZATION

On Being Different combines breadth and comprehensiveness in presenting
an introduction to the human condition and a critical analysis of mainstream North American practices and beliefs. As a thematic text it illuminates our understanding of human diversity, intrinsic to our society, and
multiculturalism, the basis of North American social organization in the
early 21st century. **An interdisciplinary and comparative perspective informs our discussion of topics and supports our argument.**

The second edition of *On Being Different* surveys major aspects of being
different—diversity—in an order we find logical, starting with culture, and
proceeding through ethnicity, race, religion, gender, sexual orientation; age
and generation; bodies, fitness, and health; class, place of residence, speech,

and family background. The book has an introduction and a conclusion that, respectively, set up and sum up the major themes of unity and diversity in contemporary multicultural North America. The book's contextual and theoretical frameworks are laid out most systematically in Chapters 3 ("Globalization, Identity, and Affinity") and 4 ("The Multicultural Society"), and again in Chapter 17 ("Conclusion"), but our theory is applied to specific topics and cases throughout the other chapters.

WHAT'S NEW IN THE SECOND EDITION

We did not change the chapter organization. Professors should feel free to assign chapters (except, probably, the first four) out of order. Many do so to reflect their individual teaching needs and approaches. Some assign only several of the book's 17 chapters. Others use the whole book.

One key change for this edition is the availability of an increasing amount of data from the U.S. 2000 Census, which have been incorporated throughout *On Being Different*. There are also several new reflection boxes and many new cases and topics. Following the advice of our reviewers, we've added new cases from around the world as well as from the United States and Canada.

Here are specific content changes, chapter by chapter:
In Chapter 1 ("Introduction"):

- There has been thorough updating, and new media examples have been added.
- The section titled "The Anthropological Perspective" has been substantially revised.

Chapter 2 ("Culture") contains:

- A new box, "United We Stand," which discusses the aftermath of September 11, 2001.
- Expanded discussions of culture and nature, and of how people use culture creatively.
- Expanded discussion of Canadian national culture.
- A new section, "The Uses of Culture."

Chapter 3 ("Globalization, Identity, and Affinity") features:

- A revised and expanded box, "From Mass Culture to Affinity Groups."
- Substantial revision and updating with data from the U.S. Census 2000.
- A new section, "Antiglobalization."

Chapter 4 ("The Multicultural Society") has:

- A new box, "Icarians in America."
- New examples of organization and agency within multicultural North America.

Chapter 5 ("Ethnicity") features:

- Thorough updating with data from the U.S. Census 2000.
- New information on ethnic diversity in Canada.

Chapter 6 ("Race: Its Social Construction") contains:

- A revised box, with a new discussion of color discrimination.
- Thorough updating with data from the U.S. Census 2000; a new discussion of how census data on race and ethnicity were gathered in 2000.
- A new discussion of silent racism.
- More attention to issues of ethnicity and race in Canada, including its "visible minorities."

Chapter 7 ("Race: Its Biological Dimensions") has:

- A new box, "You Can't Write Them Off Anymore," on innovation in public school curricula aimed at African-American children.
- New information on challenges to affirmative action.

Chapter 8 ("Religion") contains:

- Much more information on Islam.
- Much new information, including updated statistics and case studies, on religious diversity in the United States, Canada, and the world.
- A table summarizing key features of the world's major religions.
- A new section, "Social Control."
- A new section, "New and Alternative Religious Movements."
- New information on religious persecution.
- Discussion of the rave subculture within the context of secular religion.

Chapter 9 ("Gender") features:

- A new box, "Boys Will Be Men," which includes discussion of men's movements.
- A new section, "Patriarchy and Violence."
- Expanded discussions, with international scope, of the feminization of poverty and women's movements.
- Thorough updating of references and tables, including Census 2000 data.

Chapter 10 ("Sexual Orientation") has:

- A new box, "What's Sex Got to Do with It?" on gay parenting.
- A new section, "Varieties of Human Sexuality."

Chapter 11 ("Age and Generation") contains:

- New discussions of Generations X and Y.
- Thorough updating with data from the 2000 Census.
- A new section, "The Aging Process."

Chapter 12 ("Bodies, Fitness, and Health") features:

- More information on male/female contrasts in physical and mental health.

- An expanded and thoroughly updated discussion, "People with Disabilities."
- A new section, "Health and Healing in Cyberspace."

Chapter 13 ("Class") has:

- Updating on income distribution from the 2000 U.S. Census.
- A revised and updated discussion, "Poverty and Homelessness."
- A new section, "Diversity within Social Categories," discussing the intersection of race, class and culture.

Chapter 14 ("Where We Live") features:

- A new box, "It's Not Just a Zip Code; It's a Lifestyle."
- Updating from the 2000 U.S. Census.
- New discussion of reasons for migrating, in relation to jobs, region, housing, and educational status.
- New information on neighborhoods, ethnicity, and economic status.

Chapter 15 ("Speech") has:

- Information on nonverbal communication, related to gender differences.
- An expanded discussion of language and gender.
- A revised discussion of ebonics and Black English Vernacular.
- New information about discrimination based on speech.

Chapter 16 ("Family Background") features:

- A revised and shortened box, "We Are Family."
- A thoroughly updated and extensively revised discussion of changes in North American kinship patterns, based on Census 2000 data.
- Major new discussions of adoptive families, divorce, and single fathers.

Note, too, that we have modified the design of *On Being Different* so as to make it more attractive and more accessible, with new tables and figures throughout.

PEDAGOGY

This edition incorporates suggestions made by users of the first edition of *On Being Different,* as well as by nonusers whose input was solicited by McGraw-Hill. The result, we hope, is a sound, well-organized, interesting, and "user-friendly" introduction to diversity and multiculturalism.

Here are some of the distinguishing pedagogical features of this book:

Writing Style: Our students have taught us that material that is inaccessible, no matter how profound, is useless. They object even more to writing that excludes them deliberately, even when the content is of utmost importance to their intellectual development. We believe strongly that insights gained through anthropological research should be shared with as many people as possible. In this book, we write about topics that are critical, difficult, and controversial. We think that we do so in a style that is clear, enjoyable, and enlightening, in the hope of reaching all our readers and engaging them in productive conversations.

Reflection Boxes: On Being Different is written to inspire critical thinking. Each chapter starts with a box intended to give students a chance to reflect on aspects of their own life, their multicultural society, and today's complex world. Some boxes examine current events or debates, such as the controversy over ebonics. Others are more personal accounts, drawn from lived experiences that add feelings to our social science. Many boxes illustrate a point with examples from our own ethnographic research. Others rely on the findings of other anthropologists who have worked in various parts of the world. Students will recognize vignettes from their own enculturation and participation in society that demonstrate both cultural particularities and human universals.

Glossary: Each boldfaced term introduced in the various chapters is defined at the end of the book. Core anthropological concepts, as well as other social scientific terms and their meanings, expose readers to an interdisciplinary discussion of diversity and multiculturalism.

Bibliography: A bibliography of all cited references is also included. The subject matter of human diversity and multiculturalism is vast. This list of references is intended to guide students' inquiries and to encourage readers in the systematic study of more specialized knowledge in particular topics.

SUPPLEMENTS

As a full-service publisher of quality educational products, McGraw-Hill does much more than just sell textbooks. They create and publish an extensive array of print, video, and digital supplements for students and instructors. This edition of *On Being Different* includes an exciting supplements package. Orders of new (versus used) textbooks help to defray the cost of developing such supplements, which is substantial. Please consult your local McGraw-Hill representative for more information on any of the supplements.

For the Instructor: Instructor's Manual and Test Bank—this indispensable instructor supplement features chapter summaries, lecture ideas, experiential extensions, suggested films, and a complete test bank.

ACKNOWLEDGMENTS

We are grateful to many colleagues at McGraw-Hill. We thank Pam Gordon, freelance developmental editor, for her excellent ideas, suggestions, and guidance. Thanks also to Kevin Witt and Carolyn Henderson Meier, current and former sponsoring editors for anthropology at McGraw-Hill. We continue to enjoy working with Phil Butcher, McGraw-Hill's editorial director for social sciences and humanities. Conrad Kottak especially thanks Phil for his unflagging support during a friendship and association that has entered its second decade.

We thank Diane Folliard for her work as project manager, guiding the manuscript through production and keeping everything moving on schedule. It's been a delight, as always, to work with Barbara Salz, photo researcher. We thank Michael Hill for his excellent work on the supplements for both editions of *On Being Different*. We also thank Georgia Kornbluth for her copyediting; Mary Kazak for conceiving and executing the design; and Dan Loch, a knowledgeable, creative, and enthusiastic marketing manager. We are especially grateful to Tricia Lynn Fogarty for her assistance with the library research.

We are very grateful to the following prepublication reviewers of the second edition of *On Being Different* for their careful reading and useful suggestions:

ANTHONY BALZANO, SUSSEX COUNTY COMMUNITY COLLEGE

IONE Y. DEOLLOS, BALL STATE UNIVERSITY

PAUL GREBINGER, ROCHESTER INSTITUTE OF TECHNOLOGY

NAVITA CUMMINGS JAMES, UNIVERSITY OF SOUTH FLORIDA

RUTH ROBINSON SAXTON, GEORGIA STATE UNIVERSITY

SEIJI TAKAKU, MINNESOTA STATE UNIVERSITY, MANKATO

LAURA TAMAKOSHI, TRUMAN STATE UNIVERSITY

MARGARET WALLER, ARIZONA STATE UNIVERSITY

VALERIE WHEELER, CALIFORNIA STATE UNIVERSITY- SACRAMENTO

We were delighted by the enthusiasm expressed in these reviewers' comments, especially by those who have used *On Being Different* in their courses. We also thank those faculty and students who have taken the time to e-mail us with questions or comments about this book.

Anyone—student or instructor—with access to e-mail can reach us at the following addresses: ckottak@umich.edu and antkxk@panther.gsu.edu.

Our families have offered understanding, support, and inspiration during the preparation of both editions of *On Being Different*. Betty Kottak and Robert Springer have been effective sounding boards for and critics of our ideas. Our children, Juliet and Kreton Mavromatis, Nicholas Kottak, and Phillip and Robin Springer, have kept us on our toes as we have ventured to write about growing up American. Now we have Conrad Kottak's grandchildren, Lucas and Elena, to teach us new lessons.

We dedicate this book to our students, who teach us about the struggles and privileges of being citizens of the world and architects of our multicultural society.

Conrad Phillip Kottak
Ann Arbor, Michigan
ckottak@umich.edu

Kathryn A. Kozaitis
Atlanta, GA
antkxk@panther.gsu.edu

On Being Different

CHAPTER ONE

Introduction

UNITY AND DIVERSITY, ILLUSTRATED BY "STAR TREK," AN AMERICAN MYTH

The "Star Trek" myth, a familiar, powerful, and enduring force in the popular culture of the United States, can be used to illustrate the idea that popular media content often is derived from prominent values expressed in many other domains of culture. Americans first encountered the *Starship Enterprise* on NBC in 1966. The TV series *Star Trek* was shown in prime time for just three seasons. However, the series not only survives but thrives today in reruns, books, cassettes, theatrical films, and spinoff series. Revived as a regular weekly series with an entirely new cast in 1987, *Star Trek: The Next Generation* soon became the third most popular syndicated program in the United States (after *Wheel of Fortune* and *Jeopardy*). More recent spinoff series include *Deep Space Nine, Star Trek: Voyager,* and *Enterprise.*

What does the enduring mass appeal of *Star Trek* tell us about American culture? We suggest that the answer is this: "Star Trek" is a transformation of a fundamental American origin myth about unity and diversity. The same myth shows up in the image and celebration of Thanksgiving, a distinctively American holiday. Thanksgiving sets the myth in the past, and "Star Trek" sets it in the future.

Encountering the word *myth*, which comes from the Greek for "what they say," most people probably think of stories about Greek, Roman, or Norse gods and heroes. However, all societies have myths. Their central characters need not be unreal, superhuman, or physically immortal. Such tales may be rooted in actual historical events. The popular notion that a myth is untrue—indeed, that its untruth is its defining characteristic—is not only naive but shows misunderstanding of its very nature. Its scientific truth or otherwise is irrelevant. A myth is a statement about society, and our place

Thanksgiving is a national holiday celebrated by most Americans, including Protestants, Catholics, Jews, and African Americans. Kwanzaa, on the other hand, a holiday begun in 1966, which specifically celebrates African-American heritage, is of increasing importance in a multicultural society. Here Charles Tymony, front, and others sing a hymn at the 18th annual Kwanzaa candle lighting ceremony in Los Angeles in 1995. Do you celebrate a holiday like Kwanzaa?

in it and in the surrounding universe (Middleton 1967, p. x). Myths are hallowed stories that express fundamental cultural values. They are widely and recurrently told among, and have special meaning to, people who grow up in a particular culture. Myths may be set in the past, present, or future, or in fantasyland. Whether set in real time or fictional time, myths are always at least partly fictionalized.

The myths of contemporary America are drawn from a variety of sources, including such popular-culture fantasies as the *Star Wars* films, *The Wizard of Oz*, and *Star Trek*. Our myths also include real people, particularly national ancestors, whose lives have been reinterpreted and endowed with special meaning over the generations. The media, schools, churches, communities, and parents teach the national origin myths to American children. The story of Thanksgiving, for example, continues to be important. It recounts the origin of a national holiday celebrated by Protestants, Catholics, and Jews. All those denominations share a belief in the Old Testament God, and they find it appropriate to thank God for their blessings.

Again and again Americans have heard idealized retellings of that epochal early harvest. We have learned how Indians taught the Pilgrims to farm in the New World. Grateful Pilgrims then invited the Native Americans to share their first Thanksgiving. Native American and European labor, techniques, and customs thus blended in that initial biethnic celebration. Annually reenacting the origin myth, American public schools commemorate the first Thanksgiving as children dress up as Pilgrims, Indians, and pumpkins.

More rapidly and pervasively as the mass media grow, each generation of Americans writes its own revisionist history. Our culture constantly reinterprets the origin, nature, and meaning of national holidays. The collective consciousness of contemporary Americans includes TV-saturated memories of the first Thanksgiving and the first Christmas. Our mass culture has instilled widely shared images of a Peanuts-peopled Pilgrim–Indian "love-in." We also conjure up a fictionalized Nativity with Mary, Joseph, Jesus, manger animals, shepherds, three kings of Orient, a little drummer boy, and, in some versions, Rudolph the Red-Nosed Reindeer. Note that the interpretation of the Nativity that American culture perpetuates is yet another variation on the same dominant myth. We remember the Nativity as a Thanksgiving involving interethnic contacts (e.g., the three kings) and gift giving. It is set in Bethlehem rather than Massachusetts.

We impose our present on the past as we reinterpret quasi-historic and actual events, such as the sinking of the *Titanic*. For the future we do it in our science-fiction and fantasy creations. *Star Trek* places in the future what the Thanksgiving story locates in the past—the myth of the assimilationist, incorporating, melting-pot society. The myth says that America is distinctive not just because it is assimilationist but because the nation is founded on unity in diversity. (America's origin is unity in diversity. After all, we call ourselves the *United* States.) Thanksgiving and *Star Trek* illustrate the credo that unity through diversity is essential for survival, whether of a harsh winter or of the perils of outer space. Americans work, cope, and survive by sharing the fruits of specialization.

Star Trek proclaims that the sacred principles that validate American society, because they lie at its foundation, will endure across the generations, even the centuries. The original *Starship Enterprise* crew was a melting pot. Captain James Tiberius Kirk was symbolic of real history. His clearest historical prototype was Captain James Cook, whose ship, the *Endeavor*, also sought out new life and civilizations. Kirk's infrequently mentioned middle name, from the Roman general and eventual emperor, linked the captain to the earth's imperial history. Kirk was also symbolic of the original Anglo-American. He ran the *Enterprise* (America is founded on free enterprise), just as laws, values, and institutions derived from England continue to run the United States.

McCoy's Irish (or at least Gaelic) name represented the next wave, the established immigrant. Sulu was the successfully assimilated Asian American. The African-American female character Uhura, whose name means "freedom," confirmed that blacks would become partners with all other Americans. Yet Uhura was the only major female character in the original crew. Female work outside the home was much less characteristic of American society in 1966 than it is today.

One of the constant messages of *Star Trek* is that strangers, even ene-mies, can become friends. Less obviously, this message is about cultural im-perialism, the assumed irresistibility of American culture and institutions. Through Chekhov's inclusion, who could doubt that Russian nationals would one day succumb to an expansive American culture? Spock, though from Vulcan, was half human, with human qualities. We learn, therefore, that our assimilationist values will eventually not just rule the earth but ex-tend to other planets as well. By *The Next Generation*, Klingon culture, even more alien than Vulcan culture, personified by Bridge Officer Worf, had joined the melting pot. Other aliens have been added to later crews.

Even God was harnessed to serve American culture, in the person of Scotty. His role was that of the ancient Greek *deus ex machina*. He was a stage controller who "beamed" people up and down, back and forth, from earth to the heavens. Scotty, who kept society going, was also a servant-employee who did his engineering for management, illustrating loyalty and technical skill.

The Next Generation offered many analogues of the original characters. Several "partial people" served as single-character personifications of par-ticular human qualities represented in more complex form by the original crew members. Kirk, Spock, and McCoy were all split into multiple charac-ters. Captain Jean-Luc Picard possessed the intellectual and managerial at-tributes of James T. Kirk. With his English accent and Kirk-like French name, Picard, like Kirk, drew his legitimacy from symbolic association with historic western European empires. First Officer Riker (almost a Kirk ana-gram) took over from Kirk as the romantic man of action.

Spock, an alien (strange ears) who represented science, reason, and in-tellect, was split in two. One half was Worf, a Klingon bridge officer whose cranial protuberances were analogues of Spock's ears. The other was Data, an android whose brain contained the sum of human wisdom. Two female characters, an empath and the ship's doctor, were analogues of Dr. McCoy as the repository of healing, emotion, and feeling.

Mirroring a changing American culture, *The Next Generation* featured prominent black, female, and physically handicapped characters. An African-American actor played the Klingon Mr. Worf. Another, LeVar Bur-ton, became Geordi La Forge. Although blind, Geordi was not really visually impaired; he managed, through his visor, to see things other people could not. His mechanical vision expressed the American faith in technology. So did the android, Data. During its first year, *The Next Generation* had three prominent female characters. One was the ship's doctor, a working profes-sional with a teenage son. Another was an empath, the ultimate helping pro-fessional. The third was the ship's security officer.

The United States by the late 1980s had become, and by now is even more, specialized, differentiated, and professional than it was in the sixties. The greater role specificity and diversity of *The Next Generation* charac-ters reflect this. Nevertheless, both series convey the central message of the "Star Trek" myth, a message that dominates the culture that created them:

Humans are social animals. We habitually work together in a crew, team, enterprise, or, most generally, a society. We often have to subordinate our personal differences, identities, and preferences to the demands of teamwork. Shown here, a weekly team meeting at Daimler-Chrysler's Jefferson-North assembly plant in Detroit. What kinds of teams do you belong to?

Americans have varied backgrounds. Individual qualities, talents, and specialties divide us. However, we make our livings and survive as members of cohesive, efficient groups. We explore and advance as members of a crew, a team, an enterprise, or, most generally, a society. Our nation is founded on and endures through effective subordination of individual differences within a smoothly functioning multiethnic team. The team is American culture. It worked in the past. It works today. It will go on working across the generations. Orderly and progressive democracy based on mutual respect is best. Inevitably, American culture will triumph over all others—by convincing, attracting, and assimilating rather than conquering them. Unity in diversity guarantees human survival, and for this we should be thankful.

Now apply these observations about American values involving unity and diversity to a contemporary example. Some possibilities: MTV's *The Real World*, NBC's medical drama *ER*, and one of several TV programs about lawyers. Also consider issues of unity and diversity involved in the mobilization of American society following the events of September 11, 2001. How were unity and diversity expressed as the Bush administration worked to build "an international coalition against terrorism"? If you live in the South, think of how the national push toward unity changed the symbolic use of diverse flags (e.g., U.S. and Confederate). ☺

AMERICAN CULTURE AND CULTURES

In this book we draw on anthropology's distinctive comparative and cross-cultural perspectives to shed light on aspects of diversity and multicultural-ism in contemporary North America. We'll examine many forms and aspects of sociocultural diversity, based on such variables as ethnicity, race, religion, gender, age, class, occupation, region, sexual orientation, and dif-ferential "abledness." This book extends work on American culture that one of us (Conrad Kottak) has been doing since 1976. Kottak's early work on the United States focused on American mass culture and popular culture (see Kottak 1982). His main focus then was on unifying themes, values, and be-havior in American national culture—institutions and experiences that tran-scend particular regions and social divisions. Kathryn Kozaitis has studied cultural diversity in the United States, and has worked directly with a num-ber of minority groups, for more than two decades. More recently, reflecting changes in American culture and in American studies, both Kottak and Kozaitis have focused on the range of American cultures and on the role that culture is playing in the organization and transformation of North American society. Our interests in diversity, cultures, and culture as an or-ganizing principle orient this book.

A 1992 Internal Review document of the University of Michigan Ameri-can Culture Program gives a clear exposition of such a *multi*cultural model. It recognizes "the multiplicity of American cultures." It presents multicul-turalism as a new approach to the central question in American studies: What does it mean to be an American? The document suggests a shift from the study of core myths and values, and people's relationships to them as generalized Americans, to "recognizing that 'America' includes people of differing community, ethnic, and cultural histories, different points of view and degrees of empowerment." Such a perspective encourages studies of specific ethnic and other kinds of groups, rather than of the country as a whole.

We believe that the newer multicultural model and the older national approach to North American culture should not be mutually exclusive. We still detect a series of nationally relevant institutions, norms, values, and ex-pectations to which various culturally defined groups within the United States eventually subscribe. The pressure for members of an ethnic group to observe "general American values" may come not only from the mass media and other agents of national culture but also from other ethnic groups. For instance, in interviews with various ethnic groups in Los Angeles following the riots of 1992, blacks complained about Koreans. In doing so, the African Americans invoked a general American value system that included friendli-ness, openness, mutual respect, community participation, and fair play. They saw their Korean neighbors as deficient in these traits. The Koreans countered by stressing another set of American national values, involving education, family unity, discipline, hard work, and achievement.

THE ANTHROPOLOGICAL PERSPECTIVE

What does it mean to say that we approach North American cultural diversity from an anthropological perspective? A brief introduction to anthropology is needed here. Anthropology differs from other fields that study human beings because it is holistic, comparative, and global. Anthropology is **holistic** because it studies the whole of the human condition—biological and cultural variation in time and space. Anthropologists study human biology, language, society, and culture, past and present, in all cultures, ancient and modern, simple and complex. Anthropologists also study our prehuman ancestors and our nearest primate relatives—monkeys (such as baboons) and apes (such as chimpanzees and gorillas). Anthropology has four main subfields: sociocultural, archaeological, biological, and linguistic anthropology. There are historical reasons for the inclusion of these four in a single field. American anthropology developed more than a century ago out of concern for the history and cultures of the native populations of North America (American Indians). Interest in the origins and diversity of Native Americans brought together the study of customs, social life, language, and physical traits. Now anthropologists have turned their attention to contemporary North America and the range of diversity it encompasses today.

An anthropological perspective explains human nature, illuminates human similarities and differences, describes contemporary societies and cultures, and increases our empathy for human groups who struggle to achieve security and integrity. What are some examples of the value of an anthropological approach? Studies of sex and friendship among baboons shed light on how human families and communities are formed and maintained. Human growth and development, including diversity in people's height and weight, reflect differences in genetic inheritance, and their interaction with the environment. Transnational migration changes both the sending and receiving societies of migrants and refugees, who create new, hybrid cultures in their adopted homelands. People construct and maintain ethnic boundaries to distinguish themselves from others and to express their cultural integrity. Anthropology helps us understand human diversity and multiculturalism as key components of North American society.

Researchers in the field of **sociocultural anthropology,** or, simply, **cultural anthropology,** describe and attempt to interpret and explain similarities and differences among societies and cultures. To become a cultural anthropologist, one normally does **ethnography,** or ethnographic research. This firsthand, field-based study of a particular culture usually entails spending a year or more in the field, living with local people and learning about their customs. Traditional ethnographers studied small, nonliterate (without writing) populations and developed research methods appropriate to that context. "Ethnography is a research process in which the anthropologist closely observes, records, and engages in the daily life of another culture—an experience labeled as the fieldwork method—and then writes accounts of this culture, emphasizing descriptive detail" (Marcus and Fischer 1986, p. 18). Kottak has done such field research in Brazil, the western hemisphere's second most populous country, and in Madagascar, a large island off the southeastern coast of Africa. He is now studying issues of work and family among the American middle class. Kozaitis did her major fieldwork with urban Gypsies in Athens, Greece, and has subsequently worked on educational reform in the Atlanta Public Schools. In the chapters that follow, our own field experiences, along with ethnographic accounts by many others, serve as a basis for our comparative statements about aspects of human diversity across space and time.

This book reflects our belief that, despite the added value of ethnography, the survey research so typical of sociology remains indispensable for understanding large, populous nations, in which we must pay particular attention to variation. Survey researchers gather information about age, gender, religion, occupation, income, and political party preference. These characteristics—**variables,** or attributes that vary among members of a sample or population—are known to influence beliefs and behavior, including political decisions. Gender, for example, is a useful predictor of political-party affiliation and voting behavior. More men than women claim to be Republicans, and men are more likely to vote for candidates of that party than women are. Besides gender, all nations have role specializations based on age, profession, social class, and many other contrasts.

Many more variables affect social identities, experiences, and activities in a modern nation than in the small communities and local settings where ethnography grew up. Today, hundreds of factors influence our social behavior and attitudes. Such *social predictors* or *social indicators* include our religion; the region of the country we grew up in; whether we come from a town, suburb, or inner city; and our parents' professions, ethnic origins, and income levels. Because we must be able to detect, measure, and compare the influence of social indicators, many contemporary anthropological studies have a statistical foundation. Statistical analysis can support and round out an ethnographic account of local social life.

However, in the best anthropological studies of modern nations, the hallmark of ethnography remains: Anthropologists enter the community and get to know the people. They participate in local activities, networks, and associations. They observe and experience social conditions and problems. They watch the effects of national policies and programs on local life. They listen, observe, and learn. In a changing cultural context, they seek relevant questions as well as answers. The ethnographic method and its emphasis on case materials and personal relations in social research are valuable gifts that anthropology brings to the study of a complex society.

Anthropologists can transfer the personal, direct, observation-based techniques of ethnography to social groups and social networks in any setting. A combination of survey research and ethnography can provide new perspectives on life in **complex societies** (large and populous societies with social stratification and central governments).

Science, Humanities, and Mirror for Humanity

In the 21st century, the overwhelming majority of the world's population, along with a large percentage of the populations of the United States and Canada, will be descendants of the non-Western groups that anthropologists have traditionally studied. By 2025, developing countries will account for 85 percent of the world's population, compared with 77 percent in 1992 (Stevens 1992). The population of Canada is growing more rapidly than the populations of the United States or western Europe. More than half that growth is from immigration. Solutions to future North American social problems will depend increasingly on understanding non-Western cultural backgrounds.

As the field that focuses on that understanding, anthropology is simultaneously a science, a humanities field, and a mirror for humanity. It is a **science** because it is a "systematic field of study or body of knowledge that aims, through experiment, observation, and deduction, to produce reliable explanations of phenomena, with reference to the material and physical world" (*Webster's New World Encyclopedia* 1993, p. 937). Science is based on *cumulative knowledge* (Ember and Ember 1997), of which anthropology has an impressive amount. Clyde Kluckhohn (1944, p. 9) called anthropology "the science of human similarities and differences." His statement of the need for such a science still stands: "Anthropology provides a scientific basis for dealing with the crucial dilemma of the world today: how can peoples of different appearance, mutually unintelligible languages, and dissimilar ways of life get along peaceably together?"

Anthropology is also linked to the humanities, for several reasons. It applies a comparative and nonelitist perspective to the **humanities,** which study art, narratives, music, dance, and other forms of creative expression. Anthropology influences and is influenced by the humanities. For example, adopting a view of creativity in its varied social and cultural contexts, current approaches in the humanities are shifting the focus away from elite art forms toward mass and popular culture and local creative expressions. Another area of convergence between anthropology and the humanities is the view of cultural expressions as patterned texts (Ricoeur 1971; Geertz 1973). Thus "unwritten behavior, speech, beliefs, oral tradition, and ritual" (Clifford 1988, p. 39) can be approached as a corpus to be interpreted in relation to *meaning* within a particular cultural context. Anthropology, we think, is the most humanistic of the academic fields, because of its fundamental respect for human diversity. Anthropologists listen to, record, and represent voices from a multitude of nations and cultures. We strive to convince our students of the value of local knowledge, of diverse world views and perspectives.

Anthropology's longtime focus on cultural diversity should be cherished as colleges and universities increasingly require courses on diversity or multiculturalism. Kottak has noticed that many of the strongest advocates of a diversity requirement (or "race and ethnicity course," as it is called at the University of Michigan) know little about anthropology. Some people who advocate a diversity requirement only want to have other *American* voices represented, not voices from around the world, voices anthropologists have been heeding for years. Anthropologists need to get our perspectives and cumulative knowledge across to such people. This is a major goal of this book.

A final basic role is anthropology as a *mirror for humanity,* a term derived from Clyde Kluckhohn's metaphor.

> Ordinarily we are unaware of the special lens through which we look at life. It would hardly be fish who discovered the existence of water. Students who had not yet gone beyond the horizon of their own society could not be expected to perceive custom which was the stuff of their own thinking. *Anthropology holds up a great mirror to man and lets him look at himself in his infinite variety.* (Kluckhohn 1944, p. 16—his emphasis)

In making this point, we wish also to invoke the name of one of Kottak's teachers, Margaret Mead. Although Kluckhohn wrote the popular book called *Mirror for Man,* we'll always remember Mead for her unparalleled success in demonstrating anthropology's value and relevance in allowing Americans to reflect on cultural diversity and variation and the plasticity of human nature. Mead conveyed the anthropological perspective to a broad public in a way no contemporary anthropologist does. She represented anthropology so effectively because she viewed it as *a humanistic science of unique value in understanding and improving the human condition.* We share that vision of the field. Our goal here is to apply it to the cultures of contemporary North America.

CHAPTER TWO

Culture

"United We Stand"

Semester after semester, by the second week of class, at least one "white" student will exclaim, "I didn't know I had a culture!" Many Americans are surprised (and pleased) to learn that, among all the foreign and ethnic cultures that surround them, there is one culture they may claim as their own.

American culture is built on unity and diversity. Historically, the United States has been represented as a nation of White Anglo-Saxon Protestants (WASPs)—people of northern European extraction, with mostly English, but also Scottish and Welsh, ancestry. This depiction of American society has never been accurate. The boundaries of the United States have always included Native Americans (called First Nations in Canada), soon to be joined by Africans and Asians. Since its exploration by Europeans began, North America has included Spanish and French, as well as English, speakers. Today, migrants from many countries, along with the descendants of various immigrant groups, occupy North American soil. All contemporary Americans, to some extent, regardless of their national origin or ancestry (often mixed), participate in a common culture (patterned ways of behaving and thinking).

Cultural unity in American society is depicted in traditions, customs, and rituals, including Thanksgiving dinner and Valentine's Day, graduation ceremonies and bridal showers, serial monogamy, and the Super Bowl.

Americans, as a society, invent new traditions and core values that reflect social transformations. *Environmentalism* is exemplified by recycling. A concern for public health translates into safe sex and fitness programs. Other prevalent patterns in American culture include peer influence, fictive kin ties (close relationships between unrelated persons that mimic biological kinship), and living among and with strangers. Because work is the key organizing condition of our social life, we spend most hours of our day with people we don't love and, worse yet, often with people we don't like! Millions of American children are reared in child care centers and by "blended families." Retirement communities house adults who have become peripheral to the labor force and to the family. Support groups, through which Americans acquire comfort and a sense of belonging, have risen in association with numerous disorders, illnesses, and tragedies. Psychotherapists and other helping professionals, also known as "formal support systems," have become the best friends money can buy. What other examples can you think of that support the argument that Americans in fact are, and have, *a* culture?

The multicultural movement has brought a new consciousness to North Americans, who now see culture as an equal opportunity good—something all people possess. In this view, an Italian festival in New York's Little Italy is as much a signifier of culture as is *Carmen* at the opera house. Going to a concert by Gypsy Kings is as much a cultural experience as is attending Sartre's play *No Exit*. A Gay Pride celebration in Atlanta may rival Chicago's St. Patrick's Day Parade in media attention. Literature on women's culture occupies its own wall in bookstores. The disabled, as a social category, are distinguished by their abilities. To be sure, ranking of cultures persists. However, the realization that all people, including nonethnic Americans, have culture, has never been stronger.

Integral to contemporary American mass culture is human diversity. To be mainstream today increasingly means to be multicultural—exposed to and tolerant of, if not active in, a myriad of customs, traditions, and rituals. Appropriation by Americans of symbols, styles, and artifacts external to their national origins is common. Our public and private lives are permeated by forces and influences that may have little to do with our ancestral cultures, and everything to do with a common experience at a particular moment in history. A struggle, crisis, tragedy, or threat mobilizes people to unite, organize, and fight as one, transcending their differences to protect their common, human rights. At no time in recent American history was this process more evident than in fall 2001, following the September 11 terrorist attack on the United States.

Patriotism among Americans, across lines of race, ethnicity, class, age, region, and religion, arose instantaneously to counter what millions of Americans perceived as a threat to the very core of their society. There was a powerful resurgence of nationalism among citizens of the United States. The historic national ideal "Out of Many, One," in the face of threats seen by Americans as potential *ethnocide,* became reality. According to "America's Mayor," Rudolph W. Giuliani (2001),

We know that this was not just an attack on the City of New York or the United States of America. It was an attack on the very idea of a free, inclusive and civil society. The victims were of every race, religion and ethnicity, representing 80 different nations. Americans are not a single ethnic group. Americans are not of one race or one religion. We are defined as Americans by our belief in political, economic, and religious freedom, democracy, the rule of law, and respect for human life.

A self-conscious, collective expression of a common culture by a people is readily and invariably depicted in symbols. Visual markers of culture serve to construct a distinct identity, and to erect and maintain boundaries of exclusion. Artifacts, words, colors, and accessories, which people imbue with meaning, validate and strengthen a sense of peoplehood. In what ways did Americans visually express their national unity following the terrorist attacks? Pause for a moment and reflect on the landscape that surrounds you. What signs, or messages of an American culture abound as never before, and demand your attention?

Whatever the sentiments, interpretations, and uses of the American flag have been historically, this symbol of American identity was embraced, adopted, and displayed by more citizens after September 11, 2001, than ever before. At the time of this writing (February 2002), neighborhoods are still dotted by stars and stripes. Red, white, and blue, the color scheme in vogue, decorate malls, human service organizations, businesses, schools, parks,

Selling American flags in New York's Chinatown after the September 11, 2001, terrorist attack on America. What kinds of symbols do you see in the photo? What do they stand for?

and shops across rural, suburban, and urban America. Bumper stickers, scarves, hats, T-shirts, and jewelry that boast the American flag constitute a cultural commodity affordable by all and profitable for some. The colorful, lighted sign "Support Our President" welcomes patrons of an XXX-rated adult club in downtown Atlanta.

What is our take-home lesson from the tragedy that paralyzed America, and from the ways in which Americans joined as one people to grieve their loss and respond to this threat to their collective well-being? Danger begets action. Just as a personal tragedy may turn into a political crusade, the threat of genocide or ethnocide may generate nationalism and ethnocentrism. Historically, victimized populations, such as Gypsies the world over, Jews and Armenians in Europe, and Native Americans and African Americans in the United States, have responded to such threats by constructing and strengthening an inclusive in-group or nation. Social solidarity is adaptive for groups threatened by discrimination, oppression, or extinction on the basis of their cultural orientation.

As you read the rest of the book, you will understand the powerful role that culture, an adaptive capacity among humans, plays in biological survival, social reproduction, and political integrity. The proliferation of nationalism in the world, and multiculturalism, in the form of culturally defined affinity groups, in the United States and Canada is, at the core, an adaptation to death and an expression of life. Americans' solitary response to terrorism parallels the responses by minorities in our society to the groups and circumstances that threaten them. Any self-conscious collectivity, by mobilizing, uniting, and fighting for their human rights, expresses their humanity and their agency in a society that prides itself on being "the land of the free and the home of the brave." ☻

CULTURE AND ITS ASPECTS

Human beings share society (organized life in groups) with other animals. Culture, however, is distinctly human. The term **culture** refers to a way of life—traditions and customs—transmitted through learning, which play a vital role in molding the beliefs and behavior of the people exposed to them. Children learn these traditions by growing up in a society, through a process called *enculturation*. Cultures include customs and opinions, developed over the generations, about proper and improper behavior. Cultural traditions answer such questions as: How do we do things? How do we make sense of the world? How do we tell right from wrong? A culture tends to produce consistencies in behavior and thought among people who live in the same society.

A critical feature of culture is its transmission through learning. For hundreds of thousands of years, humans have had at least some of the biological capacities on which culture depends. These abilities are to learn, to think symbolically, to use language, and to use tools and other cultural means of organizing their lives and adapting to their environments.

The concept of culture has long been basic to *anthropology* (the study of human biological and cultural diversity in time and space). More than a century ago, in his classic book *Primitive Culture,* the British anthropologist Edward Tylor gave a definition of culture that is still more widely quoted than any other: "Culture . . . is that complex whole which includes knowledge, belief, arts, morals, law, custom, and any other capabilities and habits acquired by man as a member of society" (Tylor 1871/1958, p. 1). The key words here are "acquired . . . as a member of society." Tylor's definition points to beliefs and behavior that humans obtain not through biological heredity but by growing up in a particular society. As they grow up they are exposed to a specific cultural tradition. **Enculturation** is the process by which a child learns his or her culture.

Culture Is Learned   Each of us grows up in the presence of a set of rules and expectations transmitted across the generations. The ease with which children absorb any cultural tradition reflects the unique human capacity to learn. Cultural traditions, or more simply, cultures, are transmitted through learning and language. Each infant begins immediately, through learning and interaction with others, to incorporate a cultural tradition. Sometimes culture is taught directly, as when parents tell kids, "Say thank you" or "Don't talk to strangers." Culture is also learned through observation, as children pay attention to what goes on around them. Children may change their behavior because other people tell them to do so. They also learn from experience—by seeing examples of what their culture considers right and wrong and of what happens to people who violate norms.

Culture is also absorbed unconsciously. Consider how we internalize norms about how far apart people should stand when they talk. No one ever instructs us to maintain a specific distance when we speak to someone. Instead people learn their culture's idea of proper "social spacing" through a gradual process of observation, experience, and conscious and unconscious behavior modification. No one tells Latin Americans to stand closer together than North Americans do, but they learn to do so anyway as part of their cultural tradition.

Culture Is Shared   Culture is transmitted in society and across generations. We learn a culture by watching, listening and talking to, learning from, and being with other people. Individual members of a given culture share many memories, beliefs, values, expectations, and ways of thinking and acting. Enculturation unifies people by providing them with common experiences and knowledge.

Adults become agents in the enculturation of their children, just as their parents were for them. Culture constantly changes, but certain beliefs, values, and child-rearing practices persist. Consider a simple American example of enduring shared enculturation. As children, when we didn't finish a meal, our parents reminded us of starving children in some foreign country. A generation earlier, our grandparents probably said something similar to

Muslim men and boys worship in a mosque in Brunei, located in the northwest of the island of Borneo. What aspects of culture are illustrated?

our parents' pronouncement. The specific country changes (China, India, Bangladesh, Ethiopia, Somalia). Still, American enculturators go on suggesting that by eating all our brussels sprouts, broccoli, or spinach we can justify our own good fortune, compared to a hungry foreign child.

Despite the American value of individualism—including the belief that people should make up their own mind and have a right to their opinion—little of what we think is original or unique. Because of enculturation, we share our opinions and beliefs with many other people. Illustrating the power of a shared cultural background, we are most likely to feel comfortable with people from our own culture. **Culture shock** refers to disturbed feelings that often arise when one has contact with an unfamiliar culture, either in North America or, more usually, abroad. It is a feeling of alienation, of being without some of the most ordinary and basic cues of one's culture of origin. Usually culture shock passes if one stays in the new culture long enough.

Culture Is Symbolic   Cultural learning is based on the unique human capacity to use symbols (signs that have no necessary or natural connection to the things they stand for). During enculturation, people gradually internalize a system of meanings and symbols that are part of their culture. Symbolic thought is crucial to humans and to culture. The anthropologist Leslie White saw culture as:

dependent upon symbolling. . . . Culture consists of tools, implements, utensils, clothing, ornaments, customs, institutions, beliefs, rituals, games,
works of art, language, etc. (White 1959, p. 3)

For White, culture originated when our ancestors acquired the ability to
use symbols:

freely and arbitrarily to originate and bestow meaning upon a thing or
event, and, correspondingly, . . . to grasp and appreciate such meaning.
(White 1959, p. 3)

A **symbol** is something verbal or nonverbal, in a language or culture,
that comes to stand for something else. There is no obvious, natural, or necessary connection between the symbol and that which it symbolizes. A pet
that barks is no more naturally a *dog* than a *chien, Hund,* or *mbwa,* to use
the words in French, German, and Swahili for the animal we call "dog."
Language, which makes symbolic thought possible, is a distinctive possession of human beings.

Symbols may also be nonverbal. Flags can stand for countries; and
arches, for hamburger chains. Holy water is an important symbol for Roman Catholics. As is true of all symbols, the link between the symbol (water)
and what is symbolized (holiness) is arbitrary. In itself water is not holier
than milk, blood, or other natural liquids. Nor does holy water differ chem-
ically from ordinary water. Holy water is a symbol within Roman Catholicism, which is an international cultural system. A natural thing has come to
have a special meaning for Catholics. People who are enculturated in
Catholicism (raised as Catholics) share common beliefs passed on through
learning across the generations.

All human societies use symbols to create and maintain culture. The animals that are most closely related to us—chimpanzees and gorillas—have
rudimentary precultural abilities. But no other animal has elaborated cultural abilities—to learn, to communicate, and to store, process, and use information—to the extent that humans have.

Culture and Nature   Culture takes the natural biological urges we share
with other animals and teaches us how to express them in particular ways.
People have to eat, but culture teaches us what, when, and how. In many
cultures people have their main meal at noon, but most North Americans
prefer a large dinner. English people eat fish for breakfast, but North Americans prefer hot cakes and cold cereals. Brazilians put hot milk into strong
coffee, whereas North Americans pour cold milk into a weaker brew. Midwesterners dine at 5 or 6 P.M., Spaniards at 10 P.M.

Cultural habits, perceptions, and inventions mold "human nature" in
many directions. All people have to eliminate wastes from their bodies, but
some cultures teach people to defecate standing, while others tell them to
do it sitting down. A generation ago, in Paris and other French cities, it was
customary for men to urinate almost publicly, and seemingly without embarrassment, in barely shielded outdoor *pissoirs.* Our "bathroom" habits,

including waste elimination, bathing, and dental care, are parts of cultural traditions that have converted natural acts into cultural customs.

Our culture—and cultural changes—affect the ways in which we perceive nature, human nature, and the "natural." Through science, invention, and discovery, cultural advances have overcome many "natural" limitations. We prevent and cure diseases like polio and smallpox, which felled our ancestors. We use Viagra to restore sexual potency. Through cloning, scientists have altered the way we think about biological identity and the meaning of life itself. Culture, of course, has not freed us from natural threats. Hurricanes, floods, earthquakes, and other natural forces regularly challenge our wishes to modify the environment through building, development, and expansion. Can you think of other ways in which nature strikes back at people and their products?

Culture Is All-Encompassing   All people have culture, and culture is all-encompassing. Sometimes we hear someone described as "a cultured person," but all humans have culture in the anthropological sense. Culture includes much more than elite education, taste, refinement, sophistication, and appreciation of the fine arts. All people are cultured, not only artists and college graduates. The most significant cultural forces are those that affect us every day of our lives, especially those that influence children during enculturation. Culture encompasses experience that is sometimes regarded as trivial, such as exposure to popular culture. To understand contemporary North American culture, we must consider the importance of television, fast food, and sports. A rock star can be as significant as a symphony conductor, or more; a comic book, as relevant as a book-award winner.

Culture Is Integrated   Cultures are not haphazard collections of customs and beliefs but integrated, patterned systems. A **culture trait** is an individual item in a culture, such as a particular belief, tool, or practice. A **culture pattern** is a coherent set of interrelated traits. Many customs, institutions, and values form patterns. That is, they are connected and interrelated, so that if one changes, the others also change. During the 1950s, for example, the pattern was for most American women to have domestic careers as homemakers and mothers. Now it is assumed that women will get jobs outside the home. Related attitudes toward marriage, family, and children have also changed. The new pattern includes a later age at marriage, alternative child care systems, and more frequent divorce.

Cultures are integrated by their main economic activities and social patterns. They are also integrated by enduring themes, values, and attitudes. Cultures train their individual members to share certain personality traits. A set of **core values** (key, basic, or central values) integrates each culture and helps distinguish it from others. For instance, the work ethic, individualism, achievement, and self-reliance are core values that have integrated American culture for generations. Different sets of values are found as patterns in other cultures.

People Use Culture Actively   Although cultural rules tell us what to do and how to do it, people don't always do what the rules say should be done. People use their culture actively and creatively, rather than blindly following its dictates. We are not passive beings who are doomed to follow our cultural traditions like programmed robots. Instead, people can learn, interpret, and manipulate the same rule in different ways. Also, culture is contested. That is, different groups in society often struggle with one another over whose ideas, values, and beliefs will prevail. Even common symbols may have radically different *meanings* to different people and groups in the same culture. Golden arches may cause one person to salivate while another plots a vegetarian protest.

Even if they agree about what should and shouldn't be done, people don't always do as their culture directs or as other people expect. Many rules are violated, some very often (for example, automobile speed limits). Some anthropologists find it useful to distinguish between ideal and real culture. The *ideal culture* consists of what people say they should do and what they say they do. *Real culture* refers to their actual behavior as observed by the anthropologist.

Culture is both public and individual, both in the world and in people's minds. Anthropologists are interested not only in public and collective behavior but also in how *individuals* think, feel, and act. The individual and culture are linked because human social life is a process in which individuals internalize the meanings of *public* (i.e., cultural) messages. Then, alone and in groups, people influence culture by converting their private understandings into public expressions (D'Andrade 1984).

Culture Is Instrumental, Adaptive, and Maladaptive   Culture is the main reason for human adaptability and success. Other animals rely on biological means of adaptation (such as fur or blubber, which are adaptations to cold). Humans also adapt biologically—for example, by shivering when we get cold or sweating when we get hot. But in addition to biological responses, people also have cultural ways of adapting. To cope with environmental stresses we habitually use technology, or tools. We hunt cold-adapted animals and use their fur coats as our own. We turn the thermostat up in the winter and down in the summer. Or we plan action to increase our comfort. We have a cold drink, jump in a pool, or travel to some place cooler in the summer or warmer in the winter. People use culture *instrumentally*, that is, to fulfill their basic biological needs for food, drink, shelter, comfort, and reproduction.

On one level, cultural traits (e.g., air conditioning) may be called *adaptive* if they help individuals cope with environmental stresses. But, on a different level, such traits can also be *maladaptive*. That is, they may threaten a group's continued existence. Thus chlorofluorocarbons from air conditioners deplete the ozone layer and, by doing so, can harm humans and other life. Many modern cultural patterns may be maladaptive in the long run. Some examples of maladaptive aspects of culture are policies that encourage overpopulation, poor food-distribution systems, overconsumption, and industrial pollution of the environment.

There Are Levels of Culture   Cultures can be larger or smaller than nations. We may distinguish between different levels of culture: international, national, and subcultural. **International culture** is the term for cultural traditions that extend beyond national boundaries. Many culture traits and patterns have become international in scope. They have spread through migration, colonization, and the expansion of multinational organizations (like the Catholic Church). Catholics in different countries share experiences, symbols, beliefs, and values transmitted by their church. Also illustrating international culture, the United States, Canada, Great Britain, and Australia share certain traits as a result of a shared linguistic and cultural heritage from British founding fathers and mothers.

    National culture refers to experiences, beliefs, customs, and values shared by people who have grown up in the same nation, such as the United States, Canada, or Mexico. Although people who live in the same society—a nation, for example—share a cultural tradition, cultures also have internal diversity, which is the focus of this book. Individuals, families, communities, regions, classes, and other groups within a culture have different learning experiences as well as shared ones. **Subcultures** are the diverse cultural patterns and traditions associated with subgroups in the same nation. Subcultures (a problematic term, as we shall see below and in Chapter 4) may originate in ethnicity, class, region, or religion. The religious backgrounds of American Baptists, Catholics, Jews, and Muslims create subcultural differences between them. Although they share the same national culture, northern and southern Americans differ in certain culture traits and patterns. This illustrates regional subcultures.

    Nowadays, many anthropologists are reluctant to use the term *subculture*. They feel that the prefix "sub" is offensive because it means "below." "Subcultures" may thus be perceived as "less than" or somehow inferior to a dominant, elite, or national culture. In this discussion of levels of culture, we intend no such implication. Our point is simply that nations may contain many different culturally defined groups. As mentioned earlier, culture is contested. Various groups strive to promote the correctness and value of their own practices, values, and beliefs in comparison with those of other groups, or the nation as a whole.

Ethnocentrism and Cultural Relativism   **Ethnocentrism** is the tendency to use one's own cultural standards and values to judge the behavior and beliefs of people with different cultures. Ethnocentrism is a cultural universal. That is, people everywhere think that familiar explanations, opinions, and customs are true, right, proper, and moral. They regard different behavior as strange or savage.

    The opposite of ethnocentrism is **cultural relativism,** the view that behavior in one culture should not be judged by the standards of another. This position can also present problems. An extreme cultural relativist might contend that there is no superior, international, or universal morality—that the moral and ethical rules of all cultures deserve equal respect. In the extreme relativist view, Nazi Germany is evaluated as impartially as Athenian Greece. Anthropologists respect human diversity, and most anthropologists try to be objective, accurate, and sensitive in their accounts of diverse cultures. However, objectivity and sensitivity do not mean that we have to ignore certain international standards of justice and morality.

Universality, Generality, and Particularity   Anthropologists agree that learning is uniquely developed among humans, that culture is the main reason for the success of our species (*Homo sapiens*), and that any normal child can learn any cultural tradition through enculturation. Regardless of their genes, ancestry, or physical appearance, people can learn any culture. This point is illustrated by the fact that the ancestors of modern Americans and Canadians came to North America from different countries and continents, representing hundreds of different nations, cultures, and languages. However, the earliest colonists, later immigrants, and their descendants have learned to be Americans or Canadians. These diverse descendants now share, to some extent at least, a common national culture.

In studying cultural diversity, we may distinguish between the universal, the generalized, and the particular. Certain social and cultural features are universal, shared by people everywhere. Others are merely generalities, found in several or many but not all cultures. Still other traits are particularities, limited or unique to certain cultures.

Universals are the traits that tend to distinguish *Homo sapiens* from other species. Human social universals include kinship, family living, child care, and food sharing. Cultural universals include religion (belief in supernatural beings, powers, and forces) and the incest taboo (prohibition against mating with or marrying a close relative).

Cultural **generalities** are similarities that occur in many but not all cultures. One reason for generalities is diffusion—borrowing between cultures. Societies can share the same traits because of borrowing or through (cultural) inheritance from a common cultural ancestor. Other generalities originate in independent invention of the same trait or pattern in separate cultures. Similar needs and circumstances have led people in different lands to innovate and change in parallel ways. They have independently come up with the same cultural solution to a recurrent problem.

One cultural generality that is present in many but not all societies is the nuclear family, a kinship group consisting of parents and children. Many Americans view the nuclear family as a proper and natural group, but it is not universal. It was totally absent, for example, among the Nayars, who lived on the Malabar Coast of India. The Nayars lived in female-headed households, and husbands and wives did not live together.

Cultures that share many traits may, however, emphasize very different values, practices, and institutions (such as individualism, respect for ancestors, or warfare). **Particularities**—distinctive traits and patterns—lend uniqueness to cultures. Most cultures use rituals to recognize such human life cycle events as birth, puberty, marriage, parenthood, and death. But cultures vary about which event merits special celebration. Americans regard expensive weddings as more socially appropriate than lavish funerals. But the cultures of Madagascar take the opposite view. The marriage ceremony is a minor event that brings together just the couple and a few close relatives. A funeral, by contrast, is a measure of the deceased person's social position and lifetime achievement, and may attract a thousand or more.

UNIFYING FACTORS IN CONTEMPORARY AMERICAN CULTURE

Culture is shared, but all societies contain divisive as well as unifying forces. For example, people of the same tribe are separated by their residence in different villages and membership in different kin groups. Nations, although united by government, are typically divided by class, region, ethnicity, religion, and political interest groups. As we describe in more detail in Chapter 4, the idea of common culture can be used to mobilize people, to solidify group identity and solidarity, and to promote special interests.

In any society or nation, a common cultural tradition can provide one basis for uniformity among its members. Whatever unity contemporary American culture has does not rest on a particularly strong central government. Nor is national unity based on common kinship, descent, or religion. In fact, many of the commonalities of behavior, belief, and activity that enable us to speak of contemporary American culture are relatively new. They are founded on and perpetuated by recent developments, particularly in business, transportation, and the media.

When we study contrasts between rural, urban, and suburban life, or relations among social class, ethnicity, and household organization, we are focusing on variation, a very important topic and the focus of this book. When we consider the active and creative use that each individual makes of popular culture (see the next chapter), we are also describing cultural diversity. Despite increasing diversity in the United States and Canada, we can still talk about an American or a Canadian national culture. Through common experiences in their enculturation, especially through exposure to the mass media, Americans and Canadians, respectively do come to share certain knowledge, beliefs, values, and ways of thinking and acting, as is true of any culture. Many shared aspects of national culture override differences among individuals, genders, regions, or ethnic groups.

The media, especially television, have helped bring nationalism and its symbols, including cultural contrasts with the United States, to prominence in Canada. In spring 2000, a TV commercial produced in Toronto for Molson Canadian beer gained instantaneous national prominence. The ad featured the character Joe Canadian delivering what came to be known as "The Rant," which was soon to become a nationalist mantra for 30 million Canadians:

"I'm not a lumberjack or a fur trader; I don't live in an igloo, eat blubber or own a dogsled.

"I have a prime minister, not a president. I speak English and French, not American.

"I can proudly sew my country's flag on my backpack. [This refers to Canada's gender-neutral school curriculum, in which sewing is taught to both boys and girls.]

"I believe in peacekeeping, not policing; diversity, not assimilation."

Images of maple leaves and beavers flashed on the screen as Joe reached his climax:

"Canada is the second-largest land mass, the first nation of hockey and the best part of North America. My name is Joe and I am Canadian." (quoted in Brooke 2000)

The Rant seems to have spurred the government of Ontario, Canada's most populous province, to announce that starting in September 2000, each student would start the day by singing "O Canada," and (as a member of the British Commonwealth) by pledging allegiance to the queen. Although The Rant was recited by ordinary Canadians from Vancouver to Halifax, one province did not join in this affirmation of national identity. In French-speaking Quebec, which has been governed by the separatist Parti Québecois since 1994, Canadian national symbols like the flag and anthem are officially ignored, and Molson Canadian beer is not even marketed (Brooke 2000).

It is fitting that anthropology, which originated as the study of non-Western societies, extend its lens to North American society and culture. We have seen that anthropology deals with cultural universals, generalities, and uniqueness. A national culture may be seen as a particular cultural variant, as interesting as any other. Techniques developed to interpret and analyze smaller-scale societies, where sociocultural uniformity is more marked, can also contribute to an understanding of Canadian or American life—the whole and its parts.

A **native anthropologist** is one who studies his or her own culture. Native anthropologists include Americans working in the United States, Canadians in Canada, French in France, and Nigerians in Nigeria. Many of us have turned to native anthropology after having first done fieldwork elsewhere. The academic training, fieldwork abroad, and cross-cultural focus that characterize anthropology tend to provide its practitioners with a degree of detachment and objectivity that most natives lack. On the other hand, life experience as a native can also be an advantage to the anthropologist embarking on a study of his or her own culture of origin. Nevertheless, much more than when working abroad, the native anthropologist is both participant and observer, often emotionally and intellectually involved in the events and beliefs being studied. Native anthropologists should be wary of their biases as natives and should attempt to be as objective with their own culture as they are with others.

Common cultural traditions provide a basis for uniformity among members of a society or nation. Among the unifying factors in contemporary American culture are graduation celebrations (high school and college) and associated customs, such as tossing hats in the air.

Knowledge of other cultures enables us both to appreciate and to question aspects of our own. Anthropological techniques developed to describe and analyze other cultures can be applied to North America as well. Yet because natives often see and explain their behavior very differently from the way anthropologists do, Canadian and American readers may disagree with some of the analyses and interpretations presented in this book. In part this is because you are natives, who know much more about your own culture than you do about any other. Also, individuals and groups within a culture (e.g., men and women, rich and poor, old and young, blacks and whites, teachers and students) may perceive that culture very differently. American culture assigns a high value to differences in individual opinion—and to the belief that one opinion is as good as another.

A reminder about the all-encompassing nature of culture may be useful here. Culture means much more than refinement, cultivation, education, and appreciation of classics and fine arts. Native anthropologists cannot ignore popular culture, especially the mass media and their impact. That TVs outnumber toilets in American households is a significant cultural fact. Kottak's observations about Michigan college students may be generalizable to other young Americans. They visit McDonald's more often than they do houses of worship. Almost all have seen a Walt Disney movie and have attended rock concerts and football games. If these observations are true of young Americans generally, as we suspect they are, such shared experiences are major features of American enculturation patterns. Certainly any extra-terrestrial anthropologist doing fieldwork in the United States would stress them. Within the United States, the mass media and the culture of consumption have created major themes in contemporary national culture. These themes merit anthropological study.

The next chapter will consider, among other topics, the creative use that individuals and groups make of cultural forces, including media images. We will explore how, through different "readings" of the same "text," people constantly make and remake culture. Here we take a different, but complementary, approach, focusing on some of the texts that have diffused most successfully in a given national culture. Such texts spread because they are culturally appropriate and, for various cultural reasons, able to carry some sort of meaning for millions of Americans. From the popular domains of sports, TV, movies, theme parks, and fast food we may identify certain very popular texts, such as football or the "Star Trek" myth, which was examined in Chapter 1. Other texts (e.g., blue jeans, baseball, and pizza) would enable us to make similar points—that there are powerful shared aspects of contemporary American national culture and that anthropological techniques can be used to interpret them.

Football

Football, we say, is only a game, but it has become a hugely popular spectator sport. (*Monday Night Football* on ABC was the only common program included in the 10 favorite TV programs of both blacks and whites in the United States in 1996–1997.*) Like team allegiance in general, football is a sport that both unites and divides us. Most Americans share the experience of watching TV football or attending games; yet they root for different teams, often passionately. On fall Saturdays millions of people travel to and from college football games. Smaller congregations meet in high school stadiums. Millions of Americans watch televised football. Indeed, half the adult population of the United States watches the annual Super Bowl (a spectacle, however, that may do as much to divide as to unite men and women, children and adults).

Because of its mass significance, then, football is an American (as well as a Canadian) popular cultural institution that merits anthropological attention. Popular sports manage to attract people of diverse ethnic backgrounds, regions, religions, political parties, jobs, social statuses, wealth levels, and even genders, as attendance at college games will show. The popularity of football, particularly professional football, depends directly on the mass media, especially television.

Is football, with its territorial incursion, hard hitting, and violence—occasionally resulting in injury—popular because we are violent people? Are

*As reported in a CNN series, *Race in America,* June 11, 1997.

football spectators vicariously realizing their own hostile and aggressive tendencies? Anthropologist W. Arens (1981) discounts this view, pointing out that football is a peculiarly North American pastime. Baseball has become a popular sport in the Caribbean, parts of Latin America, and Japan. Basketball and volleyball are also spreading. However, throughout most of the world, soccer is the most popular sport. Arens argues that if football were a particularly good channel for expressing aggression, it would have spread (as soccer and baseball have done) to many other countries, where people have as many aggressive tendencies and hostile feelings as we do. Furthermore, he suggests that if a sport's popularity rested simply on its appeal to a bloodthirsty temperament, boxing, a far bloodier sport, would be our national pastime. Arens concludes that the explanation for football's popularity lies elsewhere, and we agree.

Arens contends that football is popular because it symbolizes certain key features of North American life. In particular, it is characterized by teamwork based on elaborate specialization and division of labor, which are pervasive features of modern life. Susan Montague and Robert Morais (1981) take the analysis a step further. They argue that Americans appreciate football because it presents a miniaturized and simplified version of modern organizations. People have trouble understanding organizational bureaucracies, whether in business, universities, or government. Football, these anthropologists argue, helps us understand how decisions are made and rewards are allocated in organizations.

Montague and Morais link football's values, particularly teamwork, to those associated with business. Like corporate workers, ideal players work hard and are dedicated to the team. Within organizations, however, decision making is complicated, and workers aren't always rewarded for their dedication and good job performance. Decisions are simpler and rewards are more consistent in football, these anthropologists contend, and this helps explain its popularity. Even if we can't figure out how General Motors and Microsoft run, any fan can become an expert on football's rules, teams, scores, statistics, and patterns of play. Even more important, football suggests that the values stressed by business really do pay off. Teams whose members work hardest, show the most spirit, and best develop and coordinate their talents can be expected to win more often than other teams do.

ANTHROPOLOGY AND AMERICAN POP CULTURE

Unlike the chapters that follow, this one has not focused primarily on variation. Instead, we have stressed experiences and enculturative forces that are common to many or most Americans. We have made several points here. One is that we can employ techniques developed to study other cultures to interpret our own. Also, we have seen that native anthropologists can contribute uniquely by coupling professional detachment with personal experience and understanding. There are some questions we should bear in mind, though, as we ponder the adequacy of our analyses and explanations: Do natives accept them or prefer them to other interpretations? Do they enable natives to make more sense of familiar phenomena? Do they fit within a comparative framework provided by data and analyses from other societies? Can the relations we detect be confirmed by researchers who independently examine the same data?

We are witnessing major changes in the material conditions of North American life—particularly in work organization and technology, including transportation and information flows. Through the mass media, institutions such as sports, movies, TV shows, theme parks, and fast-food restaurants have become powerful elements of national culture. They provide a framework of common expectation and experience overriding differences in region, class, formal religious affiliation, political sentiments, gender, ethnic group, and place of residence.

For various reasons, Americans can see themselves not just as members of a varied and complex nation but also as a population united by distinctive shared symbols, customs, and experiences. Despite its own internal diversity, then, American culture is one among many distinctive national cultures, part of the range of global cultural diversity.

MECHANISMS OF CULTURAL CHANGE

We live in a world of increasing intercultural contact, in which the pace of cultural change has accelerated enormously. Cultures in contact typically get traits from each other through borrowing or diffusion. **Diffusion,** an important mechanism of cultural change, has gone on throughout human history, because cultures have never been truly isolated. As the anthropologist Franz Boas (1940/1966) noted many years ago, contact between neighboring tribes has always existed and has extended over enormous areas. Diffusion is *direct* when two cultures trade, intermarry, or wage war on one another. Diffusion is *forced* when one culture subjugates another and imposes its customs on the dominated group. Diffusion is *indirect* when products and patterns move from group A to group C via group B without any firsthand contact between A and C. In the modern world much international diffusion is due to the spread of the mass media.

Acculturation, another mechanism of cultural change, is the exchange of cultural features that results when groups come into continuous firsthand contact. The original cultural patterns of either or both groups may be changed by this contact (Redfield, Linton, and Herskovits 1936). We usually speak of acculturation when the contact is *between* nations or cultures. Parts of the cultures change, but each group remains distinct. In situations of continuous contact, cultures exchange and blend foods, recipes, music, dances, clothing, tools, and techniques.

Independent invention—the process by which humans innovate, creatively finding new solutions to old and new problems—is another important mechanism of cultural change. Faced with comparable challenges, people in different places have innovated in similar or parallel ways, which is one reason that cultural generalities exist. One example is the independent invention of agriculture in the Middle East and Mexico. In both areas people who faced food scarcity began to domesticate crops. Over the course of history, innovations have spread at the expense of earlier practices. Often a major invention, such as agriculture, triggers a series of subsequent interrelated changes. Thus, in both Mexico and the Middle East, agriculture led to many social, political, and legal changes, including notions of property and distinctions in wealth, class, and power.

Another reason for cultural change—one that is critical for understanding contemporary North America—is **globalization.** This term refers to linkages (through transportation, migration, the media, and various economic and political processes) that are developing at an accelerating pace among people and nations throughout the world. Globalization, examined further in Chapter 3, links all contemporary people, directly or indirectly, in the modern world system.

THE USES OF CULTURE

Nowadays, "culture," as a term and as a concept, is used liberally both by people in general and by professionals. When people want to assert certain unique qualities, or to justify patterns of behavior, they may claim, "It's my culture!" Teens may distinguish themselves from other family members by claiming a "different culture." Some students use their "culture of birth" by taking a test in their native language to avoid taking courses to fulfill a foreign language requirement.

Business stresses the importance of "corporate culture." Marketers target "culture niches" to pitch products and services. Everett Rogers (1995) points out that understanding the "culture of individuals" in a system targeted for change provides change agents with information needed to design and implement effective innovations.

"Cultural competency" is a key to quality services in health, education, and welfare. Disparities in medical diagnosis and treatment affect the health status of various minorities. In the United States these minorities include African Americans, certain Spanish-speaking groups, Native North Americans, and some groups of Asian descent. In Canada they include Indians, or First Nations. Indians and Pakistanis are minorities in the United Kingdom, North Africans in France, Turks in Germany, Kurds in Turkey, and Ethiopian Jews in Israel (Geiger 2001). A primary reason for inequitable health care delivery is a lack of cultural awareness and competence by health care professionals.

The notion of "school culture" marks the speech, scholarship, administration, and teaching of American educators. Learning, curriculum development, leadership, and reform are linked to the culture of the school—its history, its social organization, its core values, and the people who define it (Deal and Peterson 1999; Kozaitis 2000). Attention to culture is intrinsic to economic development, social work, and public welfare services. Culturally compatible development requires participation by local people in plans that affect them (Kottak 1990a). Programs directed at culturally defined "client populations" rely on cultural awareness for success (Green 1982).

Nowhere is the use of culture more evident than in organized efforts by self-identified affinity groups who demand human rights on the basis of "our culture." The movement to valorize culture and identity within the African diaspora boasts *négritude*, a configuration of history, experience, ideology, and sentiment shared by blacks. The concept of *sisterhood* is equally powerful in the Women's Liberation Movement, the initial objectives of which included "the development of a women's culture" (Newton 2000, p. 114). As people with disabilities forge their own civil rights movement, they emphasize the "celebration of separate culture" (Shapiro 1993, pp, 74–104).

Understanding contemporary social movements requires appreciation of the nature, construction, and uses of culture. In Chapter 3 we discuss globalization and the active and creative ways in which people rely on culture to negotiate, adapt, and influence social transformations.

CHAPTER THREE

Globalization, Identity, and Affinity

——————— FROM MASS CULTURE TO AFFINITY GROUPS ———————

From World War II through the early 1960s, the United States was represented as "one nation indivisible." (The phrase "under God" was added to the Pledge of Allegiance in 1954.) America was seen as a "melting pot," united by mass culture, abetted by the spread of television. The draft provided a common experience for millions of men who were called up for military service. With the exception of the separate but unequal schools of the South prior to desegregation, a fairly uniform public school system taught kids nationwide to read the same stories about Dick, Jane, and their pets.

With TV a novelty and just two or three networks available, Americans shared common programming, images, and information. Mondays at nine everyone watched *I Love Lucy*. The most celebrated female extradomestic labor in 1953 was Lucy's as she rushed to the hospital to give birth to Little Ricky. On Sunday evenings, Ed Sullivan's show attracted mass audiences by headlining such decade-dominating celebrities as Elvis Presley and the Beatles. The "housewives" of the 1950s watched their soaps, and bought the laundry products for which the shows were named, using them to wash clothes purchased in downtown department stores in their new mass-produced appliances.

Although the country was (temporarily) reunited by the events of September 11, 2001, today's United States is remarkably different from the way it was 50 years ago. Contributing to the transformations have been national movements for Civil Rights, for Women's Liberation, and against the Vietnam war, as well the "White Backlash" to those movements during the 1960s and 1970s. Unity and union eventually yielded to diversity and dissension—in the United States and, eventually, in the U.S.S.R. In North America the trend toward diversification has been the result of many factors—political mobilization and identity politics (see below), immigration, and resistance to homogenization through mass media and education.

One key development in North American culture since the 1970s, especially evident in the media, is a general shift from "massification" to "segmental appeal." An increasingly differentiated nation celebrates diversity. The mass media—print and electronic—join the trend, measuring various "demographics." The media aim their products and messages at particular segments, rather than at an undifferentiated mass audience. Television, films, radio, music, magazines, and Internet forums all gear their topics, formats, and styles to particular homogeneous segments of the population (i.e., "interest groups," "affinity groups," or "target audiences"). In particular, cable TV and the videocassette recorder (VCR) have helped direct television, the most important mass medium, away from the networks' cherished mass audiences and toward particular viewing segments. Cable permits special interest audiences to choose among a multiplicity of targeted channels. They specialize in music (country, pop, rock, Latin, or "black entertainment"), sports, news (financial, weather, headline), comedy, science fiction, gossip, movies (commercial, foreign, "art," "classic"), cartoons, old TV sitcoms, Spanish language, nature, travel, adventure, history, biography, and home shopping. There even seems to be a "nun's channel." Something for every one. Nothing for everyone. The Super Bowl, the Academy Awards, and Olympics still manage to capture large national and international audiences; but in 1998, the final episode of *Seinfeld*, though it was hugely popular, could not rival the mass audience shares achieved by programs such as *Roots*, Lucy's childbirth episode, or the final episode of *M*A*S*H*.

Special-interest audiences and groups are proliferating, as part of a pattern of increasing specialization and diversification—a key feature of contemporary lives. High technology has the capacity to tear all of us apart as it brings some of us together. The Internet, fax machines, and satellite dishes work internationally to establish virtual communities and instantaneous contact. National boundaries are permeable. New units form. People participate in multiple social systems and play various roles depending on the situation.

The world navigable via computer—cyberspace—is part of a larger high-tech communications environment, which may be called advanced information technology (AIT). Other elements of this environment include computer hardware and software, modems, advanced telephone systems, digital subscriber lines (DSL), cable TV, satellite dishes, and faxing capability. One of the key features of AIT is its international scope. Along with modern transportation systems, AIT plays a key role in connecting people worldwide.

A particular cybergroup can unite people from all over the world who share a common interest. Some groups are devoted to specific health concerns or political issues. Others focus on nations and their diasporic citizenries. They provide a common forum for scholars and others interested in a particular nation, or for its citizens in various locales. Groups with a narrow focus may be based on work cultures and other *affinity groups*—groups of user-participants with common interests and/or characteristics (Harvey 1996). They may link members of a single organization, branches of that organization, or similar professionals—(ear, nose, and throat ENT) physicians all over the world. *Transecting groups* create direct communication channels between groups that previously had, or otherwise have, trouble communicating—for instance, physicians and patients.

Although AIT links the world, access to its riches is unequal both among and within nations. The "developing" nations have poorer access than do North America, western Europe, Japan, Australia, and New Zealand. Even within a "developed" nation such as the United States or Canada, socioeconomic, demographic, and cultural factors affect access to and use of cyberspace. There is privileged access to AIT by class, race, ethnicity, gender, education, profession, age, and family background. For example, young people tend to be more comfortable with AIT than old people are. Families with higher incomes tend to have better access to the whole range of high-tech items. Groups with more restricted access to AIT include minorities, the poor, females, older people, and developing nations.

Social scientists are studying ways in which AIT is fostering new social constructions of reality, and computers are changing notions of identity and the self. Virtual worlds, such as computer role-playing games, are ways of extending oneself into various forms of cybersocial interaction (Escobar 1994). People manipulate their identities by choosing various "handles," their names in cyberspace. If one engages in online communication through multiple servers, such as a university gateway, a commercial service, and various interactive websites, one may have various handles and identities. In some contexts, people manipulate ("lie about") their ages and genders and create their own cyberfantasies.

Despite certain utopian visions of the potential role of virtual networks in integrating physical communities (e.g., Kling 1996), it is doubtful that AIT will play much of a role in strengthening whole local communities—towns and cities. It is more likely that AIT will be used mainly to facilitate communication among affinity groups—relatives, friends, and people with common identities, experiences, interests, and concerns, ranging from work and business to ideology and politics. AIT will be used especially for immediate communication within groups of co-workers and members of an organization. Its main role, however, will be to establish and maintain links between physically dispersed people who have things, and come to have more things, in common. ☺

IDENTITY POLITICS AND GLOBALIZATION

In this new millennium, in the context of diffusing transnational and global institutions, existing governments are increasingly challenged. New bases for union and division are forming. One such basis is **identity politics.** As Robert D. Kaplan (1994) notes, social and political identities based on the perception of sharing a common culture, religion, (e.g., Christianity, Judaism, Islam), language, or "race" are becoming the basis of prime allegiance, rather than citizenship in a nation-state, which contains diverse social groups.

A key feature of the nation-state, or more simply, the state, is its territorial basis. Robert Carneiro sees the state as "an autonomous political unit, encompassing many communities within its territory" (1970, p. 733). Elizabeth Brumfiel describes states as "territorially extensive, administratively complex political systems in which governmental institutions monopolize the use of legal force" (1980, p. 459). States bring members of diverse groups together and oblige them to pledge allegiance to a government; but in today's world more and more people are refusing to make that pledge. Territory per se is declining as a basis of identity.

The great sociopolitical paradox of the contemporary world is that both integration and disintegration are increasing. Through the media, travel, and migration, areas of the world are linked more now than ever before. But dissolution and anarchy also surround us. Nations have dissolved, along with political blocs (the Warsaw Pact nations) and ideologies ("Communism"). Kaplan (1994) suggests that internal diversity may doom many nation-states. Identity politics fractures countries into divisions based on "race," class, ethnicity, language, religion, age, gender, and sexual orientation.

The Decline of Government

Contradicting opinions expressed every day on American call-in radio, a global perspective makes it clear that government is not getting stronger. Rather, governments are weaker, less respected, and less relevant than they were 50 years ago. Political units are being challenged worldwide. West Africa and eastern Europe are full of "failed states." The North American airwaves reveal and promote a lack of respect for government and "public servants" that is unprecedented in history. Never have so many people freely said so many disparaging things to so many others about their present and former leaders.

In nation after nation the media report actual and alleged corruption and scandals involving political figures and their cronies. Distrust of government and its representatives increases. Potential public servants are reluctant to subject themselves and their families to a system of media scrutiny that seems to have run wild. Dozens of members of the U. S. Congress decline to run for reelection.

President George H. W. Bush proclaimed that the New World Order was in the making, with the fall of the Soviet Union and the end of the Cold War; but disorder is rampant. In many places (West Africa, Somalia, Rwanda) the world seems to have reverted to feudal times. Without state socialism and Soviet support, Yugoslavia disintegrated into ministates. With no "Communist threat," First World nations have cut their support for puppet regimes and loyal Third World allies. American foreign aid to African governments decreased at precisely the time when some of them (particularly in southern Africa) started to become more democratic.

Trade and Globalization

With the end of the Cold War, the ideological, political, and military basis of international alliance has been largely replaced by a focus on trade and economic issues. A southern cone economic union took shape in South America. A similar movement is underway in southern Africa, with the end of war and repression in many nations there. In North America and Europe, multinational economic unions came into conflict with national and partisan interests. Such economic alliances include the North American Free Trade Association (NAFTA), the General Agreement on Trade and Tariffs (GATT), and the European Economic Community (EEC).

Finance is a fundamental transnational force, as capitalists look beyond national boundaries for places to invest. As Appadurai puts it, "money, commodities, and persons unendingly chase each other around the world" (1991, p. 194). Many Latin American communities, especially in Mexico and the Caribbean, have lost their autonomy because their residents now depend on cash derived from international labor migration. The United States also relies more on foreign cash. Long dominated by domestic capital, the economy of the United States is increasingly influenced by foreign investment, especially from Britain, Canada, Germany, the Netherlands, and Japan. Canada itself has the highest level of foreign economic ownership in the developed world—23 percent of company assets (Brooke 2000). The American economy has also increased its dependence on foreign labor—through both the immigration of laborers and the export of jobs.

Transnational finance and labor modify the economic control and the ethnic mix of local life. By the mid-1980s, for example, 75 percent of the buildings in downtown Los Angeles were owned at least in part by foreign capital. Up to 90 percent of multistory construction was being financed from abroad. More than 40 percent of the Angeleno metropolitan population consisted of ethnic minorities, mainly from Latin America and Asia (Rouse 1991). Business, technology, and the media have increased the craving for commodities and images throughout the world. This has forced nation-states to open to a global culture of consumption. Almost everyone today participates in this culture.

Antiglobalization

There is, of course, resistance to globalization, as 1997 elections in England, France, Canada, and Mexico illustrate. You may remember the massive and violent demonstration against the policies of the World Trade Organization (WTO), which met in Seattle in December 1999. Since then, thousands of protesters have been turning out worldwide to show their disapproval of the "globalization policies" of international agencies such as the World Trade Organization, the International Monetary Fund (IMF), and the World Bank. The Seattle demonstration drew 50,000 protesters; there were 600 arrests and one death. Police were accused of starting the violence by using excessive force. Soon thereafter, in April 2000, a Washington meeting of the World Bank and the IMF drew 10,000 protesters. Although there were 1,300 arrests, the protesters were kept from disrupting the meeting. Then, in September 2000, Prague, Czech Republic, drew 12,000 protesters against a World Bank–IMF meeting, with 900 arrests. Debt relief was pledged for 20 poor countries after Prague became a battle zone. In Genoa, Italy, in July 2001, a protest against the G-8 (group of eight major economic powers) summit meeting drew 150,000 protesters, with 200 arrests and one death (Prasso, August 6, 2001). In January 2001, in Davos, Switzerland, 1,000 protesters came to demonstrate against the World Economic Forum. Although the protesters were blockaded from the city, there were 121 arrests. This annual meeting was next held in January 2002 in New York City, where the protests were mainly peaceful.

An antiglobalization demonstration in New York City on February 2, 2002. This was a peaceful protest against the World Economic Forum being hosted in the city. What issues were addressed by the protesters?

These protesters have included cross-sections of social and economic classes and people with different political views. Prominent among them are trade union members, environmentalists, anticapitalists, and anarchists. The different groups have somewhat different goals. Debt-relief advocates want the IMF and the World Bank to forgive loans to poor countries and to replace future loans with grants for local development programs. Environmentalists seek tougher environmental impact assessments for companies and borrowers. Human right groups contend that international development policies help only big business, not poor countries and their citizens. IMF reformers accuse the fund of worsening financial crises in various countries by proscribing budget-slashing policies. Trade unionists support global labor standards. The protesters fall into two camps, those who want the agencies disbanded and those who merely want them reformed (Miller 2000).

The antiglobalists agree that "governments and international institutions put the interests of big companies ahead of those of the public on poverty reduction, the environment, human rights and jobs" (Hay 2001). They would prefer a democratically elected international agency to the current ones, which are run by nonelected officials representing the world's richest nations and corporations. IMF, World Bank, and G-8 officials respond by saying that progress and reform, though slow, are being made.

The U.S. press has been accused of biased coverage of the antiglobalization protests. Media accounts *have* tended to focus either on violence or on trade and commerce, rather than on the issues championed by protesters. According to John Giuffo (2001), the media have paid more attention to the "corporate side of these debates" than to the concerns raised by the protesters, in effect siding with the powerful international agencies that promote economic development and free trade.

MULTILOCALITY AND THE MEDIA

We have seen that *globalization* describes the accelerating links between nations and people in a world system connected economically, politically, and by modern media and transportation. With globalization, long-distance contact is easier, faster, and cheaper than ever. Although people travel more than ever, migrants and other travelers maintain their ties with home (by phoning, e-mailing, faxing, visiting, and sending money). In a sense, such people live multilocally, in different places at once. More and more people live multilocal and transnational rather than territorially confined, state-based lives.

Globalization has transplanted citizens of many nations, including participants in low-skilled, low-wage services such as housework. For example, migrant Filipina domestic workers can be found in large cities in more than 130 countries. Lacking citizenship in their host countries, they construct a compensating "sense of place and sense of community in globalization" (Parrenas 2001). Familiar products and print media move from the Philippines to European countries, and multinational networks have developed to provide support services to members of this Filipina diaspora.

The mass media assist in forming and maintaining not just cultural, but also transnational religious identities. Muslim identity, for example, has been abetted by coverage of clashes between the United States and Islamic nations, especially during the Gulf War and after September 11. As people move, they stay linked to each other and to their homeland through the media and through travel services targeted at specific ethnic, national, or religious audiences.

The media also propel a globally spreading culture of consumption, stimulating participation in the cash economy. Those who control the media have become key gatekeepers. Taking on roles played historically by political and religious leaders, they regulate public access to information. The moguls, magnates, managers, and mouths of TV and radio, including talk-show hosts, have the power to direct public attention toward some issues and away from others. Politicians and government officials also attempt to use radio and television for their own ends, and ordinary people increasingly use the media (e.g., talk radio, the Internet) to bring their concerns to the attention of fellow citizens and policymakers.

The media spread awareness of options and alternatives in products, services, "rights," institutions, and lifestyles, but they also fuel cynicism. Scandals about corruption in government, business, religion, and sports increase distrust of authorities, influencing electoral outcomes and policy. The flow of information has also encouraged people to clamor for "rights" and benefits and to demand more from familiar institutions. One result of media exposure, in the United States, Canada, and many other countries, has been to encourage accountability by government agents. Democratization of authoritarian governments has been another result of exposure to media messages, as in South Africa and the former Soviet Union, and potentially in China and Iran. According to Jim Fisher-Thompson, radio coverage of African elections "encouraged people to go out and vote and to speak out when they saw polling officials or 'government commandos' trying to interfere in the election process" (2002).

Governments, as might be expected, are not eager to give up their gatekeeping authority. Many governments take steps to restrict information flows. For example, in 1996 the U.S. Senate passed the Communications Decency Act, which the Supreme Court declared unconstitutional in 1997, as legislation aimed at pornography on the Internet. The Iranian parliament banned satellite dishes, as China has done, to limit exposure to information about external events, Western culture, and alternative models of society and government.

Reacting to Westernization and globalization, by late September 1996, Afghanistan's Taliban Movement, led by Muslim clerics, was enforcing its version of an Islamic society modeled on the teachings of the Koran (Burns 1997). Various repressive measures were instituted, limiting communication and personal freedom. The Taliban barred women from work and girls from school. Females past puberty were prohibited from talking to unrelated men. Women needed an approved reason, such as shopping for food, to leave their homes. Men, who were required to grow bushy beards, also faced an array of bans—against playing cards, listening to music, keeping pigeons, and flying kites.

To enforce their decrees, the Taliban sent armed enforcers throughout the country. These agents took charge of "beard checks" and other forms of scrutiny on behalf of a religious police force known as the General Department for the Preservation of Virtue and the Elimination of Vice (Burns 1997). By late fall 2001, the Taliban had been overthrown, and a new interim government was established in Kabul, the Afghan capital, on December 22. The collapse of the Taliban followed American bombing of Afghanistan in response to the September 11, 2001, attacks on New York's World Trade Center and Washington's Pentagon. As the Taliban yielded Kabul to victorious northern alliance forces, local men flocked to barbershops to have their beards trimmed or shaved. They were using a key Taliban symbol to celebrate the end of repression in religion's name. These images of freedom from religious oppression were transmitted around the world, even as Al Jazeera, the leading Arabic TV channel and news portal on the Internet, broadcast accounts questioning the policies and actions of the United States in Afghanistan and other Islamic nations.

The media have the capacity to liberate, opening people's minds, allowing for the expression of dissident and subaltern voices. (**Subaltern** means lower in rank, subordinate, traditionally lacking an influential role in decision making.) However, the mass media can also reinforce stereotypes and unfounded opinions and close people's minds to complexity and variety.

Fear of crime and the search for order and security are worldwide phenomena. Some fears are justified; others, exaggerated. Here again the media play a role. Waves of internationally transmitted images and information reinforce the perception that the world is a dangerous place, with threats to security and order everywhere. Who will ever forget the images of September 11? The rise of cable TV and 24-hour newscasting has blurred the distinction between the international, the national, and the local, bringing all threats closer to home. Constant rebroadcasting magnifies risk perception. Geographical distance is obscured by the barrage of "bad news" received daily from so many places. Many viewers have no idea how far away the disasters and threats really are.

NGOs AND RIGHTS MOVEMENTS

Related to the spread of identity politics and increased agitation for various kinds of "rights" is the proliferation of interest groups and nongovernmental organizations (NGOs) (local, domestic, and international). NGO formation is another major trend of contemporary political organization that poses a challenge to existing states. Currently, the allocation of aid to many "developing countries" challenges their governments by increasing the share of funds given to NGOs, which have gained prominence as social-change enablers. NGOs tend to question government authority at various levels, sometimes militantly. Activities once done by government are increasingly handled by NGOs; private voluntary organizations (PVOs), such as charities; and grass-roots organizations (GROs).

Posing yet another challenge to existing nation-states is the "rights" movement (human, cultural, animal), which has emerged within the arena of identity politics. Minority groups demand certain "rights." Larger political movements take up the cause, and media pressure becomes intense. The idea of **human rights** challenges the nation-state by invoking a realm of justice and morality beyond and superior to particular countries, cultures, and religions. Human rights are usually seen as vested in individuals. They would include the rights to speak freely; to hold religious beliefs without persecution; and to not be enslaved or imprisoned without charge. The human rights movement condemns state-perpetrated injustices. Such rights are not ordinary laws, which particular governments make and enforce. Rather, human rights are seen as inalienable (nations cannot abridge or terminate them) and metacultural (larger than and superior to individual nations and cultures).

The doctrine of human rights challenges the state by appeal to a level *above and beyond* it. Cultural rights apply to units *within* the state. **Cultural rights** are vested not in individuals but in identifiable *groups,* such as religious and ethnic minorities and indigenous peoples. Cultural rights include a group's ability to preserve its culture, to raise its children in the ways of its forebears, to continue its language, and to not be deprived of its economic base by the nation-state in which it is located (Greaves 1995, p. 3). The province of Quebec, for example, has enjoyed a special place among Canada's 10 provinces because of its special linguistic and cultural history.

Certain rights are codified: Nation-states have agreed to them in writing. Four United Nations documents—the UN Charter; the Universal Declaration of Human Rights; the Covenant on Economic, Social, and Cultural Rights; and the Covenant on Civil and Political Rights—contain nearly all the human rights that have been internationally recognized. However, almost all these rights are seen as vested in *individuals* rather than groups. As Thomas Greaves (1995) notes, nation-states have been slow to recognize group rights (see Chapter 4). The concept of group rights may seriously challenge government sovereignty, by legitimating fundamental loyalties to segments *within* the state, thus undermining the state's hegemony.

Many countries have signed pacts endorsing, for cultural minorities in nation-states, such group rights as self-determination, some degree of home rule, and the right to practice the group's religion, culture, and language. Greaves (1995) points out that because cultural rights are mainly uncodified, their realization must rely on the same mechanisms that create them—pressure, publicity, and politics. Such rights have been pushed by a wave of political assertiveness throughout the world. We will see American manifestations of this process in Chapter 4. The media, NGOs, tribal associations, and other collectivities play a prominent part in the rights movement. The push for human rights has been fairly peaceful, working through the law and established political channels, in the western hemisphere; but the battle to promote minority interests has been much more disruptive, involving warfare, ethnic conflict, separatism, and genocide in eastern Europe and Africa.

Two junior rangers display the new Nunavut flag during a ceremony in Iqaluit, Nunavut, Canada, on April 1, 1999, celebrating the new territory. As big as western Europe, Nunavut, led by the Inuit, represents the first major change in the map of Canada since Newfoundland joined the nation in 1949.

The notion of indigenous **intellectual property rights (IPR)** has arisen in an attempt to conserve each society's cultural base—its core beliefs and principles. IPR is claimed as a group right—a cultural right, allowing indigenous groups to control who may know and use their collective knowledge and its applications. Much traditional cultural knowledge has commercial value. Examples include ethnomedicine (traditional medical knowledge and techniques), cosmetics, cultivated plants, foods, folklore, arts, crafts, songs, dances, costumes, and rituals. According to the IPR concept, a particular group may determine how indigenous knowledge and its products may be used and distributed, and the level of compensation required.

Indigenous peoples, such as the Inuit of Canada, increasingly fight for increased cultural autonomy. One major Inuit victory was a pact signed in December 1991, in which Canada agreed to set the boundaries for a self-governing Inuit homeland. On May 5, 1992, voters in Canada's Northwest

Territories authorized its split into two separate territories—one for the Inuit. Extending almost to Greenland, the eastern territory covers an area a third larger than Alaska. It is inhabited by 20,500 "Eskimos," who prefer the name Inuit. The Inuit now administer this area, which they call Nunavut, meaning "our land." They have received direct title to about 20 percent of the land within Nunavut. As an economic jump-start for this homeland, they were also to receive at least $1.4 billion over 14 years (Farnsworth 1992; see also http://www.nunavut.com/basicfacts/english/basicfacts.html).

As in the rights discussion, issues involving property and ownership are also debated at levels *within* the state (e.g., IPRs of minorities) and *beyond* the state. Challenging the state from above is the idea of global morality. This notion of a moral order that transcends the moral codes of particular societies has been abetted by environmentalist NGOs. One prominent example is the idea that resources within nations (e.g., biodiversity, rain forests) belong to the world. Such a claim challenges national sovereignty. Not surprisingly, nations reject it. Brazilians, for example, are incensed when northerners suggest that the Amazon is a global resource.

DIASPORAS AND POSTMODERNITY

Arjun Appadurai characterizes today's world as a "translocal," "interactive system" that is "strikingly new" (1990, p. 1). Whether as refugees, migrants, tourists, terrorists, pilgrims, proselytizers, identity politicians, laborers, business people, development workers, employees of nongovernmental organizations (NGOs), soldiers, sports figures, or media-borne images, people are on the move.

So significant a process is transnational migration that many Mexican villagers find "their most important kin and friends are as likely to be living hundreds or thousands of miles away as immediately around them" (Rouse 1991, p. 9). Yet we have seen that many migrants lead multilocal lives, as they regularly phone or visit their native communities, send back cash, or watch "ethnic TV" in North America. Dominicans in New York City, for example, have been described as living "between two islands"—Manhattan and Santo Domingo (Grasmuck and Pessar 1991). Many Dominicans, like migrants from other countries, migrate to the United States temporarily, seeking cash to transform their lifestyles when they return to their homelands.

With so many people "in motion," the unit of anthropological study expands from the local community to the **diaspora**—the offspring of an area who have spread to many lands. **Postmodernity** describes our time and situation—today's world in flux, with people on the move who have learned to manage multiple identities depending on place and context. In its most general sense, **postmodern** refers to the blurring and breakdown of established canons (rules or standards), categories, distinctions, and boundaries. The word is taken from **postmodernism**—a style and movement in architecture that succeeded modernism, beginning in the 1970s. Postmodern architecture rejected the rules, geometric order, and austerity of modernism. Modernist buildings were expected to have a clear and functional design. Postmodern design is "messier" and more playful. It draws on a diversity of styles from different times and places—including popular, ethnic, and non-Western cultures.

Postmodernism extends "value" well beyond classic, elite, and Western cultural forms. *Postmodern* is now used to describe comparable developments in music, literature, and visual art. From this origin, *postmodernity* describes a world in which standards, contrasts, groups, boundaries, and identities are opening up, reaching out, and breaking down.

AGENCY

The active role of individuals in making and remaking culture is called **agency.** Any cultural product—a ceremony, an artifact, an ideology, or a media-borne image—can be considered a **text.** This term applies to something that can be creatively "read," interpreted, and assigned meaning by anyone (a "reader") who receives it. We note that such meanings may be very different from what the original creators of the text imagined. (The reading or meaning that the creators intended, or the one that the elites consider to be the right meaning, can be called the **hegemonic reading.**)

Illustrating agency, "readers" constantly produce their own meanings, some of which may resist or oppose the hegemonic meaning of the text. Or readers may focus on the antihegemonic aspects of a text. Slaves in the American South did this when they preferred the biblical story of Moses and deliverance to the hegemonic lessons of obedience their masters taught them.

In his book *Understanding Popular Culture* (1989), John Fiske argues that each individual's use of popular culture is a creative act (an original "reading" of a text). (For example, Madonna, the Grateful Dead, and *Star Wars* mean something different to each of their fans.) As Fiske puts it, "the meanings I make from a text are pleasurable when I feel that they are *my* meanings and that they relate to *my* everyday life in a practical, direct way" (1989, p. 57). All of us creatively "read" magazines, books, music, television, films, celebrities, politicians, and other popular culture products.

Also illustrating agency, individuals often manipulate ideas and images to express resistance. Fiske points out that through their use of popular culture, for example, people can symbolically oppose the unequal power relations they face each day—in the family, at work, and in the classroom. Variant forms, interpretations, and readings of culture, sometimes harnessed by political movements, can express discontent and resistance by individuals and groups who are or feel oppressed.

The meaning of culture is neither intrinsic nor imposed. It is locally manufactured and revised. People assign their own meanings and value to the texts, messages, ideologies, and products they receive. Those meanings are influenced by their cultural backgrounds and experiences (but, as we have seen, individuals and groups within a society also vary in their interpretations, actions, and reactions). When forces from world centers enter new societies they are **indigenized**—modified to fit the local culture. This is true of cultural forces as different as fast-food, music, housing styles, science, terrorism, celebrations, and political ideas and institutions (Appadurai 1990).

For example, Michaels (1986) found the film *Rambo* to be popular among aborigines in the deserts of central Australia. They had manufactured their own set of meanings from the film, but their reading was very different from the one in the minds of the movie's creators. The Native Australians saw Rambo as a representative of oppressed minorities, battling the white officer class. This reading expressed their negative feelings about white paternalism and existing race relations. The Native Australians also created tribal ties and kin links between Rambo and the prisoners he was rescuing. All this made sense to them, based on their experience. Native Australians are disproportionately represented in their nation's jails, and their most likely liberator would be someone with a personal kin link to them. These readings of *Rambo* were relevant meanings produced *from* the text, not *by* it (Fiske 1989).

Some social commentators see contemporary flows of people, technology, finance, information, and ideology as a cultural imperialist steamroller. This view overlooks the role of agency—the selective, synthesizing activities of human beings as they deal with cultural forces, images, and messages, and as they mobilize against perceived injustices. Having examined the role of globalization in cultural creation and exchange, we are ready to focus specifically on cultural unity and diversity in contemporary North America.

CHAPTER FOUR

The Multicultural Society

------------------------------ Icarians in America ------------------------------

On Labor Day weekend in 2001, New York City was bathed in sunlight. Its streets, shops, restaurants, and theaters were packed with locals and visitors there to celebrate leisure. Days before the terrorist attack on the World Trade Center, the world's capital offered its hospitality to those who were there to play, as it accommodated those who were there to work.

The city's Hilton Hotel was especially vibrant. From dawn to dawn the lobbies buzzed with joyful guests engaged in a frenzy of enthusiastic greetings, affectionate embraces and kisses, and endless chit-chat marked by "Greeklish" (a mix of Greek and English words). The 2001 national convention of the "Pan-Icarian Brotherhood of America—ICAROS" was in progress. Kozaitis (not an Icarian) was present to participate in what was to become a potent display of not only an "imagined community," but a self-consciously constructed affinity group whose members exhibit "connection" and "an identity of our own."

Icaria is one of the Northeastern Aegean Islands, a rather small and not well known place in a part of Greece distinguished by its physical and cultural diversity, due in part to its association with Turkey and an Asian heritage. At present many self-identified Icarians reside in Athens, Greece, but most live in the United States. More than 2,000 families participate in the annual celebration of their unified identity as Icarians, Greeks, and Americans. Proud of their financial success and professional achievements, Icarians in the United States attribute their political strength to the community they call ICAROS, which they have created in America. Recalling stories of discrimination, exclusion, racism, and poverty left behind by the early immigrants from Icaria, their descendants are planning an elaborate centennial celebration of the Brotherhood, to be held in 2003. As one Icarian leader put it, "It has taken us 100 years to establish ourselves as a community, but look at us now. We live in our own world, and we live well at that!"

The more financially secure and socially integrated members of an ethnic group are, the more likely they are to erect and maintain cultural boundaries of distinction. Why? Because they can afford it! This is especially true in multicultural societies like the United States and Canada. Kozaitis observed a reportedly affluent population, self-identified as "ethnic," whose members express their appreciation for a host society that nurtures its diversity. Most impressive was the presence of adolescents and young adults at this convention. Their investment in cultural continuity was especially clear in their parties, which young and old alike describe as a mating ground from which new families spring year after year.

Members of ICAROS articulate a rhetoric of ethnic pride and cultural authenticity. Specific religious and linguistic habits, music, food, and dance permit them to distinguish themselves from Icarians in Greece, from other regionally identified Greeks in America, such as the Pan-Thisvian Society (of which Kozaitis is a member), and from "all others." The ICAROS logo features Icarus, the son of Daedalus. A well-known figure in Greek mythology, Icarus serves as a symbol of the Icarians' common past. (Icarus fell and died tragically after using artificial wings that his father constructed; they were held together by wax, which melted when he flew too close to the sun to escape from the Labyrinth, a maze in which the king of Crete kept the Minotaur, the half-man–half-bull born to his queen after she mated with a sacred bull.) Members of ICAROS claim ownership of the mythical place in which "man's imagination to fly" has its beginnings. They use the terms "brother" and "sister" to refer to one another in conversation or print. Core values, such as the nuclear and extended family, endogamy, higher education, financial prosperity, and bipatriotism, are celebrated and transmitted to the young who, by their participation in this event and community, embrace and reproduce. (Bipatriotism refers to loyalties, identity, and participation in two societies.)

Every community is organized according to its history and geography, the material resources at its disposal, political relations, patterned behavior, and a system of core beliefs. People assert their *agency* to create communities which they imbue with meaning and power. In the process, they construct their history, which new generations review, reproduce, or change, not always consciously. Financially and socially secure in the United States, Icarians construct what they perceive to be a culture of their own, rooted in and sustained by Icarian traditions, customs, rituals, and values. Markers of an Icarian heritage are obvious. They include particular surnames, the *Ikariotiko* (an Icarian dance), and a local dialect of modern Greek. But the building blocks of this community are American made and, therefore, are culturally hybrid.

ICAROS follows American protocols of community organization. A national president leads this community, assisted by a vice president, a secretary, a treasurer, and a counselor. The community is further delineated according to six districts spanning all states and Canada, each district led by its own governor. Members are associated with one of 25 local chapters, each with its own national representative. Three chairmen, three directors, and a secretary are in charge of the Pan-Icarian Foundation, a charitable organization designed to raise funds and finance scholarships, summer youth camps in Icaria, a University Chair in Hellenic Studies, a residential retirement facility in Greece, and other community projects. During the reunion in New York, Greek was spoken intermittently in casual conversations, but most of the business meetings were conducted in English. Their content focused on "being and becoming Icarian in America." ICAROS is a product and a creation of a multicultural society. Its members have woven a cultural tapestry that includes elements of Ikaria, contemporary Greece, and mainstream American culture.

Human agency, the collective capacity of human beings to construct culture within historic and political processes, is easily realized in a society whose mainstream thrives on diversity. The case at hand illustrates that it is precisely the sociocultural advantages of being in the mainstream that empower ICAROS to cultivate a distinct collective identity. To be sure, a threat to a people's integrity can generate the collective will to resist oppression and to mobilize for cultural survival. The black, feminist, and gay movements attest to this principle, as do more recent organized efforts by the aged and people with disabilities to ensure their human rights. As this book demonstrates, agency, and its attendant expression of culture as power, is a key feature of the multicultural society. ☺

THE POWER OF CULTURE

Increasingly, North Americans—individuals and groups—are constructing identities on the basis of culture. That is, people use culture (shared knowledge, values, and experience) to organize society into cohesive groups with political, economic, educational, and moral goals. In the past, anthropologists tended to see culture as a given, rather than as a basis for *new* social identities. The tendency has been to portray culture as something passive, ages old, enduring, inherited. Culture (tradition) was seen as something unifying a whole society rather than a force capable of segmenting society into cohesive subgroups. The conventional view of culture has been that it was a social glue binding people through their common past rather than something being continually created and reworked in the present. The new emphasis, and a focus of this book, is on the role of human agency. This refers to the actions that individuals, especially leaders and mobilizers of culturally defined groups, take in making and remaking cultural identities.

Multiculturalism (from here on abbreviated as MC) is a volatile force. MC pervades the worlds of work, politics, public service, and personal relations. We confront elements of MC as we work, vote, socialize, and watch television. MC influences marketers of products, lobbyists advocating political change, physicians recommending treatment plans, architects designing accessible office buildings, and executives seeking to enhance diversity management among personnel.

Although MC is pervasive, its formal study has received too little attention. Consequently, MC remains a mystery to many, a burden to some, and a threat to others. The understanding of MC is hindered further by seeing it as an independent variable, when it is actually a symptom of larger changes. MC is not a neutral model; because of its political implications, it has advocates and opponents.

Based on the idea of culture, MC also has social, ideological, political, and economic dimensions. In this book we present MC in its context and totality—as a social condition, an idea, a movement, and part of our economy. We also explore the causes of its emergence.

CONCEPTUALIZING CULTURAL DIVERSITY

Basic to modern nation-states is socioeconomic stratification—differential access to resources, including the means of production. Stratification and segmentation (the division of society into discrete groups) produce a multiplicity of ranked cultural units, along with evaluations of their intrinsic worth. Efforts to expose, challenge, and change this ranking system constitute the crux of the movement known as MC. Our discussion of MC begins with a consideration of key features of diversity in contemporary North America.

Cultural diversity refers to variation in institutions, traditions, language, customs, rituals, beliefs, and values. All nations have such internal variation. Recent settlers of North America trace their origins to Europe, Africa, Asia, and Latin America. Within the United States and Canada many groups claim a particular heritage (e.g., ethnic roots) that distinguishes them from other such groups and from a mainstream, dominant national culture (Takaki 1993). Other kinds of groups are based on a common occupational status and identity. Still other expressions of diversity involve contrasts among rural, urban, and suburban lifestyles.

Another set of groups is defined by perceptions of reality, **cognitive ties**—what people know or think they know. *Knowing* complements two other kinds of social alignment: (1) *being*—social links corresponding to primordial ties such as kinship, descent, caste, or religion—and (2) *doing*—membership reflecting the civic ties that characterize nation-states, such as residence and participation in a district, county, state, province, or other governmental or administrative unit and its affairs, including work (Geertz 1963). In contemporary North America, cognitive ties compete, and coexist, with primordial and civic ties. These three means of social organization breed a variety of cultural units.

The presence of variety in contemporary North America is a given. MC, by contrast, particularly its political manifestation, is a North American achievement, a contemporary construction. MC stands for (1) the *acknowledgment* of variation, (2) the *belief* that all cultural segments merit equal value, scholarly interest, and social representation, and (3) the *practice* of seeking economic, political, and cultural parity for minority groups. MC differs from its predecessors, assimilation and pluralism. Each term corresponds to a way of dealing with diversity and a period in North American history.

Assimilation

Assimilation refers to the merging of groups and their traditions within a society that endorses a single common culture. Assimilation requires minorities to adopt the traits of the dominant culture. Assimilation was encouraged during the Great Immigration around 1900 and through World War II. This model applied mainly to the White Anglo-Saxon Protestants (WASPs) who have dominated the United States since its English colonization, and the European immigrants who followed, including Germans, Irish, Italians, and Russians. Native North American Indians, the first settlers of the New World, and the Africans who began to arrive in the 17th century as slaves were not easy candidates for assimilation. These groups, who were clearly different in physical appearance (phenotype) from the whites, were excluded from full assimilation. "White ethnics," by contrast (i.e., non-WASP Europeans), were encouraged to embrace the motto *e pluribus unum*, to forge one nation out of many nationalities.

The idea of a melting pot assumes that immigrants want to emulate the dominant group and seek to melt into one people. Blending is neither democratic nor selective. Rather, assimilation assumes that all groups that have had lower or marginal status would choose, and ought, to adopt dominant traits as their own. However, the assimilationist model has several flaws. Absorption into a mass culture means erasing prior cultural traits and identities—changing names, dress, speech, values, and behavior. Such adjustments foster "passing" or "fitting in." Assimilation requires internal, psychological allegiance to the dominant group as well as external, physical similarity. People who look like the dominants are most likely to blend in. Consider the first-generation American-born descendant of Greek peasants, Demetrios Demosthenis. By graduating from an Ivy League college, changing his name to James Demos, and dressing in preppy garb, he manages to become the "Ralph Lauren poster child." However, these markers in themselves don't get him far on Wall Street. His stature of 6 feet, fair skin, light-brown hair, and midwestern English combine to give him the stamp of social approval.

Assimilation rejects the value of ethnic customs. Loyalty to traditions from the old country declines as immigrants and their offspring negotiate upward mobility. On the other hand, evident racial differences and categories do not assimilate. Race isn't as malleable as ethnicity is. The African-American physician may be mistaken for a secretary in a medical office. A third-generation professor of Japanese descent is asked about his immigration status. The college student of mixed Korean and Anglo-Saxon heritage is still labeled Korean.

The assimilationist model focuses on individuals, not groups. That is, individuals merge; groups do not. Theoretically, a Yugoslav in the United States can assimilate to the dominant culture, as can an immigrant from Pakistan, or an African American from a rural area. However, Yugoslavs, Pakistanis, and African Americans do not assimilate into the mainstream collectively.

The assimilationist model assumes and emphasizes a single cultural core. This presumption of a normal national pattern of values and behavior can differentiate numerous marginal and peripheral groups. From these subcultures, the elite may select "qualified" individuals to join the privileged class, offering them access to resources and cultural capital.

Pluralism

Pluralism, not to be confused with the plural society concept to be discussed in Chapter 5, holds that ethnic *and* racial difference should be allowed to thrive, so long as such diversity does not threaten dominant values and norms. This view emerged in the 1970s, in the context of migration from eastern and southern Europe and Asia, and growing participation by African Americans and Hispanics in the labor force, higher education, and the Civil Rights movement. Unlike assimilation, pluralism embraces racial as well as ethnic differences. However, its emphasis is on *moral relativism,* a social ethic rooted in *tolerance* of diversity, rather than *acceptance* and *appreciation* of collective behavior that may contradict or threaten a dominant culture.

Notions derived from social Darwinism underlie pluralism. One is the idea that social groups compete for resources and power, and that they win or lose in the struggle for existence because of intrinsic qualities that make particular groups more or less fit than others. Pluralism interprets the relative fortune of groups through stereotypes involving their assumed strengths and weaknesses. East Indians, for example, may be perceived as ambitious, but the family orientation of Mexican Americans may be seen as impeding their mobility. While tolerating diversity, pluralism does not question the need for a dominant culture, nor does it challenge stratification. Pluralists may praise the festive spirit of Greek Americans, but a Greek president is somehow implausible. Also, pluralism regards ethnic boundaries as firm, cultural borders as static, and identities as fixed. Pluralists speak of "*the* Italians," "women," "Asians," "homosexuals," and "blacks," creating a monolithic image and ignoring diversity, often substantial, within the group.

Multiculturalism

Multiculturalism differs from assimilation and pluralism (1) by recognizing a multiplicity of legitimate cultural cores, or centers; (2) by acknowl-
edging cultural criteria as the source of group formation; and (3) by
promoting democratization and equity among groups. Assimilation and
pluralism are founded on the maxim *e pluribus unum* (out of many, one).
MC, by contrast, introduces a new ethos: In one, many. Society is seen not
as various traditions blending into one heritage, but as the coexistence of
many heritages and newly invented traditions within a single nation-state.

MC is manifest in many forms. First is MC as fait accompli, a neutral
condition describing present-day society and rooted in demographic reality.
The vital statistics of our population depict its global origins, phenotypical
variety, occupational diversity, and mosaic of cultural traits. Heterogeneity
is a social fact. In a generation North America has undergone a fundamental transformation. Increasingly our society is organized according to the
conceptualization, regulation, and management of difference.

Second is MC as ideology, a doctrine that influences our economic, political, and social systems. As a new moral order, MC pushes society toward sociocultural equity. The various segments of our population, along with their
institutions, behavior, and beliefs, are seen as having legitimacy and value.

Third, MC is manifest in policy and laws that seek to redress economic,
political, and social inequities. MC combats discrimination based on such
factors as origin, sex, and age. As policy, MC supports legal rights that government and private industry extend to persons by virtue of their citizenship
and their membership in a category. MC influences all domains of society,
including education and the media. Diversity is mainstreamed in workshops
and school curriculum reform and through media images.

MC as decorum permeates personal relations. Business transactions, romantic liaisons, friendships, and casual conversations are regulated by *political correctness,* the unwritten law and etiquette of contemporary society.

The most salient manifestation of MC is as **identity,** a psychosocial and
political orientation that individuals internalize and that is shared by people
united by a common status or experience. MC as identity is expressed in the
formation of **affinity groups,** aggregates that rival such institutions as the
family, neighborhood, and local community, as "the nursery of human nature" (Cooley 1909). Affinity groups are like the reference groups of modern
societies, such as political parties, religious affiliations, or professional organizations (Hyman 1942).

Affinity groups have emerged from, and often because of, subcultural
status. Implicit in the term *subcultures* is a hierarchical relation between
those units and a national culture. They are identified as subcultures by a
dominant, and presumably more valuable, culture of comparison. The prefix
sub denotes "below," therefore "less than," a higher culture. MC, by contrast,
conceptualizes "the other" as simply different, in a conscious attempt to establish equity between different segments of the population. Affinity groups

depend on action and politics for their existence. They are consciously constructed by people who share a common *experience* of living. They proliferate as black diaspora women, Asian Pacific homosexual men, the American Association of Retired Persons (AARP), and hundreds of other identities.

MC has overt and covert forms. This distinction affects the ways in which diversity is recognized and mobilized. Overt diversity includes variation in skin color, sex, or age. Such markers as mode of dress and accent also denote difference, and symbols alert us to variation in our midst. We see diversity when Indian women use a velvety dot (*bindia*) on their forehead to show they are married, when Jewish men wear a *yarmulke,* or when poor people wait in the rain to get into a soup kitchen. External markers, including the phenotype, subject groups to judgment. However, when valuation is based mainly on appearance, it is likely to be flawed or unfair; it may entail enhanced status for some or denial of rights for others.

Covert diversity can also be genuine and powerful. Orientations that may be concealed include class, religion, sexual preference, country of origin, and natal region. Bearers of hidden traits are advantaged by their ability to "pass," or to control their expression situationally and contextually. Consider the lesbian who presents herself as "straight" in a competition for a job. But pretending to be something one is not takes a psychological toll. The dominant etiquette may suggest that certain identities remain concealed. But consciousness raisers and mobilizers (community organizers) may try to bring such covert identities to the surface and use them for affirmative action. Others may then resent the public expression and spread of formerly concealed identities by social movements aimed at what they perceive as special rights. Taking pride in once-hidden identities, activists may strive to make the identity apparent—for example, through organization, speech, mannerisms, or dress.

MC is a new *social contract* in the making. Its chief organizing principle is *culture*. Political activism has spread awareness of difference within North America. MC validates the past and present contributions of various culturally defined groups. For example, black activists have stressed key roles played by African Americans in the economic development of the United States. MC exposes inequality, such as educational and economic disparities when Mexican Americans and Puerto Ricans are compared with other Americans. MC also advocates sociocultural parity, for example, the inclusion of women's or African-American studies in the core undergraduate curriculum.

THEORY OF MULTICULTURALISM

MC denotes a pattern of sociocultural integration for contemporary societies. Central to MC as a form of social integration is its relation to political power and its effectiveness in promoting change. In its most popular and palatable form, MC acknowledges human diversity. Its ethical relativism assumes that variation should be lateral rather than hierarchical. In other words, the various culturally defined groups within the multicultural society should be valued equally, with equal rights and status, rather than existing in a hierarchy, in which some groups rank higher than others. MC reveals the capacity of culture—specifically ideas, symbols, and political views—to create social realities.

Sociocultural Transformation

Technological change is the prime mover of social and cultural transformation. Simple technology is associated with slow change, whereas complex technical advances speed the alteration of economic, political, and social institutions (White 1949/1969; Harris 1979; Lenski, Lenski, and Nolan 1991). The Industrial Revolution, which began in England in the mid-18th century, led to the rapid concentration of people in cities. Contemporary technological progress, especially in transportation and the electronic media, has produced the Information Revolution. Human life is now determined chiefly by access to and application of technology and ideas in a global market economy. Concomitant with developing forms of economic and social organization are systems of meaning that people adopt to shape, define, and justify their lives. One of the most compelling features of contemporary societies is the role that culture itself, particularly human action and symbolism, plays in organizing and integrating our lives.

In nonindustrial societies, primordial attachments, including heritage, territory, descent, and marital alliances, are the main forms of sociocultural integration. Such societies may offer a fairly coherent and congenial way of life for their members. Hunting and gathering groups feature homogeneity, social and cultural unity, and political and economic equality, with stratification limited to gender and age. Members share resources, quality of life, and a common system of meaning.

Following the invention of agriculture, an increase in economic specialization was accompanied by the growth of social and political stratification. Agrarian communities were linked to cities, nation-states, and market economies. Kinship diminished as a cultural force, as formal economic, political, and religious institutions assumed a larger role in regulating interpersonal relations. Formal education supplemented enculturation as a socializing force. This also increased specialization and social inequality.

Later, with the Industrial Revolution, the dominant source of collective consciousness became people's relation to the production and consumption of goods in a market-oriented society. Occupational identities, loyalties, and ties assumed a new prominence. Economic specialization intensified, along with the formality and complexity of government, education, and religion.

Today's high-tech economy, based on services and information processing, has produced new forms of social organization. People now have social identities based not only on "who they are" and "what they do" but also on "what they know." Senses of self and of belonging are increasingly fueled by ideational energy. People who share political, psychological, and cognitive orientations establish new groups and identities. In North America, identities based on culture coexist with, but dominate, those with more conventional roots, such as ancestry, territory, and original homeland.

As old comfort zones erode, new ones emerge to meet our needs. Large-scale forces are pushing people worldwide into a general state of fragmentation, imbalance, disequilibrium, insecurity, and confusion. Correspondingly, people struggle, using culture as an organizing strategy, to build a congenial way of life and a coherent identity based on shared experience and meaning.

Multiculturalism in the North American Mainstream

MC expresses our need to belong. Today's North Americans are building relations, bonds, and loyalties through common knowledge. We may call this form of integration **ideational solidarity.** The needs to belong and to resist inequality translate into voluntary group construction, with the creation of charters for collective rights (Featherstone 1990; King 1991).

The global organization of work moves people and cultural content across national boundaries, creating a diverse workforce (Johnston 1994). People may sever existing ties and create new ones. Individuals often abandon, or modify, old patterns of behavior and thought and invent others for a new location (Wolf 1982). Today, social integration relies less on a shared past and territory, or descent, than it does on a shared present and political position.

What do we mean when we speak of culture as an integrative, mobilizing force? A culture may develop when individuals who are subjected to similar conditions, share similar experiences, and have similar interests organize and unite. Individual interests and rights are merged, articulated, and valorized as group interests and collective rights. The psychosocial plight of persons becomes the social plight of a group, a process that transforms the personal into the political.

When a personal predicament is articulated as a sociocultural phenomenon, it often warrants economic accommodation and attains political legitimacy. For example, when a homosexual seeks validation and protection as an American citizen, he does not talk about his sexual behavior. Rather, he marches in a pride parade along with thousands of other "Queer Nationalists" and displays a sign that reads: "It's about Human Rights, Stupid!" *MC is more than human diversity, personal preference, and artifacts. It is the political organization of culture in contemporary nation-states.* A striking feature of contemporary society is the active role that individuals are playing in constructing and defining culture.

Individuals who are **mobilizing agents** constitute another determinant of MC. These are elite members of minority groups, who also belong to the national elite. Often they are artists and intellectuals with access to major social institutions, especially education and the media. Their effectiveness reflects their strength and advantages as the privileged of the underprivileged. They have the technical means, including the written word, to contest inequity. In doing so, they give voice to a group of "others" marked by ethnicity, race, gender, and other social classifications. They fight exploitation of their "own kind" and mobilize others to work for reform.

The commercialization of MC has also influenced North American society. The entrepreneurial spirit reigns in the Western world of cultural production. Corporations consider segments of the gay market, the Hispanic market, and the senior market as they produce and advertise goods, services, and information. Some of them hire cultural consultants to assess the consumer tastes of a racially and ethnically diverse population. Clever marketers have generated *xenomania*, love of anything "otherly," from ethnic prints, jewelry, food, and music, to spiritualism. At home, Americans, particularly young educated ones, may display foreign artifacts, such as African masks in an Irish Catholic household.

The marketing of MC also benefits people who produce and sell items associated with their own native culture, heritage, or present culture of reference. Shops specializing in African goods, Native American objects, and

Illustrating the urban face of multicultural North America are these signs in English, Spanish, and Chinese on a building in New York City. What products are being advertised?

international gifts are a booming business in metropolitan centers. Ethnic enclaves and areas with concentrated gay and lesbian populations have specialty shops for local customers and interested visitors. Confirming diversity's mass appeal are catalogs that target goods, services, and ideas to specific cultures. Americans are consumers, and MC is a hot commodity.

Jennifer Steinhauer (1997) describes ways in which some large retail chains have started targeting cultural diversity, focusing especially on the fastest-growing ethnic group in the United States, the 35 million Americans of Hispanic origin. Previously, such chains as Sears and J.C. Penney did centralized buying, which was compatible with an assimilationist model, the notion that all Americans would want the same things. Now, signaling the significance of MC and diversity in the American mainstream, micromerchandising extends to varied groups and tastes. For example, Sears stores in Asian neighborhoods carry rice cookers and what buyers perceive to be suitable clothing sizes. Houston Sears offers western wear in February for Rodeo Week. But Hispanic customers in Texas get the most attention, because there are so many of them (one-third of the state's populace), linked by language, if not by a homogeneous culture.

MC started its penetration of retailing with grocery stores, to accommodate ethnic food preferences, and the trend has spread to other retail chains. In 1997, Sears had 148 stores concentrating on Hispanic shoppers in eight states. J.C. Penney had 120. Circuit City arranges for items bought in its American stores to be picked up by friends and relatives at affiliated outlets in Mexico.

A tour of the East Los Angeles Sears store, which caters to Spanish speakers, found subtle differences in almost every department. The women's department carried smaller sizes than other Sears stores did, and men's jeans had narrower waists and shorter inseams. Colors for women were brighter; and skirts, shorter. Custom-made curtains had been eliminated in favor of sewing machines (Steinhauer 1997).

Effective multicultural marketing recognizes in-group variation. Retailers do not stock each Hispanic-oriented store in exactly the same way. Products may be geared toward middle-class Cuban shoppers in Miami, immigrants from Mexican towns in Los Angeles, and students of Puerto Rican ancestry in New York. Some retail executives try to tweak stores, region by region. According to a merchandise manager quoted by Steinhauer, "Southern Californian Mexican-American is very different from a San Antonio Mexican-American" (1997).

Mainstream companies are also aiming sales pitches at homosexuals as part of efforts to reach segments of the general consumer market. Stuart Elliott (1997) notes that images associated with gay men and lesbians have become increasingly prevalent in print advertisements for products as disparate as Absolut vodka, American Express traveler's checks, Subaru automobiles, and Gardenburger vegetable patties. Such images are also turning up on TV, in commercials aimed at general audiences as well as gay and lesbian consumers. The spots feature same-sex couples, celebrities known to be homosexuals, drag performers, and even transsexuals. As of mid-1997, British and Canadian spots with kissing male and female couples, for Guinness and Molson Dry beers, had been made (Elliott 1997).

The Center of Cultural Production

As a social movement, MC takes aim at a particular social order. The United States features an elaborate system of ordering—of classifying and ranking groups. People are divided into status *groups,* including sociocultural *peripheries* organized by *varied social and cultural criteria of membership.* The society is culturally diverse, with social segments that remain symbolically subordinate to a ruling elite. A dominant culture of comparison is formed by occupants of *a center,* who possess a *standardized set of credentials and qualifications.* To borrow from Marx's paradigm, they own and control the means and relations of cultural production.

The culture of power is increasingly **heteromorphic,** that is, varied in appearance. Activists tend to stereotype the center as a monolithic world of wealthy WASP males. Actually, the emerging culture of power, thriving on cultural capital, selects for certain types of individuals, frequently regardless of sex, age, origin, class of birth, regional roots, sexual orientation, race, or religion. Such people are distinguished by actual or potential commercial success in the world of cultural production. The worth that society grants them is based on certain *constants:* production, profit, and creativity. The market value of imagination increases when it is articulated as information, viewpoint, design, technology, service, standard of production, and criteria for defining and improving the human condition. The polarity between the privileged and the underprivileged is marked less and less by conventional contrasts like black and white, male and female, or straight and gay. A more compelling dichotomy is that between the chosen and the rejects—the culturally fit and the others.

The center reinforces its legitimacy by constantly affirming its superior quality, morality, and value. The ranked segmentation of people, the media manipulation of group images, and the deliberate devaluation ("dissing") of certain social segments are intrinsic to this process.

The battle to maintain credibility by the dominant group may use *naturalization,* linking social stratification to biological and psychological factors. Intrinsic features of biology and psychology may be invoked to justify discrimination against those who fail to meet standards of production in a market economy. The idea of a natural hierarchy has been used to justify sexism, classism, racism, heterosexism, and ageism.

Another way to justify the subordination of groups is *rationalization,* the scientific justification of inferiority, which the center presents as fact. The value of the cultural content associated with ranked segments is measured against the dominant culture of comparison. By constructing skewed definitions of other groups, the dominant one sets the standard for human worth.

Justifications of stratification are imbued with a myth, a master fiction that supports inequality among groups. The master fiction of contemporary market societies, including our own, emphasizes the opposition of culture and subculture. Before MC, culture had been presented as mass, official, formal, real, desirable, and true. By contrast, subculture referred to folklore, to alternative, unofficial, exotic, limited, segmental, or vulgar patterns of behavior and thought. The dominant culture reinforced the assumed relation between cultural value and commercial success.

Agency and Resistance

But this has changed. In a multicultural society, minority cultures deemed inferior by dominant standards of value respond by creating standards of their own. Leaders of those communities, whose inherent "bifocality" informs them of the operative rules in both the dominant and the minority group, mobilize their members to invest and develop inwardly, in opposition to outgroup definitions of humanity. These manifestations of MC contradict what Antonio Gramsci (1971) refers to as the "spontaneous consent" that subordinates give to the centralized, dominant culture in nation-states. Rather, MC demonstrates the effects of planned resistance to state policies that do not meet the needs, or represent the interests, of many Americans.

Individuals are more easily assimilated and accommodated than are clusters. They are also more easily ignored. It is more difficult to assimilate, or obliterate, culturally organized communities. They demand and receive political attention. Persistence of a dominant culture in contemporary nation-states breeds many other culturally organized groups who compete for resources, legal protection, and a meaningful life.

Illustrating agency and resistance, Mirta Ojito (1997) describes how hundreds of residents of New Britain, Connecticut, created an organization called Puerto Rican Organization for Unity and Dignity (PROUD) to combat prejudice there. The impetus was a report in which some local business leaders blamed Puerto Ricans for the city's lack of economic progress. They said Puerto Rican workers were lazy and unreliable, with poor family values and language skills. The only solution for New Britain, they said, was to rid the city of the Puerto Ricans, who, they claimed, strained the city's public housing and financial resources.

The report caused such a stir that several business leaders apologized for their comments, and two of them lost their leadership positions. Not content with these acts of contrition, Puerto Ricans in New Britain contacted the Puerto Rican Legal Defense and Education Fund, a national advocacy group based in New York, which, in turn, asked the federal government to investigate the handling of public money (which had financed the report) in New Britain.

Historically, New Britain has been a city of immigrants (Irish, Germans, Italians, Poles, and Puerto Ricans), with the last ones to arrive traditionally blamed for alleged shortcomings. By the late 1990s, however, with the loss of jobs in the hardware industry, the city's economic situation had never been as bleak. Anti-immigrant sentiment had become so pronounced, according to PROUD, that some New Britain business leaders felt emboldened to vent private feelings in a public document (Ojito 1997).

The report spurred heated meetings, demonstrations, and the formation of PROUD. In a letter to town leaders, members of PROUD made several demands. They sought to serve on public boards and city commissions and to have a voice in the city's economic planning. The anti-Hispanic rhetoric in the report ignited the Hispanic community, propelled its mobilization, and forced business people to pay attention. Puerto Ricans made up 16 percent of New Britain's population in the 1990 Census, increasing to 27 percent in 2000. PROUD forced the city to recognize the purchasing power and voting significance of an organized Puerto Rican population.

The increasing political sophistication of Puerto Ricans in New Britain, moving from anger to specific demands and, later, to active participation, is similar to what has happened among Hispanic groups across the United States. "It's like someone lit a keg and it is ready to go," observed Lisa Navarrete, the public information director of the National Council of La Raza, the largest Hispanic civil rights organization in the United States. Ms. Navarrete pointed to 1996 voting records (5.2 million Hispanic votes were cast in the presidential election nationwide, a jump of more than a million from 1992) as an example of how Hispanic citizens are influencing politics (Ojito 1997). Hispanics cast 7 percent of votes in the 2000 presidential election, versus 5 percent in 1996 (*Migration News* 2000).

For one more example of Hispanic agency, see the 2000 PBS documentary "The Forgotten Americans" or visit the website http://www.pbs.org/klru/forgottenamericans. The focus is some 500,000 people living in neighborhoods on the South Texas–Mexico border. The communities of Las Colonias consist predominantly of Mexican-American families who live in abject poverty. Many lack running water and electricity in their homes. Traditionally, these people, who are U.S. citizens, have had only rudimentary representation. Recently, residents have formed a grass-roots effort to lobby for economic development funds. They have organized themselves into a political force that works with lawmakers to take action on behalf of the community and its human rights.

MC depends on human agency, the organized efforts of leaders of disadvantaged groups (and their followers). Their role as *culture makers* has given life to patterns of culture and thought that question, contradict, and often defy the center. However, their work does not eliminate a center altogether. Rather, it constructs a new dominant core by infusing it with personnel and influences from varied peripheries. Another structural manifestation of MC is the creation of multiple centers, or **culturelets,** within the nation-state. Transformation of the center forces Americans to adjust by constructing such smaller structures based on culture, through which they achieve participation and social integration, and within which they meet emotional and spiritual needs.

MULTICULTURALISM: THE MASTER MOVEMENT

We have seen that MC involves political mobilization—organized activity seeking social change. Contemporary society produces culturally differentiated groups, whose leaders and other members work to achieve social and political legitimacy. A global information economy, an increasingly diverse population, and the decline of state influence in daily life are factors that encourage interest groups to work to realize self-determination, security, and meaning. As a master social movement, MC encompasses all the particular movements in progress, such as the Afrocentric movement and the women's movement. MC seeks to liberate and democratize all minority groups that occupy the peripheries of society. This effort has fueled awareness of stratification in North America, the elevation of culture as power, and an appreciation of culture as an agent of social change.

As a movement, MC emphasizes conscious, directed change. Advocates fight for parity for all segments of the population. This focus differs from the civil rights outlined by the U.S. Constitution, which guarantees fundamental freedoms to *individuals*. The prospect of extending civil, or human, rights to all distinct *groups* in one nation-state is more challenging. But the technology of our Information Age facilitates communication and collaboration for a common cause or mission.

Over the past several decades, social movements have produced significant changes in North America. The Civil Rights movement of the 1950s and 1960s eliminated legal segregation and gained rights for African Americans. The women's liberation movement sought for women the same economic, social, and political rights that men enjoy. The Civil Rights Act of 1964 spurred federal action against institutional discrimination based on race and sex. Later, affirmative action was implemented to ensure more equal representation of African Americans, women, and other minorities in the economy and education, spheres historically dominated by white men. To enhance equity in the labor force, the Equal Employment Opportunity Commission (EEOC) investigates discriminatory practices within social institutions.

More recently, collective efforts to secure the civil rights of homosexuals, or those who define themselves as gay, lesbian, or bisexual, have helped change the ways in which Americans view and judge love, psychosexual orientation, sexual behavior, and gender identity. Legislation to protect the legal rights of domestic partners, including people of the same sex who live together and declare long-term commitment, is gaining slow acceptance. Also pursuing organized efforts are people with disabilities, the elderly, and other groups who feel their interests and needs are not being met by formal institutions.

MC differs from prior social movements in that it represents a variety of collective interests, rather than those of a single category. There are several reasons for the rise and success of MC. First is actual or perceived differential access to resources. For example, women now judge their success and comparable worth in the labor market by comparison with men (England

1992). The global women's movement continues to fight for greater political participation by women (Davis, Leijenaar, and Oldersma 1991). African Americans compare their representation in our economy, education, and social life with that of other Americans (Wilson 1984; Lichter 1989). Afro-centrism draws on race and culture as organizing principles, promoting African patterns and perspectives as a strategy in seeking the cultural autonomy of African Americans (Asante 1987, 1988).

Second is actual or perceived economic alienation. Our economy breeds ageism, prejudice and discrimination against the elderly, who are displaced as a group. Economic factors encourage retirement from official labor participation and thus from social ties linked to an occupational status. More important, the economy rewards production, speed, efficiency, and profit. These criteria tend to marginalize and devalue groups that don't measure up to market demands, including the elderly and people with disabilities (Butler 1975). The disabilities civil rights movement combats inaccurate views of people with disabilities and fosters their socioeconomic integration. These efforts have resulted in the Rehabilitation Act of 1973 and the Americans with Disabilities Act of 1990 (Shapiro 1993).

Third is actual or perceived inequality in citizenship rights. Failure to extend legal protection to all citizens spurs organized corrective efforts. For example, the gay movement battles homophobia and negative stereotypes of homosexuals, gays, lesbians, and bisexuals, and fights to extend their civil and constitutional rights (Mohr 1988). The success of this movement owes much to the composition of its personnel, its concentration of white, educated men and women, who are generally members of the middle and upper classes. The collective capacity to articulate the movement's mission as a question of human rights transforms sexual orientation from a private matter into a public issue.

Fourth is actual or perceived inferior cultural status. Besides their economic and political disadvantages, certain categories of Americans also suffer from prejudice and discrimination on the basis of their traditions and customs. Rural Americans, the poor, Southerners, Native Americans, Mexican Americans, and Puerto Ricans are differentiated from dominant cultural norms because of their *cultural difference*. They are also subordinated and discriminated against for their presumed *cultural inferiority*. A Puerto Rican who speaks with an accent is more likely to be judged unqualified for public office than one without an accent. Similarly, expression of certain agrarian values, for example, "freedom from supervision, flexibility of work pace, and daily independence," subjects farmers to prejudice and limits the degree of integration and political parity farm workers can achieve in large-scale agribusiness (Barlett 1993, p. 79).

Native Americans have faced cultural subordination since the early settlers from Europe distinguished "primitive" native culture from "progressive" European culture. Recently, Native Americans have organized to reclaim lands, to demand control over reservations, to construct their own social standing in national society, and to assert pride in their cultural heritage

Over the past several decades, social movements have produced significant changes in North America. Here some 150 people march in Boston's second Disability Pride Day. The event aims at celebrating the lives of people with disabilities, educating the general public, and demonstrating that disability is a natural part of the human experience. Speakers at the event stressed rights to equal access and participation in society. This photo shows that people of many backgrounds, ages, and identities are unified politically by the disability movement.

and identity (Josephy 1982; Fost 1991). Similarly, educated and politically active Latinas and Latinos have worked collectively to improve the socio-cultural standing of Hispanics who, like Native Americans, suffer from both material deprivation and cultural discrimination.

For example, James Engstrom examines problems and solutions reflecting Mexican migration to Dalton, Georgia. The local carpet industry welcomes the immigrant labor force, but local political leaders and residents complain about the strain the Mexicans place on the local economy and school system. Through an exchange program with a Mexican university, co-funded by industrialists and school officials, the community now benefits. Graduates of that university now work as teachers' aides in the local schools. Engstrom notes that the carpet industry, "a loud and respected voice in the community, is publicly articulating a positive response to immigration and is celebrating the new multiculturalism of Dalton" (2001, p. 53).

As a political movement, MC seeks to promote the interests of all groups that have faced discrimination. Some disadvantaged social segments lack the resources and personnel that political movements require. The Afrocentric movement, the women's movement, and the gay movement have succeeded because the ranks of each include a strong elite, which effectively advances the political agenda. These three movements constitute the basis of such mini-intracommunity and cross-community movements as lesbians of color.

All the particular movements by self-defined collectivities combine to create a master movement. Seeking economic prosperity, political legitimacy, cultural integrity, personal security, and human worth for all Americans, the multicultural society has several stances and goals. It questions the superiority and value of a cultural center. It focuses energies on "decentering," on recognizing a multiplicity of cultural cores within a single society. MC challenges the naturalized hierarchy of groups within the labor market and society. MC recognizes permeable group boundaries, fluid social identities, and multiple memberships and statuses of North Americans. It reinforces the expression of personal identity through culturally organized groups. It emphasizes group-determined definitions, needs, and interests. It encourages in-group cultural production and representation of collective agony and rage as prerequisites to collective action. MC promotes the use of culture as a source of power—identity politics that rely on numbers and political consensus. It generates institutionalized, group-determined practices for self-protection, preservation, and reproduction. It advocates absolute cultural relativism in society. MC is rooted in a rapidly integrating world system with a proliferation of culture-based groups. The discontent felt by such groups and the mobilization by minority elites across different groups foster collaboration aimed at social reform.

CHAPTER FIVE

Ethnicity

"HOW ETHNIC!"

Consider the expression "How ethnic!" What images, associations, and meanings come to mind? Does this phrase convey certain physical characteristics, such as skin color, hair texture, or facial features? What cultural attributes, for example, speech, dress style, or religious beliefs, do you think of as being ethnic? Is ethnicity absolute and salient, or tentative and conditional?

Now utter the phrase yourself. Pay attention to your intonation. What impressions, sentiments, and judgments surface when you observe or imagine ethnicity? Do you feel liberated, threatened, disgusted, or amused? In what ways do these feelings and values inform your behavior and attitude toward people and artifacts? Are you likely to show empathy or antagonism toward a classmate who is ethnic? Do you find it easier to attend an ethnic festival or to pursue a romantic relationship with a person who is labeled ethnic? How do you justify your opinions and actions with respect to ethnic people? Do you feel ethnic yourself?

The remark "How ethnic!" was uttered by a couple of restaurant patrons to describe, and to judge, the maitre d' who escorted them to their table. The subject was convinced the comment was derogatory. He knew that their description was misguided. Since the patrons were Caucasian, he wondered if they were referring to his dark skin, his accent, or his body type. Could it be his occupation? It surely was not his uniform; he was dressed in a tuxedo.

Regardless of the cues that may have sparked their impression, the subject was left feeling devalued—different and less-than. Behind the ethnic image was an immigrant from India, a member of a high caste, and the son of two physicians. His father had been dean of a medical school. He had been raised among an intellectual elite. Himself an internist, he had taken a temporary restaurant job to help support his family, while he and his wife awaited a residency license to practice medicine in the United States. One's objective, visible ethnic status doesn't always correspond to one's subjective, essential identity.

Traditions, customs, and ceremonies that are the bedrock in one society may be modified or ignored by immigrants who settle in another. Behavior that confirms a woman's status in an Indian caste system changes when she migrates to North America as an urban professional. Lifestyle requirements in a new society vary, and may even contradict, how people act in their country of birth, despite the constancy of ethnic identity. For example, a Filipina science teacher in Brazil lives differently from a Filipina pianist in Chicago. Both live differently from the way a Filipina housekeeper in Athens, Greece, lives. Difference in the cultural life of each is linked to class, profession, and the host society, but all identify ethnically as Filipinas.

Ethnic groups do select particular symbols, rituals, sacred laws, and special feast days to help them preserve a sense of a shared heritage. For Greek Americans, higher education and economic success American-style are primary objectives. Yet they may also be adamant about transmitting the Greek language and Orthodox religion to their American-born children. Middle- and upper-class African Americans sometimes draw on Black English Vernacular (BEV) to reinforce in-group solidarity and affirm shared experience in multicultural America.

Adoption of American core values and practices may incorporate people who ascribe to themselves a Guatemalan, a Chinese, or a Nigerian identity into the educational and economic elite of the United States. It is common for people who claim attachment to an ethnic group or an ethnic identity to behave and think like mainstream Americans. Consider the predicament of a group of Asian college women who maintain strong loyalties to in-group dietary, sexual, and social rules. However, as college students, they participate in spring break, student protests, internships, and the junior-year-abroad program. These habits facilitate alliances with non-Asian peers and secure them a place in mainstream American college culture. One American-born student of Pakistani immigrant parents describes his life as a "double closet." Beliefs, rituals, and ceremonies that he shares with his family and other Pakistanis are unknown to his American friends, teachers, and colleagues. Conversely, his parents and relatives are oblivious to his "other life"—habits and customs of the American college scene.

Today many people live by two or more cultural codes of conduct, depending on the society that hosts them at different times in their lives. Mexicans who work seasonally in the United States maintain a sense of

People may observe two or more cultural codes of conduct depending on the society that hosts them at different times in their lives. Mexicans who work seasonally in the United States, such as these strawberry workers in California, maintain a sense of binationalism, affiliation with two nation-states.

binationalism, affiliation with two nation-states. Dominicans who live and work in the United States have formed a *transnational community,* cultural patterns, loyalties, and social relations that are regionally rooted but linked to larger systems. An American ambassador stationed in Costa Rica for four years contends with a dual track in the enculturation of his adolescent children. They must learn and practice customs native to Costa Rica and also observe American traditions and rituals. Brazilian immigrants in New York City are there "in body, not soul." They work as low-wage employees to earn enough money to be able to return to Brazil and maintain a middle-class lifestyle there (Margolis 1994).

Ethnicity no longer implies lower class, or inferior social status. Recent waves of migration from Asia, particularly India, Japan, and the Philippines, include a high percentage of physicians, engineers, scientists, and academics. These middle- and upper-middle-class professionals maintain regular contact with friends, relatives, and colleagues in their country, or culture, of birth. They are proficient in their native language. They may speak it preferentially, remain active in the politics of their homeland, and observe native holidays and feast days. This increasingly large segment of the American population identifies itself, and is identified by others, as ethnic. However, a close examination of lifestyle also reveals strong allegiance to mainstream American habits and values. Ethnic diversity is as prevalent among mainstream Americans as is American mainstream culture among ethnic-identified individuals and groups. In fact, some of the more lavish exhibits of ethnic identity come from individuals and groups who have high status within the North American cultural hierarchy. As one middle-class professional immigrant put it, "We can afford to be ethnic!" ☺

ETHNICITY AND SOCIAL STATUSES

We know from previous chapters that culture is a powerful organizing force that is shared, learned, symbolic, patterned, all-encompassing, adaptive, and maladaptive. Now we consider more closely and specifically the relation between culture and ethnicity. Ethnicity is based on cultural similarities and differences in a society or nation. The similarities are with members of the same ethnic group; the differences are between that group and others.

As with any culture, members of an **ethnic group** *share* certain beliefs, values, habits, customs, and norms because of their common background. They define themselves as different and special because of cultural features. This distinction may arise from language, religion, historical experience, geographic isolation, kinship, or race (see the next two chapters). Markers of an ethnic group may include a collective name, belief in common descent, a sense of solidarity, and an association with a specific territory, which the group may or may not hold (Ryan 1990, pp. xiii, xiv).

Ethnicity means identification with, and feeling part of, an ethnic group and exclusion from certain other groups because of this affiliation. Ethnic feeling and associated behavior vary in intensity within ethnic groups and countries and over time. A change in the degree of importance attached to an ethnic identity may reflect political changes (Soviet rule ends—ethnic feeling rises) or individual life cycle changes (young people relinquish, or old people reclaim, an ethnic background).

We saw in Chapter 2 that people may participate in multiple levels of culture. The various culturally organized segments of a society, including ethnic groups in a nation, have different learning experiences as well as shared ones. Cultural diversity within a nation is associated with ethnicity, class, region, religion, and other factors. Individuals often have more than one group identity. People may be loyal, depending on circumstances, to their neighborhood, school, town, state or province, region, nation, continent, religion, ethnic group, or interest group (Ryan 1990, p. xxii). In a complex society like the United States or Canada, people constantly negotiate their social identities. All of us wear different hats, presenting ourselves sometimes as one thing, sometimes as another.

The term **status** can be used to refer to such "hats"—to any position that determines where someone fits in society. Social statuses include parent, professor, student, factory worker, Democrat, shoe salesperson, labor leader, ethnic-group member, and thousands of others. People always occupy multiple statuses (e.g., Hispanic, Catholic, infant, brother). Among the statuses we occupy, particular ones dominate in particular settings, such as son or daughter at home and student in the classroom.

An **ascribed status** is one that people have little or no choice about occupying. Age is an ascribed status; people can't choose not to age. Race and ethnicity are usually ascribed; people are born members of a certain group and remain so all their lives. An **achieved status,** by contrast, is one that isn't automatic but comes through traits, talents, actions, efforts, activities, and accomplishments.

In many societies an ascribed status is associated with a position in the social/political hierarchy. **Minority groups** are subordinate. They have inferior power and less secure access to resources than do **majority groups,** which are superordinate, dominant, or controlling. Minorities need not have fewer members than the majority group does. Women in the United States and blacks in South Africa have been numerical majorities but minorities in terms of income, authority, and power. Often ethnic groups are minorities. When an ethnic group is assumed to have a biological basis, it is called a **race.** Discrimination against such a group is called **racism**. The next two chapters consider race in social and biological perspective.

Minority groups are obvious features of stratification in the United States. The 2000 poverty rate was 7.5 percent for non-Hispanic whites, 22.1 percent for blacks, and 21.2 percent for Hispanics (U.S. Census 2000). Comparing the native-born with the foreign-born populations of the United States, the poverty rate was 10.7 percent for the former and 15.7 percent for the latter. Naturalized U.S. citizens, however, had a lower poverty rate (9.7 percent) than that of either natives or foreign-born (overall) (U.S. Census 2000). Census data consistently confirm the inequality that continues to affect African Americans, Hispanics, and Pacific Islanders. Inequality shows up consistently in unemployment figures and in median household income. In 2000, median household incomes in the United States stood at $30,439 for African Americans and $33,447 for Hispanics (both figures are all-time highs), and in the same year it was $45,904 for non-Hispanic whites. Note that although the African-American income figure reached an all-time high, the figure for whites was 51 percent higher (U.S. Census 2000).

Status Shifting

Sometimes statuses, particularly ascribed ones, are mutually exclusive. It's hard to bridge the gap between black and white or male and female (although some rock stars have seemed to be trying to do so). Sometimes, taking a status or joining a group requires a conversion experience, acquiring a new and meaningful identity, such as becoming a "born again" Christian, or "coming out of the closet."

Some statuses aren't mutually exclusive but contextual. People can be both black and Hispanic or both a mother and a senator. One identity is used in certain settings, another in different ones. We call this the situational negotiation of social identity. When ethnic identity is flexible and situational (Moerman 1965), it can become an achieved status. B. Benedict (1970), Despres (1975), and B. Williams (1989) all stress the fluidity and flexibility of ethnicity.

Hispanics, for example, may move through levels of culture (shifting ethnic affiliations) as they negotiate their identities. *Hispanic* is an ethnic category based mainly on language. It includes whites, blacks, and racially mixed Spanish speakers. There are also Native American, and even Asian, Hispanics. *Hispanic* lumps together millions of people of diverse geographic origin—Puerto Rico, Mexico, Cuba, El Salvador, Guatemala, the Dominican Republic, and other Spanish-speaking counties of Central and South America and the Caribbean. *Latino* is a broader category, which can also include Brazilians (who speak Portuguese).

A 53 percent increase in the number of Mexican Americans fueled a 13 million rise in the number of Hispanic Americans between 1990 and 2000. The national origins of American Hispanics/Latinos in 2000 were as follows:

National Origin	Millions of People
Mexican American	20.6
Puerto Rican	3.4
Cuban	1.2
Central American	1.7
South American	1.4
Dominican	0.8
Other Hispanic/Latino origin	6.1
Total	35.3

Source: http://www.census.gov/Press-Release/www/2001/cb01-81.html.

Mexican Americans (Chicanos), Cuban Americans, and Puerto Ricans may mobilize to promote general Hispanic issues (e.g., opposition to English-only laws), but they act as three separate interest groups in other contexts. Cuban Americans are richer on average than Chicanos and Puerto Ricans are, and their class interests and voting patterns differ. Cubans often vote Republican, but Puerto Ricans and Chicanos generally favor Democrats. Some Mexican Americans whose families have lived in the United States for generations have little in common with new Hispanic immigrants, such as those from Central America. Many Americans, especially those fluent in English, claim Hispanic ethnicity in some contexts but shift to a general American identity in others.

It would appear that the label "Hispanic" is used chiefly by Northeasterners in the United States, and by the U.S. Census Bureau. This practice is misleading because it implies that all Spanish-speaking groups have the same cultural identity, and that they are all of Spanish extraction. We know that Spanish-speaking populations in the United States and Canada also claim Native American and African ancestry. Furthermore, they distinguish themselves not only according to region or country of origin but also with political labels that signify in-group cultural construction. For example, the label "Latino" includes all peoples of Latin American origin, while the classification "Chicano" refers specifically to a political and ideological consciousness among Mexican Americans (Russell 1994).

As social categories, including ethnic labels, proliferate in our increasingly diverse society, some people have trouble deciding on their social identity, on a label that fits. One day a Korean-American student asked Kottak, following his lecture on the social construction of race and ethnicity (see the next chapter), what she was, in ethnic terms. She had been born and raised in the United States by parents from Korea. She told Kottak about visiting Korea, meeting her relatives there, and being considered by them—and feeling herself—American. She finds it hard to feel Korean. In the United States she is labeled Asian, Oriental, or Asian American. But she doesn't feel much in common with other Asians and Asian Americans, like Chinese, Japanese, Vietnamese, Laotians, and Cambodians. After the discussion, she concluded that a reasonable ethnic label for her was Korean American. Happily, she had found an ethnic identity, important in the contemporary United States.

ETHNIC GROUPS, NATIONS, AND NATIONALITIES

What is the relation between an ethnic group and a nation? The term **nation** was once synonymous with a tribe or an ethnic group. All three of these terms referred to a single culture sharing a single language, religion, history, territory, ancestry, and kinship. Thus one could speak interchangeably of the Seneca (American Indian) nation, tribe, or ethnic group. Now *nation* has come to mean a **state,** an independent, centrally organized political unit, a government. *Nation* and *state* have become synonymous. Combined in **nation-state** they refer to such an autonomous political entity, a country, like the United States or Canada.

Because of migration, conquest, and colonialism, most nation-states are not ethnically homogeneous, and the term *nation-state* is then a misnomer. Another reason for ethnic diversity is that states sometimes manipulate ethnicity and encourage ethnic divisions for political and economic ends. No more than one-fourth of all countries are ethnically homogeneous. Of 132 nation-states existing in 1971, Connor (1972) found just 12 (9 percent) to be ethnically homogeneous. In another 25 (19 percent), a single ethnic group accounted for more than 90 percent of the population. Forty percent of the countries contained more than five significant ethnic groups.

In a later study, Nielsson (1985) classified only 45 (27 percent) of 164 states as "single nation-group" (i.e., ethnic group) states (with one ethnic group accounting for more than 95 percent of the population). Identified as the three most homogeneous were North Korea, South Korea, and Portugal. Nielsson's study actually underestimates the ethnic diversity of modern states. There is reason to question the ethnic homogeneity of some of the countries on his list, such as Japan (see the next chapter). Further, many of the countries he lists are now multiethnic because of increased immigration.

Nationalities and Imagined Communities

Ethnic groups that once had, or wish to have or regain, autonomous political status (their own country) are called **nationalities.** In the words of Benedict Anderson (1991), they are "imagined communities." Even when they become nation-states, they remain imagined communities, because most of their members, though feeling deep comradeship, will never meet as an actual community (Anderson 1991, pp. 6–10). They can only imagine that they all participate in the same social entity.

Anderson traces western European nationalism, which arose in England, France, and Spain, back to the 18th century. He stresses that language and print played a crucial role in the growth of European national consciousness. The novel and the newspaper were "two forms of imagining" communities (consisting of all the people who read the same sources and thus witnessed the same events) that flowered in the 18th century (Anderson 1991, pp. 24–25).

Over time, political upheavals and wars have divided many imagined national communities that arose in the 18th and 19th centuries. The German and Korean homelands were split after wars, according to Communist and capitalist ideologies. World War I dispersed the Kurds, who remain only an imagined community. Forming a majority in no state, Kurds are a minority group in Turkey, Iran, Iraq, and Syria. Similarly, Azerbaijanis, who are related to Turks, were a minority in the former Soviet Union, as they still are in Iran.

Migration is another reason certain ethnic groups live in different nation-states. Massive migration in the decades before and after 1900 brought Germans, Poles, and Italians to Brazil, Canada, and the United States. Chinese, Senegalese, Lebanese, and Jews have spread all over the world. Some of these (e.g., descendants of Germans in Brazil and the United States) have assimilated to their host nations and no longer feel connected to the imagined community of their origin.

In creating multitribal and multiethnic states, colonialism often erected boundaries that fit poorly with prior cultural divisions; but colonial institutions also helped create new imagined communities beyond nations. A good example is the idea of **négritude** (black association and identity) developed by dark-skinned intellectuals from the Francophone (French-speaking) colonies of West Africa and the Caribbean.

ETHNIC TOLERANCE AND ACCOMMODATION

Ethnic diversity may be associated with positive group interaction and co-existence or with conflict (discussed below). There are nation-states in which multiple cultural groups live together in reasonable harmony.

Cultural Assimilation

Assimilation was discussed in the last chapter as a historically specific ideology for dealing with cultural diversity. Assimilation describes the process of change that a minority ethnic group may experience when it moves to a country where another culture dominates. By assimilating, the minority adopts the patterns and norms of its host culture. It is incorporated into the dominant culture to the point that it no longer exists as a separate cultural unit. Not only is the assimilationist model historically specific, it is also culturally specific. Some countries, such as Brazil, are more assimilationist than others are. Germans, Italians, Japanese, Middle Easterners, and east Europeans started migrating to Brazil late in the 19th century. These immigrants all assimilated to Brazilian culture, which has Portuguese, African, and Native American roots. The descendants of the immigrants speak the national language (Portuguese) and participate in national culture. During World War II, Brazil, which was on the Allied side, forced assimilation by banning instruction in any language other than Portuguese, especially in German.

Brazil has been more of a melting pot than have the United States and Canada, in which ethnic groups have always retained more distinctiveness and self-identity. Kottak remembers his first visit, in 1984, to the southern Brazilian city of Porto Alegre, the site of mass migration by Germans, Poles, and Italians around 1900. Transferring an expectation derived from his North American culture to Porto Alegre, he asked for a tour of the city's ethnic neighborhoods. The tour guide couldn't understand what Kottak was talking about. Except for a Japanese-Brazilian neighborhood in the city of São Paulo, the idea of an ethnic neighborhood has been alien to Brazil.

The Plural Society

Assimilation is not inevitable. Ethnic distinctions can persist despite generations of interethnic contact. Through a study of three ethnic groups in Swat, Pakistan, Fredrik Barth (1958/1968) challenged an old idea that interaction always leads to assimilation. He showed that ethnic groups can be in contact for generations without assimilating and can live in peaceful coexistence.

Barth (1958/1968, p. 324) used the term *plural society*, which he extended to the entire Middle East, for a society combining ethnic contrasts and economic interdependence. (Do not confuse this term with the concept of pluralism, discussed in Chapter 4.) He borrowed the term from J. S. Furnivall (1944), who first used it to describe the Netherlands East Indies, now Indonesia. It has also been used for Caribbean societies (Smith 1965). Furnivall's plural Indonesia consisted of three main ethnic groups: the colonialists (the Dutch), the dominated natives (the Indonesians), and a middle group of merchants and small-scale businesspeople (Chinese immigrants). The comparable groups in the Caribbean were European colonialists, African slaves and their descendants, and Asian (especially Indian) immigrants. Furnivall saw domination and potential conflict as inevitable features of the plural society, which he believed would shatter without strong colonial rule.

Barth (1958/1968, p. 324) offered a more optimistic take on plural societies. Specifically he saw a **plural society** as one that combines ethnic contrasts, ecological specialization—that is, use of different environmental resources by each ethnic group—and the economic interdependence of those groups. Consider his description of the Middle East (in the 1950s): "The 'environment' of any one ethnic group is not only defined by natural conditions, but also by the presence and activities of the other ethnic groups on which it depends. Each group exploits only part of the total environment, and leaves large parts of it open for other groups to exploit." The ecological interdependence (or, at least, the lack of competition) between ethnic groups may be based on different activities in the same region or on longtime occupation of different regions in the same nation-state.

In Barth's view, ethnic boundaries are most stable and enduring when the groups occupy different ecological niches. That is, they make their living in different ways and don't compete. Ideally, they should depend on each other's activities and exchange with one another. When different ethnic groups exploit the *same* ecological niche, the militarily more powerful group will normally replace the weaker one. If they exploit more or less the same niche, but the weaker group is better able to use marginal environments, they may also coexist (Barth 1958/1968, p. 331). Given such niche specialization, ethnic boundaries, distinctions, and interdependence can be maintained, although the specific cultural features of each group may change. By shifting the analytic focus from individual cultures or ethnic groups to *relations* between cultures or ethnic groups, Barth (1958/1968, 1969) has made important contributions to ethnic studies.

Multiculturalism and Ethnic Identity

As we saw in Chapter 4, the view of cultural diversity in a country as something good and desirable is a key feature of multiculturalism (MC). The multicultural model is the opposite of the assimilationist model, in which minorities are expected to abandon their traditions and values, replacing them with those of the majority. MC promotes the affirmation and practice of cultural/ethnic traditions. A multicultural society socializes individuals not only into the dominant (national) culture but also into an ethnic culture. Thus in the United States, millions of people speak both English and another language, eat both American and ethnic foods, celebrate both

In the United States and Canada, multiculturalism is of growing importance. Especially in large cities like Toronto (shown here), people of diverse backgrounds attend ethnic fairs and festivals and feast on ethnic foods. What are some other expressions of multiculturalism in your society?

national and ethnic religious holidays, and study both national and ethnic group histories. MC succeeds best in a society whose political system promotes freedom of expression and in which there are many and diverse culturally organized groups.

In the United States and Canada, MC is of growing importance. As we saw in the previous chapter, this reflects an awareness that the number and size of ethnic groups have grown dramatically in recent years. If this trend continues, the ethnic composition of the United States will change dramatically (see Figure 5–1).

Even now, because of immigration and differential population growth, whites are outnumbered by minorities in many urban areas. For example, of the 8,008,278 people living in New York City in 2000, 27 percent were black, 27 percent Hispanic, 10 percent Asian, and 36 percent other—including non-Hispanic whites. The comparable figures for Los Angeles (which has 3,694,820 people) were 11 percent black, 47 percent Hispanic, 9 percent Asian, and 33 percent other—including non-Hispanic whites (Census 2000, http://www.census.gov). Table 5–1 illustrates ethnic diversity in Canada, based on the most recently available census figures—1996.

One response to ethnic diversification and awareness has been for many whites to reclaim ethnic identities (e.g., Albanian, Serbian, Lithuanian) and to join ethnic associations. Some such groups are new. Others have existed

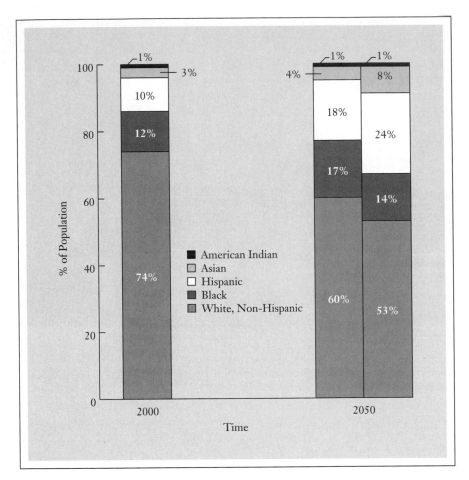

FIGURE 5–1 The proportion of the American population that is white and non-Hispanic is declining. Consider two projections of the ethnic composition of the United States in A.D. 2050. The first assumes an annual immigration rate of zero; the second assumes continuation of the current level of immigration, about 880,000 immigrants per year. With either projection, the non-Hispanic white proportion of the population declines dramatically.
Source: Conrad P. Kottak, *Mirror for Humanity: A Concise Introduction to Cultural Anthropology,* 3rd ed. Copyright © 2003 by The McGraw-Hill Companies, Inc. Reprinted by permission of the publisher.

for decades, although they lost members during the assimilationist years of the 1920s through the 1950s.

MC seeks ways for groups to understand and interact that depend on respect for differences. MC stresses the interaction of ethnic groups and their contribution to the country. It assumes that each group has something to offer and learn from the others, and it uses legal and political means to advance these beliefs.

We see evidence of varied ethnicity and multiculturalism all around us. Seated near you in the classroom are students whose parents were born in

TABLE 5–1. Top 25 Ethnic Origins in Canada, 1996*

Total population	28,528,125
1. Canadian	8,806,275
2. English	6,832,095
3. French	5,597,845
4. Scottish	4,260,840
5. Irish	3,767,610
6. German	2,757,140
7. Italian	1,207,475
8. Aboriginal	1,101,955
9. Ukrainian	1,026,475
10. Chinese	921,585
11. Dutch	916,215
12. Polish	786,735
13. South Asian	723,345
14. Jewish	351,705
15. Norwegian	346,310
16. Welsh	338,905
17. Portuguese	335,110
18. Swedish	278,975
19. Russian	272,335
20. Hungarian	250,525
21. Filipino	242,880
22. American	211,790
23. Spanish	204,360
24. Greek	203,345
25. Jamaican	188,770

*Includes single and multiple responses.
Source: http://www.statcan.ca/english/census96/feb17/eo1can.pdf.

other countries. Islamic mosques have joined Jewish synagogues and Christian churches in American cities. To help in exam scheduling, colleges inform professors about the main holidays of many religions. You can attend ethnic fairs and festivals; watch ethnically costumed dancers on television; eat ethnic foods, even outside ethnic restaurants; and buy ethnic foods at your supermarket. Some such foods (e.g., bagels, pasta, tacos) have become so familiar that their ethnic origin is fading from our memories. There is even a popular shrine celebrating the union of diversity and globalization: At Disneyland and Walt Disney World we can see and hear a chorus of ethnically costumed dolls drone on that "it's a small world after all." All these exemplify growing tolerance and support of ethnic groups in contemporary society.

Several forces, some considered in previous chapters but meriting restatement here, have propelled North America away from the assimilationist model toward MC. First, MC reflects the recent large-scale migration, particularly from the less-developed countries to the developed nations of North America and western Europe. MC is related to globalization: People use modern means of transportation to migrate to nations whose lifestyles they learn about through the media and from tourists who increasingly visit their own countries.

The decline of many Third World governments breeds insecurity, and violence and genocide within states create refugees. Also fueling migration is rapid population growth, coupled with insufficient jobs (both for educated and uneducated people), in the less-developed countries. As traditional rural economies decline or mechanize, displaced farmers move to cities, where they and their children are often unable to find jobs. As people in the less-developed countries get better educations, they seek more skilled employment. They hope to partake in an international culture of consumption that includes such modern amenities as refrigerators, televisions, and automobiles.

Contrary to popular belief, the typical migrant to the United States or Canada isn't poor and unskilled; rather, he or she is middle class and fairly well educated. Educated people migrate for several reasons. Often they can't find jobs to match their skills in their countries of origin (Grasmuck and Pessar 1991; Margolis 1994). Also, they are knowledgeable enough to manipulate international regulations. Many migrants have been raised to expect a lifestyle that their own nations can offer to just a few. On arrival in North America or western Europe, immigrants find themselves in democracies where citizens are allowed, or even encouraged, to organize for economic gain and a fair share of resources, political influence, and cultural respect. The most-educated immigrants often become political organizers and advocates of MC.

Ethnic identities are used increasingly to form organizations aimed at enhancing the group's economic competitiveness and political clout (B. Williams 1989). Michel Laguerre's (1984) study of Haitian immigrants in New York City shows that they made no conscious decision to form an ethnic group. Rather, they had to mobilize to deal with the discriminatory structure (racist in this case, since Haitians tend to be black) of American society. Ethnicity (their common Haitian creole language and cultural background) was the basis for their mobilization. Haitian ethnicity then distinguished them from American blacks and other ethnic groups seeking similar resources and recognition. In studying ethnic relations, it is not enough to look at the cultural content of the ethnic group. Equally important are the structural constraints and the political/economic context in which ethnic differentiation develops.

Chapter 4 showed us that, although ethnic groups often face discrimination, their members are not passive victims. Immigrants tend to be dynamic, creative, and courageous people, determined to enhance their chances in the modern world system. Ethnic groups mobilize for political action, often with economic goals. Their members also consciously manipulate multiple identities. Individual choice and purpose are evident in everyday expressions of ethnicity.

In a study of Yemeni Arabs in New York City, Staub (1989) stresses that Yemeni immigrant ethnicity is not static, but achieved, situational, and flexible. Still, specific cultural content is also evident: traditional concepts (e.g.,

honor and shame), ethnic poetry, distinctive foods, dialects, local and regional history, exclusive ethnic social and political clubs, ethnic political
events (called festivals), and dancing. They prefer Yemeni ethnic identity to
the more general label *Arab.*

One side effect of the new immigration and the rise of MC has been to
inspire old ethnic groups to strengthen their identity and fight for their
rights. One example is Native American success, in the United States and
Canada, in reclaiming traditional property rights. In Michigan and Wisconsin, for example, Indians have used the court system to establish privileged
hunting and fishing rights, at the expense of hunters, sport fishers, and
commercial fishers.

In the face of globalization, much of the world, including the entire
democratic West, is experiencing an ethnic revival. The new assertiveness of
long-resident ethnic groups extends to Basques and Catalans in Spain, the
Bretons and Corsicans in France, and the Welsh and Scots in the United
Kingdom. And, as we have seen, the United States and Canada have been
leading the movement toward the multicultural society.

ROOTS OF ETHNIC CONFLICT

Ethnicity, based on perceived cultural similarities and differences in a society or nation, can be expressed in peaceful multiculturalism or in discrimination or violent interethnic confrontation. Culture is both adaptive and
maladaptive. The perception of cultural differences can have disastrous effects on social interaction. The roots of ethnic differentiation—and therefore, potentially, of ethnic conflict—can be political, economic, religious,
linguistic, cultural, or racial. Why do ethnic differences often lead to conflict
and violence? The causes include a sense of injustice because of resource
distribution, economic or political competition, and reaction to discrimination, prejudice, and other expressions of threatened or devalued identity
(Ryan 1990, p. xxvii).

Prejudice and Discrimination

Ethnic conflict often arises in reaction to prejudice (attitudes and judgments) or discrimination (action). **Prejudice** means devaluing (looking
down on) a group because of its assumed behavior, values, capabilities, or
attributes. People are prejudiced when they hold stereotypes about groups
and apply them to individuals. **Stereotypes** are fixed ideas, often unfavorable, about what members of a group are like. Prejudiced people assume
that members of the group will act as they are "supposed to act" (according
to the stereotype) and interpret a wide range of individual behaviors as evidence of the stereotype. They use this behavior to confirm their stereotype
(and low opinion) of the group.

Discrimination refers to policies and practices that harm a group and its members. Discrimination may be de facto (practiced, but not legally sanctioned) or de jure (part of the law). An example of de facto discrimination is the harsher treatment that American minorities, compared with other Americans, tend to get from the police and the judicial system. This unequal treatment isn't legal, but it happens anyway. Segregation in the southern United States and apartheid in South Africa are two examples of de jure discrimination which are no longer in existence. In the United States de jure segregation has been illegal since the 1950s. The South African apartheid system was abandoned in 1991. In both systems, by law, blacks and whites had different rights and privileges. Their social interaction ("mixing") was legally curtailed. Slavery, of course, is the most extreme and coercive form of legalized inequality; people are treated as property.

We can also distinguish between attitudinal and institutional discrimination. With **attitudinal discrimination,** people discriminate against members of a group because they are prejudiced toward that group. For example, in the United States members of the Ku Klux Klan have expressed their prejudice against blacks, Jews, and Catholics through verbal, physical, and psychological harassment.

The most extreme form of anti-ethnic (attitudinal) discrimination is **genocide,** the deliberate elimination of a group through mass murder. The United Nations defines genocide as acts "committed with intent to destroy, in whole or in part, a national, ethnical, racial, or religious group, as such" (Ryan 1990, p. 11). Strongly prejudicial attitudes (hate) and resulting genocide have been directed against people viewed as standing in the way of progress (e.g., Native Americans) and people with jobs that the dominant group wants (e.g., Jews in Hitler's Germany, Chinese in Indonesia).

In other examples of genocide, dictator Joseph Stalin's assault on ethnic groups in the Soviet Union led to their forced relocation, mass starvation, and murder. Twenty million people died. The Turks massacred 1.8 million Armenians during World War I. Nazis murdered 6 million Jews. More recently, the Indonesian government waged a genocidal campaign against the people of East Timor. Yet more recent examples of genocide occurred in Bosnia, Rwanda, and Burundi.

Institutional discrimination refers to programs, policies, and institutional arrangements that deny equal rights and opportunities to, or differentially harm, members of particular groups. This form of discrimination is usually less personal and intentional than attitudinal discrimination is, but it may be based on a long history of inequality that also includes attitudinal bias. One example of institutional discrimination is what Bunyan Bryant and Paul Mohai call **environmental racism,** "the systematic use of institutionally based power by whites to formulate policy decisions that will lead to the disproportionate burden of environmental hazards in minority communities" (1991, p. 4). Thus, toxic waste dumps tend to be located in areas with nonwhite populations.

Environmental racism is discriminatory but not always intentional. Sometimes toxic wastes *are* deliberately dumped in areas whose residents are considered unlikely to protest, because they are poor, powerless, disorganized, or uneducated. In other cases property values fall after toxic waste sites are located in an area. The wealthier people move out, and poorer people, often minorities, move in, to suffer the consequences of living in a hazardous environment.

African Americans and Hispanics on average have shorter lives, greater infant mortality, and higher murder rates than whites do, for institutional reasons. They are more likely than whites are to live in impoverished, high-crime areas with inadequate access to health care and to opportunities and services generally. This current lack of access reflects a long history of discrimination, both attitudinal and institutional.

Another example of institutional discrimination is that social and economic shifts harm certain groups more than others. African Americans have been hurt especially by the change from a manufacturing economy to one based on services and information processing. Factories, where people with a high school education used to find well-paid (usually unionized) employment, were traditionally located in cities. Now they have moved to the suburbs, necessitating a difficult and costly commute for city dwellers, including many African Americans. The service jobs now available to comparably educated people in urban areas tend to pay much less than the old manufacturing jobs did. Many minorities have not benefited as much from a changing American society as majority groups or even new immigrants have.

Chips in the Mosaic

Although the multicultural model is increasingly prominent in North America, ethnic competition and conflict are also evident. We hear increasingly of conflict between new arrivals, like Central Americans and Koreans, and long-established ethnic groups, like African Americans. Ethnic antagonism flared in South-Central Los Angeles in spring 1992, in rioting that followed the acquittal of the four white police officers who were tried for the videotaped beating of Rodney King (Abelmann and Lie 1995).

Angry blacks attacked whites, Koreans, and Hispanics. This violence expressed frustration by African Americans about their prospects in an increasingly multicultural society. A *New York Times*/CBS News poll conducted May 8, 1992, just after the Los Angeles riots, found that blacks had a bleaker outlook than whites did about the effects of immigration on their lives. Only 23 percent of the blacks felt they had more opportunities than recent immigrants, compared with twice that many whites (Toner 1992).

Were they right? A 1997 report by the National Academy of Sciences found that competition with immigrants did slightly reduce the wage and job prospects of low-skilled American workers, especially high school dropouts. In New York City and Los Angeles, some black workers had lost their jobs to immigrants. Elsewhere, however, immigration had little impact on the opportunities of blacks, because most blacks did not live in places with large concentrations of immigrants (Pear 1997).

The report found that immigrants had "a negative fiscal impact at the state and local level, but a larger positive impact at the federal level, resulting in an overall positive impact for the United States" in the long run. This is because immigrants tend to arrive as young workers and "will help pay the public costs [i.e., Social Security and Medicare] of the aging baby-boom generation" (Pear 1997). In the main, the report concluded, most Americans are enjoying a healthier economy as a result of the increased supply of labor and lower prices that result from immigration.

But in the short run and in certain areas, such benefits may remain hidden, leading to interethnic conflict. South-Central Los Angeles, where most of the 1992 rioting took place, is an ethnically mixed area, which used to be mainly African American. As blacks have moved out, there has been an influx of Latin Americans (Mexicans and Central Americans). The Hispanic population of South-Central Los Angeles increased by 119 percent in a decade, as the number of blacks declined by 17 percent. By 1992 the neighborhood had become 45 percent Hispanic, almost equaling the black population (48 percent). Many store owners in South-Central Los Angeles were Korean immigrants.

Korean stores were hard hit during the 1992 riots, and more than a third of the businesses destroyed were Hispanic-owned. A third of those who died in the riots were Hispanics. These mainly recent migrants lacked deep roots to the neighborhood. As Spanish speakers, they faced language barriers (M. Newman 1992). Many Koreans also had trouble with English.

Koreans interviewed on ABC's *Nightline* on May 6, 1992, recognized that blacks resented them and considered them unfriendly. One man explained, "It's not part of our culture to smile; in Asia people who smile are considered airheads" (he hesitantly chose the word). African Americans interviewed on the same program did complain about Korean unfriendliness. "They come into our neighborhoods and treat us like dirt." These comments suggest a shortcoming of the multicultural perspective: Ethnic groups (blacks here) expect other ethnic groups in the same nation-state to assimilate to some extent to a shared (national) culture. The African Americans' comments invoked a general American value system that includes friendliness, openness, mutual respect, community participation, and fair play. Los Angeles blacks wanted their Korean neighbors to act more like generalized Americans and good neighbors.

Whatever their ethnic background, people can't hope to live in social isolation from the communities from which they derive their livelihoods. They have to take steps to adapt. Some African Americans jointly interviewed with a few Koreans by ABC told the store owners they could improve relations in the neighborhood by hiring one or two local people. The Koreans said they couldn't afford to hire nonrelatives.

One way in which Koreans in cities like New York and Los Angeles have succeeded economically is through family enterprise. Family members work together in small grocery stores, like those in South-Central Los Angeles, pooling their labor and their wealth. Korean culture stresses the value of education. Children, supervised and encouraged by their parents, study hard to do well in school. In a society whose economy is shifting from manufacturing toward specialized services and information processing, good jobs demand education beyond high school. When Asian parents encourage their children to study and work hard, with such careers in mind, their educational goals also fit certain general American ideals. Work and achievement are American values that the Korean Americans being interviewed invoked to explain their behavior. (Family solidarity is also a general American value, but the specific meaning of *family* varies between groups.) The Koreans also felt that they couldn't succeed financially if they had to hire nonrelatives.

Yet without efforts designed to gain local social acceptance, storekeepers (of whatever ethnic group) will continue to face looting, boycotts, and other **leveling mechanisms.** This term refers to customs or social actions that operate to reduce differences in wealth and bring standouts in line with community norms. Leveling mechanisms surface when there is an expectation of community solidarity and economic similarity, especially shared poverty, and when some people appear to be profiting more than, or at the expense of, others.

Harassment of and violence against racially and ethnically defined groups remain prevalent in North America, as in many other countries. Following the terrorist attack on America on September 11, 2001, many people of Middle Eastern and South Asian descent have been victimized unjustly by "racial and ethnic profiling." Civilians and law enforcement officers have harassed people whose physical appearance or cultural markers suggest Middle Eastern origins. In response, some religious leaders have organized interfaith services to emphasize a common spirituality among Christians, Jews, and Muslims, a movement toward a "religiously pluralistic America."*

Aftermaths of Oppression

Other reasons for ethnic conflict include such forms of discrimination as forced assimilation, ethnocide, and cultural colonialism. A dominant group may try to destroy the cultures of certain ethnic groups (**ethnocide**) or force them to adopt the dominant culture (**forced assimilation**). Many countries have penalized or banned the language and customs of an ethnic group, including its religious observances. One example of forced assimilation is the anti-Basque campaign that the dictator Francisco Franco (who ruled between

*www.nytimes.com/2001/09/14/national/14ISLA.html?ex=1001491750&ei=1&en=6e114f39f.

1939 and 1975) waged in Spain. Franco banned Basque books, journals, newspapers, signs, sermons, and tombstones and imposed fines for using the Basque language in schools. His policies led to the formation of a Basque terrorist group and spurred strong nationalist sentiment in the Basque region (Ryan 1990, 1995).

A policy of **ethnic expulsion** aims at removing groups that are culturally different from a country. There are many examples, including Bosnia-Herzegovina in the early 1990s. Uganda expelled 74,000 Asians in 1972. The neofascist parties of contemporary western Europe advocate repatriation (expulsion) of immigrant workers (West Indians in England, Algerians in France, and Turks in Germany).

A policy of expulsion may create **refugees**—people who have been forced (involuntary refugees) or who have chosen (voluntary refugees) to flee a country, to escape persecution or war. For example, Palestinian refugees moved to camps in Egypt, Jordan, and Lebanon after the Arab-Israeli wars of 1948 and 1967 (Ryan 1990, 1995).

Colonialism, another form of oppression, refers to the political, social, economic, and cultural domination of a territory and its people by a foreign power for an extended time (Bell 1981). The British and French colonial empires are familiar examples of colonialism. We can extend the term to the former Soviet empire, once known as the Second World.

Using the labels "First World," "Second World," and "Third World" is a common, although clearly ethnocentric, way of categorizing nations that may be defined here. The *First World* refers to the "democratic West," traditionally conceived in opposition to a Second World ruled by communism. The First World includes Canada, the United States, western Europe, Japan, Australia, and New Zealand. The *Second World* refers to the Warsaw Pact nations, including the former Soviet Union, the socialist and once-socialist countries of eastern Europe and Asia. Proceeding with this classification, the less-developed or "developing" countries make up the *Third World*.

The frontiers imposed by colonialism weren't usually based on, and often didn't reflect, preexisting cultural units. In many countries, colonial nation-building left ethnic strife in its wake. Thus, over a million Hindus and Muslims were killed in the violence that accompanied the division of the Indian subcontinent into India and Pakistan. Problems between Arabs and Jews in Palestine began during the British mandate period.

Multiculturalism may be growing in North America, but the opposite is happening in the former Soviet empire, where ethnic groups (nationalities) are demanding their own nation-states. The flowering of ethnic feeling and conflict as the Soviet Union disintegrated illustrates that years of political repression and ideology provide insufficient common ground for lasting unity. **Cultural colonialism** refers to internal domination by one group and its culture/ideology over others. One example is the domination over the former Soviet empire by Russian people, language, and culture, and by communist ideology. The dominant culture makes itself the official culture. This is reflected in schools, the media, and public interaction. Under Soviet rule,

ethnic minorities had very limited self-rule in republics and regions controlled by Moscow. All the republics and their peoples were to be united by
the core doctrine of socialist internationalism. One common technique in cultural colonialism is to flood ethnic areas with members of the dominant ethnic group. Thus, in the former Soviet Union, ethnic Russian colonists were
sent to many areas to diminish the cohesion and clout of the local people.

The Commonwealth of Independent States is all that remains of the Soviet Union. In this group of new nations, ethnic groups (nationalities) are
seeking to establish separate and viable nation-states based on cultural
boundaries. This celebration of ethnic autonomy is part of an ethnic flores-
cence that, as surely as globalization and transnationalism, is a trend of the
new millennium.

CHAPTER SIX

Race: Its Social Construction

──────────── **"I AM THE ORIGINAL SEOUL BROTHER!"** ────────────

Joseph Simplicio (2001) describes a classroom lesson he did with prekindergarten children who were interested in skin color. He used M&M candies to show that things can look different on the outside but be the same on the inside. Young children start noticing skin color differences as early as age three or four. Years after their graduation, Simplicio's high school students have returned to tell him they still remember that particular lesson, which he believes helps kids develop tolerance and an understanding of diversity.

"Don't judge a book by its cover." The proverb warns against determining the value of something simply by the way it looks. Why haven't we learned to apply this principle to our interactions with human beings? To what extent would ethnic conflict and racial violence diminish if we more consistently sought knowledge of humanity beyond appearance? What might our world look like without the imprints of slavery, colonialism, and the Holocaust?

Freudian theory suggests that within the first few minutes of having met someone, we know how we feel about that person. We determine almost instantaneously our course of action toward the new acquaintance. Stories about love at first sight are all too familiar. So are experiences of spontaneous, on-sight rejection, avoidance, and dismissal, be we the senders or recipients of such interpersonal responses. We *look* with our eyes, but *see* with our hearts, our instincts, and our history. We like, and protect, that which is familiar and comforting, and, especially, that which resonates with our sense of reality, righteousness, and survival. Intergroup relations, including race-based ones, mirror interpersonal strategies that work for self-preservation.

For a moment, assume the task of drawing a mental picture of the person who claims to be "the original Seoul brother." What associations come to mind? What does the person look like? Imagine his body type, his facial features, and other physical attributes, such as his skin pigmentation and the texture of his hair. Consider his intellectual, emotional, and social attributes. How much education does he have? What language or languages does he speak? Is he employed, religious, wealthy, gregarious? How does he dress? How does he spend his leisure time? How do you feel about him?

Now try to interpret his self-definition. What possible stories, experiences, and meanings does his statement reveal? What might be *original* about him? How does his reference to Seoul, and the obvious pun, inform your interpretation? What meanings do you infer from his use of the term *brother?* Are there others *just* like him? Try to classify these people. What criteria of membership did you select? How much value does this group merit?

Finally, *listen* carefully to his claim, "I am the original Seoul brother!" What sentiments do you hear in his *voice*, that is, his *representation* or definition of himself? Do these vary from the sentiments that you generated about him? If so, how? If there are differences between his and your depiction, how do you account for them?

If you find it challenging to complete this exercise with a single person as your focus, imagine the effort that a thorough understanding of a group or a population requires. Failure to achieve an accurate account and appreciation of a race-based group of people results in racism (beliefs about categorical superiority and inferiority of socially defined groups assumed to share biological characteristics). Organized efforts by contemporary groups deemphasize a racial definition by redefining themselves by ethnic or cultural criteria. Thus Jesse Jackson's proclamation to rename black Americans as African Americans has resulted in both a more positive self-image and more political credibility for this group.

The subject of our story defines himself as a "war baby." He was born in Seoul, South Korea, the "proud son" of a Korean mother and an African-American father. "Everyone sees me as black. But I'm more than that; my nature is mixed, and my culture is rich." By emphasizing his ethnic heritage, this man asserts a different-but-equal status. He resists the stigma that often accompanies a biologically based identity. In addition, he is adamant about his cosmopolitan orientation. He has lived in the United States since he was six years old. He claims American citizenship and nationality. He has traveled in India and plans to move to Brazil. His self-representation communicates pride and assurance with respect to his ancestry as a Korean, by his reference to *Seoul,* and his kinship to and affinity for African Americans, by his reference to *brother.* The structure of his *performance* when he speaks of himself—that is, his body language, his voice modulation, speech pattern, gestures, and facial expression—tells of a man much more complex than his appearance, *colored* by phenotype and a janitor's uniform, attest.

As part of the Civil Rights movement of the 1960s and later events, political activists and antiracist artists and intellectuals of various ethnic backgrounds united in efforts to combat racism and institutional discrimination.
To do so, they accepted the argument that human beings are racially distinct, even though it was this idea that had fueled racism and racial consciousness in the first place. To remedy historical inequities involving
people of color, these well-meaning reformers accepted racial categorization
as valid. They assumed that the best way to achieve equity was through
race-based initiatives, such as affirmative action. This strategy proved useful in increasing access to resources and privileges by people of color.

However, this approach accentuates race-based differentiation and
stratification. It makes race a primary criterion for the allocation and distribution of goods, services, and value. In this case, judging the book by its
cover is justified by those who believe that privilege has always been linked
chiefly to appearance (that is, race) rather than substance (that is, culture).
Some argue that historically the people who have dominated economically,
politically, and socially have done so because they are white, a race of another color. However, this perspective is misinformed and misguided. The
fact that privilege and power have been the properties of whites and
continue to be to a significant degree is incidental. The proximity that historically a European minority had to technological development and environmental exploitation is the primary determinant of the wealth, power, and
prestige that whites are associated with. All Europeans are not privileged
and powerful, any more than are all white people in North America. European peasants and poor whites in the United States and Canada are socioculturally differentiated and subordinated much like other racially defined
minorities. Their access to privilege and power is limited and controlled.
Whiteness may be considered generally an asset, but it does not equal inherent economic, political, or social superiority.

Socioeconomic divisions are enforced by elites of many *colors* who control economic, political, and cultural power. One of the consequences of ex-
ternally structured segmentation and stratification is the construction of
internal solidarity, loyalties, and habits by individuals. Such cohesion serves
to distinguish and protect one group of people from another. From its in-
ception as a classification, race has served as a basis for separating peoples,
for protecting some and exploiting others. The Nazi party used race and
racism to justify the extermination of millions of Jews and Gypsies in its
intent to enforce German nationalism. Afrocentrists rely on race and racial-
centrism to mobilize, organize, and unite the "black Atlantic," encompassing descendants of the slavery-driven African diaspora.

Race is still perceived as either a stigma or a marker of superiority. Racial
distinctions perpetuate inequalities and reinforce misconceptions about the
nature and culture of social groups. However, mainstream Americans are beginning to understand today, as Brazilians have always known, that race is no
longer as simple as black and white. Reminders come from celebrities like
Tiger Woods; members of such advocacy groups as the Multiracial Americans

of Southern California, Interracial/Intercultural Pride, and its offshoot, Generation Pride (a group of teenagers of interracial background in the San Francisco Bay area); and the debate over adding a new, multiracial category to the U.S. Census forms. Contrary to Flip Wilson's assertion "What you see is what you get!," and more consistent with the stance of our Seoul brother, what we get from the varied individuals and groups that make up our society is much more than what we view. Culture, regardless of its racial cover, must be read critically and conscientiously, like any book, if it is to be understood and before it can be judged, let alone recommended. ☺

RACE AND RACISM

This chapter and the next one will examine *race* as a cultural construct and as a discredited biological term. Detailed discussion of examples from different cultures will show that race, like ethnicity in general, is a matter of cultural categories and organization, rather than biological reality. That is, ethnic groups, including races, derive from contrasts perceived and perpetuated in particular societies, rather than from scientific classifications based on common genes.

Members of a group may consider themselves or be defined by others as different and special because of their language, religion, geography, history, ancestry, or physical traits. When an ethnic group is assumed to have a biological basis (shared blood or genetic material), it is called a *race*.

More than 50 years ago, the anthropologist Ruth Benedict realized that "in World history, those who have helped to build the same culture are not necessarily of one race, and those of the same race have not all participated in one culture. In scientific language, culture is not a function of race" (Benedict 1940, Chapter 2). Despite ample evidence backing her statement, faulty associations between heredity and society continue to distort the status of certain groups. To what extent has the construct *race* been used to rank human beings and to discriminate against them? How does race serve as a basis for group inclusion, identity, and solidarity?

Our tendency to classify and to stratify people by their appearance continues today despite decades of scientific evidence contradicting natural and absolute divisions of humanity. Abolition and the Civil Rights movement failed to end racial consciousness. We still hear discussions of the needs of the black race and accusations against the white race. The ranking of human groups based on assumed shared biological traits has been prominent in international and interpersonal relations for centuries. Unequal access to strategic resources, such as employment and education, disproportionately affects peoples of color.

Moral worth has also been unequally allocated. So strong is the perceived link between economic or political status and virtue that we tend to evaluate people by category rather than by their personal qualities. Attention to race often outweighs consideration of individual moral worth. Parents may warn their children against "mixing blood" by interracial marriage. Offspring of mixed unions may struggle to determine, and to assert, a satisfactory racial identity.

Racism rests on the notion that some groups are inherently inferior to others, and therefore should be dominated by other, presumably inherently superior, groups. In the United States, until the 1960s, domination of blacks was institutionalized and backed by the government. African Americans were denied civil rights and full participation in national economic, political, and social life. Racism continues. Remarks such as "Mexicans in California are like the blacks in the South," and acts such as locking the car doors when a Hispanic-looking youth approaches exemplify the tendency of whites to equate nonwhiteness with inferiority or danger.

However, practices that promote social inequality coexist with acts, policies, and programs designed to combat racism. Belief in biopsychological equality of human groups informs the work of **antiracists,** who reject ideas and practices based on presumed innate superiority and inferiority of groups. Antiracist strategies include refusal to behave according to one's prescribed racial category and participation in activities to combat racism.

Legislation has played a vital role in increasing social equality. Federal action against racism includes the Civil Rights Act of 1964, which fought segregation in public facilities and employment, the Voting Rights Act of 1965, and the Fair Housing Act of 1968. Affirmative action refers to a set of policies designed to increase the participation of African Americans and other minorities in settings and positions traditionally dominated by privileged whites. These policies, whose legal status is currently in question, require institutions and employers to admit and hire members of historically underrepresented groups.

The Civil Rights movement in general, and the black movement in particular, fostered a reevaluation of race as a concept and category. This process has accelerated through the **Afrocentric** orientation of many African Americans and the native movements of other minorities. Race and culture have been reclaimed, redefined, and reinterpreted by minority leaders and their followers. In this new ownership, the classification denotes strength, not weakness; privilege, not victimization; and freedom rather than confinement. Trying to correct past injustices, leaders declared race the basis of their unity, identity, and power. They used race as a basis for explaining discrimination and mobilizing self-reflection and solidarity. The collective voice of these cultural architects of color proclaimed, "It's about race, everybody!" (Table 6–1 presents some statistics about African Americans in the United States.)

Ideas and practices that promote inequality among races reflect cultural bias, not science or justice. Racial stratification and racism have economic and political determinants. In opposition, the mobilizing agents of racial and ethnic identity groups devise strategies to enhance opportunities, awareness, pride, and quality of life for their members. Such movements

TABLE 6–1. Some Facts about African Americans

Population

In 2000, there were about 35.5 million African Americans, 12.3 percent of the U.S. population.

In 2000, 54 percent of all African Americans lived in the South (versus 33 percent of whites), 18 percent in the Northeast, 19 percent in the Midwest, and 8 percent in the West.

The nation's African-American population is young, with an estimated median age of 30, five years younger than the median for the U.S. population as a whole.

The African-American population is expected to grow more than twice as fast as the white population between 1995 and 2020, reaching 45.1 million. After 2016, more African Americans than non-Hispanic whites would be added to the U.S. population each year.

Businesses

Between 1987 and 1997, the number of businesses owned by African Americans almost doubled, growing from 424,165 to 823,499.

Between 1987 and 1992 receipts for black-owned firms rose 63 percent, compared with 67 percent for the United States as a whole.

Education

In 2000, 78 percent of African Americans aged 25 and over had a high school diploma, versus 51 percent in 1980 (and 88 percent for whites in 2000).

In 2000, 16.5 percent of African Americans 25 and over had a college degree or higher, versus 8 percent in 1980. (The corresponding figures for whites were 28 percent in 2000, compared with 18 percent in 1980.)

Marriage and family

In 1980, 45 percent of African-American women 15 years old and over were married. By 2000, the percentage had dropped to 30.5 percent. The corresponding figures for African-American men were 49 and 38.5 percent.

Considering the percentage of families headed by women, with no husband present, the 2000 figure was 44 percent for African Americans, versus 13 percent for non-Hispanic whites.

In 1998, the typical African-American family consisted of 3.4 members, larger than the average of 3.0 members for non-Hispanic white families but smaller than the average of 3.9 members for Hispanic families.

Occupations and earnings

African-American women, age 16 and over, were more likely than white women to participate in the labor force (64 percent versus 61 percent). For men the reverse was true, with 68 percent participation by African Americans and 74 percent by whites.

In 2000, the proportion of African-American men in managerial and professional jobs was 18 percent, versus 32 percent for white men. African-American men were twice as likely as white men to work in service occupations (19 percent versus 9 percent).

For women in 2000, 25 percent of African-American women, versus 35 percent of white women, worked in managerial and professional occupations.

Income and poverty

Median household income of African Americans increased from $20,032 in 1993 to $30,439 in 2000, the highest ever, in terms of real income. The 2000 figure for

TABLE 6–1. (continued)

non-Hispanic whites was $45,856. Half (51 percent) of African-American married-couple families had incomes of $50,000 or more, compared with 60 percent of non-Hispanic whites.
Between 1993 and 2000, poverty rates dropped for African Americans (from 33 percent to 22 percent) and for whites (from 12 percent to 8 percent).

Source: Collins 1996; and U.S. Census 2002.

have helped reduce disparities, but they have not ended hierarchy. Contemporary examples of members of subordinate groups who participate in dominant social spheres—for example, the African-American engineer, the Native-American journalist, or the Latino senator—do not negate the fact of culture-based but biology-justified group subordination.

Barbara Trepagnier (2001) sets forth the idea of *silent racism*. Some "well-meaning white people . . . do not commit overtly racist acts or make intentionally racist statements, and they are concerned about racism," yet they still may play a role in constructing racist acts (Trepagnier 2001, p. 142). Rather than the binary categories of "racist" and "nonracist," there is a continuum of racial awareness, and people are racist to various degrees. Trepagnier assembled focus groups of white women who had identified themselves as concerned about racism. She discovered two forms of silent racism in her study: feelings of superiority by members of the dominant group (whites) and stereotypical images of others, reflecting their belief in inherent racial differences.

Optimal understanding of any construct requires critical analysis of its origins as well as its nature. Has humanity been racially ordered since antiquity? What circumstances generated racism? When did diverse ways of life become subject to valuation? Is racism a cultural universal? How are races and racism conceived in different cultures? Do humans possess a racist gene? If so, should we assume that efforts to abolish racism are futile?

Many Americans assume that racism has always existed and that it is intrinsic to humanity. People of European descent are specially targeted for being innately racist. Frank Snowden, Jr., dispels this myth in his analysis of intergroup relations in the ancient world (1970, 1983, 1992, 1995). He relies on classical studies and ancient art to show that Europeans and Africans coexisted in the ancient world and that social relations and business transactions occurred free of discrimination based on skin color or other physical features.

According to Snowden, the ancient Greeks and Romans accepted the physical and cultural diversity in their midst. For example, they used the term *Ethiopian* for the dark-skinned peoples who lived south of Egypt. Portrayals of African blacks by Greeks and Romans spanned a range of physical types and a gradation of skin color. Degree of coloration (e.g., blackest,

Hispanics can be of any race. Hispanic is a label that crosscuts racial contrasts such as that between black and white. Racial diversity even exists within a particular Hispanic category, such as Puerto Rican. These Puerto Rican girls celebrate the festival Betances at a housing development in Boston. The festival commemorates a Puerto Rican hero who worked to abolish slavery.

less sunburned, and mildly dark) and contrasts by physical features (thick lips and tightly curled hair) denote recognition of a range of human diversity. Ancient art and literature also acknowledged variety in customs and social practices, for instance, facial scarification. The Greeks and Romans ascribed variations in physical characteristics and cultural markers partly to environmental influences and partly to intermarriage between members of different groups (Snowden 1995).

RACE, ETHNICITY, AND CULTURE

It is not possible to define races biologically. Only cultural constructions of race are possible, even though the average citizen conceptualizes race in biological terms. The belief that races exist and are important is much more common among the public than it is among scientists. Most Americans, for example, believe that their population includes biologically based races to which various labels have been applied. These labels include white, black, yellow, red, Caucasoid, Negroid, Mongoloid, Amerindian, Euro-American, African American, Asian American, and Native American.

We hear the words *ethnicity* and *race* frequently, but North American culture doesn't draw a very clear line between them. As an illustration, consider two articles in the *New York Times* of May 29, 1992. One, discussing the changing ethnic composition of the United States, stated (correctly) that

Hispanics "can be of any race" (Barringer 1992, p. A12). In other words, *Hispanic* is an ethnic category that crosscuts racial contrasts such as that between black and white. The other article reported that during the Los Angeles riots of spring 1992, "hundreds of Hispanic residents were interrogated about their immigration status on the basis of their *race* alone [emphasis added]" (Mydans 1992a). Use of *race* here seems inappropriate, because *Hispanic* is usually perceived as referring to a linguistically based (Spanish-speaking) ethnic group rather than a biologically based race. Since these Los Angeles residents were being interrogated because they were Hispanic, the article was actually reporting on ethnic, not racial, discrimination. However, given the lack of a precise distinction between race and ethnicity, it is probably better to use the term *ethnic group* instead of *race* to describe *any* such social group, for example, African Americans, Asian Americans, Irish Americans, Anglo Americans, or Hispanics.

THE CULTURAL CONSTRUCTION OF RACE

Races are ethnic groups assumed by members of a particular culture to have a biological basis, but actually race is culturally constructed. The races we hear about every day are cultural, or social, rather than biological categories. In Charles Wagley's terms (1959/1968), they are **social races**—groups assumed to have a biological basis but actually defined in a culturally arbitrary, rather than a scientific, manner. Many Americans mistakenly assume that *whites* and *blacks*, for example, are biologically distinct and that these terms stand for discrete races; but these labels, like racial terms used in other societies, really designate culturally perceived rather than biologically based groups.

Hypodescent: Race in the United States

How is race culturally constructed in the United States? In American culture, one acquires his or her racial identity at birth, as an ascribed status, but race isn't based on biology or on simple ancestry. Take the case of the child of a racially mixed marriage involving one black and one white parent. We know that 50 percent of the child's genes come from one parent and 50 percent from the other. Still, American culture overlooks heredity and classifies this child as black. This rule is arbitrary. From genotype (genetic composition), it would be just as logical to classify the child as white.

American rules for assigning racial status can be even more arbitrary. In some states, anyone known to have any black ancestor, no matter how remote, is classified as a member of the black race. This is a rule of **descent** (it assigns social identity on the basis of ancestry), but of a sort that is rare outside the contemporary United States. It is called **hypodescent** (Harris and Kottak 1963) (*hypo* means "lower") because it automatically places the children of a union or mating between members of different groups in the minority group. Hypodescent helps divide American society into groups that have been unequal in their access to wealth, power, and prestige.

Millions of Americans have faced discrimination because one or more of their ancestors happened to belong to a minority group. We saw in Chapter 5 that governments sometimes manipulate ethnicity and encourage ethnic divisions for political and economic ends. The following case from Louisiana is an excellent illustration of the arbitrariness of the hypodescent rule and of the role that governments (federal or state) play in legalizing, inventing, or eradicating race and ethnicity (B. Williams 1989). Susie Guillory Phipps, a light-skinned woman with Caucasian features and straight black hair, discovered as an adult that she was black. When Phipps ordered a copy of her birth certificate, she found her race listed as colored. Since she had been "brought up white and married white twice," Phipps challenged a 1970 Louisiana law declaring anyone with at least one-thirty-second "Negro blood" to be legally black. Although the state's lawyer admitted that Phipps "looks like a white person," the state of Louisiana insisted that her racial classification was proper (Yetman 1991, pp. 3–4).

Cases like Phipps's are rare, because racial and ethnic identities are usually ascribed at birth and usually don't change. The rule of hypodescent affects blacks, Asians, Native Americans, and Hispanics differently. It's easier to negotiate Indian or Hispanic identity than black identity. The ascription rule isn't as definite, and the assumption of a biological basis isn't as strong.

To be considered Native American, one ancestor out of eight (great grandparents) or four (grandparents) may suffice. This depends on whether the assignment is by federal or state law or by an Indian tribal council. The child of a Hispanic may (or may not, depending on context) claim Hispanic identity. Many Americans with an Indian or a Latino grandparent consider themselves white and lay no claim to minority group status.

Something like hypodescent even works with the classification of sexual orientation in the United States. Bisexuals are lumped with gays and lesbians rather than with heterosexuals. These statuses (sexual orientations) are often viewed as ascribed (no choice) rather than achieved (ambivalent or changing sexual preference possible).

The controversy that erupted in 1990–1991 over the casting of the Broadway production of the musical Miss Saigon offers a final illustration of the cultural construction of race in the United States. The musical had opened a few years earlier in London, where the Filipina actress Lea Salonga played Kim, a young Vietnamese woman. Another major role is that of the Eurasian (half-French, half-Vietnamese) pimp known as the Engineer. For the New York production the producer, Cameron Mackintosh, wanted Salonga to play Kim and the English actor Jonathan Pryce, who had originated the part in London, to play the Engineer. Actors' Equity must approve the casting of foreign stars in New York productions. The union voted that Mackintosh couldn't cast Pryce, a Caucasian, in the role of a Eurasian. The part should go to an Asian.

In this case the American hypodescent rule was being extended from the offspring of black-white unions to Eurasians (here, French-Vietnamese). Again, the cultural construction of ethnicity is that children get their social identity from the minority parent—Asian rather than European. This cultural construction of ethnicity also assumes that all Asians (e.g., Vietnamese, Chinese, and Filipinos) are the same. Thus it's okay for Filipinos to play Vietnamese or even Eurasians, but an Englishman can't play a half-French Eurasian.

In fact, Vietnamese and Filipinos are farther apart in language, culture, history, and ancestry than French and English are. It would be more logical (based on language, culture, and common ancestry) to give the Engineer's part to an English actor than a Filipino one. But Actors' Equity didn't see it that way. (The most "correct" choices for the part would have been a French man, a Vietnamese man, or a Eurasian of appropriate background.)

When Actors' Equity vetoed Pryce, Mackintosh canceled the New York production of *Miss Saigon*. Negotiations continued, and *Miss Saigon* eventually opened on Broadway, with a well-integrated cast, starring Pryce and Salonga (whose demanding part was shared, for two performances per week, with a Chinese-American actress). After Pryce and Salonga left the production, until its closing in January 2001, the three main Asian (Vietnamese) parts, including the Eurasian Engineer, were usually played by Filipinos.

The culturally arbitrary hypodescent rule—not logic—is behind the notion that an Asian is more appropriate to play a Eurasian than a Caucasian is. Hypodescent governs racial and ethnic ascription in the United States and channels discrimination against offspring of mixed unions, who are assigned minority status. But, as the case of *Miss Saigon* illustrates, and as we have seen in previous chapters, what has been used against a group can also be used to promote the interests of that group. There has been a shortage of parts for Asian and Asian-American actors. In this case they used the hypodescent rule as a basis for political action—to stake their claim to Eurasian as well as Asian parts.

The U.S. Census Bureau has gathered data by race since 1790. Initially this was done because the Constitution specified that a slave counted as three-fifths of a white person and because Indians were not taxed. The racial categories included in the 1990 Census were White, Black or Negro, Indian (American), Eskimo, Aleut or Pacific Islander, and Other. A separate question asked about Spanish-Hispanic heritage. Check out Figure 6–1 for the racial categories in the 2000 census. What changes do you notice?

An attempt by social scientists and interested citizens to add a "multiracial" census category has been opposed by NAACP and the National Council of La Raza. As the *Miss Saigon* incident demonstrates, racial classification is a political issue, involving access to resources including parts, jobs, voting districts, and federal funding of programs aimed at minorities. The hypodescent rule results in all the population growth being attributed to the minority category. Minorities fear their political clout will decline if their numbers go down.

→ **NOTE: Please answer BOTH Questions 5 and 6.**

5. Is this person Spanish/Hispanic/Latino? *Mark* ⊠ *the* **"No"** *box if **not** Spanish/Hispanic/Latino.*

☐ **No,** not Spanish/Hispanic/Latino   ☐ Yes, Puerto Rican
☐ Yes, Mexican, Mexican Am., Chicano   ☐ Yes, Cuban
☐ Yes, other Spanish/Hispanic/Latino — *Print group.* ↘

| | | | | | | | | | | | | | | | | | | | |

6. What is this person's race? *Mark* ⊠ **one or more races** *to indicate what this person considers himself/herself to be.*

☐ White
☐ Black, African Am., or Negro
☐ American Indian or Alaska Native — *Print name of enrolled or principal tribe.* ↘

| | | | | | | | | | | | | | | | | | | | |

☐ Asian Indian   ☐ Japanese   ☐ Native Hawaiian
☐ Chinese   ☐ Korean   ☐ Guamanian or Chamorro
☐ Filipino   ☐ Vietnamese   ☐ Samoan
☐ Other Asian — *Print race.* ↘   ☐ Other Pacific Islander — *Print race.* ↘

| | | | | | | | | | | | | | | | | | | | |

☐ Some other race — *Print race.* ↘

| | | | | | | | | | | | | | | | | | | | |

FIGURE 6–1 Reproduction of questions on race and Hispanic origin from Census 2000
Source: U.S. Census 2000, questionnaire.

Changes in North American Racial Classification

But things are changing. Choice of "some other race" in the U.S. Census more than doubled from 1980 (6.8 million) to 2000 (more than 15 million), suggesting imprecision in and dissatisfaction with the existing categories (Mar 1997).

In the year 2000, Americans numbering 274.6 million (out of 281.4 million censused) reported they belonged to one race, as follows:

White	75.1
Black or African American	12.3
American Indian and Alaska Native	0.9
Asian	3.6
Native Hawaiian and other Pacific Islander	0.1
Some other race	5.5

Hispanics totaled 35.3 million, or about 13 percent, of the total U.S. population. Nearly 48 percent of Hispanics identified themselves as white alone,

The number of interracial marriages and children is increasing. Interracial, biracial, or multiracial children who grow up with both parents undoubtedly identify with particular qualities of either parent. It is troubling for many of them to have so important an identity as race dictated by the arbitrary rule of hypodescent. It may be especially discordant when racial identity doesn't parallel gender identity, for example, for boys with a white father and a black mother or girls with a white mother and black father.

and about 42 percent as "some other race" alone. In the 2000 census, 2.4 percent of Americans, or 6.8 million people, chose a first-ever option of identifying themselves as belonging to more than one race. About 6 percent of Hispanics reported two or more races, as compared to less than 2 percent of non-Hispanics.*

The number of interracial marriages and children is increasing, with implications for the traditional system of American racial classification. "Interracial," "biracial," or "multiracial" children who grow up with both parents undoubtedly identify with particular qualities of either parent. It is troubling for many of them to have so important an identity as race dictated by the arbitrary rule of hypodescent. It may be especially discordant when racial identity doesn't parallel gender identity—for example, boys with a white father and a black mother, or girls with a white mother and a black father.

How does the Canadian census compare with the American census in its treatment of race? The most recent Canadian census data, gathered every five years, is for 1996. Rather than race, the Canadian census asks about "visible minorities." That country's Employment Equity Act defines such groups as "persons, other than aboriginal peoples [a.k.a. First Nations in Canada, Native Americans in the United States] who are non-Caucasian in race or non-white in colour" (Statistics Canada 2001). The 1996 census was

*http://www.census.gov/Pres-Release/www/2001/cb01cn61.html.

TABLE 6–2. Visible Minority Population of Canada, 1996 Census

	Number	Percent
Total Population	**28,528,125**	**100.0**
Total visible minority population	3,197,480	11.2
Chinese	860,150	3.0
South Asian	670,590	2.4
Black	573,860	2.0
Arab/West Asian	244,665	0.8
Filipino	234,195	0.8
Southeast Asian	172,765	0.6
Latin American	176,970	0.6
Japanese	68,135	0.2
Korean	64,835	0.2
Other visible minority	69,745	0.2
Multiple visible minority	61,575	0.2
Nonvisible minority	25,330,645	88.8

Source: Statistics Canada 2001.

the first to gather systematic data on visible minorities—for the purpose of assessing employment equity. Similar to affirmative action in the United States, Canada's Employment Equity Act was a response to the political organization of diversity in that country. Table 6–2 shows that "Chinese" and "South Asian" are Canada's largest visible minorities. Note that Canada's total visible minority population of 11.2 percent contrasts with a comparable figure of about 25 percent for the United States in the 2000 Census. In particular, Canada's black 2 percent population contrasts with the American figure of 12.3 percent for African Americans, while Canada's Asian population is significantly higher than the U.S. figure of 3.6 percent on a percent basis. Only a tiny fraction of the Canadian population (0.2 percent) claimed multiple visible minority affiliation, compared with 2.4 percent claiming "more than one race" in the United States in 2000.

Not Us: Race in Japan

American culture ignores considerable diversity in biology, language, and geographic origin as it socially constructs race in the United States. North Americans also overlook diversity by seeing Japan as a nation that is homogeneous in race, ethnicity, language, and culture, an image the Japanese themselves cultivate. Thus in 1986 prime minister Nakasone created an international furor by contrasting his country's supposed homogeneity (responsible, he suggested, for Japan's success in international business at that time) with the ethnically mixed United States. To describe Japanese society Nakasone used *tan'itsu minzoku,* an expression connoting a single ethnic-racial group (Robertson 1992).

Japan is hardly the uniform entity Nakasone described. Some dialects of Japanese are mutually unintelligible, and scholars estimate that 10 percent of the national population of 124 million are minorities of various sorts. These include aboriginal Ainu, annexed Okinawans, outcast *burakumin,* children of mixed marriages, and immigrant nationalities, especially Koreans, who number more than 700,000 (De Vos, Wetherall, and Stearman 1983).

Americans tend to see Japanese and Koreans as alike, but the Japanese stress the difference between themselves and Koreans. To describe racial attitudes in Japan, Jennifer Robertson (1992) uses Kwame Anthony Appiah's (1990) term *intrinsic racism*—the belief that a perceived racial difference is a sufficient reason to value one person less than another.

In Japan the valued group is majority ("pure") Japanese, who are believed to share "the same blood." Thus the caption to a printed photo of a Japanese-American model reads: "She was born in Japan but raised in Hawaii. Her nationality is American but no foreign blood flows in her veins" (Robertson 1992, p. 5). Something like hypodescent also operates in Japan, but less precisely than in the United States, where mixed offspring automatically become members of the minority group. The children of mixed marriages between majority Japanese and others, including Euro-Americans, may not get the same racial label as their minority parent, but they are still stigmatized for their non-Japanese ancestry (De Vos and Wagatsuma 1966).

How is race culturally constructed in Japan? The majority Japanese define themselves by opposition to others, whether minority groups in their own nation or outsiders—anyone who is "not us." Aspects of phenotype (detectable physical traits, such as a perceived body odor) are considered part of being *racially different by opposition.* Other races don't smell as "we" do. The Japanese stigmatize Koreans by saying they smell different, as Europeans also do. The Japanese contend that Koreans have a pungent smell, which they mainly attribute to diet. Koreans eat garlicky foods and spicy kimchee. Japanese also stereotype their minorities with behavioral and psychological traits. Koreans are seen as underachievers, crime-prone, and working-class, in opposition to dominant Japanese, who are positively stereotyped as harmonious, hardworking, and middle class (Robertson 1992).

The "not us" should stay that way; assimilation is generally discouraged. Cultural mechanisms, especially residential segregation and taboos on interracial marriage, work to keep minorities "in their place." (Still, many marriages between minorities and majority Japanese do occur.) However, perhaps to give the appearance of homogeneity, people (e.g., Koreans) who become naturalized Japanese citizens are expected to take Japanese-sounding names (De Vos et al. 1983; Robertson 1992).

In its construction of race, Japanese culture regards certain ethnic groups as having a biological basis, when there is no evidence that they do. The best example is the burakumin, a stigmatized group of at least 4 million outcasts, sometimes compared to India's untouchables. The burakumin are physically and genetically indistinguishable from other Japanese. Many of them pass as (and marry) majority Japanese, but a deceptive marriage can end in divorce if burakumin identity is discovered (Aoki and Dardess 1981).

Burakumin are perceived as standing apart from the majority Japanese lineage. Through ancestry and descent (and thus, it is assumed, blood, or genetics) burakumin are "not us." Majority Japanese try to keep their lineage pure by discouraging mixing. The burakumin are residentially segregated in neighborhoods (rural or urban) called *buraku,* from which the racial label is derived. Compared with majority Japanese, the burakumin are less likely to attend high school and college. When burakumin attend the same schools, they face discrimination. Majority children and teachers may refuse to eat with them because burakumin are considered unclean.

In applying for university admission or a job and in dealing with the government, Japanese must list their address, which becomes part of a household or family registry. This list makes residence in a buraku, and likely burakumin social status, evident. Schools and companies use this information to discriminate. The best way to pass is to move so often that the buraku address eventually disappears from the registry. Majority Japanese also limit race mixture by hiring marriage mediators to check out the family histories of prospective spouses. They are especially careful to check for burakumin ancestry (De Vos et al. 1983).

The origin of the burakumin lies in a historic tiered system of stratification (from the Tokugawa period, 1603–1868). The top four ranked categories were warrior-administrators (*samurai*), farmers, artisans, and merchants. The ancestors of the burakumin were below this hierarchy, an outcast group who did unclean jobs, like animal slaughter and disposal of the dead. Burakumin still do related jobs, including work with animal products, like leather. The burakumin are more likely than majority Japanese are to do manual labor, including farm work, and to belong to the national lower class. Burakumin and other Japanese minorities are also more likely to have careers in crime, prostitution, entertainment, and sports (De Vos et al. 1983).

Like blacks in the United States, the burakumin are class-stratified. Because certain jobs are reserved for the burakumin, people who are successful in those occupations (e.g., shoe factory owners) can be wealthy. Burakumin have also found jobs as government bureaucrats. Financially successful burakumin can temporarily escape their stigmatized status by travel, including foreign travel.

Today most discrimination against the burakumin is de facto rather than de jure. It is strikingly like the discrimination—attitudinal and institutional—that blacks have experienced in the United States. The burakumin often live in villages and neighborhoods with poor housing and sanitation. They have limited access to education, jobs, amenities, and health facilities. In response to burakumin political mobilization, Japan has dismantled the legal structure of discrimination against burakumin and has worked to improve conditions in the buraku. Still, Japan has yet to institute American-style affirmative-action programs for education and jobs. Discrimination against nonmajority Japanese is still the rule in companies. Some employers say that hiring burakumin would give their company an unclean image and thus create a disadvantage in competing with other businesses (De Vos et al. 1983).

In contrast to the burakumin, who are citizens of Japan, most Japanese Koreans are not. Koreans, who form one of the largest minorities in Japan (about 750,000 people), continue, as *resident aliens,* to face discrimination in education and jobs. They lack citizens' health care and social service benefits, and government and company jobs don't usually go to non-Japanese.

Koreans started arriving in Japan, mainly as manual laborers, after Japan conquered Korea in 1910 and ruled it through 1945. During World War II, there were more than 2 million Koreans in Japan. They were recruited to replace Japanese farm workers who left the fields for the imperial army. Some Koreans were women (numbering 70,000 to 200,000) forced to serve as prostitutes ("comfort women") for Japanese troops. By 1952 most Japanese Koreans had been repatriated to a divided Korea. Those who stayed in Japan were denied citizenship. They became resident aliens, forced, like Japanese criminals, to carry I.D. cards, which resentful Koreans call "dog tags." Unlike most nations, Japan doesn't grant automatic citizenship to people born in the country. One can become Japanese by having one parent born in Japan and living there three successive years (Robertson 1992).

Like the burakumin, many Koreans (who by now include third and fourth generations) fit physically and linguistically into the Japanese population. Most Koreans speak Japanese as their primary language, and many pass as majority Japanese. Still, they tend to be segregated residentially, often in the same neighborhoods as burakumin, with whom they sometimes intermarry. Koreans maintain strong kin ties and a sense of ethnic identity with other Koreans, especially in their neighborhoods. Most Japanese Koreans qualify for citizenship but choose not to take it, because of Japan's policy of forced assimilation. Anyone who naturalizes is strongly encouraged to take a Japanese name. Many Koreans feel that to do so would cut them off from their kin and ethnic identity. Knowing they can never become majority Japanese, they choose not to become "not us" twice.

Phenotype and Fluidity: Race in Brazil

There are more flexible, less exclusionary ways of constructing social race than those used in the United States and Japan. Along with the rest of Latin America, Brazil has less exclusionary categories, which permit individuals to change their racial classification. Brazil shares a history of slavery with the United States, but it lacks the hypodescent rule. Nor does Brazil have racial aversion of the sort found in Japan. The history of Brazilian slavery dates back to the 16th century, when Africans were brought as slaves to work on sugar plantations in northeastern Brazil. Later, Brazilians used slave labor in mines and on coffee plantations. The contributions of Africans to Brazilian culture have been as great as they have been to American culture. Today, especially in areas of Brazil where slaves were most numerous, African ancestry is evident.

The system that Brazilians use to classify biological differences contrasts with those used in the United States and Japan. First, Brazilians use many more racial labels (more than 500 have been reported [Harris 1970]) than Americans or Japanese do. In 1962, in northeastern Brazil, Kottak found 40 different racial terms in use in Arembepe, then a village of only 750 people (1999). Through their classification system Brazilians recognize and attempt to describe the physical variation that exists in their population. The system used in the United States, by recognizing only three or four races, blinds Americans to an equivalent range of evident physical contrasts. Japanese races, remember, don't even originate in physical contrasts. Burakumin are physically indistinguishable from other Japanese but are considered to be biologically different.

The system that Brazilians use to construct social race has other special features. In the United States one's race is an ascribed status; it is assigned automatically by hypodescent and doesn't usually change. In Japan race is also ascribed at birth, but it can change when, say, a burakumin or a naturalized Korean passes as a majority Japanese. In Brazil racial identity is more flexible, more of an achieved status. Brazilian racial classification pays attention to phenotype. **Phenotype** refers to an organism's evident traits, its manifest biology—anatomy and physiology. There are thousands of evident (detectable) physical traits, ranging from skin color, hair form, and eye color (which are visible), to blood type, color blindness, and enzyme production (which become evident through testing). A Brazilian's phenotype, and racial label, may change due to environmental factors, such as the tanning rays of the sun.

For historical reasons, darker-skinned Brazilians tend to be poorer than lighter-skinned Brazilians are. When Brazil's Princess Isabel abolished slavery in 1889, the freed men and women received no land or other reparations. They took what jobs were available. For example, the freed slaves who founded the town of Arembepe, which Kottak has been studying since 1962, turned to fishing. Many Brazilians, including slave descendants, are poor because they lack a family history of access to land or commercial wealth and because upward social mobility is difficult. Continuing today, especially in cities, it is poor, dark-skinned Brazilians, on average, who face the most intense discrimination.

Given the correlation between poverty and dark skin, the class structure affects Brazilian racial classification, so that someone who has light skin and is poor will be perceived and classified as darker than a comparably colored person who is rich. The racial term applied to a wealthy person who has dark skin will tend to "lighten" the skin color, which gives rise to the Brazilian expression "money whitens." In the United States, by contrast, race and class are correlated, but racial classification isn't changed by class. Because of hypodescent, racial identity in the United States is an ascribed status, fixed and lifelong, regardless of phenotype or economic status. One illustration of the absence of hypodescent in Brazil is that there, unlike in the United States, full siblings may belong to different races, if they are phenotypically different.

Arembepe has a mixed and physically diverse population, reflecting generations of immigration and intermarriage between its founders and outsiders. Some villagers have dark skin color; others, light. Facial features, eye and hair color, and hair type also vary. Although physically heterogeneous, Arembepe has been economically homogeneous—few local residents have risen out of the national lower class. Given such economic uniformity, wealth contrasts don't affect racial classification, which Arembepeiros base on the physical differences they perceive among individuals. As physical characteristics change (sunlight alters skin color, humidity affects hair form), so do racial terms. Furthermore, racial differences are so insignificant in structuring community life that people often forget the terms they have applied to others. Sometimes they even forget the ones they've used for themselves. To reach this conclusion, Kottak made it a habit to ask the same person on different days to tell him the races of others in the village (and his own). In the United States Kottak is always white or Euro-American, but in Arembepe he got lots of terms besides *branco* (white). He could be *claro* (light), *louro* (blond), *sarará* (light-skinned redhead), *mulato claro* (light mulatto), or *mulato* (mulatto). The racial term used to describe him or anyone else varied from person to person, week to week, even day to day. Kottak's best informant, a man with very dark skin color, changed the term he used for himself all the time, from *escuro* (dark) to *preto* (black) to *moreno escuro* (dark brunet).

The American and Japanese racial systems are creations of particular cultures rather than scientific, or even accurate, descriptions of human biological differences. Brazilian racial classification is also a cultural construction, but Brazilians have developed a way of describing human biological diversity that is more detailed, fluid, and flexible than the systems used in most cultures. Brazil lacks Japan's racial aversion, and it also lacks a rule of descent like that which ascribes racial status in the United States (Harris 1964; Degler 1970).

The operation of the hypodescent rule helps us understand why the populations labeled black and Indian (Native American) are growing in the United States but shrinking in Brazil. American culture places all mixed children in the minority category, which therefore gets all the resultant population increase. Brazil, by contrast, assigns the offspring of mixed marriages to intermediate categories, using a larger set of ethnic and racial labels. A Brazilian with a white (*branco*) parent and a black (*preto*) parent will almost never be called *branco* or *preto* but instead by some intermediate term, of which dozens are available. The United States lacks intermediate categories, but those categories are swelling in Brazil. Brazil's assimilated Indians are called *cabôclos* (rather than *índios*, or a specific tribal name, like Kayapó or Yanomami). With hypodescent, by contrast, someone may have just one of four or eight Indian grandparents or great-grandparents and still feel Indian, be so classified, and even have a tribal identity.

For centuries the United States and Brazil have had mixed populations, with ancestors from Native America, Europe, Africa, and Asia. Although races have mixed in both countries, Brazilian and American cultures have constructed the results differently. The historic reasons for this contrast lie mainly in the different characteristics of the settlers of the two countries. The mainly English early settlers of the United States came as women, men, and families, but Brazil's Portuguese colonizers were mainly men—merchants and adventurers. Many of these Portuguese men married Native American women and recognized their racially mixed children as their heirs. Like their North American counterparts, Brazilian plantation owners had sexual relations with their slaves; but the Brazilian landlords more often freed the children that resulted, for demographic and economic reasons. (Sometimes these were their only children.) Freed offspring of master and slave became plantation overseers and foremen and filled many intermediate positions in the emerging Brazilian economy. They were not classed with the slaves but allowed to join a new intermediate category. No hypodescent rule ever developed in Brazil to ensure that whites and blacks remained separate (see Harris 1964; Degler 1970).

In the next chapter we turn to purportedly more scientific treatments of race, but we shall see that culture again plays a decisive role. We'll also see how scientists do deal with the important matter of human biological variation. And we'll also consider claims for relationships between race and the inheritance of attributes such as intelligence and sports abilities.

CHAPTER SEVEN

Race: Its Biological Dimensions

--------------- "YOU CAN'T WRITE THEM OFF ANYMORE!" ---------------

Jeff, a senior engineering student at Georgia Tech, reached this conclusion after working with fourth graders in an Atlanta public school. As a "science partner" to a classroom teacher, Jeff, along with more than 500 other college students in Atlanta, helped implement an innovative program designed to engage children in hands-on science lessons.

These college science partners learned valuable lessons of their own. In focus groups and reflection sessions, they expressed surprise that "these children are really smart!" "They so want to learn; they just don't have the chance," explained Jyothi, a premed student at Emory University. A psychology major spoke more to the point: "Before I started working with these kids I thought they were lazy, or dumb, and that they didn't really care about school, or learning. Now I know these children *can* learn!"

Why the surprise? What preconceptions about pupils in the Atlanta Public Schools (APS) do these statements reveal? What demographic profile comes to your mind as you read these statements by your peers?

Kozaitis conducts participatory action research in a project aimed at systemic change within the Atlanta Public Schools. The goal is to develop science literacy among teachers and students. The program, called Elementary Science Education Partners (ESEP), was funded by the National Science

Foundation (NSF). This agency supports the development of science literacy among groups traditionally underrepresented in science, math, and technology. These include racially defined and ethnic minorities, females, rural students, and other communities in high-need school districts and high-poverty inner cities.

The Atlanta initiative served an urban, financially stressed school district with more than 30,000 children and some 1,600 teachers. Of the children, 91 percent are African Americans, three-quarters (76 percent) of whom qualify for free or reduced-priced lunches. Eighty-one percent of the teachers in APS are women; of them, 69 percent are African Americans. Previously the science education offered by APS had been limited by severe shortages involving time, materials, curriculum, and instruction. ESEP encouraged APS to form partnerships with several local colleges and universities, in a collaborative effort to improve science teaching in the district's 70 elementary schools.

The NSF's investment in these teachers and students is based on the premise that *"All* children can learn." NSF's mission contradicts racist proposals that attribute differences in academic achievement across groups to genes (Herrnstein and Murray 1994; Rushton 1995). Unequal access by minorities to science education is due more to socioeconomics and politics than to innate ability.

Despite overwhelming evidence that race is not a biological reality, racist ideas continue to flourish, as justification for separating and subordinating individuals and groups. Consider the Puerto Rican physician who insists, "Blacks are on welfare because they can't help it"; an educator who wonders, "Why don't black people speak English as well as immigrants?"; and an immigrant minister who states that his daughters "can marry any one they want, except a Jew or a black."

For more than half a century, anthropologists, beginning with Franz Boas (1940/1966) and later Ashley Montagu (1962, 1963, 1964), have shown that the concept of race does not explain human evolution. Nor are races fixed categories with innate characteristics, abilities, and inclinations. The correlation between biology and the academic achievements of certain groups is not only incorrect, but unjust and dangerous. Nowhere is this more evident than in the annual ritual of setting up millions of children (and their teachers) for failure by administering standardized tests which leave most American students feeling incompetent.

As the ESEP project demonstrates, all children can and do learn, given the necessary resources, a student-centered pedagogy, close supervision, and emotionally engaged teachers. Culturally informed, participatory strategies can transform "school failures" into enthusiastic and successful students. Once-powerless teachers have become self-conscious agents of change. Conventional administrators have become innovative leaders.

Just as impressive is the transformation of privileged undergraduates into committed agents of change. Given their preconceptions about poor people, black children, and inner-city teachers, the college students who worked as "science partners" were amazed at the humanity behind the stereotypes. Each semester, for five years, Kozaitis facilitated a series of focus groups and reflection sessions with hundreds of college students turned "service learners." Direct contact between the college students and public school children raised questions about cultural stratification and social responsibility. The undergraduates agreed that the ESEP experience taught them "more about life, education, and society than any traditional college course."

They learned directly about the relation between class and academic success, about institutional and interpersonal racism as a barrier to social equality, and about their own agency as social reformers. They gained an appreciation for teaching as a profession, teachers as agents of enculturation, and children as delightful human beings (college students reported little or no contact with children during their tenure in college other than the APS students).

Through their experience in hands-on social science, middle- and upper-middle-class college students learned the most important lesson of all. In the words of one graduating senior and future medical student, "All my life I thought that my academic success was natural, that I was just naturally smart. Now I know that my own achievement, and that of my friends, has more to do with our cultural background." On cue, following the unanimous nods of agreement in the room, Kozaitis asked, "What implications does this insight have for making sense of your life's work?" After a long silence, one speaker, in a collective voice, uttered, "You can't write them off anymore."

What do you think? ☻

RACIAL CLASSIFICATION

In Chapter 6 we saw, through cross-cultural evidence from the United States, Japan, and Brazil, that races are culturally constructed categories, which may have little to do with actual biological differences. The validity of race as a scientific concept in biology has also been discredited. Historically, scientists have approached the study of human biological diversity from two main directions: (1) **racial classification,** a now-rejected approach that seeks to assign human beings to categories based on assumed common ancestry, (2) and the current **explanatory approach,** which strives to discover the *causes* of specific human biological differences. In this chapter we'll review each approach. First we'll consider the problems with racial classification, which led to its rejection as a scientific concept. Then we'll offer an example of the explanatory approach to human biological diversity.

Racial classification has fallen out of favor in biology for several reasons. The main reason is that scientists have trouble placing specific groups of people into isolated and distinct racial units. A race is supposed to reflect shared *genetic* material, but scholars have tended to use *phenotypical* traits (usually skin color) for racial classification. There are several problems with a phenotypical approach to race. First, which traits should be primary in assigning people who look different to different races? Should races be defined by height, weight, body shape, facial features, teeth, skull form, or skin color? Like their fellow citizens, early European and American scientists gave priority to skin color. The phenotypic features, such as skin color, that were most apparent to those early scientists were also the very characteristics that had been assigned arbitrary cultural value for purposes of discrimination. Genetic variation (e.g., differences in blood types or groups) that was not directly observable was not used in cultural ways, nor did it figure in early racial classification.

Many school textbooks and encyclopedias still proclaim the existence of three great races: the white, the black, and the yellow. Such simplistic racial classification was compatible with the political use of race as a power device during the colonialist period of the late nineteenth and early twentieth centuries. The tripartite scheme kept white Europeans neatly separate from their African and Asian subjects. Colonial empires began to break up, and scientists began to question established racial categories, after World War II.

Politics aside, one obvious problem with color-based racial labels is that the terms don't accurately describe skin color. White people are more pink, beige, or tan than white. Black people are various shades of brown, and yellow people are tan or beige. But these terms have also been dignified by more scientific-*sounding* synonyms: Caucasoid, Negroid, and Mongoloid.

Another problem with the tripartite scheme is that many human populations don't neatly fit into any one of the three "great races." For example, where does one put the Polynesians? **Polynesia** is a triangle of South Pacific islands formed by Hawaii to the north, Easter Island to the east, and New Zealand to the southwest. Does the bronze skin color of Polynesians place them with the Caucasoids or the Mongoloids? Some scientists, recognizing this problem, enlarged the original tripartite scheme to include the Polynesian race. Native Americans present an additional problem. Are they red or yellow? Again, some scientists add a fifth race—the red, or Amerindian—to the major racial groups.

Many people in southern India have dark skins, but scientists have been reluctant to classify them with black Africans because of their Caucasoid facial features and hair form. Some, therefore, have created a separate race for these people. What about the Australian aborigines, hunters and gatherers native to the most isolated continent? By skin color, one might place some Native Australians in the same race as tropical Africans. However, similarities to Europeans in hair color (light or reddish) and facial features have led some scientists to classify them as Caucasoids. But there is no evidence that Australians are closer genetically or historically to either of these groups than they are to Asians. Recognizing this problem, scientists often regard Native Australians as a separate race.

Finally, consider the San ("Bushmen") of the Kalahari Desert in southern Africa. Scientists have perceived their skin color as varying from brown to yellow. Those who regard San skin as yellow have placed them in the same category as Asians. In theory, people of the same race share more recent common ancestry with each other than they do with any others; but there is no evidence for recent common ancestry between San and Asians. More reasonably, the San are classified as members of the Capoid (from the Cape of Good Hope) race, which is seen as being different from other groups inhabiting tropical Africa.

Similar problems arise when any single trait is used as a basis for racial classification. An attempt to use facial features, height, weight, or any other phenotypical trait is fraught with difficulties. For example, consider the Nilotes, natives of the upper Nile region of Uganda and Sudan. Nilotes tend to be tall and to have long, narrow noses. Certain Scandinavians are also tall, with similar noses. Given the distance between their homelands, to classify them as members of the same race makes little sense. There is no reason to assume that Nilotes and Scandinavians are more closely related to each other than either is to shorter (and nearer) populations with different kinds of noses.

Would it be better to base racial classifications on a combination of physical traits? This would avoid some of the problems mentioned above, but others would arise. First, skin color, stature, skull form, and facial features (nose form, eye shape, lip thickness) don't go together as a unit. For example, people with dark skin may be tall or short and have hair ranging from straight to very curly. Dark-haired populations may have light or dark skin, along with various skull forms, facial features, and body sizes and shapes. The number of combinations is very large, and the amount that heredity (versus environment) contributes to such phenotypical traits is often unclear.

There is a final objection to racial classification based on phenotype. The phenotypical characteristics on which races are based supposedly reflect genetic material that is shared and that has stayed the same for long time periods. But phenotypical similarities and differences don't necessarily have a genetic basis. Because of changes in the environment that affect individuals during growth and development, the range of phenotypes characteristic of a population may change without any genetic change. There are several examples. In the early 20th century, the anthropologist Franz Boas (1940/1966) described changes in skull form among the children of Europeans who had migrated to the United States. The reason for this was not a change in genes, for the European immigrants tended to marry among themselves. Some of their children had been born in Europe and merely raised in the United States. Something in the new environment, probably in the diet, was producing this change. We know now that changes in average height and weight produced by dietary differences in a few generations are common and have nothing to do with race or genetics.

EXPLANATORY APPROACHES TO HUMAN BIOLOGICAL DIVERSITY

Traditional racial classification assumed that biological characteristics were determined by heredity and stable (immutable) over long periods of time. We now know that a biological similarity doesn't necessarily indicate recent common ancestry. Dark skin color, for example, can be shared by tropical Africans and Native Australians for reasons other than common ancestry. It is not possible to *define races* biologically. Still, scientists have made much progress in *explaining* variation in human skin color, along with many other expressions of human biological diversity. We shift now from classification to *explanation,* in which natural selection plays a key role.

First recognized by Charles Darwin and Alfred Russell Wallace, **natural selection** is the process by which nature selects the forms most fit to survive and reproduce in a given environment, such as the tropics. Over the years, the less fit organisms die out and the favored types survive by producing more offspring. The role of natural selection in producing variation in skin color will illustrate the explanatory approach to human biological diversity. Comparable explanations have been provided for many other aspects of human biological variation, some of which are discussed in the next section.

Explaining Skin Color

Skin color is a complex biological trait, influenced by several genes—just how many isn't known. **Melanin,** the primary determinant of human skin color, is a chemical substance manufactured in the epidermis, or outer skin layer. The melanin cells of darker-skinned people produce more and larger granules of melanin than do those of lighter-skinned people. By screening out ultraviolet radiation from the sun, melanin offers protection against a variety of maladies, including sunburn and skin cancer.

Before the sixteenth century, most of the world's very dark-skinned populations lived in the **tropics,** a belt extending about 23 degrees north and south of the equator, between the Tropic of Cancer and the Tropic of Capricorn. The association between dark skin color and a tropical habitat existed throughout the Old World, where hominids have lived for millions of years. The darkest populations of Africa evolved not in shady equatorial forests but in sunny open grassland, or savanna, country.

Outside the tropics, skin color tends to be lighter. Moving north in Africa, for example, there is a gradual transition from dark brown to medium brown. Average skin color continues to lighten as one moves through the Middle East, into southern Europe, through central Europe, and to the north. South of the tropics skin color is also lighter. In the Americas, by contrast, tropical populations do not have very dark skin. This is because the settlement of the New World, by light-skinned Asian ancestors of Native Americans, was relatively recent, probably dating back no more than 30,000 years.

How, aside from migrations, can we explain the geographic distribution of skin color? Natural selection provides an answer. In the tropics, with intense ultraviolet radiation from the sun, unprotected humans face the threat of severe sunburn, which can increase susceptibility to disease. This confers a selective *dis*advantage (i.e., less success in surviving and reproducing) on lighter-skinned people in the tropics (unless they stay indoors or use cultural products, like umbrellas or lotions, to screen sunlight). Sunburn also impairs the body's ability to sweat. This is a second reason light skin color, given tropical heat, can diminish the human ability to live and work in equatorial climates. A third disadvantage of having light skin color in the tropics is that exposure to ultraviolet radiation can cause skin cancer (Blum 1961). A fourth factor affecting the geographic distribution of skin color is vitamin D production by the body. W. F. Loomis (1967) focused on the role of ultraviolet radiation in stimulating the manufacture of vitamin D by the human body. The unclothed human body can produce its own vitamin D when exposed to sufficient sunlight. But in a cloudy environment that is also so cold that people have to dress themselves for much of the year (such as northern Europe, where very light skin color evolved), clothing interferes with the body's manufacture of vitamin D. The ensuing shortage of vitamin D diminishes the absorption of calcium in the intestines. A nutritional disease known as **rickets,** which softens and deforms the bones, can develop. In women, deformation of the pelvic bones from rickets can interfere with childbirth. During northern winters, light skin color maximizes the absorption of ultraviolet radiation and the manufacture of vitamin D by the few parts of the body that are exposed to direct sunlight. On the other hand, there has been selection against dark skin color in northern areas because melanin screens out ultraviolet radiation.

Considering vitamin D production, light skin is an advantage in the cloudy north but a disadvantage in the sunny tropics. Loomis suggested that in the tropics, dark skin color protects the body against an *overproduction* of vitamin D by screening out ultraviolet radiation. Too much vitamin D can lead to a potentially fatal condition **(hypervitaminosis D),** in which calcium deposits build up in the body's soft tissues. The kidneys may eventually fail. Gallstones, joint problems, and circulation problems are other symptoms of hypervitaminosis D.

This discussion of skin color shows that common ancestry, the presumed basis of race, is not the only reason for biological similarities. Here natural selection has made a major contribution to this example of human diversity.

The racial approach to human biological diversity has been abandoned because of the faulty assumptions and problems involved in assigning humans to discrete races, which are assumed to reflect close common ancestry. Guided by the scientific method, biologists and anthropologists now focus on specific biological differences, such as skin color, and try to explain them. We have seen that skin color, along with other biological similarities between geographically separate groups, may reflect independent genetic adaptation to similar natural selective forces rather than common ancestry.

Lactose Intolerance

Many biological traits that illustrate human adaptation, such as skin color, are not under simple genetic control. Genetic determination of such traits may be likely but unconfirmed, or several genes may interact to influence the trait in question. Sometimes there is a genetic component, but the trait also responds to stresses encountered during growth. We speak of phenotypical adaptation when adaptive changes occur during the individual's lifetime. Phenotypical adaptation is made possible by biological plasticity—our ability to change in response to the environments we encounter as we grow.

For example, genes and phenotypical adaptation work together to produce a biochemical difference between human groups: the ability to digest large amounts of milk—an adaptive advantage when other foods are scarce and milk is available, as it is in dairying societies. All milk, whatever its source, contains a complex sugar called *lactose*. The digestion of milk depends on an enzyme called *lactase*, which works in the small intestine. Among all mammals except humans and some of their pets, lactase production ceases after weaning, so that these animals can no longer digest milk.

Lactase production and the ability to tolerate milk vary between populations. About 90 percent of northern Europeans and their descendants are lactose tolerant; they can digest several glasses of milk with no difficulty. Similarly, about 80 percent of two African populations, the Tutsi of Rwanda and Burundi in East Africa and the Fulani of Nigeria in West Africa, produce lactase and digest milk easily. Both these groups are herders. However, such nonherders as the Yoruba and Igbo in Nigeria, the Baganda in Uganda, the Japanese and other Asians, Eskimos, South American Indians, and many Israelis cannot digest lactose (Kretchmer 1972/1975).

However, the variable human ability to digest milk seems to be a difference of degree. Some populations can tolerate very little or no milk, but others are able to metabolize much greater quantities. Studies show that people who move from no-milk to low-milk diets to high-milk diets increase their lactose tolerance; this suggests some phenotypical adaptation. We can conclude that no simple genetic trait accounts for the ability to digest milk. Lactose tolerance appears to be one of many aspects of human biology governed both by genes and by phenotypical adaptation to environmental conditions.

THE CASE FOR CULTURAL VERSUS BIOLOGICAL DETERMINATION OF PHYSICAL ATTRACTIVENESS AND SPORTS ABILITIES

One way in which the environment affects human biology is through natural selection. Certain traits that are favored in particular environments confer a selective advantage on the organisms that have them. Such organisms have a better chance of surviving and reproducing than do organisms that

Twin Wade on the left is bigger and taller than his brother Wyatt. How can this be if they are identical?

lack those advantageous or adaptive traits. If those traits have a genetic basis, they will tend to be transmitted to descendants, and the favored type will increase its numbers in successive generations. In this way the environment can change a population's typical phenotype by favoring the genes that produce the favored phenotype.

In the long run, over the generations, environmental forces may thus produce phenotypical change in a population through natural selection. In this case the change in typical phenotype rests on corresponding changes in the population's gene pool. However, the discussion of lactose tolerance as a form of phenotypical adaptation has illustrated another way in which the environment affects human biology. Environmental forces mold phenotype during human growth and development, from infancy to adulthood. Identical twins, who share exactly the same genetic makeup, may look radically different as adults if one has been raised in the high Andes and the other has grown up at sea level. They will also differ if one has grown up with an adequate diet, while the other has been nutritionally deprived for years. In other words, during the individual lifetime, particularly during growth and development to adulthood, environmental forces can have a profound effect on phenotype.

Culture is a key environmental force determining how human bodies will grow and develop. Culture constantly molds human biology. Food preferences and dietary patterns, for example, influence human biology, as we saw in the discussion of lactose tolerance. Cultural traditions also promote certain activities and abilities, discourage others, and set standards of physical well-being and attractiveness. Physical activities, including sports, which are influenced by culture, help build phenotype. For example, North American girls are encouraged to pursue, and therefore do well in, competitive

Years of swimming sculpt a distinctive physique: an enlarged upper
torso, a massive neck, and powerful shoulders and back. Shown here is
the Dutch swimmer Inge de Bruijn, who won multiple medals at the
2000 summer Olympics in Sydney.

track and field, swimming, diving, and many other sports. Brazilian girls, by
contrast, have not fared nearly as well in international athletic competition
involving individual sports as have their American and Canadian counterparts. Why are girls encouraged to excel as athletes in some nations but discouraged from physical activities in others? Why don't Brazilian women,
and Latin women generally, do better in most athletic categories? Does it
have to do with racial differences or cultural training?

    Cultural standards of attractiveness influence sports participation and
achievement. Americans run or swim not just to compete but to keep trim
and fit. Brazil's beauty standards accept more fat, especially in female buttocks and hips. Brazilian men have had some international success in swimming and running, but Brazil rarely sends female swimmers or runners to
the Olympics. One reason Brazilian women avoid competitive swimming in
particular is that sport's effects on phenotype. Years of swimming sculpt a
distinctive physique—an enlarged upper torso, a massive neck, and powerful shoulders and back. Successful female swimmers tend to be big, strong,

and bulky. The countries that produce them most consistently are the United States, Canada, Australia, Germany, Scandinavia, the Netherlands, and Russia, where this phenotype isn't as stigmatized as it is in Latin countries. Swimmers develop hard bodies, but Brazilian culture says that women should be soft, with big hips and buttocks, not big shoulders. Many female swimmers in Latin America choose to abandon the sport rather than the feminine body ideal.

Culture, not race, also helps us understand many or most of the differences in the sports success of blacks and whites. Cultural factors help explain why blacks excel in certain sports and whites in others. In American public schools, parks, sandlots, and city playgrounds, African Americans have access to baseball diamonds, basketball courts, football fields, and tracks. However, because of restricted economic opportunities, many black families can't afford to buy hockey gear or golf or ski equipment, take ski vacations, pay for tennis lessons, or belong to clubs with tennis courts, pools, or golf courses. In the United States mainly light-skinned suburban boys (and increasingly, girls) play soccer, the most popular sport in the world. In Brazil, however, soccer is the national pastime of all males—black and white, rich and poor. There is wide public access. Brazilians play soccer on the beach and in streets, squares, parks, and playgrounds. Many of Brazil's best soccer players, including the world-famous Pelé, have dark skin. When blacks have opportunities to do well in soccer, tennis, golf, or any other sport, they are physically capable of doing as well as whites.

Why does contemporary North America have so many black football and basketball players and so few black swimmers and hockey players? The answer lies mainly in cultural factors, including variable access and social stratification. Many Brazilians practice soccer, hoping to play for money for a professional club. Similarly, American blacks are aware that certain sports have provided career opportunities for African Americans. They start developing skills in those sports in childhood. The better they do, the more likely they are to persist, and the pattern continues. Culture—specifically, differential access to sports resources—has more to do with sports success than race does.

THE CASE FOR CULTURAL VERSUS BIOLOGICAL DETERMINATION OF INTELLIGENCE

No discussion of the biological dimensions of race would be complete without considering the purported relation between race and IQ. Are there genetically determined differences in the learning abilities of races, classes, and ethnic groups? We know of no convincing evidence for biologically based contrasts in intelligence between rich and poor, black and white, or men and women. Environmental variables—particularly educational, economic, and social background—provide much better explanations for performance on intelligence tests by such groups. Tests cannot help but reflect the cultural training and life experiences of those who develop and administer them. All tests are to some extent culture-bound and biased. Equalized environmental opportunities show up in similar test scores.

We have seen that, as scientists have shifted from racial *classification* to the *explanation* of human biological diversity, race is no longer considered a valid biological concept. Race has meaning only in social, cultural, and political terms. Over the centuries groups with power have used racial ideology to justify, explain, and preserve their privileged social positions. Dominant groups have declared minorities to be *innately,* that is, biologically, inferior. Racial ideas have been used to suggest that social inferiority and presumed shortcomings (in intelligence, ability, character, or attractiveness) are immutable and passed across the generations. This ideology defends stratification as inevitable, enduring, and natural—based in biology rather than society. Thus, the Nazis argued for the superiority of the Aryan race, and European colonialists asserted the existence of a "white man's burden." South Africa institutionalized apartheid. Again and again, to justify exploitation of minorities and native peoples, those in control have proclaimed the innate inferiority of the oppressed. In the United States the supposed superiority of whites was once standard segregationist doctrine. Belief in the biologically based inferiority of Native Americans has been an argument for their slaughter, confinement, and neglect.

However, anthropologists know that most of the behavioral variation among human groups rests on culture rather than biology. The cultural similarities revealed through thousands of ethnographic studies leave no doubt that capacities for cultural evolution are equivalent in all human populations. There is also excellent evidence that within any stratified (class-based) society, differences in performance between economic, social, and ethnic groups reflect their different experiences and opportunities. (Stratified societies, remember, are those with marked differences in wealth, prestige, and power between social classes.)

Stratification, political domination, prejudice, and ignorance continue to exist. They propagate the mistaken belief that misfortune and poverty result from lack of ability. Occasionally, doctrines of innate superiority are even set forth by scientists, who, after all, tend to come from the favored stratum of society. One of the best-known examples is Jensenism, named for the educational psychologist Arthur Jensen (Jensen 1969; Herrnstein 1971), its leading proponent. Jensenism is a highly questionable interpretation of the observation that African Americans, on average, perform less well on intelligence tests than Euro-Americans and Asian Americans do. Jensenism asserts that blacks are hereditarily incapable of performing as well as whites do. Writing with Charles Murray, Richard Herrnstein makes a similar argument in the 1994 book *The Bell Curve,* to which the following critique also applies (see also Jacoby and Glauberman 1995).

Environmental explanations for test scores are much more convincing than are the genetic arguments of Jensen, Herrnstein, and Murray. An environmental explanation does not deny that some people may be smarter than others. In any society, for many reasons, genetic and environmental, the talents of individuals vary. An environmental explanation does deny, however, that these differences can be generalized to whole populations. Even when talking about individual intelligence, however, we have to decide which of several abilities is an accurate measure of intelligence.

Psychologists have devised various kinds of tests to measure intelligence, but there are problems with all of them. Early intelligence tests required skill in manipulating words. Such tests do not accurately measure learning ability for several reasons. For example, individuals who have learned two languages as children (bilinguals) don't do as well, on average, on verbal intelligence tests as do those who have learned a single language. It would be absurd to suppose that children who master two languages have inferior intelligence. The explanation seems to be that because bilinguals have vocabularies, concepts, and verbal skills in both languages, their ability to manipulate either one suffers a bit. This would seem to be offset by the advantage of being fluent in two languages.

Education isn't the same thing as enculturation, the universal process by which children internalize their culture by learning how they are supposed to act. **Education,** which refers to the acquisition of more formal knowledge, normally occurs in a place called a school. Education, which tends to be found in nation-states, exposes certain—not all—people in a society to a body of formal knowledge or lore. Education is a strategic resource to which there is differential access based on stratification. All nations have educational systems, but access to the full range of educational possibilities is always unequal.

Tests reflect the experience of the people who devise them—educated people in Europe and North America. It isn't surprising that middle- and upper-class children do best, because they are more likely to share the test makers' educational background, knowledge, and standards. Numerous studies have shown that performance on Scholastic Achievement Tests (SATs) can be improved by coaching and preparation. Parents who can afford $500 or more for an SAT preparation course enhance their kids' chances of getting high scores. Standardized college entrance exams are similar to IQ tests in that they have claimed to measure intellectual aptitude. They may do this, but they also measure type and quality of high school education, linguistic and cultural background, and parental wealth. No test is free of class, ethnic, and cultural biases.

Tests can measure only phenotypical intelligence, the product of a particular learning history, rather than genetically determined learning potential. IQ tests use middle-class experience as a standard for determining what should be known at a given chronological age. Furthermore, tests are usually administered by middle-class white people who give instructions in a dialect or language that may not be totally familiar to the child being tested. Test performance improves when the cultural, socioeconomic, and linguistic backgrounds of takers and examiners are similar (Watson 1972).

Recognizing the difficulties in devising a culture-free test, psychologists have developed several nonverbal tests, hoping to find an objective measure that is not bound to a single culture. In one such test, individuals score higher by adding body parts to a stick figure. In a maze test, subjects trace their way out of various mazes. The score increases with the speed of completion. Other tests also base scores on speed, for example, in fitting geometric objects into appropriately shaped holes. All these tests are culture-bound because our culture stresses speed and competition, whereas most nonindustrial cultures do not.

We offer several examples of cultural biases in testing. Such biases affect performance by people in other societies and by different groups within the same society, such as Native Americans in the United States. Many Native Americans have grown up on reservations or under conditions of urban or rural poverty. They have suffered social, economic, political, and cultural discrimination. In one study, Native Americans scored the lowest (a mean of 81, compared with a standard of 100) of any minority group in the United States (Klineberg 1951). But when the environment during growth and development includes opportunities similar to those available to middle-class Americans, test performance tends to equalize. Consider the Osage Indians, on whose reservation oil was discovered. Profiting from oil sales, the Osage did not experience the stresses of poverty. They developed a good school system, and their average IQ was 104. Here the relationship between test performance and environment is particularly clear. The Osage did not settle on the reservation because they knew oil was there. There is no reason to believe these people were innately more intelligent than were Indians on different reservations. They were just luckier, and afterward they benefited from their good fortune.

Similar links between social, economic, and educational environment and test performance show up in comparisons of American blacks and whites. At the beginning of World War I, intelligence tests were given to approximately one million American army recruits. Blacks from some northern states had higher average scores than did whites from some southern states. At that time northern blacks got a better public education than many southern whites did, so their superior performance wasn't surprising. That southern whites did better, on average, than southern blacks also was expectable, given the unequal school systems then open to whites and blacks in the South.

Racists tried to dismiss the environmental explanation for the superior performance of northern blacks compared with southerners by suggesting selective migration, that smarter blacks had moved north. However, it was possible to test this hypothesis, which turned out to be false. If smarter blacks had moved north, their superior intelligence should have been evident in their school records while they were still living in the South. It was not. Furthermore, studies in New York, Washington, and Philadelphia showed that as length of residence in those cities increased, test scores also rose.

Studies of identical twins raised apart also illustrate the impact of environment on identical heredity. In a study of 19 pairs of twins, IQ scores varied directly with years in school. The average difference in IQ was only 1.5 points for the 8 twin pairs with the same amount of schooling. It was 10 points for the 11 pairs with an average of five years' difference. One subject, with 14 years more education than his twin, scored 24 points higher (Bronfenbrenner 1975).

These and similar studies provide overwhelming evidence that test performance measures background and education rather than genetically determined intelligence. For centuries Europeans and their descendants have extended their political and economic control over much of the world. They colonized and occupied environments that they reached in their ships and conquered with their weapons. Most people in the most powerful contemporary nations—located in North America, Europe, and Asia—have light skin color. Some people in these currently powerful countries may incorrectly assert and believe that their position rests on innate biological superiority. Remember (as we saw in the last chapter) that a prime minister of Japan has made such a claim.

We are living in and interpreting the world at a particular time. In the past there were far different associations between centers of power and human physical characteristics. When Europeans were barbarians, advanced civilizations thrived in the Middle East. When Europe was in the Dark Ages, there were civilizations in West Africa, on the East African coast, in Mexico, and in Asia. Before the Industrial Revolution, the ancestors of many white Europeans and North Americans were living more like precolonial Africans than like current members of the American middle class. There is every reason to doubt that preindustrial Europeans would excel on 20th-century IQ tests.

Testing and Affirmative Action

We are individuals, but we also belong to groups with whose other members we share backgrounds, behavior patterns, values, interests, expectations, strengths, and weaknesses, which influence our likelihood of success in particular domains. One such domain is higher education, in which affirmative-action policies have been used to increase the proportion of minorities in the student body. Today, however, colleges and universities with affirmative-action policies face increased legal and political challenges.

In 1997, the Center for Individual Rights in Washington, D.C., sued the University of Michigan on behalf of white students claiming that efforts to increase campus diversity by admitting black and Hispanic students with lower test scores and grades violated the Constitution. This suit followed a similar one against the University of Texas and a referendum in California

(Proposition 209) that ended racial preferences in admissions. California and Texas are now forbidden to use race in university admissions.

It is claimed that affirmative-action policies lead universities to use different, and lower, standards for minorities. The standards mentioned in the legal challenges are national test scores (whose limitations have been discussed above) and grade-point averages. The average test scores of black and Latino students are below those of whites. This phenomenon cuts across all income groups.

On the other side of the issue, responding to the affirmative-action ban, the Mexican-American Legal Defense and Educational Fund sued the state of Texas, contending that its high school graduation exam, on which black and Mexican-American students fail at a much higher rate than non-Hispanic whites do, is discriminatory (Bronner 1997). A special issue of the *Journal of Blacks in Higher Education* argues that "African Americans are struggling to overcome 200 years of white supremacy and educational segregation" and need affirmative action to progress (Bronner 1997).

Educators face a quandary. How can fairness and equal opportunity be combined with maintenance of student bodies that reflect national diversity? How, fairly and legally, can diversity and multiculturalism be mainstreamed in the college setting? It is feared that primary use of scores, rather than more qualitative criteria, will result in virtual racial segregation. Furthermore, there is reason to question whether SAT scores and their professional-school equivalents are the best predictors of academic and career success. The *Journal of Blacks in Higher Education* reported that in 1951, Martin Luther King, Jr., took the Graduate Record Exam for admission to a doctoral program at Boston University. His verbal aptitude score was below average. Yet King is now viewed as a verbal hero, one of the greatest orators in American history (Bronner 1997).

In the previous section we saw that test performance varies with environmental conditions and opportunities. It also varies over time. Writing in the *American Psychologist,* Wendy Williams and Stephen Ceci (1997) conclude that the black-white gap in IQ testing has decreased. They cite work by James Flynn, who found that for the previous 65 years IQ scores had been increasing in every country where they were measured. IQ scores of black Americans are about where white ones were two generations ago. This suggests, according to Williams (in Bronner 1997), that there is greater malleability in such tests than was previously believed. IQ tests, like SATs, are open to such influences as the sophistication or urban nature of the society in which one lives. Supporting that view, researchers at Washington University in St. Louis compared IQ test scores of blacks and whites in their last year of high school and again at the end of college. Blacks improved their scores more than four times as much as whites did, cutting the IQ gap in half (Bronner 1997). The college experience itself may explain the faster rate of increase in average test scores by blacks.

Claude Steele of Stanford University suggests that blacks and women absorb negative self-images from the environment, driving down their scores on standardized tests (Bronner 1997). Steele (1997) found that when blacks taking a test were told that such tests showed no distinction in white-black scores, they did as well as the white test-takers. But when they were told nothing or had to check off their race on a form before starting, their scores were lower. The findings for women were similar.

The challenge to affirmative action is ongoing. Two suits against the University of Michigan are currently (as of 2002) under appeal. The initial hearing judge in one case supported, but in the other case opposed, the university's affirmative action policies. In 2001 a federal appeals court ruled unconstitutional the admissions policy of the University of Georgia, which gave bonus points to nonwhite applicants to increase diversity in the student body. Firestone quotes the judges of the U.S. Court of Appeals for the 11th Circuit: "Racial diversity alone is not necessarily the hallmark of a diverse student body, and race is not necessarily the only, or best, criterion for determining the contribution that an applicant might make to the broad mix of experiences and perspectives that create diversity" (2001). Some university affirmation action programs now give priority to students in poverty, not only students of African American, Hispanic, and Asian origin (Marciniak 2001).

One solution is to end the use of standard tests for college admissions. Almost 300 American colleges, including Bates College in Maine, no longer require test scores from their applicants (Bronner 1997). Bates College's internal data show that those who did not submit their scores but were admitted got 160 points less than those who did submit their scores. Yet the two groups show no difference in grades or graduation rates (Bronner 1997). The lower scorers included not only minority students but also whites from working-class backgrounds, students who grew up speaking another language at home, more women than men, and musicians and athletes. Bates's no-test policy had helped double its minority representation (Bronner 1997).

CHAPTER EIGHT

Religion

"UNIVERSAL TRUTH IS EVERYWHERE"

Concern with a supreme being, sacred principles, or higher truth is a cultural universal. It is as old as humanity itself, and intrinsic to the human condition. Even people who claim to be atheists (those who deny the existence of God) or agnostics (those who believe that the existence of any supreme power or force is unknown, or unknowable) may admit to having had a religious experience.

Like culture in general, religion is malleable and adaptive. A religious system responds to change within and outside the cultural and social context of its birth to meet the needs of its bearers. Immigrants can interpret and express their native religions in ways that reflect life in a new society. In North America we find many religious systems, along with a wide variation in the expression of particular religions that reflect other factors, such as socioeconomic status.

Consider, for example, the performance of the Hindu ritual *Satyanarayana Puja* by Indian immigrants. Hinduism emphasizes freedom from the material world through purification of desires and the elimination of personal identity. The ultimate goal of a devotee is to master one's senses and to recognize and speak the higher truth. According to Hinduism, humans can alleviate sufferings and sorrows and gain salvation by performing the Satyanarayana Puja. Many Hindus in the United States perform this Puja in their homes, facilitated by a priest.

Hindus believe that the Puja will bring happiness, peace of mind, and wealth in this life and salvation beyond. One must gather his or her friends and relatives and perform the Puja with devotion and according to tradition. Enacted by former members of a high Indian caste who are presently middle-class professionals in the United States, the Puja takes on a new form to fit American society. Its content remains authentic to fulfill the needs of the participants. As an invited family friend and observer of a Puja, Kozaitis was impressed by an unfamiliar sequence of rites (ceremonial acts) supplemented by characteristically American cultural elements.

The ceremony was to start at 3:30 PM. It began promptly, but some guests arrived late. None of the 30 guests were related to the hosts. Most were colleagues and neighbors. Along with the hosts, the eight Indians in attendance were the only genuinely engaged participants. The other guests were sympathetic spectators. Some were there to support the hosts; others, to offer symbolic consent to the ritual itself: the primacy of "higher truth" which, as the hosts explained, "is omnipresent." Implicit in this statement is the idea that one does not need to be an Indian or a Hindu to take part in the Puja. This notion justified the presence of an American, white majority in the room, a condition that reflected the new status of the hosts as professionals and as (socially) American themselves.

Everyone spoke English except the priest, who spoke in an ancient language. The dress of the Indians signified their in-group status. Others were dressed more casually. A few children attended the ritual. Others, consistent with the age segregation that characterizes American life, watched television and played video games in the basement. All the adults sat in the "sacred space" that hours earlier had been an ordinary family room.

The ritual followed procedural and sequential requirements. One wall of the room was designated as the location of the ritual performance. Flowers, fruits, and other foods were arranged on a fabric-covered surface that resembled a small altar. Taped to the wall were photographic reproductions of Lord Ganesha, Navagraha, Ashtadikpalak, Panchalokapalkas, and Satyanarayana, to which the Puja is performed. The host family and the priest sat next to the altar, facing and handling the artifacts. The priest said several prayers. The guests gazed at a scene that was visually engaging but, for most present, meaningless.

The participants offered fruits, ghee, milk, curd, butter, wheat flour, sugar, and honey to God. Among the ritual artifacts were Tropicana orange juice and Kroger milk. In India, participants would have used freshly squeezed juice and milk from the cows. After the Puja was over, the parents and their two children took turns reading, in English, the *Satyanarayan Katha* (stories treated by Hindus as sacred truth). The ritual ended with the distribution of *prasadam* (a blessed food). Everyone conformed by accepting and consuming the prasadam.

The contrast between the engaged, devoted performers and the disengaged, illiterate audience diminished as the ritual progressed to its third stage, the feast. In India the ritual ends by having participants consume the various blessed foods. Segregated by gender, participants sit around the altar and eat from common bowls. In the United States, the last part of the ritual changed to meet the expectations of outsiders. The hostess prepared a buffet table, with a number of pots filled with ordinary food (unblessed by the priest), stacked dishes, napkins, and forks. Now everyone knew what to do. People stood in line, chatted about the food, filled their plates, and sought seating on the patio. Some ate in small groups, others in pairs. Others ate standing alone. Several conversations went on simultaneously.

The scene took on a middle-class American character. Most people didn't know each other. Introductions preceded many of the chats. People asked each other what they did to earn a living and stated their own occupations. Others gave updates about their projects, summer jobs, and career interests, convinced one another of how busy they were, discussed the pros and cons of professional development, and debated the quality of one school over another. The conversations revealed the social reality of all who were present, including the hosts. No one discussed the Puja. The emphasis had shifted from eternal, higher, and universal truth to temporal, concrete, and specifically American, if not individualistic, ego-centered concerns.

Still, like all rituals, the Puja fulfilled certain fundamental spiritual and social needs of the hosts. As for the guests, this event marked yet one more exposure to cultural diversity in the North American mainstream. ☺

CHURCH AND STATE

Religion is a cornerstone of North American diversity. Our system of religious pluralism evolved as people fled countries where religious difference and dissent were not respected. Those founding fathers and mothers, seeking to preserve religious freedom, also brought strong, and still influential, religious values to the New World. Like ethnicity and national heritage, religion is the basis of identities, organization, and common activity—sometimes with the goal of changing public policy. Increasingly, religion and religious views have entered the political realm, where ads have gone so far as to declare that a vote for a particular candidate is "a sin against God." On the political left, leaders have targeted evangelicals and warned against fundamentalist involvement in politics. On the right, candidates campaigning as "concerned Christians" have accused those who oppose their views of Christian-bashing.

The U.S. Constitution says government should be neutral but accommodating toward religion. Churches are, however, subject to laws and regulations that affect the rest of the community, including the tax code. Religious institutions are exempt from taxes on funds raised for activities directly related to their religious mission or that serve a charitable purpose. This exemption includes money raised to support the acquisition and up- keep of a place of worship and staff compensation. Funds raised for chari- table activities, such as food drives for the hungry or collections for overseas victims of persecution, are also exempt from taxation. Electoral politics, however, is not a tax-free activity. Contributions to political candidates are not tax-deductible, and groups that work to elect candidates are not tax- exempt. Religious groups have the right to engage in such activity, but they cannot continue to operate as a tax-exempt organization, although some of them have attempted to do so.

The government of the United States is supposed to guarantee and pro- tect religious liberty without establishing religion. Rooted in the First Amendment to the U.S. Constitution is the doctrine that government must show neither official approval nor disapproval of religion. The principle of government neutrality means not favoring one religion over another or over no religion at all. Most Americans say they believe in God, and most also have some kind of religious affiliation. But the U.S. government holds no of- ficial religious view and is enjoined against seeking to promote one. Supreme Court Justice Sandra Day O'Connor stated this principle in a 1984 case:

> The Establishment Clause prohibits government from making adherence to a religion in any way relevant to a person's standing in the political com- munity. Government can run afoul of that prohibition in two principal ways. One is excessive entanglement with religious institutions. . . . The sec- ond and more direct infringement is government endorsement or disap- proval of religion. Endorsement sends a message to non-adherents that they are outsiders, not full members of the political community, and an accom- panying message to adherents that they are insiders, favored members of the political community. Disapproval sends the opposite message. (Quoted in Freeman 1994)

Article VI, Section 3 of the U.S. Constitution declares that "no religious test shall ever be required as a qualification to any office or public trust un- der the United States" (Freeman 1994). Both left and right have occasionally ignored that constitutional mandate. One example was in 1988, when a presidential candidate said he would only appoint Christians or Jews to his cabinet. He wouldn't feel comfortable with an advisor from some other background, he said. Such a blanket exclusion of Muslims, Buddhists, and atheists, for example, regardless of their personal qualifications, violated the Constitution's prohibition on religious tests.

Castelli (1984) and Freeman (1994) argue for the need to respect religious differences, views, and values in political debates. Whether Roman Catholic, Christian fundamentalist, or New Age religionist, no American should be ex- cluded from politics or publicly denigrated because of his or her religious views. Yet some leaders who claim to be victims of religious bigotry are them- selves guilty of belittling opponents because of religious differences. Politi- cians routinely insult minority religions or religious views—for example, "New Age philosophy"—in an attempt to marginalize their opposition.

Politics and Religion

With religion as with other components of multiculturalism, we recognize diversity within cultural segments and formal institutions and that different groups have their own agendas. Castelli (1984) and Freeman (1994) suggest that political leaders typically claim to represent a broader constituency than they actually do represent. One example is politicians who refer to their backers as Christians and who claim to speak for those Christians. This claim may also suggest that people with different views are not real Christians. In fact, Christians, even evangelicals, belong to diverse denominations and have varied political opinions.

Still, many southern white Protestant fundamentalists no doubt share with feminists, gay rights activists, and African-American leaders the perception that dominant social institutions (such as government and the media) have little use and respect for their beliefs, practices, and values. Like the other groups, fundamentalists (the "Religious Right") also coalesce (most notably as the Christian Coalition) and work to influence electoral outcomes and public policy. Such people see themselves as the real American mainstream (the silent majority), whose voice too long has been silenced by special interest groups (e.g., homosexuals and "feminazis") clamoring for special rights and by cultural elites (liberals) seen as controlling media and the government. And the other affinity groups and their identity politicians fear, oppose, and preach against the Religious Right as ardently and stridently as the Christian Coalition does against its perceived enemies. Here religion links up with media and politics, especially through the spread of religious TV (televangelism) and talk radio. Liberals oppose by honing identity politics and voting for Democrats, whereas conservatives and Republicans dominate talk radio, complaining about the perceived celebration of special rights, liberalism, and immorality in government and the media.

RELIGION AND SOLIDARITY

In previous chapters we have stressed the role of political mobilization and solidarity in the formation of social identities and culturally organized groups within a society. Historically, religion has been a potent force for social union and division. Like racial and ethnic identities, those based on religion can both unite us, as members of a congregation or social body, and create division by separating us from other congregations.

The anthropologist Anthony F. C. Wallace has defined **religion** as "belief and ritual concerned with supernatural beings, powers, and forces" (1966, p. 5). Religion is a formal social institution which, for individuals, may provide coherence, meaning, and direction in life. Also, inculcating a social (religious) identity, religion, especially through its rituals, serves to create temporary or permanent union among people who carry out the same rituals. One role of religious beliefs and rites is regularly to affirm, and thus to maintain, the solidarity of a religion's adherents. ("A family that prays together stays together.")

According to Roy Rappaport (1974), several features distinguish religious **rituals** from other kinds of behavior and thus make religion different from the other forces of social unity and division examined so far. Rituals are formal; that is, they are stylized, repetitive, and stereotyped. People perform them in special (sacred) places and at set times. Rituals include liturgical orders, set sequences of words and actions invented prior to the current performance of the ritual in which they occur.

One example of religious ritual in a sacred place is the *hajj*—the pilgrimage to Mecca, the most sacred of Muslim sites. The hajj can be taken by any member of a family, but many families go together. The hajj is expected of all Muslims, depending on their financial and physical capabilities (Bhardwaj 1998). Pilgrims to Mecca, where the prophet Muhammad was born, visit its many holy sites. The *Kaaba*, a building that Abraham and Ishmael, the patriarchs of Islam, are believed to have built, stands in the center of Mecca's great mosque, as does the Black Stone, reportedly given to Abraham by the angel Gabriel. Another important shrine is a well reportedly used by Hagar, Ismael's mother. Pilgrims usually carry out their journey during the lunar year's last month, *Dhu al-Hijja* in the Islamic calendar. Several symbolic rituals are performed by pilgrims, including wearing a white shroud, later saved to be their burial garb, and the circling seven times of the *Kaaba*. People gain a sense of solidarity through their common identity as pilgrims. Muslims who have completed the hajj may use celebratory titles, *Hajji* and *Hajjah* (for men and women, respectively), throughout their lives. Some 2 million pilgrims travel to Mecca annually (Microsoft Encarta Encyclopedia 2002).

Rituals convey information about the participants and their traditions. As they are reenacted year after year, generation after generation, rituals translate enduring messages, values, and sentiments into observable actions. Rituals are social acts. Inevitably, some participants are more committed than others are to the beliefs that lie behind the rites. However, just by taking part in a joint public act, the performers signal that they accept a common social and moral order, one that transcends their status as individuals. Participation in a ritual can thus be a powerful force for mobilization.

Ritualized Changes in Status and Identity

Rituals called **rites of passage** are often associated with a change from one place, condition, status, or stage of life to another. Found worldwide, such rites can be individualistic or collective. An example of an individualistic rite of passage was the Vision Quest of Native Americans, especially the Indians who lived in the Great Plains of North America. In order to move from boyhood to manhood, a youth separated himself from his community. During isolation in the wilderness, often with fasting and drug consumption, the young man would see a vision, which would become his personal

Religion is a formal social institution which, for individuals, may provide coherence, meaning, and direction in life. Also, inculcating a social identity, religion, especially through its rituals, serves to create temporary or permanent union among those who carry out the same rituals. This Russian Orthodox woman takes holy communion by kissing the cross, as those behind her in line also will do.

guardian spirit. He would return to his community and be regarded as an adult. The rite of passage had changed his identity.

Contemporary rites of passage include confirmations, baptisms, bar and bat mitzvahs, and fraternity hazing. Passage rites make a public statement about changes in status, such as from boyhood to manhood or from non-member to sorority sister.

All rites of passage have three phases: separation, margin, and aggregation. In the first phase, people withdraw temporarily from ordinary society. In the third, they reenter society, having completed the rite. The margin phase is the most interesting. It is the period between states, the limbo during which people have left one place or state but have not yet entered the next. This is called the *liminal phase* of the rite (V. W. Turner 1969/1995). **Liminality** has certain characteristics. Liminal people occupy ambiguous social positions. They exist apart from ordinary distinctions and expectations. They are in a time out of time, cut off from ordinary society. A series of contrasts may serve symbolically to demarcate liminality from regular life (see Table 8–1).

Often, passage rites are collective, with a group of people enduring them together. Examples include teenage boys being jointly circumcised, fraternity

TABLE 8–1. Contrasts Between Liminality and Ordinary Social Life

Liminality	Normal Social Structure
Transition	State
Homogeneity	Heterogeneity
Communitas	Structure
Equality	Inequality
Anonymity	Names
Absence of property	Property
Absence of status	Status
Nakedness or uniform dress	Dress distinctions
Sexual continence or excess	Sexuality
Minimization of sex distinctions	Maximization of sex distinctions
Absence of rank	Rank
Humility	Pride
Disregard of personal appearance	Care for personal appearance
Unselfishness	Selfishness
Total obedience	Obedience only to superior rank
Sacredness	Secularity
Sacred instruction	Technical knowledge
Silence	Speech
Simplicity	Complexity
Acceptance of pain and suffering	Avoidance of pain and suffering

Source: Reprinted with permission from Victor W. Turner, *The Ritual Process: Structure and Anti-structure,* (New York: Aldine de Gruyter), © 1969 Victor W. Turner.

or sorority initiates, men at military boot camps, football players in summer training camps, and women becoming nuns. The most notable social aspect of collective liminality is **communitas** (V. W. Turner 1969/1995), an intense community spirit, a feeling of great solidarity, equality, and togetherness. People experiencing liminality together form a community of equals. The distinctions that existed before and that will exist afterward are temporarily forgotten. Liminal people face the same conditions, are treated the same, and must act alike. Liminality may be marked ritually and symbolically by reversals of ordinary behavior. For example, sexual taboos may be intensified or, conversely, sexual excess may be encouraged.

Baptism is a liminal ritual for Protestants (more or less so depending on the specific church). The baptismal rite may involve sacred instruction prior to the ritual, wearing uniform clothing (e.g., a white robe), transition from the unbaptized state to the baptized state (involving spiritual rebirth), silence (during the ritual), acceptance of discomfort (being dunked in cold water), and communitas with others being baptized at the same time.

Liminality is basic to every passage rite. Furthermore, in certain societies, including our own, liminal symbols may be used to set off one religious group from another and from society as a whole. Such permanent

liminal groups (e.g., sects, brotherhoods, and cults) are found most characteristically in complex societies—nation-states. Such liminal features as hu-
mility, poverty, equality, obedience, sexual abstinence, and silence may be
required for all sect or cult members. Those who join such a group agree to
its rules. As if they were undergoing a passage rite—but in this case a never-
ending one—they may rid themselves of their previous possessions and cut
themselves off from former social links, including those with family members. Identity as a member of the group is expected to transcend individuality. Cult members often wear uniform clothing. They may try to reduce
distinctions based on age and gender by using a common hair style (shaved
head, short hair, or long hair). The Heaven's Gate cult, whose mass suicide
garnered headlines in 1997, even used castration to increase **androgyny**
(similarity between males and females). With such cults (as in the military),
the individual, so important in American culture, is submerged in the collective. This is one reason Americans are so fearful and suspicious of cults.
In a variety of contexts, liminal features mark diversity by signaling the distinctiveness or sacredness of groups, persons, settings, and events. Liminal
symbols mark entities and circumstances as extraordinary, outside and beyond ordinary social space and routine social events.

RELIGIOUS DIVERSITY

Overwhelmingly, the United States remains a Protestant country. Yet, in the
face of large-scale immigration from Roman Catholic countries, its Protestant population share has declined substantially, from 67 percent in 1967 to
56 percent in 2000 (Table 8–2). Still, in both years the number of Protestants
substantially exceeded that of Catholics, who now make up 27 percent of
the population. In Canada, by contrast, Catholics outnumber Protestants, a

**TABLE 8–2. Religious Composition (in Percentages) of the Populations
of the United States, 1967 and 2000, and Canada, 1981 and 1991**

	United States		Canada	
	1967	2000	1981	1991
Protestant	67%	56%	41%	36%
Catholic	25	27	47	46
Jewish	3	2	1	1
Other	3	7	3	4
None given	2	8	7	12

Source: Statistical Abstract of the United States 2001, p. 56, Table 66. 1991, and Census of Canada,
http://www.StatCan.ca.

difference that has grown more substantial in the past decade. In both countries, reflecting immigration, especially from Asia, membership in the "other"
religious category has increased—to 7 percent in the United States in 2000,
versus just 2 percent in 1967. The number of censused people who did not
offer a religious preference has also risen in both countries, to 8 percent in
the United States and 12 percent in Canada. This would seem to indicate a
rising secularism in both nations.

The organized religions and churches represented in the United States
and Canada include, but are not limited to, Christianity, Judaism, Islam,
Hinduism, and Buddhism. On the basis of the latest available figures, Christianity dominates in both countries, with more than 80 percent of the population. In order, Canada's other major organized religions are Eastern
Orthodox (1.4 percent), Judaism (1.2), Islam (0.9), Buddhism (0.6), Hinduism (0.6), and Sikh (0.5). In the United States, equivalent figures are not
available, but the order of membership is Judaism, Eastern Orthodox, Islam, Buddhism, Hinduism, and Sikh.

Justin Long (1998) concludes that while every other religion is gaining
converts in North America,[*] Christianity, growing at 0.8 percent annually—
slightly less than the region's population growth rate of 0.9 percent—is los-
ing them. Among Christians, Pentecostals (increasing at 1.3 percent) and
Evangelicals (1.1 percent) have the highest growth rates. Buddhism (2.4
million North American members), at 2.8 percent annually, is growing three
times as fast as Christianity. North America's 1.2 million Hindus have an annual growth rate of 3.4 percent. Numbering 26 million in 1998 (versus 1
million in 1900), the nonreligious have an annual growth rate of 1.1 percent
(mostly through births to nonreligious homes). Atheists have grown from
2,000 in 1900 to 1.4 million today, and are maintaining a growth rate of 2
percent (Long 1998).

Both the United States and Canada have marked regional variation in
religious affiliation and church membership. In Canada the province of
Quebec has the largest concentration of Roman Catholics. In the United
States the Jewish population, only 2 percent nationally, is significantly
larger in New York state (9 percent) and New York City. Southerners
(75 percent) are more likely to belong to a church or temple than are midwesterners (72 percent), easterners (67 percent), or, especially, westerners
(60 percent), as shown in Table 8–3. However, the rate of actual church attendance is similar throughout the country. The most Christian states are
Utah, whose population is almost 80 percent Christian, with the nation's
largest concentration of Mormons, and North Dakota (almost 76 percent
Christian). The least religious state is Nevada. Less than a third of the population there belongs to a congregation.

---

[*]North America, as defined by the United Nations, includes Bermuda, Canada, Greenland, St.
Pierre and Miquelon, and the United States.

TABLE 8–3. U.S. Church, Synagogue (etc.) Membership (in Percentages) by Age Group and Region, 1999

	Percentage
Age Group	
18–29	68%
30–49	64
50–64	72
65 and older	82
Region	
North	67%
Midwest	72
South	75
West	60

Source: Statistical Abstract of the United States 2000, p. 62, Table 75.

Religious affiliation also varies with age (Table 8–3). Older people are more likely to belong to a congregation than younger people are. The proportion of affiliated people is 68 percent among those 18–29 years old, rising to 82 percent among Americans 65 and older. This is probably both a cohort effect and an age effect. That is, older people tend to be more religious both because they grew up at a more religious time in American history and because there is a tendency to seek religious consolation and think about the afterlife as the end of life draws nearer.

The World's Major Religions

Information on the world's major religions is provided in Table 8–4. Based on people's claimed religions, Christianity is the world's largest, with some 2 billion members. Islam, with 1.2–1.3 billion practitioners, is next, followed by Hinduism, Buddhism, and Chinese traditional religion, also known as Chinese folk religion and Confucianism. More than a billion people in the world either claim no religion or say they are atheists. Worldwide Islam is growing faster than Christianity, about 2.9 percent annually, versus 2.3 percent for Christianity, whose growth rate is the same as the rate of world population increase (Ontario Consultants 2001; Adherents.com 2001).

Within Christianity, there is variation in the growth rate. There were an estimated 680 million "born-again" Christians (e.g., Pentecostals and evangelicals) in the world in 2001, with an annual worldwide growth rate of 7 percent, versus just 2.3 percent for Christianity overall. The global growth rate of Roman Catholics and other non-Protestant Christians is estimated at only 1.3 percent, compared to a Protestant growth rate of 3.3 percent per year (Winter 2001).

TABLE 8–4. Religions of the World

Religion	Date Founded	Sacred Texts	Members (millions)	Percent of World
Christianity	30 C.E.	Bible	2,015	33 (dropping)
Islam	622 C.E.	Qur'an and Hadith	1,215	20 (growing)
No religion*	No date	None	925	15 (dropping)
Hinduism	1500 B.C.E.	Veda	786	13 (stable)
Buddhism	523 B.C.E.	Tripitaka	362	6 (stable)
Atheists	No date	None	211	4
Chinese folk religion	270 B.C.E.	None	188	4
New Asian religion	Various	Various	106	2
Tribal religions	Prehistory	Oral tradition	91	2
Other	Various	Various	19	<1
Sikhism	1500 C.E.	Guru Granth Sahib	16	<1
Judaism	No consensus	Torah, Talmud	18	<1
Shamanists	Prehistory	Oral tradition	12	<1
Spiritism			7	<1
Confucianism	520 B.C.E.	Lun Yu	5	<1
Baha'i Faith	1863 C.E.	Most Holy Book	4	<1
Jainism	570 B.C.E.	Siddhanta, Pakrit	3	<1
Shinto	500 C.E.	Kojiki, Nohon Shoki	3	<1
Zoroastrianism	No consensus	Avesta	0.2	<1

*Persons with no religions, agnostics, freethinkers, humanists, secularists, etc.
Source: http://religioustolerance.org/worldrel.htm. Reprinted by permission of Ontario Consultants on Religious Tolerance.

The website Adherents.com classifies 11 world religions according to their degrees of internal unity and diversity. Listed first in Table 8–5 (next page) are the most cohesive/unified groups. Listed last are the religions with the most internal diversity. The list is based mainly on the degree of doctrinal similarity among the various subgroups. To a lesser extent it reflects diversity in practice, ritual, and organization. (The list includes majority manifestations of each religion, as well as subgroups that the larger branches may label "heterodox.") How would you decide whether a value judgment is implied by this list? Is it better for a religion to be highly unified, cohesive, monolithic, and lacking in internal diversity, or to be fragmented, schismatic, multifaceted, and abounding in variations on the same theme? Over time, such diversity can give birth to new religions—for example, Christianity arose from Judaism, Buddhism from Hinduism, Baha'i from Islam, and Sikhism from Hinduism. Within Christianity, Protestantism developed from Roman Catholicism.

TABLE 8–5. Classical World Religions Ranked by Internal Religious Similarity

Most Unified

Baha'i
Zoroastrianism
Sikhism
Islam
Jainism
Judaism
Taoism
Shinto
Christianity
Buddhism
Hinduism

Most Diverse

Source: Adherents.com. Reprinted by permission of adherents.com.

Protestant Values

Different religions promulgate different values. North America is overwhelmingly Christian, and Protestantism is the dominant religion in the United States. Despite the proliferation of Protestant sects and other religions, the English-derived Protestant values of the founding fathers and mothers of the United States continue to influence American society and culture.

Most forms of Christianity, including Protestantism, illustrate a distinctive type of religion, which Robert Bellah (1978) has called the world-rejecting religion. The first such religions arose in ancient civilizations, along with literacy and a specialized priesthood. These religions are so named because of their tendency to reject the natural (mundane, ordinary, material, secular) world and to focus instead on a higher (sacred, transcendent) realm of reality. The divine is a domain of exalted morality to which humans can only aspire. Salvation through fusion with the supernatural is the main goal of such religions. To some extent at least, most Americans have been influenced by such religious doctrines.

Notions of salvation and the afterlife dominate Christian ideologies. However, most varieties of Protestantism lack the hierarchical structure of earlier monotheistic religions, including Roman Catholicism. With a diminished role for the priest (minister), salvation is directly available to individuals. Regardless of their social status, Protestants have unmediated access to the supernatural. The individualistic focus of Protestantism offers a close fit with capitalism and with American culture. Protestantism has coevolved with the former for some 400 years and with the latter for over 200 years.

In his influential book *The Protestant Ethic and the Spirit of Capitalism* (1920/1958), the social theorist Max Weber linked the spread of capitalism to the values preached by early Protestant leaders. Weber saw European Protestants, and eventually their American descendants, as more successful financially than Catholics. He attributed this difference to the values stressed by their religions. Weber saw Catholics as more concerned with immediate happiness and security. Protestants were more ascetic, entrepreneurial, and future-oriented, he thought.

Capitalism, said Weber, required that the traditional attitudes of Catholic peasants be replaced by values fitting an industrial economy based on capital accumulation. Protestantism placed a premium on hard work, an ascetic life, and profit seeking. Early Protestants saw success on earth as a sign of divine favor and probable salvation. According to some Protestant credos, individuals could gain favor with God through good works. Other sects stressed predestination, the idea that only a few mortals had been selected for eternal life and that people could not change their fates. However, material success, achieved through hard work, could be a strong clue that someone was predestined to be saved.

The English Puritan variety of Protestantism, eventually transferred to North America, stressed work and discouraged leisure, worldly pleasures, and the enjoyment of life. "An idle hand is the Devil's workshop." Waste of time was a deadly sin because labor was a duty demanded by God. The Puritans valued the simplicity of the middle-class home, condemning ostentation as worldly enjoyment. Profits, the fruits of successful labor, could be given to the church or reinvested; but they could not be hoarded, because excess wealth might lead to temptation. People could increase their profits as long as they remembered the common good and avoided harmful, illegal, greedy, or dishonest activity.

According to Weber, the change in world view produced by the Protestant Reformation nourished the development and spread of modern industrial capitalism. However, residues of the traditional Catholic peasant mentality resisted and slowed the pace of change. Early Protestants who produced more than they needed for subsistence and tried to make a profit stirred up the mistrust, hatred, and moral indignation of others. Facing such suspicion and possible ostracism from the community, successful innovators had to have strong character to persevere and maintain the confidence of their customers and workers.

Weber also argued that rational business organization required the removal of industrial production from the home, its setting in peasant societies. Protestantism made such a separation possible by emphasizing individualism: Individuals, not families or households, would be saved or not. Interestingly, given the connection that is usually made with morality and religion in contemporary American discourse about family values, the family was a secondary matter for Weber's early Protestants. God and the individual reigned supreme.

Today of course, in North America as throughout the world, people of many religions and with diverse world views are successful capitalists. Furthermore, the old Protestant emphasis on honesty and hard work often has little to do with today's economic maneuvering. Still, there is no denying that the individualistic focus of Protestantism was compatible with the severance of ties to land and kin that the Industrial Revolution demanded. These values remain prominent in the religious background of the people of the United States.

Social Control

If the faithful truly internalize a system of religious rewards and punishments, their religion becomes a powerful means of controlling their beliefs, behavior, and what they teach their children. Religion has meaning to individuals. It helps them cope with adversity and tragedy and provides hope that things will get better. Sinners can repent and be saved, or they can go on sinning and be damned. Lives can be transformed through spiritual healing or rebirth.

Many people engage in religious activity because they believe it works. Prayers get answered. Faith healers heal. Sometimes it doesn't take much to convince the faithful that religious actions are efficacious. Many Native American people in southwestern Oklahoma use faith healers at high monetary costs, not just because it makes them feel better about the uncertain, but because it works (Lassiter 1998). Each year legions of Brazilians visit a church, Nosso Senhor do Bomfim, in the city of Salvador, Bahia. They vow to repay "Our Lord" (Nosso Senhor) if healing happens. Showing that the vows work, and are repaid, are the thousands of *ex votos,* plastic impressions of every conceivable body part, that adorn the church, along with photos of people who have been cured.

Religion works through sacred force. It also works by getting inside people and mobilizing their emotions—their joy, their wrath, their righteousness. Émile Durkheim (1912/1961), a prominent French social theorist and scholar of religion, described the collective "effervescence" that can develop in religious contexts. Intense emotion bubbles up. People feel a deep sense of shared joy, meaning, experience, communion, belonging, and commitment to their religion.

The power of religion affects action. When religions meet, they can coexist peacefully, or their differences can be a basis for enmity and disharmony, even battle. Religious fervor has inspired Christians on crusades against the infidel and has led Muslims to wage jihads, holy wars against non-Islamic peoples. Throughout history, political leaders have used religion to promote and justify their views and policies.

To ensure proper behavior, religions offer rewards, such as the fellowship of the religious community, and punishments, such as the threat of being cast out or excommunicated. "The Lord giveth and the Lord taketh away." Many religions promise rewards for the good life and punishment for the bad. Your physical, mental, moral, and spiritual health, now and forever, may depend on your beliefs and behavior.

Religions, especially the formal organized ones typically found in state societies, often prescribe a code of ethics and morality to guide behavior. The Judaic Ten Commandants lay down a set of prohibitions against killing, stealing, adultery and other misdeeds. Crimes are breaches of secular laws, as sins are breaches of religious strictures. Some rules (e.g., the Ten Commandants) proscribe or prohibit behavior; others prescribe behavior. The Golden Rule, for instance, is a religious guide: Do unto others as you would have them do unto you. Moral codes are ways of maintaining order and stability. Codes of morality and ethics are constantly repeated in religious sermons, catechisms, and the like. They become internalized psychologically. They guide behavior and produce regret, guilt, shame, and the need for forgiveness, expiation, and absolution when they are not followed.

Religions also maintain social control by stressing the temporary and fleeting nature of this life. They promise rewards (and/or punishment) in an afterlife (Christianity) or reincarnation (Hinduism and Buddhism). Such beliefs serve to reinforce the status quo. People can accept what they have now, knowing they can expect something better in the afterlife or the next life, if they follow religious guidelines. Under slavery in the American South, the masters taught portions of the Bible, such as the story of Job, that stressed compliance. The slaves, however, seized on the story of Moses, the promised land, and deliverance.

RELIGION AND CHANGE

Religion helps maintain social order, but it can also be an instrument of change, sometimes even revolution. As a response to conquest or foreign domination, for example, religious leaders often undertake to alter or revitalize a society. In its Islamic Revolution, Iranian ayatollahs marshaled religious fervor to create national solidarity and radical change. We call such movements *nativistic movements* (Linton 1943) or *revitalization movements* (Wallace 1956).

Fundamentalists seek order based on strict adherence to purportedly traditional standards, beliefs, rules, and customs. Christian and Islamic fundamentalists recognize, decry, and attempt to redress change, yet they also contribute to change. In a worldwide process, new religions challenge established churches. In the United States, for example, conservative Christian TV hosts have become influential broadcasters and opinion shapers. In Latin America evangelical Protestantism is winning millions of converts from Roman Catholicism.

Contemporary North America has witnessed a certain decline in formal organized religions and a rise of secularism. Atheists and secular humanists are not just bugaboos for religious conservatives. They really do exist, and they, too, are organized. Like members of religious groups, they use varied media, including print and the Internet, to communicate among themselves. Just as Buddhists can peruse *Tricycle: The Buddhist Review,* secular humanists can find their views validated in *Free Inquiry,* a quarterly identifying itself as "the international secular humanist magazine." Secular humanists speak out against organized religion and its "dogmatic pronouncements" and "supernatural or spiritual agendas" and the "obscurantist views" of religious leaders who presume "to inform us of God's views" by appealing to sacred texts (Steinfels 1997).

New and Alternative Religious Movements

Even as society appears to be growing more secular, and in the context of the fragmentation and collapse of traditional institutions mentioned in earlier chapters, some middle-class people have also turned to spiritualism in search of the meaning of life. Spiritual orientations serve as the basis of new social movements. Some white people have appropriated the symbols, settings, and purported religious practices of Native Americans and, in Australia, of Native

Even as society appears to be growing more secular, some middle-class people have turned to spiritualism, seeking the "meaning of life." The "Anastasia" movement is a new age movement that stresses a return to nature. Its followers have smeared their bodies with mud as part of their beliefs near Gelendgik in Russia's Krasnodar region on September 6, 1999.

Australian, for New Age religions. And natives have strongly protested the use of their sacred property and places by these groups.

The New Age movement, which emerged in the 1980s, draws on and blends cultural elements from multiple traditions. It advocates change through individual personal transformation, rather than through political action. According to Lisa Aldred (2000), its adherents are mainly white, middle to upper middle class, middle aged, and college educated. Some New Agers construct their beliefs and practices mainly around Native American religion, following "plastic medicine men," people who claim to have been taught by "authentic" medicine men.

Native American activists decry the appropriation and commercialization of their spiritual beliefs and rituals, as when "sweat lodge" ceremonies are held on cruise ships, with wine and cheese served. Native Americans complain that New Agers romanticize their rites and images, thus obscuring the continuing socioeconomic and political problems that Indians face. They see the appropriation of their ceremonies and traditions as theft. In defense, the New Agers cite the First Amendment right of religious freedom; they assert that spirituality cannot be owned. Indians counter with examples in which entrepreneurs have incorporated, copyrighted, and sought trademark protection for ceremonies, books, and themes based on Native American spirituality (illustrating intellectual property rights, or IPRs, as was discussed in Chapter 3).

Witchcraft has been around for generations, but it joins today in the mobilization and celebration of multiculturalism. At the Cathedral of the Pines, a New Hampshire religious park, people of all denominations were allowed to hold services. But witches (Wiccans) were initially excluded.* The dispute was resolved through meetings with the Witches' Anti-Discrimination Lobby (WADL), the Cathedral of the Pines, and the New Hampshire Commission for Human Rights. Wiccans received access to the park equal with other religious groups. The park even offered a permanent site to be consecrated as a Wiccan sacred space (Ontario Consultants 1996).

New religious movements have varied origins. Some have been influenced by Christianity, others by Eastern (Asian) religions, still others by mysticism and spiritualism, especially in the so-called New Age religions. Religion also evolves in tandem with science and technology. For example, the Raelian Movement, a religious group centered in Switzerland and Montreal, promotes cloning as a way of achieving eternal life. Raelians believe that extraterrestrials called *Elohim* artificially created all life on earth. The

---

*According to one Wiccan's Web page, Wicca is a contemporary Neo-Pagan religion, and witchcraft is the practice of "natural magic." Not all Wiccans practice magic, and not all witches are Wiccans. Wiccans are concerned about conservation and ecology and believe that both animate and inanimate objects possess a spirit, which forms part of the Whole. According to this Web page, Wicca celebrates the life forces of nature as personified by the Goddess and her consort, the God. See www.geocities.com/Athens/3038/wicca.html.

group has established a company called Valiant Venture Ltd., which offers infertile and homosexual couples the opportunity to have a child cloned from one of the spouses (Ontario Consultants 1997).

Scientology promotes the idea that humans need to think rationally and to control their disturbing emotions to achieve spiritual enlightenment and salvation. In Scientology, spiritual entities called *thetans* are believed to occupy human bodies in successive lives. Although not part of the physical universe, the thetan has become entangled with it. In the process, it acquired a reactive mind, which responds emotionally to anything that recalls painful and traumatic experiences. Salvation is the process by which that reactive mind is reduced and finally eliminated, allowing the individual to live to his or her full potential. Scientology aims at enabling individuals to recall, confront, and overcome the effects of unhappy events of the past. The ultimate goal is for the thetan to exist outside the physical realm and so outside the body. This condition has analogies with the Christian conception of the saved soul (Hubbard 1997).

In the United States the official recognition of a religion entitles it to a modicum of respect and certain benefits, such as exemption from taxation on its income and property (as long as it does not engage in political activity). Not all would-be religions receive official recognition. For example, Scientology is recognized as a church in the United States but not in Germany. In 1997 U.S. government officials spoke out against Germany's persecution of Scientologists as a form of human rights abuse. Germans protested vehemently, calling Scientology a dangerous nonreligious political movement, with between 30,000 and 70,000 German members.

Religious persecution is ages old. Communist governments have suppressed the practice and manifestations of many religions. In many nations, unofficial religions are marginalized and at least partially hidden. Often, intolerance is expressed in stated doubts about their "true" religious nature. One example is "Yoruba religion," a term applied to perhaps 15 million adherents in Africa, as well as to millions of practitioners of syncretic or blended religions (with elements of Catholicism and spiritism) in the western hemisphere. Forms of Yoruba religion include santeria (in the Spanish Caribbean and the United States), candomblé (in Brazil), and vodoun (in the French Caribbean). Yoruba religion, with roots in precolonial nation states of West Africa, has spread far beyond its religion of origin, as part of the African diaspora. It remains an influential, identifiable religion today, despite suppression, such as by Cuba's Communist government. There are perhaps 3 million practitioners of santeria in Cuba, plus another 800,000 in the United States. At least 1 million Brazilians participate in candomblé, also known as macumba.

Voodoo (or "vodoun") traces its origins to Yoruba, Dahomey, and Fon in Africa. Blended with Catholicism, it is practiced mainly in Haiti, Cuba and Benin. Usually described as a syncretic (mixed) religion, vodoun has been called the Haitian form of santeria; others consider santeria the Spanish

form of vodoun. There are probably between 2.8 and 3.2 million practitioners (Ontario Consultants 2002), many (perhaps most) of whom would name
something else, such as Catholicism, as their religion.

Secular Religion

In previous chapters we saw that individuals make creative and interpretive
use of popular culture. Remember John Fiske's (1989) contention that each
individual's use of popular culture is an original, interpretive, potentially
meaningful, reading of a text. Through this process, it is possible for apparently secular settings, things, and events to acquire intense meaning for individuals who have grown up in their presence and perceiving their
significance. Some anthropologists see religious rituals as distinguished
from other kinds of behavior by special emotions, nonutilitarian intentions,
and supernatural entities. But others define ritual more broadly. Writing
about football, Arens (1981) pointed out that behavior can simultaneously
have sacred and secular aspects. On one level, football is simply a sport; on
another, it is a public ritual.

In the context of comparative religion, the conflation of secular and sacred is not surprising. Long ago, the French sociologist/anthropologist
Émile Durkheim (1912/1961) pointed out that almost everything, from the
sublime to the ridiculous, has in some societies been treated as sacred. The
distinction between sacred and profane doesn't depend on the intrinsic
qualities of the sacred symbol. In Australian totemic religion, for example,
sacred beings include such humble creatures as ducks, frogs, rabbits, and
grubs, whose inherent qualities could hardly have given rise to the religious
sentiment they inspire.

Madagascar's tomb-centered ceremonies are times when the living and
the dead are joyously reunited, when people get drunk, gorge themselves,
and enjoy sexual license. Perhaps the gray, sober, ascetic, and moralistic aspects of many religious events in North America, in taking the fun out of religion, force us to find religion (i.e., truth, beauty, meaning, passionate
involvement) in fun. Many Americans seek in such apparently secular contexts as rock concerts, movies, and sports what other people find in religious
rites, beliefs, and ceremonies.

The rave youth subculture, which started in Great Britain in the late
1980s, quickly spread to North America. Hundreds or thousands of young
people (average age 15–25) gather for raves—all night dance parties with
techno music in fields, clubs, garages, or warehouses. There is usually an
entrance fee, so middle-class youths are mainly involved, although the
movement's roots are working-class British (Hutson 2000). Ravers' slogan is
PLUR (peace, love, unity, respect). Use of the drug ecstasy ("the hug drug")
has been common at raves. Responding to criticism from parents and police, most raves nowadays are regulated or held in clubs. Even so, unregulated outdoor raves still thrive in the South and Midwest, according to Scott
Hutson (2000), who did an ethnographic study of ravers.

Hutson (2000) compares raves to other spiritual subcultures that claim altered states of consciousness. While most scholars see raves as a form of hedonistic escape, Hutson found similarities to spirituality and shamanism in the meaningful and therapeutic effects ravers claim to experience. Many ravers equate their experiences to religious or transcendental transformations. Factors that may induce transcendental experiences include flashing lights, dancing, and the repetitive percussive nature of the techno music. Common at raves are two types of symbols: "primitive" or tribal symbols and futuristic symbols, such as friendly aliens, space ships, and computer imagery. Like the New Age movement, the rave subculture uses hybrid and decontextualized symbols, but these symbols have significant meaning for the ravers. According to Hutson (2000), they refer to distant societies, ancestral tribal times, and the prospect of a perfect future, all idealized in the rave imagination. Hutson argues further that ravers experience communitas, in Turner's sense. He compares this group consciousness to that which has been long associated with Grateful Dead concerts, and which exists among Deadheads (Grateful Dead fans). No matter how new it may seem, cultural, including religious, diversity always has ties to the past.

CHAPTER NINE

Gender

BOYS WILL BE MEN

"You're a woman now!" If you are a female reader, your mother, older sister, grandmother, or aunt may have declared you "a woman" after your first menses when you were about 12 years old. Menstruation is a developmental phase in a girl's life. After it, she feels, thinks, and behaves more and more like a woman.

Menstruation signals a biological, psychological, and social transition. Pubescent girls may begin regularly to perform adult tasks—housekeeping, child care, and meal preparation. In many societies, adolescent girls bear and raise their own children. Among Gypsies in Greece, soon after finishing elementary school, girls assume a dual adult role as homemaker, which includes mothering, and income wage earner (Kozaitis 1997).

When do boys hear the phrase "You're a man now"? Boys go through puberty at about 14 years of age. For teen boys, however, manhood isn't a biological and private accomplishment, but a social and public achievement. Generally boys become men by completing a developmental task, one that demonstrates their ability to participate productively in society. Comparative mythology, literature, and ethnography inform us that boys must claim and prove their manhood in the public sphere. Rites of passage, as discussed in

Chapter 8, often transform boys into men. Such a transition may entail collective circumcision, military duty, getting a job, or marriage.

Even when males succeed economically and socially, they still face the stereotypes that men are less mature and less stable than women are, and that "boys will be boys." Greek Gypsy women characterize men as "irresponsible," "useless," "unreliable," and "childish" (Kozaitis 1993). North American culture associates men with "fear of commitment" and the idealized status of the "playboy." For women midlife is associated with wisdom and maturity, whereas for men it often produces a "crisis" that triggers regression into behaviors associated with youth. Is play a constant craving for men? Amusement, recreation, fun: How can we explain perpetual play-seeking behavior—often secretive, self-indulgent, or illegal—among men? What types of gratification do men seek in activities that society may deem "irresponsible," "frivolous," or "immoral?"

The recent Men's Movement is an expressive form of political organization that arose among middle-class, adult white men. Inspired by Robert Bly's book, *Iron John*, these men take part in planned sessions and rituals. They share common experiences, seek their "inner boy," honor their fathers, and retrieve their "essential manhood" (Kimmer and Kaufman 1993). Participants in the Men's Movement, like those in the Women's Movement, promote community development and social reform, to liberate themselves and find self-fulfillment. How might we explain and interpret men's efforts to forge a movement of their own? Why do men need an affinity group to identify, fight for, and celebrate their "manhood"?

The same economy that has generated a huge female extradomestic labor force has produced a workforce of men for whom job security and a stable marriage are no longer givens. The Men's Movement, including its all-male retreats, allows men to assert qualities, sensibilities, and privileges they may have denied themselves in the process of becoming adults, and to defy, deny, and reject conventional categories of manhood.

Critics of the Men's Movement, most notably the National Organization of Women (NOW), accuse its participants of advancing a political agenda, of essentializing traditional assumptions about gender, and of reproducing power inequalities between men and women. For example, critics charge the "Promise Keepers," a Christian men's organization, which has drawn more than 2.6 million men to 62 stadium rallies in recent years, with making organized efforts to promote the "traditional family" and to repeal women's rights by asserting male dominance. Disputing such charges, the Promise Keepers report they include women and men from different ethnic and cultural affiliations at their retreats and in their activities.

The growth of the Men's Movement has parallels with the development of the Women's Movement. It began as a response to actual and perceived socioeconomic subordination. Its founders were middle-class whites; it eventually integrated members of color. Males have mobilized to organize and construct a special space and place in society, seeking liberation from socialization felt to be constraining and oppressive. Like the other move-ments discussed in this book, the Men's Movement helps constitute, and is constituted by, a multicultural society. As a social system, multiculturalism requires the development and proliferation of culturally organized units of status and identity. Threat mobilizes popular agency, which leads to the for-mation of affinity groups. Members of the Men's Movement, like those of other such groups, claim their human right to be persons first. ☺

NATURE, NURTURE, AND GENDER

Because anthropologists study biology, society, and culture, they are in a unique position to comment on nature (biological predispositions) and nur-ture (environment) as determinants of human behavior. Human attitudes, values, and behavior are limited not only by our genetic predispositions—which are often difficult to identify—but also by our experiences during en-culturation. Our attributes as adults are determined both by our genes and by our environment during growth and development.

Debate about the effects of nature and nurture proceeds today in scien-tific and public arenas. **Biological determinists** assume that some—they differ about how much—of human behavior and social organization is bio-logically determined. **Cultural determinists** find most attempts to link be-havior to genes unconvincing. They assume that human evolutionary success rests on flexibility, or the ability to adapt in various ways. Because human adaptation relies so strongly on cultural learning, we can change our behavior more readily than members of other species can.

The nature-nurture debate emerges in the discussion of human sex-gender roles and sexuality. Men and women differ genetically. Women have two X chromosomes, and men have an X and a Y. The father determines a baby's sex because only he has the Y chromosome to transmit. The mother always provides an X chromosome.

The chromosomal difference is expressed in hormonal and physiologi-cal contrasts. Humans are sexually dimorphic. **Sexual dimorphism** refers to marked differences in male and female biology, besides the contrasts in breasts and genitals. Men and women differ not just in primary (genitalia and reproductive organs) and secondary (breasts, voice, hair distribution) sexual characteristics but in average weight, height, and strength.

Just how far, however, do such genetically and physiologically deter-mined differences go? What effect do they have on the way men and women act and are treated in different societies? On the cultural determinist side, anthropologists have discovered substantial variability in the roles of men and women in different societies. The anthropological position on sex-gender roles and biology has been stated as follows:

Anthropologists have documented substantial variability in the roles of men, women, and children in different cultures. Despite sexual dimorphism, biology is not destiny. In many societies women do heavy work. In India in 1993, these young women carry baskets of coal to the top of a lime kiln. The majority of workers at such kilns are women and children.

> The biological nature of men and women [should be seen] not as a narrow enclosure limiting the human organism, but rather as a broad base upon which a variety of structures can be built. (Friedl 1975, 6)

Sex differences are biological, but *gender* encompasses all the traits that a culture assigns to and inculcates in males and females. *Gender*, in other words, refers to the cultural construction of male and female characteristics (Rosaldo 1980b). Given the "rich and various constructions of gender" within the realm of cultural diversity, Susan Bourque and Kay Warren (1987) note that the same images of masculinity and femininity do not always apply.

Margaret Mead did an early ethnographic study of variation in gender roles. Her book *Sex and Temperament in Three Primitive Societies* (1935/ 1950) was based on field work in three societies in Papua New Guinea: Arapesh, Mundugumor, and Tchambuli. The extent of personality variation in men and women in these three societies on the same island amazed Mead. She found that, among the Arapesh, both men and women acted as Americans have traditionally expected women to act—in a mild, parental, responsive way.

Among the Mundugumor, in contrast, both men and women acted as she believed we expect men to act—fiercely and aggressively. Tchambuli men were "catty," wore curls, and went shopping, but Tchambuli women were energetic and managerial, and they placed less emphasis on personal adornment than did the men. Drawing on their more recent case study of the Tchambuli, whom they call the Chambri, Errington and Gewertz (1987), while recognizing gender malleability, have disputed the specifics of Mead's account.

There is a well-established field of feminist scholarship within anthropology (di Leonardo 1991; Miller 1993; Nash and Safa 1986; Rosaldo 1980b; Strathern 1988). Anthropologists have gathered systematic ethnographic data about gender in many cultural settings (Mukhopadhyay and Higgins 1988; Morgen 1989; Kimmel and Messner 1995; Peplau 1999; Bonvillain 2001). We can see that gender roles vary with environment, economy, adaptive strategy, and type of political system. Before we examine the cross-cultural data, some definitions are in order.

Gender roles are the tasks and activities that a culture assigns to the sexes. Related to gender roles are **gender stereotypes**, which are oversimplified but strongly held ideas about the characteristics of males and females. **Gender stratification** describes an unequal distribution of rewards (socially valued resources, power, prestige, and personal freedom) between men and women, reflecting their different positions in a social hierarchy (Light, Keller, and Calhoun 1997).

In stateless societies, gender stratification is often more obvious in regard to prestige than it is in regard to wealth. In her study of the Ilongots of northern Luzon in the Philippines, Michelle Rosaldo (1980a) described gender differences related to the positive cultural value placed on adventure, travel, and knowledge of the external world. More often than women, Ilongot men, as headhunters, visited distant places. They acquired knowledge of the external world; amassed experiences there; and returned to express their knowledge, adventures, and feelings in public oratory. They received acclaim as a result. Ilongot women had inferior prestige because they lacked external experiences on which to base knowledge and dramatic expression. On the basis of Rosaldo's study and findings in other stateless societies, Ong (1989) argues that we must distinguish between prestige systems and actual power in a given society. High male prestige may not entail economic or political power held by men over their families.

GENDER ROLES, STRATIFICATION, AND THE ECONOMY

Several studies have shown that economic roles affect gender stratification. In one cross-cultural study, Peggy Sanday (1974) found that gender stratification decreased when men and women made roughly equal contributions to subsistence. She found that gender stratification was *greatest* when the women contributed either *much more* or *much less* than the men did.

This finding applied mainly to food producers, not to foragers (people who subsist by hunting and gathering). In foraging societies, gender stratification was most marked when men contributed much *more* to the diet than women did. This was true among the Inuit and other northern hunters and fishers. Among tropical and semitropical foragers, by contrast, gathering usually supplies more food than hunting and fishing do. Gathering is generally women's work. Men usually hunt and fish, but women also do some fishing and may hunt small animals. With gathering prominent, gender status tends to be more equal than it is when hunting and fishing are the main subsistence activities.

Gender status is also more equal when the domestic and public spheres are not sharply separated. (*Domestic* means within or pertaining to the home.) Strong differentiation between the home and the outside world is called the **domestic-public dichotomy** or the *private-public contrast*. The outside world can include politics, trade, warfare, or work. Often when domestic and public spheres are clearly separated, public activities have greater prestige than domestic ones do. This can promote gender stratification, because men are more likely to be active in the public domain than women are. Cross-culturally, women's activities tend to be closer to home than men's are. Thus, another reason hunter-gatherers have less gender stratification than food producers do is that the domestic-public dichotomy is more developed among food producers.

A division of labor linked to gender has been found in all societies. However, the particular tasks assigned to men and women don't always reflect differences in strength and endurance. Food producers often assign the arduous tasks of carrying water and firewood and of pounding grain to women. In 1967 in the former Soviet Union, women filled 47 percent of factory positions, including many unmechanized jobs requiring hard physical labor. Most Soviet sanitation workers, physicians, and nurses were women (Martin and Voorhies 1975). Many jobs that men do in some societies are done by women in others, and vice versa.

Certain roles are more sex-linked than others. Men are the usual hunters and warriors. Given such weapons as spears, knives, and bows, men make better fighters because they are bigger and stronger on average than are women in the same population (Divale and Harris 1976). The male hunter-fighter roll also reflects a tendency toward greater male mobility.

Gender among Foragers (Hunter-Gatherers)

In foraging societies, women are either pregnant or lactating during most of their childbearing period. Late in pregnancy and after childbirth, carrying a baby limits a woman's movements, even her gathering. However, among the Agta of the Philippines (Griffin and Estioko-Griffin, eds. 1985), women not only gather but also hunt with dogs while carrying their babies. Still, given the effects of pregnancy and lactation on mobility, it is rarely feasible for women to be the primary hunters (Friedl 1975). Warfare, which also requires mobility, is not found in most foraging societies, nor is interregional trade well developed. Warfare and trade are two public arenas that contribute to status inequality of males and females among food producers.

The Ju/'hoansi San illustrate the extent to which the activities and spheres of influence of men and women may overlap among foragers (Draper 1975). Traditional Ju/'hoansi gender roles were interdependent. During gathering, women discovered information about game animals, which they passed on to the men. Men and women spent about the same amount of time away from camp, but neither worked more than three days a week. The Ju/'hoansi saw nothing wrong in doing the work of the other gender. Men often gathered food and collected water. A general sharing ethos dictated that men distribute meat and that women share the fruits of gathering.

Patricia Draper's field work among the Ju/'hoansi is especially useful in showing the relationships between economy, gender roles, and stratification, because she studied both foragers and a group of former foragers who had become sedentary. Draper studied sedentary Ju/'hoansi at Mahopa, a village where they herded, grew crops, worked for wages, and did a small amount of gathering. Their gender roles were becoming more rigidly defined. A domestic-public dichotomy was developing. Doing less gathering, women were more confined to the home. Boys could gain mobility through herding, but girls' movements were more limited. The equal and communal world of the bush was yielding to the social features of sedentary life. A differential ranking of men according to their herds, houses, and sons began to replace sharing. Males came to be seen as the more valuable producers.

If there is some degree of male dominance in every contemporary society, it may be because of changes such as those which have drawn the Ju/'hoansi into wage work, market sales, and thus the world capitalist economy. An interplay between local, national, and international forces influences systems of gender stratification (Ong 1989). In traditional foraging societies, however, egalitarianism extended to the relations between the sexes. The social spheres, activities, rights, and obligations of men and women overlapped. Foragers' kinship systems tend to be bilateral (calculated equally through males and females) rather than favoring either the mother's side or the father's side. Foragers may live with either the husband's or the wife's kin, and they often shift between one group and the other.

One last observation about foragers: It is among them that the public and private spheres are least separate; hierarchy is least marked; aggression and competition are most discouraged; and the rights, activities, and spheres of influence of men and women overlap the most. Our ancestors lived entirely by foraging until 10,000 years ago. Despite the popular stereotype of the club-wielding caveman dragging his mate by the hair, relative gender equality is a much more likely ancestral pattern.

Gender among Horticulturalists

Gender roles and stratification among cultivators vary widely, depending on specific features of the economy and social structure. Demonstrating this, Martin and Voorhies (1975) studied a sample of 515 horticultural societies, representing all parts of the world. They looked at several variables, including descent and postmarital residence, the percentage of the diet derived from cultivation, and the productivity of men and women.

Women were found to be the main producers in horticultural societies. In 50 percent of those societies, women did most of the cultivating. In 33 percent, contributions to cultivation by men and women were equal. In only 17 percent did men do most of the work. Anthropologists distinguish between matrilineal societies, in which descent is traced through women only, and patrilineal societies, where descent is traced through men only. Women tended to do a bit more cultivating in matrilineal than in patrilineal societies. They dominated horticulture in 64 percent of the matrilineal societies versus 50 percent of the patrilineal ones.

Reduced Gender Stratification—Matrilineal, Matrilocal Societies

Cross-cultural variation in gender status is related to rules of descent and postmarital residence (Friedl 1975; Martin and Voorhies 1975). Among horticulturalists with matrilineal descent and *matrilocality* (residence after marriage with the wife's relatives), female status tends to be high. Matriliny and matrilocality disperse related males, rather than consolidating them. By contrast, patriliny and *patrilocality* (residence after marriage with the husband's kin) keep male relatives together, an advantage in warfare. Matrilineal-matrilocal systems tend to occur in societies where population pressure on strategic resources in minimal and warfare is infrequent.

Women tend to have high status in matrilineal, matrilocal societies for several reasons. Descent-group membership, succession to political positions, allocation of land, and overall social identity all come through female links. Among the matrilineal Malays of Negeri Sembilan, Malaysia (Peletz 1988), matriliny gave women sole inheritance of ancestral rice fields. Matrilocality created solidary clusters of female kin. These Malaysian women had considerable influence beyond the household (Swift 1963). In such matrilineal contexts, women are the basis of the entire social structure. Although public authority may be assigned to the men, much of the power and decision making may actually belong to the senior women.

Anthropologists have never discovered a **matriarchy**, a society ruled by women. Still, some matrilineal societies, including the *Iroquois* (Brown 1975), a confederation of tribes in aboriginal New York, show that women's political and ritual influence can rival that of the men.

We saw that gender status among foragers was most equal when there was no sharp separation between male and female activities and between public and domestic spheres. However, gender stratification can also be reduced by roles that remove men from the local community. We now refine our generalizations: It is sharp contrast between male and female roles *within the local community* that promotes gender stratification. Gender stratification may be reduced when women play prominent local roles, while men pursue activities in a wider, regional system. Iroquois women, for example, played a major subsistence role, while men left home for long periods. As is usual in matrilineal societies, *internal* warfare was uncommon. Iroquois men waged war only on distant groups; this could keep them away for years.

Iroquois men hunted and fished, but women controlled the local economy. Women did some fishing and occasional hunting, but their major productive role was in horticulture. Women owned the land, which they inherited from matrilineal kinswomen. Women controlled the production and distribution of food.

Iroquois women lived with their husbands and children in the family compartments of a communal longhouse. Women born in a longhouse remained there for life. Senior women, or *matrons*, decided which men could join the longhouse as husbands, and they could evict incompatible men. Women therefore controlled alliances between descent groups, an important political job in tribal society.

Iroquois women thus managed production and distribution. Social identity, succession to office and titles, and property all came through the female line, and women were prominent in ritual and politics. Related tribes made up a confederacy, the League of the Iroquois, with chiefs and councils.

A council of male chiefs managed military operations, but chiefly succession was matrilineal. It went from brother to brother, or from a man to his sister's son. The matrons of each longhouse nominated a man as their representative. If the council rejected their first nominee, the women proposed others until one was accepted. Matrons constantly monitored the chiefs and could impeach them. Women could veto war declarations, withhold provisions for war, and initiate peace efforts. In religion, too, women shared power. Half the tribe's religious practitioners were women, and the matrons helped select the others.

Reduced Gender Stratification—Matrifocal Societies

Nancy Tanner (1974) also found that the combination of male travel and a prominent female economic role reduced gender stratification and promoted high female status. She based this finding on a survey of the **matrifocal** (mother-centered, often with no resident husband-father) organization of certain societies in Indonesia, West Africa, and the Caribbean. Matrifocal societies are not necessarily matrilineal. A few are even patrilineal.

For example, Tanner (1974) found matrifocality among the Igbo of eastern Nigeria, who are patrilineal, patrilocal, and polygynous. Each wife had her own house, where she lived with her children. Women planted crops next to their houses and traded surpluses. Women ran the local markets, while men did the long-distance trading.

In a case study of the Igbo, Ifi Amadiume (1987) noted that either sex could fill male gender roles. Before Christian influence, successful Igbo women and men used wealth to take titles and acquire wives. Wives freed husbands (male and female) from domestic work and helped them accumulate wealth. Female husbands were not considered masculine but preserved their femininity. Igbo women asserted themselves in women's groups, including those of lineage daughters, lineage wives, and a communitywide women's council led by titled women. The high status and influence of Igbo women rested on the separation of males from local subsistence and on a marketing system that allowed women to leave home and gain prominence in distribution and—through these accomplishments—in politics.

Increased Gender Stratification—Patrilineal-Patrilocal Societies

The Igbo are unusual among patrilineal-patrilocal societies, many of which have marked gender stratification. Martin and Voorhies (1975) link the decline of matriliny and the spread of the **patrilineal-patrilocal complex** (consisting of patrilineality, patrilocality, warfare, and male supremacy) to pressure on resources. Faced with scarce resources, patrilineal-patrilocal cultivators such as the Yanomami of Venezuela and Brazil often wage warfare against other villages. This favors patrilocality and patriliny, customs that keep related men together in the same village, where they make strong allies in battle. Such societies tend to have a sharp domestic-public dichotomy, and men tend to dominate the prestige hierarchy. Men may use their public roles in warfare and trade, and may use their greater prestige to symbolize and reinforce the devaluation or oppression of women.

The patrilineal-patrilocal complex characterizes many societies in highland Papua New Guinea. Women work hard growing and processing subsistence crops, raising and tending pigs (the main domesticated animal and a favorite food), and doing domestic cooking, but they are isolated from the public domain, which men control. Men grow and distribute prestige crops, prepare food for feasts, and arrange marriages. The men even get to trade the pigs and control their use in ritual.

In densely populated areas of the Papua New Guinea highlands, male-female avoidance is associated with strong pressure on resources (Lindenbaum 1972). Men fear all female contacts, including sex. They think sexual contact with women will weaken them. Indeed, men see everything female as dangerous and polluting. They segregate themselves in men's houses and hide their precious ritual objects from women. They delay marriage, and some never marry.

By contrast, the sparsely populated areas of Papua New Guinea, such as recently settled areas, lack taboos on male-female contacts. The image of woman as polluter fades, heterosexual intercourse is valued, men and women live together, and reproductive rates are high.

Homosexual Behavior among the Etoro

One of the most extreme examples of male-female sexual antagonism in Papua New Guinea comes from the *Etoro* (Kelly 1976), a group of 400 people who subsist by hunting and horticulture in the Trans-Fly region. The Etoro also illustrate the power of culture in molding human sexuality. The following account applies only to Etoro males and their beliefs. Etoro cultural norms prevented the male anthropologist who studied them from gathering comparable information about female attitudes. Etoro opinions about sexuality are linked to their beliefs about the cycle of birth, physical growth, maturity, old age, and death.

Etoro men believe that semen is necessary to give life force to a fetus, which is said to be placed within a woman by an ancestral spirit. Because men are believed to have a limited supply of semen, sexuality saps male vitality. The birth of children, nurtured by semen, symbolizes a necessary (and unpleasant) sacrifice that will lead to the husband's eventual death. Heterosexual intercourse, which is required only for reproduction, is discouraged. Women who want too much sex are viewed as witches and are considered hazardous to their husbands' health. Etoro culture permits heterosexual intercourse on only about 100 days a year. The rest of the time it is tabooed. Seasonal birth clustering shows that the taboo is respected.

So objectionable is heterosexuality that it is removed from community life. Coitus can occur neither in sleeping quarters nor in the fields, but only in the woods—and there it is risky because poisonous snakes, the Etoro say, are attracted by the sounds and smells of sex.

Although coitus is discouraged, homosexual acts are viewed as essential. Etoro believe that boys cannot produce semen on their own. To grow into men and eventually give life force to their children, boys must acquire semen orally from older men. From the age of 10 until adulthood, boys are inseminated by older men. No taboos are attached to this. Homosexual activity can go on in the sleeping area or garden. Every three years a group of boys at about the age of 20 are formally initiated into manhood. They go to a secluded mountain lodge, where they are visited and inseminated by several older men.

Etoro homosexuality is governed by a code of propriety. Although homosexual relations between older and younger males are culturally essential, those between boys of the same age are discouraged. A boy who gets semen from other youths is believed to be sapping their life force and stunting their growth. When a boy develops very rapidly, this suggests that he is ingesting semen from other boys. Like a sex-hungry wife, he is shunned as a witch.

Etoro homosexuality rests not on hormones or genes but on cultural traditions. The Etoro share a cultural pattern, which Gilbert Herdt (ed. 1984) calls ritualized homosexuality, with some 50 other tribes in Papua New Guinea, especially in that country's Trans-Fly region. These societies illustrate one extreme of a male-female avoidance pattern that is widespread in Papua New Guinea and in patrilineal-patrilocal societies.

Patriarchy and Violence

Patriarchy describes a political system ruled by men in which women have inferior social and political status, including basic human rights. Barbara Miller (1997), in a study of systematic neglect of females, describes women in rural northern India as "the endangered sex." Societies that feature a full-fledged partilineal-patrilocal complex, replete with warfare and intervillage raiding, also typify patriarchy. Patriarchy extends from tribal societies like the Yanomami to state societies like India and Pakistan.

Although more prevalent in certain social settings than in others, family violence and domestic abuse of women are worldwide problems. Domestic violence certainly occurs in neolocal-nuclear family settings, such as Canada and the United States. In Canada, 62 percent of murdered women are killed by their husbands or domestic partners, compared to 50 percent in Pakistan (Kantor 1996). Cities, with their impersonality and isolation from extended kin networks, are breeding grounds for domestic violence.

We have seen that gender stratification is typically reduced in matrilineal, matrifocal, and bilateral societies in which women have prominent roles in the economy and social life. When a woman lives in her own village, she has kin nearby to look after and protect her interests. Even in patrilocal polygynous settings, women often count on the support of their co-wives and their sons in disputes with potentially abusive husbands. However, such settings, which tend to provide a safe haven for women, are retracting rather than expanding in today's world. Isolated families and patrilineal social forms have spread at the expense of matrilineality. Many nations have declared polygyny illegal. More and more women, and men, find themselves cut off from their original families and extended kin.

With the spread of the women's rights movement and the human rights movement, attention to domestic violence and abuse of women has increased. Laws have been passed, and mediating institutions established. Brazil's female-run police stations for battered women provide an example, as do shelters for victims of domestic abuse in the United States and Canada. Even so, patriarchal institutions persist in what should be a more enlightened world.

GENDER AND INDUSTRIALISM

The domestic-public dichotomy has also applied to gender stratification in industrial societies, including the United States and Canada. However, gender roles have been changing rapidly in North America. The "traditional" idea that "a woman's place is in the home" actually emerged in the United States as industrialism spread after 1900. Earlier, pioneer women in the Midwest and West had been recognized as fully productive workers in farming and home industry. Under industrialism, attitudes about gendered work came to vary with class and region. In early industrial Europe, men, women, and children had flocked to factories as wage laborers. American slaves of both sexes had done grueling work in cotton fields. With abolition, southern African-American women continued working as field hands and domestics. Poor white women labored in the South's early cotton mills. In the 1890s more than one million American women held menial and repetitious unskilled factory positions (Margolis 1984; Martin and Voorhies 1975).

After 1900, European immigration produced a male labor force willing to work for wages lower than those of American-born men. Those immigrant men moved into factory jobs that previously had gone to women. As machine tools and mass production further reduced the need for female labor, the notion that women were biologically unfit for factory work began to gain ground (Martin and Voorhies 1975).

Maxine Margolis (1984, 2000) has shown how gendered work, attitudes, and beliefs have varied in response to American economic needs. For example, wartime shortages of men have promoted the idea that work outside the home is women's patriotic duty. During the world wars the notion that women are unfit for hard physical labor faded. Inflation and the culture of consumption have also spurred female employment. When prices and/or demand rise, multiple paychecks help maintain family living standards.

The steady increase in female paid employment since World War II also reflects the baby boom and industrial expansion. American culture has traditionally defined clerical work, teaching, and nursing as female occupations. With rapid population growth and business expansion after World War II, the demand for women to fill such jobs grew steadily. Employers also found that they could increase their profits by paying women lower wages than they would have to pay returning male war veterans.

Woman's role in the home has been stressed during periods of high unemployment, although when wages fall or inflation occurs simultaneously, female employment may still be accepted. Margolis (1984) contends that changes in the economy lead to changes in attitudes toward and about women. Economic changes paved the way for the contemporary woman's movement, which was also spurred by the publication of Betty Friedan's book *The Feminine Mystique* in 1963 and the founding of the National Organization of Women (NOW) in 1966. The movement in turn promoted expanded work opportunities for women, including equal pay for equal work. Between 1970 and 2000 the female percentage of the American work force rose from 38 to 47 percent. In other words, almost half of all Americans who work outside the home are women. Some 66 million women now have paid jobs, compared to 75 million men. Women now fill more than half (54 percent) of all professional jobs (*Statistical Abstract of the United States*, 2001, 367, 380). And it's not mainly single women working, as once was the case. Table 9–1 presents figures on the ever-increasing cash employment of American wives and mothers.

Note in Table 9–1 that the cash employment of American married men has been falling, while that of American married women has been rising. There has been a dramatic change in behavior and attitudes since 1960, when 89 percent of all married men worked, compared with just 32 percent of married women. The comparable figures in 2000 were 77 percent and 61 percent. Ideas about the gender roles of males and females have changed.

Table 9–1. Cash Employment of American Mothers, Wives, and Husbands, 1960–2000*

Year	Percentage of Married Women, Husband Present, with Children Under 6	Percentage of All Married Women[a]	Percentage of All Married Men[b]
1960	19	32	89
1970	30	40	86
1980	45	50	81
1990	59	58	79
2000	63	61	77

*Civilian population 16 years of age and older.
[a]Husband present.
[b]Wife present.
Source: *Statistical Abstract of the United States*, 2001, Table 577, p. 373; Table 575, p. 372.

Table 9-2. Earnings in the United States by Gender and Job Type for Year-Round Full-Time Workers, 2000*

	Median Annual Salary		Ratio of Earnings, Female/Male	
	Women	Men	2000	1989
Median earnings	$25,532	$33,592	76	68
By Job Type				
Executive/administrative/ managerial	35,672	52,728	68	61
Professional	37,700	50,804	74	71
Sales	21,164	35,568	60	54
Service	16,432	21,528	76	62

*By occupation, longest job held.
Source: Based on data in *Statistical Abstract of the United States*, 2001, Table 621, p. 403.

Compare your grandparents and your parents. Chances are you have a working mother, but your grandmother was a stay-at-home mom. Your grandfather is more likely than your father to have worked in manufacturing and to have belonged to a union. Your father is more likely than your grandfather to have shared child care and domestic responsibilities. Age at marriage has been delayed for both men and women. College educations and professional degrees have increased. What other changes do you associate with the increase in female employment outside the home?

Table 9–2 details employment in the Unites States in 2000 by gender, income, and job type. Notice that the income gap between women and men was widest in sales, where women averaged 60 percent of the male salary. Overall the ratio rose from 68 percent in 1989 to 76 percent in 2000.

Today's jobs are not especially demanding in terms of physical labor. With machines to do the heavy work, the smaller average body size and lesser average strength of women are no longer impediments to blue-collar employment. The main reason we don't see more modern-day Rosies working alongside male riveters is that the U.S. workforce itself is abandoning heavy-goods manufacture. In the 1950s two-thirds of American jobs were blue collar, compared to less than 16 percent today. The location of those jobs has shifted within the world capitalist economy. Third World countries with cheaper labor produce steel, automobiles, and other heavy goods less expensively than the United States can, but the United States excels at services. The American mass education system has many inadequacies, but it does train millions of people for service- and information-oriented jobs, from sales clerk to computer operator.

The Feminization of Poverty

Alongside the economic gains of many American women stands an opposite extreme: the feminization of poverty. This refers to the increasing representation of women (and their children) among America's poorest people. Women head over half of U.S. households with incomes below the poverty line. In 1959 female-headed households accounted for just one-fourth of the American poor. Since then, that figure has more than doubled.

Married couples are much more secure economically than single mothers are. The data in Table 9–3 demonstrate that the average income for married-couple families is more than twice that of families maintained by a woman. The average one-earner family maintained by a woman had an annual income of $26,164 in 1999. This was less than one-half the mean income ($56,827) of a married-couple household.

TABLE 9–3. Median Annual Income of U.S. Households, by Household Type, 1999

	Number of Households (1000s)	Median Annual Income (Dollars)	Percentage of Median Earnings Compared with Married-Couple Households
All households	104,705	$40,816	72
Family households	72,025	49,940	88
Married-couple households	55,311	56,827	100
Male earner, no wife	4,028	41,838	74
Female earner, no husband	12,687	26,164	46
Nonfamily households	32,680	24,566	43
Single male	14,641	30,753	54
Single female	18,039	19,919	35

Source: Based on data from *Statistical Abstract of the United States*, 2001, Table 663, p. 434.

With machines to do the heavy work, the smaller average body size and lesser
average strength of women are no longer impediments to blue collar employment.
Shown here, a woman manager works side by side with an auto mechanic.

The feminization of poverty is not just a North America trend. The percentage of female-headed households has been increasing worldwide. In western Europe, for example, it rose from 24 percent in 1980 to 31 percent in 1990. The figure ranges from below 20 percent in certain South Asian and Southeast Asian countries to almost 50 percent in certain African countries and the Caribbean (Buvinic 1995).

Why must so many women be solo household heads? Where are the men going, and why are they leaving? Among the causes are male migration; civil strife (with men away fighting); divorce; abandonment; widowhood; unwed adolescent parenthood; and, more generally, the idea that children are women's responsibility. Globally, households headed by women tend to be poorer than are those headed by men. In one study, the percentage of single-parent families considered poor was 18 percent in Britain, 20 percent in Italy, 25 percent in Switzerland, 40 percent in Ireland, 52 percent in Canada, and 63 percent in the United States.

It is widely believed that one way to improve the situation of poor women is to encourage them to organize. New women's groups can in some cases revive or replace traditional forms of social organization that have been disrupted. Membership in a group can help women to mobilize resources, to rationalize production, and to reduce the risks and costs associated with credit. Organization also allows women to develop self-confidence and to decrease dependence on others. Through such organization, poor women throughout the world are working to determine their own needs and priorities, and to change things so as to improve their social and economic situation (Buvinic 1995).

WHAT DETERMINES VARIATION IN GENDER ISSUES?

We see then that gender roles and stratification have varied widely across cultures and through history. Among many foragers and matrilineal cultivators, there is little gender stratification, which, however, is the norm in patrilineal-patrilocal societies. When women lose their productive roles, the domestic-public dichotomy may be accentuated and gender stratification sharpened. With industrialism, attitudes about gender vary in the context of female extradomestic employment. Gender is flexible and varies with cultural, social, political, and economic factors. The variability of gender in time and space suggests that it will continue to change. The biology of the sexes is not a narrow enclosure limiting humans but a broad base upon which a variety of structures can be built (Friedl 1975; Bonvillan 1995). We continue our examination of sex-gender issues in Chapter 10, on sexual orientation, after a brief examination of media portrayals of gender roles.

The Impact of the Mass Media on Sex-Gender Roles

In contemporary societies, the media both reflect and influence sex-gender roles. Media portrayals are texts, which can be read as lessons about a culture and cultural change. Consider the portrayal of men and women on American TV. In 1975, American prime-time shows had three men for every woman. By the mid-1980s, the ratio was equalizing. Forty-seven percent of 143 new characters introduced in 1984 were female (Gunter 1986). In Brazil, where productions called *telenovelas* (soap-opera-like serial dramas, in which domestic settings predominate) are popular, TV programs have always had a more equal sex ratio than American prime-time shows did before the mid-1980s. Brazilian television, usually set at home, is faithful to the fact that in the home there are as many females as males. (American sitcoms and soap operas also have more balanced sex ratios than do other program types, particularly the male-dominated action series [Gunter 1986].)

By the 1980s American television was balancing its sex ratio to mirror a changing reality. As more and more real-life women entered the workforce, more and more television characters were female. Women increasingly populate the workplace settings that dominate programming. Long ago, *The Mary Tyler Moore Show* helped usher in the era of unmarried workplace women in American *televisionland*. By the mid-1980s the never-married woman had become the modal American TV female (55 percent). Divorced (10 percent) and widowed (9 percent) women reduced the percentage of married women to 26 percent. By the mid-1980s three-fourths of the adult female characters being introduced to American television had paid employment (National Commission on Working Women 1984). The trend continues today with the powerful physicians, including surgeons, of *E.R.*, and the professional women who populate series as different as *The X-Files*, *Alias*, and *Law and Order*.

The female characters of Brazilian TV more often gain their social status through a strategic marriage than through education, hard work, or professional careers (see Chapter 13). This illustrates different cultural values about work, individual achievement, and family connections (see Chapter 16). Brazilian feminists often criticized the prominent telenovelist Janete Clair, alleging that her female characters (particularly her long-suffering heroines) were too dominated by their husbands and lovers. However, since the mid-1970s, independent women and working women have become somewhat more common on Brazilian television.

Research that Kottak (1990b) and his Brazilian colleagues did on the impact of television on attitudes in Brazil found that televiewing correlated consistently and strikingly with liberal sex-gender views on social issues. This provided one of the strongest and clearest confirmations in that study of television's impact on attitudes. The statistical analysis showed that Brazilian television strongly influenced sex-gender views. Heavy viewers were strikingly more liberal than were people who watched television less frequently. Habitual viewers were much less traditional in their opinions about such social issues as whether women belong at home, should work when their husbands earn well, should work when pregnant, should go to bars, should leave a husband they no longer love, and should pursue men they are interested in, and about whether men should cook and wash clothes and whether parents should talk to their children about sex.

The world transmitted by Brazilian television (particularly *telenovelas*) draws on an urban-modern reality in which sex roles *are* less traditional than in the mainly rural communities where Kottak and his associates did their research. This liberalization was one of the strongest pan-Brazilian effects, with little variation between the seven towns studied in the research project. There is every reason to believe that television may have similar effects when its content is similar and nontraditional across cultures. Television certainly influences the career aspirations and life ambitions of contemporary North Americans; thus it plays a part in changing sex-gender roles across time as well as across cultures.

CHAPTER TEN

Sexual Orientation

—————————— WHAT'S SEX GOT TO DO WITH IT? ——————————

In 1977, Florida banned adoption by self-identified gay men and lesbians. The law allowed gay men and lesbians to act as foster parents, but it mandated the removal of children under four years old from gay households, to be put up for adoption by heterosexual couples. The rationale? Sexual orientation.

Diversity in sexual preference and behavior is as old as humanity. The public and political expression of sexual orientation, however, is very much a contemporary phenomenon. Today we speak of "sexual minorities," as we do of racial, ethnic, and religious minorities. The social implications of sexual orientation as a self-conscious, collective identity, especially as these concern parenting by homosexual men and women, are ambiguous and controversial.

There are men, women, and children who use terms such as "gay dad," "lesbian mom," "gay family," "gay parenting," and "gay adoption" to describe their family arrangements. These people face an uphill battle as they seek acceptance by relatives, neighbors, colleagues, peers, and government. Integration into a local community or school is often a source of anxiety for these parents and kids, who may view their own home life as "normal."

North America has never witnessed more diversity in kinship and family organization than at present. However, Americans still maintain idealized standards of love, sex, marriage, family, and community. Anthropologists distinguish between *ideal* and *real* culture to explain discrepancies between how people think, or hope, their way of life is and how they actually live. Each year Kozaitis surveys her students about how they define "family." When she asks about America's *real* kinship organization, most students recognize the

American family as a fluid system with diverse domestic and household con-
figurations. To her question "What constitutes the *ideal* family unit in our society?", however, students respond with some variant of the following: "a
legally married man and woman, who live with their biological children happily ever after, till death do them part." While the latter definition identifies
different genders and children as a requirement of family, it does not specify
the actual sexual orientation of the marital and parental partners.

Consider some questions: Are legally married men and woman always
heterosexual? Do heterosexuals inevitably raise better-adjusted children than
homosexuals do? Do women make better parents than men? Are fathers less
qualified to raise children than mothers are? Neither men nor women,
whether straight or gay, are natural caretakers. Parenting potential and performance are linked to the cultural systems in which men and women are em-
bedded. For example, in hunting-gathering societies, women contribute to
subsistence as much as or more than men do. Such a division of labor encourages participation in child rearing by men. In North America's industrial
economy of the 1950s, the bias for male work outside the home left child rearing to women, who stayed home. This arrangement reinforced the idea of fathers as categorically breadwinners, and mothers as categorically nurturers.

In today's services and information society, men and women, regardless
of their sexual orientation, compete for similar extradomestic jobs and are
likely to assume responsibilities at home that are more nearly equal than
were their parents' or grandparents' domestic responsibilities. Women's increasing extradomestic labor has reduced their participation in domestic and
child-rearing work, providing men with opportunities to express their "feminine side." The absence of women at home increases the likelihood of "male
caretakers." Nowhere is this more evident than in the case of gay fathers.
Like their lesbian counterparts, homosexual fathers are a diverse group. They
include single, divorced, and even heterosexually married men, with children
from a heterosexual mating. Other gay men first establish a gay lifestyle, then
later seek to become parents. The number of gay fathers is estimated at between 1 and 3 million (Silverstein 2000), but discrimination against them by
courts prevails with respect to custody, foster care, and adoption.

Research contradicts popular stereotypes that gay fathers are likely to
raise homosexual sons (Bozett 1989) and that homosexual parents are more
likely to abuse children sexually than their heterosexual counterparts are
(Barret and Robinson 1990; Patterson 1992). Studies show that homosexual
and heterosexual fathers have similar approaches to problem solving, commitment to parenting, and level of intimacy and engagement with their children (Silverstein 2000). Parental qualifications are more a sociocultural
than a biological matter. Competent parenting correlates with impulses to
protect the young; skills to socialize them; and a commitment to caring for,
and about, them indefinitely. Parenthood signifies adulthood, not heterosexuality. "Fathering" and "mothering" are equal opportunity privileges for
mature, healthy, and responsible adults regardless of sex, gender, or sexual
orientation.

At the 2000 Million Mom March, gay Americans expressed their determination to be recognized as parents. Represented at the march were divorced homosexual men and women, claiming a human right, to maintain contact with their children. Other, childless, adults demanded that gay couples be allowed to adopt unwanted children currently in foster care "Any kind of parenting is better than no parenting," they proclaimed. In 2002 one of the movement's best-known mobilizing agents, Rosie O'Donnell, raised national awareness of gay parenting by announcing her own status as a lesbian domestic partner and parent.

Creating and maintaining a healthy, stable family is a tall order for anyone to achieve, regardless of sexual orientation. To raise productive, well-adjusted kids from birth to young adulthood and beyond is even harder. Most Americans give it a shot; some succeed better than others do. Success in parenthood would seem to have more to do with love than with sex. Homosexual as well as heterosexual persons intend and choose to become parents. Men and women who can provide a safe, supportive, and nurturing home for children, especially for kids abandoned by their biological, most likely heterosexual, parents, are asking for the right to create families of their own. Gay men and women may ask, "What's sex got to do with it?" What do you think? ☺

THE NATURE AND CULTURE OF SEXUAL ORIENTATION

Sexual orientation is a human attribute. It is natural, biologically programmed, and cultural, linked to rules and habits. Enculturation regulates and directs the **libido** (sexual energy) toward varied expressions. Sexual desire is inborn, a human universal. However, patterns of flirting, courting, dating, loving, and lovemaking vary across time and space. Premarital sex may have outraged your grandparents, as arranged marriages, common in India, may offend some of you today. The sex drive is to erotic orientations and sexual practices as hunger is to nutritional standards and eating habits.

To some extent at least, all human activities and preferences, including erotic expression, are learned and malleable. **Sexual orientation** is the patterned way in which a person views and expresses the sexual component of his or her personality; it refers to a person's habitual sexual attraction to and activities with persons of the opposite sex, **heterosexuality;** the same sex, **homosexuality;** or both sexes, **bisexuality. Asexuality,** indifference toward or lack of attraction to either sex, is also a sexual orientation. All four of these forms are found in contemporary North America and throughout the world. But each type of desire and experience holds different meanings for individuals and groups. For example, an asexual disposition may be acceptable in some places but may be perceived as a character flaw in others. Bisexuality may be a private orientation in Mexico, rather than socially sanctioned and encouraged as among the Sambia of Papua New Guinea.

Most people ascribe to and conform to one of these labels, albeit not always self-consciously. Most heterosexuals are oblivious to the cultural construction of the sex drive. They consider the sexual dimension of their lives natural and normal. People assume, and most hope, that they will bear and rear heterosexual children. A recent warning by gay activists that read "Don't assume your preschoolers are straight!" disturbs parents who never consider that their kindergartner is anything but "normal."

The most critical gauge of sexual orientation is one's experiences in *eros* (sexual love), what in psychoanalysis is known as the *life instinct*. This is an impulse, a spontaneous inclination or incitement, to become intimate with a person or type of person. Sexual love gratifies a basic human need. It preserves physical and mental health, provided it is socially sanctioned. Eros is distinguished from *philia* (friendship), the most enduring form of love, born out of higher faculties, and *agape* (humanitarianism), or love for humanity. Erotic love may inspire creativity, productivity, and psychological fulfillment, even when morality and law forbid the physical expression of erotic longings. Desire, combined with genuine, psychic attachment between two individuals, results in what Socrates called "divine madness." Do you remember the last time you fell in love? How did you feel? That state of being hints at your sexual orientation.

Erotic fantasies and autoerotic practices also reveal aspects of one's sexual orientation. Habits of masturbation reveal one's sexual impulses and tendencies. Indicators of sexual proclivity may include possession and use of erotic paraphernalia, for example, books, videos, and sex toys. People often associate sexual orientation with essential being, or a true inner self. One's fantasy life may be homoerotic or heteroerotic, may include orgies or threesomes, may involve pain, or may consistently feature a best friend's wife. Law, morality, guilt, habit, and fear channel psychosexual potential into sociosexual behavior.

Included in the sexual component of personality is one's tendency to be **monogamous** (the practice of having only one sexual partner at a time), to have multiple partners simultaneously, to "cruise on the side" (pursue anonymous sexual contacts in public places, such as parks, bathrooms, and rest stops), to practice adultery, or to be celibate. In the North American mainstream, monogamy is a cultural ideal; but among middle-class urban Greeks, adultery is reportedly institutionalized. A favorite sound bite in conversations among Greeks is that "between 2:00 and 5:00 P.M. (the normal rest period of a workday), half of Athens is sleeping with the other half." The capacity and expression of one's sexual desires reflect enculturation and vary contextually over time, in degree and intensity.

It's common to hear people discuss their sexual preferences in terms of temperament, height, hair and skin color, age, and body weight. However, one's **sexual fit** combines physical traits with psychosocial sensibilities. This fit, that is, a particular set of characteristics that activates one's libido, reappears in different potential partners during one's life span. When a man rejects sexual advances by a woman, he may say, "She's not my *type*." Moreover,

Sexual life has both private and public manifestations. Public displays of affection vary in intensity and interpretation from one society to another. Would this scene from Cannes, France, be out of place on Main Street in your city or town?

the partner of choice at different periods in life typically matches one's own psychosocial and intellectual stage of development. Thus a man may divorce his wife because "we've grown apart and have little in common."

We also project the sexual component of our personality by our gender identity (gender-based ideas and activities to which an individual ascribes and by which he or she is defined socially). Most people align a private sexual disposition (e.g., heterosexual male) with the socially appropriate public persona (married man, or husband). Others maintain what by societal standards are incompatible markers of identity, such as private homosexual inclinations with a public heterosexual relationship. Still others choose different identities and statuses situationally and contextually.

Sexual life has both private and public manifestations. In the United States 50 years ago premarital sex was kept secret, and interracial dating was discouraged or prohibited. (Within some communities in North America these activities are still taboo.) In North America adultery is usually private behavior. Kissing and flirting are public and socially acceptable. Among the poor in some societies, depending on the economic needs of the household, some women, and men, alternate between being faithful spouses and obligatory prostitutes. They serve as sexual partners for material rewards, including food, clothes, and school supplies. Like much social behavior, sexual conduct isn't simply a matter of personal choice. Whom we love, how much, and in what way, has to do both with individual wishes and discretion and with social sanctions and survival.

Sexual activity or fantasy does not necessarily correspond with sexual orientation. For example, homosexual experiences during specific periods in the life cycle (e.g., adolescence) or time spent in gender-segregated institutions, or as a recreational outlet, do not necessarily convert the heterosexual. Likewise, a homosexual orientation doesn't necessarily prohibit one from participating in heterosexual relationships, claiming a straight identity, or marrying heterosexually. Consider the college junior who, during her third year abroad in Italy had sex regularly with a native woman. The student described the experience as *"an act* of intimacy; I don't ever have to sleep with another woman again. I know I'm heterosexual." Even a dominant sexual orientation does not define one in absolute terms.

One's sexual identity is a primary indicator of status, but it is not necessarily and not always accurate. Participation in homosexual encounters that many self-identified heterosexuals may perceive as "experimentation," "growing as a person," or "a phase," may in fact reflect a homosexual orientation and, eventually, result in a gay identity. A person who declares a bisexual identity may be denying or hiding a predominant orientation, typically homosexuality. Another may simply be expressing sexual attraction to, or actual experiences with, both sexes. Consider the young man who spent his entire college career trying to convince himself and everyone around him that "we're all bi." Several heterosexual and homosexual affairs later, the same man sought "to marry a man." "There is, however," he said, "one woman that I would marry, but she's taken." Today he is "married" to a man, "the love of my life," as he described his partner.

Sexual orientation is neither pure nor absolute. Sexuality is learned, flexible, and situational. Variability in sexual need, capacity, and expression prevails across individuals and groups. An individual may feel and display varied erotic impulses throughout the life cycle. A man dates several women as a single person but remains faithful to his wife once married. A straight-identified lesbian marries a man and raises children with him. A male homosexual sex worker "retires" to marry a woman. A married-with-children gay man and lesbian pursue homosexual liaisons. A bisexual man spends six months a year with his wife in one country and the other six months with his male lover in another. These examples, all drawn from the real world, illustrate that sexual orientation is a highly complex, multifaceted, and individual matter.

Our society recognizes four main types of sexual orientation: heterosexuality, homosexuality, bisexuality, and asexuality. However, variation in sentiment and activity *within* each category is probably greater than that *between* these labels. What we do with our body and psyche, how frequently, under what circumstances, and with whom, is more complicated than simply the anatomy of our partners. Sexual sensibilities and acts exist along a continuum. A more accurate and responsible way to discuss variety in sexual orientation is to speak about homo-, hetero-, or bisexual *acts,* and not homosexuals, heterosexuals, and bisexuals. People practice such acts, or combinations of such acts, at different times, to varying degrees, and under particular conditions.

Social categories, including those generated by sexual minorities, are terms of convenience. They also serve as markers of distinction and identity. Classifications help us to make sense of human variety and to manage social relations in a rapidly changing, complex world. Social labels are also useful to individuals because they provide actual or perceived psychosocial connections, legal and often economic protection, and political or civic validation. It is important to distinguish between self-constructed labels and those that others impose on groups. For example, members of the gay community often use the label "breeders" to describe heterosexuals. Equally offensive may be the label "homosexuals," which nongays use to reduce gays to merely sexual creatures. In this book we conform to the use of classifications only as a communication device and not as proclamations of absolute essential or social statuses.

CHANGING PATTERNS AND VIEWS OF SEXUAL ORIENTATION

Because most people practice heterosexuality, they assume it to be "just human nature." Any other type of eroticism is, therefore, a puzzle. People are less likely to wonder, "What causes sexual orientation?" than they are to ask, "Where does homosexuality come from?" Generations of Westerners, steeped in the Judeo-Christian heritage, distinguish between moral and legal sexual behavior, as in that characteristic of heterosexual unions, and all other "deviant" or, at best, alternative forms of sexuality (Foucault 1978).

In the Middle Ages sexuality was evaluated as behavior, what people did. Deviation from publicly approved procreative sex between a married couple was viewed as perverted. In many Western societies, homosexuality was severely punished, sometimes by death. Puritan values equated sexual pleasure with sin, a sentiment that still holds true in some parts of the United States. Throughout the 18th and 19th centuries, all forms of nonreproductive sex were considered deviant and morally offensive. Homosexual acts in particular, judged to be nothing more than sex for pleasure, were interpreted as a "condition" with which certain types of persons were afflicted.

Greater public attention to human sexuality led to its interpretation as an innate state of being. Persons who pursued heterosexual lifestyles were considered proper. Those who were known to practice homosexuality were identified and classified as homosexuals. In many societies, sexual categorization led to a distinction between the stigmatized "monsters" and the citizens. The perceived defects of the former category, composed of homosexuals, were presumed to be psychological and inherent to an individual, as were the characteristics of heterosexuals, the socially protected category. During the 19th century, sexuality was polarized as male-female and homosexual-heterosexual. This interpretation emphasized a congenital basis for sexuality. The prevalent belief was that sexual attraction was inborn and permanent.

The rise of scientific medicine in the late 19th and early 20th centuries promoted a view of human sexuality as a matter of health, physical and mental. Clinical and popular impressions of sexual orientation emphasized a polarity between right and wrong, good and bad, and healthy and unhealthy sexuality. Heterosexuality was deemed healthy; and homosexuality was considered an illness, a condition that could be cured. Health professionals and the populace wondered about the biological and mental nature of homosexuality as a pathology. Clinicians classified persons who practiced homosexuality as abnormal and debated the etiology (cause) of this illness. Treatment strategies for "patients" would include commitment to an institution, analysis, castration, and sterilization. Same-sex practices came to be known as *closet homosexuality*, meaning secrecy and maintenance of a double life.

Sigmund Freud contributed to the medicalization of sexuality. However, he stressed the plasticity (capable of being molded) of sexual orientation. He proposed that all humans are innately capable of bisexuality, but that normal libidinal development results in heterosexuality. Freud's perspective on sex emphasized that humans are social creatures. Biopsychological instincts are shaped and directed by a cultural milieu to accommodate societal regulations and to conform to social norms. Freud was situated in the social and cultural context of early 20th century Vienna. Heterosexuality was in fact the normative pattern of psychosocial development and interpersonal relations in his time and place.

Heterosexuality in general, and reproductive sex in particular, remained the dominant cultural code of human sexuality throughout the Western world well after World War II. The starkest demonstration of heterosexism in recent history is the extermination by the Nazis of thousands of persons suspected of being homosexual. Fascists threw perceived homosexuals into prison cells and concentration camps, along with millions of Jews and thousands of Gypsies. It would be another generation before Westerners, and North Americans in particular, would learn that same-sex relations were more common and more complex than both the psychosocial model and the biomedical model had proposed.

Understanding of the social construction of sexual orientation heightened with the publication of Alfred Kinsey's studies in the mid-20th century (Kinsey, Pomeroy, and Martin 1948; Kinsey et al. 1953). Kinsey and his colleagues documented self-reported sex practices in the United States. Their findings concluded that sexual orientation exists in gradations and not in a dichotomy of polar heterosexuality and homosexuality. Kinsey proposed a 7-point rating scale in which 0 signified exclusive heterosexuality and 6 signified exclusive homosexuality. His data showed that about 4 percent of males and 2 percent of females had an exclusively same-sex orientation. This research also suggested that people don't fit neatly into discrete categories of sexual behavior and fixed orientations. Most people are capable of responding, and many do respond, psychosexually to members of both sexes. Sexual feelings and psychic responses may change over the life span of a person.

Variability in sexual practices and meanings among Americans was confirmed by a national comprehensive survey conducted by Michael, Gagnon, Laumann, and Kolata (1994). These researchers verified that the majority of the U.S. population practices heterosexuality. Nine percent of men and 4 percent of women reported some homosexual activity during their life span. A slightly smaller percentage (7 percent of men and almost 4 percent of women) reported same-sex experiences during childhood or early adolescence. Most striking about this study is its attention to sexual orientation as an identity, not just a fantasy, proclivity, or practice. Out of 3,432 respondents, ranging in age from 18 to 59, 2.8 percent of men and 1.4 percent of women reported a partial or total homosexual identity. This number is small compared to that of persons claiming a heterosexual identity. Nonetheless, the existence of even a small percentage of homosexually identified persons is important. Understanding the nature, culture, and variety of human sexuality within North American society and in the world is likely to lead to greater integration and protection of people who for centuries have been misunderstood and, therefore, misjudged and punished.

VARIETIES OF HUMAN SEXUALITY

In any society, individuals will differ in the nature, range, and intensity of their sexual interests and urges. No one knows for sure why such individual sexual differences exist. Part of the answer may be biological, reflecting genes or hormones. Another part may have to do with experiences during growth and development. Whatever the reasons for individual variation, culture always plays a role in directing individual sexual urges toward a collective norm—and such sexual norms vary from culture to culture.

What do we know about variation in sexual norms from society to society, and over time? A classic cross-cultural study (Ford and Beach 1951) found wide variation in attitudes about masturbation, bestiality (sex with animals), and homosexuality. Even in a single culture, such as the United States, attitudes about sex differ with socioeconomic status, region, and rural versus urban residence. However, even in the 1950s, prior to the "age of sexual permissiveness" (the pre-HIV period from the mid-1960s through the 1970s), research showed that almost all American men (92 percent) and more than half of American women (54 percent) admitted to masturbation. In the famous Kinsey report (Kinsey, Pomeroy, and Martin 1948), 37 percent of the men surveyed admitted having had at least one sexual experience leading to orgasm with another male. In a later study of 1,200 unmarried women, 26 percent reported same-sex sexual activities.

Attitudes about sex in other cultures differ strikingly, as Kottak has found in contrasting the cultures he knows best—the United States, urban and rural Brazil, and Madagascar. During his first stay in Arembepe, Brazil, when he was 19 years old and unmarried, young men told him details of their experience with prostitutes in the city. Arembepe's women were also more open about their sex lives than North American women were at that time.

Arembepeiros talked about sex so willingly that Kottak wasn't prepared for the silence and avoidance of sexual subjects he encountered in Madagascar. He did discover from city folk that, as in many non-Western societies, traditional ceremonies were times of ritual license, when normal taboos lapsed and Betsileo men and women engaged in what Christian missionaries described as "wanton" sexuality. Only during his last week in Madagascar did a young man in the village of Ivato, where Kottak had spent a year, take him aside and offer to write down the words for genitals and sexual intercourse. The young man could not say these tabooed words, but he wanted Kottak to know them so that his knowledge of Betsileo culture would be as complete as possible.

Neither Kottak nor Kozaitis has ever worked in a society with institutionalized homosexuality of the sort that exists among several tribes in Papua New Guinea, such as Etoro, Kaluli (Schieffelin 1976), or Sambia (Herdt 1981, 1986). The Kaluli believe that semen has a magical quality that promotes knowledge and growth. Before traveling into alien territory, boys must eat a mixture of semen, ginger, and salt to enhance their ability to learn a foreign language. At age 11 or 12, a Kaluli boy forms a sexual relationship with an older man chosen by his father. (This man cannot be a relative, because that would violate the Kaluli incest taboo.) The older man has anal intercourse with the boy. The Kaluli cite the boy's peach-fuzz beard, which appears thereafter, as evidence that semen is promoting growth. The young Kaluli men also have homosexual intercourse at the hunting lodges, where they spend an extended period learning the lore of the forest and the hunt from older bachelors.

Homosexual activities were absent, rare, or secret in only 37 percent of 76 societies for which data were available in the Ford and Beach study (1951). In the others, various forms of homosexuality were considered normal and acceptable. Sometimes sexual relations between people of the same sex involved transvestism on the part of one of the partners. However, this was not true of male-male sex among the Sudanese Azande, who valued the warrior role (Evans-Pritchard 1970). Prospective warriors—young men aged 12 to 20—left their families and shared quarters with adult fighting men, who paid bridewealth for, and had sex with, them. During this apprenticeship, the young men performed the domestic duties of women. Upon reaching warrior status, these young men took their own younger male brides. Later, upon retiring from the warrior role, Azande men married women. Flexible in their sexual expression, Azande males had no difficulty in shifting from sex with older men (as male brides), to sex with younger men (as warriors), to sex with women (as husbands). (See Murray and Roscoe 1998.)

There appears to be greater cross-cultural acceptance of homosexuality than of masturbation. Most societies in the Ford and Beach (1951) study discouraged masturbation. However, this study assessed only the social approval of sexual practices, not their actual frequency. As in our own society, socially disapproved sex acts are more widespread than people admit.

Flexibility in human sexual expression seems to be an aspect of our primate heritage. Both masturbation and homosexual behavior exist among chimpanzees and other primates. Male bonobos (pygmy chimps) regularly engage in a form of mutual masturbation known as "penis fencing." Females get sexual pleasure from rubbing their genitals against those of other females (de Waal 1997). Our primate sexual potential is molded by culture, the environment, and reproductive necessity. Heterosexuality is practiced in all human societies—which, after all, must reproduce themselves—but alternatives are also widespread (Rathus, Nevid, and Fichner-Rathus 2000). The sexual component of human personality—just how we express our "natural" sexual urges—is a matter that culture and environment determine and limit.

THE SOCIAL CONSTRUCTION
OF SEXUAL ORIENTATION

Sexual orientation is more than a biological craving or character trait. It is also a social phenomenon. Each society maintains particular, and prevalent, views about what sexuality is and ought to be. We acquire our sense of sexual status and identity through membership in a social group. Our sense of "Who am I?" and "Who am I, *really*?" comes from our lived experiences and interaction with other human beings within and outside our own group. The difference between being labeled mentally ill, a mother's worst nightmare, a dyke, a lesbian, or a human being depends a great deal on one's social relationships. A woman who grew up in a small town thinking she was "weird" describes her "coming out" process and subsequent integration into the lesbian community as her having been "reborn; I could be myself!"

Historically and cross-culturally the sex drive and sexual behavior among humans reflect particular sociopolitical conditions as much as biopsychological cravings. For example, classical Athens was divided into two parts. One was a political and social elite composed exclusively of men, who were citizens. The subordinate category included all others—women, slaves, foreigners (barbarians), and children, all of whom were denied civil rights to varied degrees. Sexual morality and behavior mirrored this hierarchy. Free men, always the dominant, insertive "penetrators," had sexual relations with social inferiors, the "penetrated" partners, regardless of gender. Homosexual unions between elite men, including teachers and students, were viewed as acceptable behavior, indeed the highest form of intimacy.

All societies require heterosexuality for reproduction. Social groups want to reproduce themselves biologically and culturally. However, as we have seen, many societies tolerate homosexual activities, and some endorse them. We saw that Azande (southern Sudan) warriors "married" young men to satisfy their sexual needs until they were socially ready to marry a woman and have children. Homosexual acts are part of initiation rites among the Etoro and the Sambia of Papua New Guinea. Dahomey girls of West Africa prepared for marriage by having homosexual relations with older women. Among the Ju'/hoansi of the Kalahari, young girls are sexually active with each other before they have heterosexual relations. These societies recognize heterosexual or homosexual *acts*, not *persons*, and certainly not *groups*.

Cultural codes of sexual expression dictate whether an act is legal, normal, deviant, or pathological. Actual yet abnormal sexual conduct in our society includes necrophilia (an erotic attraction to or fascination with corpses), pedophilia (sexual desire by adults for children), pederasty (sodomy between an adult male and a boy), sadomasochism (sexual pleasure from inflicting or receiving physical and psychological pain), and bestiality (sexual contact between a person and an animal).

Incest is interpreted and managed differently across human societies. Among the Yanomami of Venezuela and Brazil, sex with certain first cousins is acceptable, whereas sex with other kinds of first cousins is forbidden. The legality of sex with cousins varies by state in the United States. In Greece sex between all first cousins is considered incestuous.

Mainstream North Americans hold fairly strict standards of what constitutes rape and sexual harassment compared with other Western societies. We are familiar with normative social ethics such as "No means no!" A man may hesitate to compliment a woman on her new haircut because he fears offending or insulting her. A young woman in Greece learns to expect, and manage, sexual attention from men. But many mainstream American girls are taught to discourage it by deemphasizing their femininity and sexuality.

Also, display of affection toward children varies in intensity and interpretation from one society to another. In Greece it is common to see parents and other adult relatives, even nonbiological kin, "suck" a child, "bite it," "pinch it," and "eat it," without causing alarm. Demonstrative relatives in one culture may be accused of child abuse or incest in our own society.

Societies attribute different *meaning* to sexual activities. In some New Guinea societies, homosexual relations between boys and senior warriors are obligatory. Boys live with men for an extended period of time, during which they are sexually active. The local belief system holds that masculinity is achieved through sexual contact with men, but social adulthood ultimately involves heterosexual marriage and procreative sex. In our own society, a man who admits to his fiancée or friends that he had homosexual experiences during childhood or adolescence is likely to find that they will raise questions about his masculinity. This perspective contrasts with those of contemporary Greece and Brazil, where homosexual activity, particularly by dominant (penetrating) partners, or "tops," does not threaten their perceived masculinity.

Compare these cultures with the perception and treatment of public bi-sexuals in the United States, Great Britain, and other Western societies. These individuals are often criticized and marginalized by both heterosexuals and homosexuals for *their difference*. They are often accused of being latent homosexuals, selfish, or confused. This popular response to bisexuals in the United States demonstrates lack of awareness not only of the range of human sexuality but also of its relationship to the cultural context in which it is expressed.

Enculturation directs social and sexual relations between boys and girls. The Lepcha of Sikkim in northern India consider sexuality proper behavior, comparable to eating or drinking. Sexual freedom is normative, and girls become sexually active before puberty. In contrast, some Middle Eastern societies (e.g., Saudi Arabia) enforce segregation between men and women and prohibit sexual and social relations between boys and girls. Heterosexual relations among the young, particularly adolescents, are shunned in some rural areas of Mediterranean Europe. In Greek villages, where chastity and virginity are considered a strong component of a young woman's dowry, girls are taught to avoid public contact with boys and men. A young girl may be spanked or beaten by her father or brother if she is caught with a young man. In contrast, Kozaitis (1993) observed that among the Roma (Gypsies) of Athens, Greece, adults encourage romantic relations between prepubescent boys and girls to ensure endogamy (marriage between members of the same social group) and, thus, cultural reproduction.

Societies also vary in the number of genders they recognize. Cross-cultural evidence supports the existence of a third gender in some societies. Examples include the **berdaches** found in some Native American groups. Berdaches were different from both men and women. They were biological men who dressed in women's clothing and were sexual partners to heterosexual male warriors. Berdaches were not marginalized; they were integrated fully in the economic and political life of their societies (Callender and Kochems 1983). In India a group known as the **hijras** are viewed as neither men nor women. Biological males, they undergo an operation to have their genitals removed. They are transformed into hijras, a third gender, who exaggerate female dress codes and decorum. They identify themselves as followers of the Hindu deity, Bahuchara Mata, and perform life-cycle ceremonies, such as the birth of a child. They also earn a living as prostitutes, serving as sexual partners to men (Nanda 1990).

Historically and cross-culturally, sexual behavior and ideology reveal economic and political conditions. What is considered normal, proper, deviant, or alternative differs from one society to another. In the United States we find variation in sexual beliefs and practices within and across segments of the population. Our market-oriented society nurtures individualism, supports personal choice, poses obstacles to marriage and procreative sex, and fosters gender symmetry. Indirectly, it encourages recreational sex, a menu of sexual pleasures that includes premarital and extramarital sex, bisexuality, homosexuality, and serial monogamy. Increased female participation in the labor force launched a social movement in the 1960s that fueled a sex-gender revolution. Puritanism may still exist as a cultural ideal, but our society contains an unprecedented diversity in sexual sentiment, belief, and experience. In earlier chapters we saw that the black movement introduced *race* as an organizing principle. Later the feminist movement established *gender* as a constitutive basis for social organization. Now we turn to the gay movement and see how *desire* may form a basis for culture.

THE POLITICAL ORGANIZATION
OF SEXUAL ORIENTATION

Sexual diversity is not only a demographic fact. It is also a political reality. The shift from an industrial to a services-and-information economy and growing female participation in the workforce have altered our perceptions of sex, sexuality, and sex-gender roles. North American households have changed form and become more diverse (see Chapter 16). By the 1970s dual-career couples and two-income families had become common models of mainstream American life. Broken families, blended families, and single-parent households are increasingly common.

Along with these changes came new cultural values, illustrated by terms like *career woman, independent woman, working mother, singlehood, sexual freedom,* and *gender equality*. A sexual revolution born out of economic and political changes challenged the basis of our social order. In 1973 the American Psychiatric Association declassified homosexuality as a disease. Choice in sexual expression became more accessible and popular among mainstream, particularly educated, North Americans, including persons with same-sex desires. More open diversity in sexual interests, beliefs, and actions threatened our society's standard of the traditional family.

The feminist movement played an important role in changing ideas and behavior about human sexuality. Being *female* became the basis upon which (mainly middle-class and upper-income white) women organized socially and politically to promote gender equality. Women became a category that required political attention. The public interest in *sex-gender roles* expanded to include sex. Women sought freedom, signified by choice in all aspects of life, including sexual partners, premarital sex, extramarital sex, and same-sex relationships.

Interpersonal contact between men and women became more common in the workplace and, more generally, in the public, extradomestic arena. Increased contact among all kinds of people outside the boundaries of traditional family life generated greater sensitivity to the sexual *self* and *other*. Distance from domestic, procreative roles also promoted awareness of sexual potential and preferences.

Types and degrees of desire and intimacy were publicly expressed. Men and women learned to manage, interpret, and adapt in ways that reinforced self-fulfillment and not necessarily communal well-being. Economic and political institutions supported and rewarded the "me generation," which, among its many quests, sought sexual gratification.

The liberation of men in general, and homosexual men in particular, followed the women's liberation movement. Gay men and lesbians fought as individuals, as two separate constituencies, and as a unified body for public acknowledgment of their oppression and for their freedom. Consistent with the national climate of sexual liberation in the 1970s, sexual fulfillment and self-actualization became key goals of the gay and lesbian movement. More important, individual activists fought to change mass opinion and public policy. Men and women who for centuries had been outlaws, marginals, and accused of living in sin demanded to be recognized and treated like citizens.

The distinction between the terms *homosexual* and *gay* or *lesbian* is perhaps the most important one to appreciate. As we saw earlier, **homosexual** is a term used to describe *sexual desire and activity* between persons of the same sex. **Gay** and **lesbian** stand for *a way of life* by persons who desire, and have sex with, persons of the same sex. The classification "gays and lesbians" refers to a community of experience that homosexual-identified individuals share, and construct in an ongoing fashion.

Political mobilization among gay men and lesbians seeks citizenship rights and privileges: the right to a safe, healthy, and gratifying life within the structure and norms of gay culture, as this is constructed in various Western societies. The gay movement assumes (1) that sexual desire forms the basis for building a community and (2) that individuals, through collective action, can alter society by expressing a particular configuration of needs, feelings, and experiences. Gays and lesbians seek the freedom to pursue and design a way of life that offers self-fulfillment, security, and legitimacy.

Gay and lesbian activists emphasize that sexual orientation is a human attribute. Like race and gender, it should be understood as an aspect of human nature and validated as a social practice. The contemporary gay and lesbian movement has several goals. The primary ones include protection from discrimination related to housing, employment, health, health insurance, *domestic partnerships* (legalization of same-sex marriages), parenting, and kinship (Weston 1991; Melymuka 2001).

Individuals whose sexual nature and culture have cost them a comfortable status in mass society pursue and develop a society of their own. To belong to a primary social group, such as an affinity group, is a biopsychological imperative. The driving collective force of today's constructed "soul groups" is social legitimacy, not erotic fulfillment. One may pursue a liaison for sexual pleasure, but one joins a group or becomes a member of a community for social comfort and protection.

Organized efforts for civil rights by gay and lesbian activists have helped establish a gay culture (Herdt 1992). This way of life is distinguished by standards, norms, values, and symbols that its members invent, practice, and reproduce. The gay community is an aggregate of human beings, not

The contemporary Gay and Lesbian Movement has several goals. The primary ones include protection from discrimination related to housing, employment, health, health insurance, domestic partnerships (legalization of same-sex marriages), parenting, and kinship. Shown here, a gay family, with couple, son, uncle, and aunt, participate in a Gay Heritage parade in New York City in 1998. The kinship term on one T-shirt is obscured. What do you imagine it says?

just individuals defined by their sexual interests and practices. The onset of AIDS shifted attention to humanistic and political support within the gay community and by society at large. Gay-born social institutions include ceremonies and "rituals of deliverance," such as "commitment ceremonies" and the annual Gay and Lesbian Pride Day Parade (Browning 1994).

As many gay and lesbians report, gay culture provides a home for persons who may be rejected, marginalized, and punished by other citizens, including employers, colleagues, and, most important, members of their own family. In cities such as San Francisco, New York, Toronto, and Atlanta, sexual minorities occupy a physical space that constitutes home and community.

"Queer Nation" encompasses all gays, lesbians, bisexuals, and transgendered persons. "We're here! We're queer! Get used to it!" assert Queer Nationals. In their effort to dispute and diminish discrimination by outsiders, gay and lesbian activists claim the right to represent the needs of "our own kind." Demonstrations and rallies by Queers in public settings, such as shopping malls and parks, express anger associated with oppression. Unification of persons with same-sex desires and partnerships, regardless of race, ethnicity, gender, or age, strengthens the movement and symbolizes internal power and determination to "be who we are!" Today, gay men and lesbians, as individuals and as a collective, have greater access to political and economic power than at any time in the history of North America.

The term *queer* may be derogatory when used by heterosexuals, or "straights." But today it has become a label that gays and lesbians claim to refer to same-sex relations and to a range of desires, identities, and behaviors. Most important, this category rejects all others that are either imposed by outsiders on the gay community or express conventional, heterosexist practices and morality. Queer Nation stands for, cultivates, and promotes a particular culture. It emphasizes the principle that gays and lesbians are human first. As a social category, Queers challenge conventional models and morality related to sexual pair bonding, courting patterns, love, romance, and reproduction. Perceptions of sex and gender as fixed categories break down as blending, flexing, and bending gender orientations become more common.

Gay and lesbian intellectuals and academics are building "Queer theory," concepts and frameworks that demonstrate the relationship between society, politics, culture, and sexuality. "Queer Studies" has developed into a field of study in its own right (Abelove, Barale, and Halperin 1993). Gay, lesbian, bisexual, and transgendered organizations have proliferated throughout the country's college and university campuses.

Today labels and identities such as gay and lesbian connote political choices, not sexual idiosyncrasies. The phrase "I am a lesbian" may denote a female's realization that she is physically and psychologically attracted to women, that she prefers sexual intimacy with and the companionship of women, or that she has sex exclusively with females (Faderman 1991). Today a woman may use the same words to distinguish herself socially and politically from other women and men. In this case, emphasis is placed not on *being*, on what one *is* psychosexually, but on *becoming*, what one *has become* socioculturally and politically. Lesbianism is not only a sexual category, it's a political affinity, "a synonym for sisterhood, solidarity, and affection" (Weeks 1991). To identify as a lesbian today, a woman reveals conscious association with or participation in a way of life—allegiance to a segment of society marked by such cultural criteria as particular intellectual orientations, recreational activities, social rituals, dress codes, political activities, and spiritual outlets.

Our society, and the kind of work and family roles it requires, encourages gender flexibility on all fronts. Accordingly, mainstream norms and ideas about sex and gender are changing to embrace diversity in psychosocial profiles among most Americans. Human diversity is intrinsic to every social group. The gay and lesbian community is not an exception. As the numbers grow, so does intracommunity variation in class, ethnicity, religion, age, sexual tastes and styles, and other personality and social traits. Diversity, and even stratification, within the gay community is more prevalent than it is between gays and straights.

Homoerotic feelings and homosexual tendencies probably exist in all human societies. But a gay *culture* is a characteristic of few, including northwestern Europe, Canada, and the United States. Cross-cultural studies show that non-Western societies may recognize same-sex activities as integral and necessary to the overall social structure (Herdt 1997). People may practice same-sex activities that are ritualized and culturally *sanctioned*; they *reinforce* rather than *threaten* the social order. In contrast, Westerners in general and North Americans in particular have tended to disapprove of same-sex desire and relationships; but they increasingly tolerate a gay and lesbian community or culture. Our market society may discourage homosexual behaviors, even as it generates a gay community.

This chapter has focused on another component of human diversity and multiculturalism. Sexual orientation is a biocultural universal that reflects the social organization and structure of particular human societies. The multicultural society accommodates, accepts, and integrates variety in sexually organized *lifestyles* not simply *orientations*. Sexual gratification has never dictated cultural identity or social status. Heterosexuals do not pursue romantic relationships, marriages, and social connections to satisfy sexual fantasies and needs, any more than do homosexuals, bisexuals, transgendered persons, or any other kind of sexually identified individuals. A sexual culture, like all cultures, is less about sex, and more about affinity.

CHAPTER ELEVEN

Age and Generation

───────── To Age is Human; to Age Ungracefully, American ─────────

On her 40th birthday, a woman announces, "From now on, I will always be 36!" To celebrate the event she asks her friends to wear black. The party features black balloons, dishes, napkins, and eating utensils. Banners read "Over the hill." A man observes his sixtieth birthday similarly. "Well," he remarks as he blows out his birthday candles, "it's downhill from here!" To what extent are these interpretations of aging uniquely American? What factors might be influencing such perceptions of growing old?

Knowing and reporting age is one of the first developmental tasks of childhood, second only perhaps to saying one's name. Adults typically ask children, "How old are you?" The brief dialogue usually ends with the adult rewarding the child with compliments such as "You're a good girl!" or "You're a big boy!" We learn very early that chronological age (number of years since birth) *ought* to correspond to maturity (capacity and performance of socially desirable thoughts and actions).

Attention to age denotes social expectations and cultural values by which individuals are judged. We expect the four-year-old to know her ABCs, the nine-year-old to bathe and dress himself, the adolescent to drive responsibly, and the adult to support herself financially. Social convention dictates when a youth is invited to sit at "the adults' table," the timing for "leaving home," and the age at which perfectly healthy adults must retire from the labor force.

In North America aging biologically and socially is celebrated during childhood and adolescence. Children can't wait to become grown-ups. Little girls imitate women by playing dress-up. Little boys pretend to shave. Children are eager to earn money by accepting responsibility for chores. Adolescents look forward to expressing their sexual freedom, having a car, and being on their own. Growing *up* is desirable, but growing *old* is not.

In our society the enthusiasm for aging diminishes as people reach adulthood. To ask a woman her age is still considered taboo. The midlife crisis is a familiar rite of passage for many Americans. By the time men, and increasingly women, reach middle adulthood (the forties), they measure the value of their life by occupationally linked accomplishments, for example, position, status, and annual income. Anxieties about aging escalate as adults become "the elderly." Compulsory retirement from gainful employment; increased isolation from family ties; and, for many seniors, physical decline force many older people into a life of perceived, or actual, disengagement.

All living organisms age biologically. Participation in a life course, maturation, physiological capacity relative to biological age, and age-related risks of mortality constitute a universal, genetically programmed process. However, as a sociocultural process, aging varies in structure, content, and meaning. For example, Greek-American elderly in Chicago report that the crowning glory of one's life is a good family. Implicit in this core value (if not always a fact) is that having a good family during one's *yerondamata* (old age) guarantees social security for elderly who are not integrated in the dominant senior culture of our society (Kozaitis 1987).

Age is a key dimension of one's cultural identity and social status. In many nonindustrial societies, people continue to work until they become frail, injured, or ill. In societies in which the elderly control land, property, technology, and knowledge, they also have authority and power, and they are repositories of tradition and wisdom. Seniors hold positions of prestige and leadership and contribute to the security and prosperity of family and community. This is particularly true of small-scale, slowly changing, nonliterate societies that rely on the old for economic security, social guidance, political protection, and cultural integrity.

By contrast, today's industrial societies rely on up-to-date, state-of-the-art skills and information. A market economy that depends on new and rapidly changing technology and knowledge favors younger workers and forces many elders into early retirement. Compared with agrarian societies, today's older generation may be less directly involved in its adult children's private lives, including decisions about lifestyle, courtship, marriage, and child rearing. However, among the poor, the wealthy, and some ethnic groups in industrial nations, the elderly do maintain a strong position within families by offering persistent financial and psychological support to their children and grandchildren. Kozaitis (1993) found that the Roma of Athens, Greece, insisted that "our children's children are twice our children." These Gypsies invest vigorously in securing land, property in the form of gold, and desirable marriage alliances for their children and grandchildren.

In contemporary North America old age is defined chiefly in terms of years, labor participation, accumulation of wealth, and eligibility for federal entitlements. Many Americans retire from the labor force at age 65. The rest of their life they are supported by investments, retirement funds, and government programs. Middle-class retirees often live long distances from their children and withdraw from family decision making. Many elderly people move to retirement communities, frequently in warm regions of the country. The quality of these vary; some resemble apartment buildings that accommodate "the young old" who are capable of independent living. More frail elderly move to complexes that specialize in assisted living. Many people spend their last years of life in convalescent homes where they receive round-the-clock care.

Gerontological research shows that aging does not result in loss of intelligence, change in personality, or altered political orientation. Why then are older people often seen as a social burden? Social scientists have treated the elderly as a contemporary social problem, to be investigated and understood. Research foci include **ageism** (prejudice and discrimination against the elderly), physical decline, social isolation, depression, poverty, and abuse from family members. **Geriatrics** has become a recognized specialty in medicine, and **gerontology** has gained legitimacy among the professions, both as a field of study and as practice. Students who want to work with old people pursue a degree or certificate that qualifies them to serve the elderly in some professional capacity. Today, "elder care" is more than a logo; it is a viable economic niche in a market that thrives on services and information.

Is the graying of America actually a social problem? Consider the number of retirement communities that require designers, architects, builders, and managers to construct and maintain them. Travel, a major pursuit of persons in their golden years, helps support airline agents, tour guides, hotel clerks, and cruise line personnel. Many retailers, journalists, psychiatrists, accountants, and fitness experts earn their living by meeting elder-specific needs. Hundreds of nurses, physicians, social workers, janitors, cooks, and administrators depend on nursing homes to supply them with salaries and benefits. Is it any wonder that our society, despite its apparent contempt for aging, invests in prolonging life biomedically?

In today's North America, both children and the elderly tend to be excluded from contributing directly to the formal economy as producers. Segregation into care facilities for kids and old people, by those who can afford the services, relieves the "sandwich generation" of many child and elder care responsibilities that might otherwise devolve on adult children. Actually, the perception that our growing elder population has become "the young man's burden" is erroneous. Think of all the younger people that the elderly support to take care of them and meet their special needs. Even if many seniors are not contributing resources to their biological kin, they are certainly a key economic resource for many American families.

For their part, the elderly are actively constructing a culture of their own. Their number alone justifies their collective status and identity. About 12 percent of Americans are over 65 years of age. By the mid-21st century this segment will comprise about 20 percent of the U.S. population. Cultural differences and similarities characterize seniors within and across socioeconomic class, ethnicity, age, and gender. However, age-based cultural construction is evident by the number of senior citizen organizations, agencies, and centers designed to meet the social and recreational needs of older adults, living quarters, and specialized services and benefits. Most seniors pursue new, or previously neglected, interests and engage in activities that reinforce new psychological ties and social membership. These include volunteer work, continuing education, travel, hobbies, and part-time work. Elders are gradually, but not always consciously, participating in a culture of their own.

As in the other culture-based movements (e.g., those related to ethnicity and sexual orientation), organization and development of collective consciousness and group rights is left in the hands of an active elite. For example, the status and destiny of elderly American women is negotiated most forcibly by middle-class, middle-aged, educated women. A growing number of older women have adopted the label *crone* to call attention to and celebrate their wisdom, accomplishments, and spirituality (Kreilkamp 1994; Losee 1997). Interest in growing old is also evident in the number of journals and books on the topic. These include *Encore: A Bi-Monthly Magazine Celebrating the Return of the Crone; The Crone: Woman of Age, Wisdom, and Power;* and *Amazons, Bluestockings and Crones: A Feminist Dictionary.* The crone movement has its own manifesto titled "Honoring the Crone in All of Us." The movement seeks to raise members' consciousness about older women's issues, including death and dying, sexuality, housing, and spirituality (Kreilkamp 1994; Losee 1997). (These concerns are obviously not unique to older women.)

In this rapidly changing Information Age, the technical skills of older people may become obsolete, their pace may be too slow, and their strength limited. What the elderly *do have* is experience in many of life's main concerns, such as citizenship, friendship, family planning, child-rearing, career development, peace of mind, marital harmony, and human development. Such insight is a resource that elders can provide and that younger generations can use. We live in a period of human history in which most of us are overinformed and underenlightened. Resigned to a peer culture that a market society supports and reinforces, we are denied understanding of aging and the human life course that is gained best from intergenerational relationships. Consistent and meaningful exchange across generations and the understanding of humanity that it yields would, at the very least, urge us to celebrate birthdays without complaints, and at most, lead us to grow old gracefully and meaningfully. ☺

AGES AND COHORTS

Age is like many of the other social principles we have examined so far. Age unites and divides us, and it can be a basis for ranking. But age is unlike our

People of the same age or cohort share certain enculturative influences, experiences, recollections, preferences, and behavior. What are some generational markers of the twenty-first century American teenagers shown here?

other ascribed statuses—ethnicity, race, or gender, for example—in that we can expect to experience more than one, in fact several, age-based statuses during our lives. Most North Americans can join Sir Paul McCartney in wondering, "Will you still need me, will you still feed me, when I'm 64?" (although most 64-year-olds, indeed most 84-year-olds, are perfectly capable of feeding themselves).

The social significance of age differences is demonstrated by our many terms designating age categories and attributes. Babies, infants, toddlers, children, kids, juveniles, preteens, adolescents, teens, young, yuppies, adults, middle-aged, midlife crisis, maturity, old, seniors, elderly—many of the most common labels we use for our fellow citizens are based on age. Some of the categories have adjectives attached, suggesting stereotypes associated with that age category, for example, terrible twos. Some labels incorporate multiple social contrasts—yuppies are young urban professionals. The term *yuppie* blends age with residence (city) and occupation (professional), with a hint of class (upscale). *Retiree*, based on former work status, also implies a certain age range.

Two kinds of age-based statuses—age and generation, or cohort—are roughly comparable to what anthropologists call **age grades** and **age sets.** Thus, we can expect to go through certain age phases, categories, or grades, like infancy, childhood, adolescence, the college years, young adulthood, middle age, and old age. But also, by virtue of when we were born and what we experienced during our formative years, many of us belong to a culturally named generation, which is like an age set (see below). Thus, as *baby boomers* or *generation Xers*, we share or have shared certain enculturative influences, experiences, recollections, preferences, and behavior. Members of a generation, cohort, or age set share common memories. For example, the assassination of President John F. Kennedy was a defining event for boomers, as the stock market crash of October 1929, followed by the Great Depression, was for their parents. For what generation was September 11, 2001, a defining event? If we live to be 100 years old, we'll pass through the same age grades as everyone else, but we'll always belong to our age set, cohort, or generation.

Generations are distinguished by patterns of collective identity, behavior, beliefs, and values. *Generation X* includes some 17 million Americans born between 1961 and 1975. Market researchers associate this generation with self-indulgence, a sense of entitlement, materialism, prolonged adolescence, disregard for authority, and high distress levels, but also with commitment to a balanced way of life. For example, Generation X women seek a lifestyle that may be less profitable financially, but more fulfilling psychologically (Gutner 2002).

Generation Y includes Americans born between 1976 and 1994 (or 1999, according to some definitions). Also known as the "millennium generation" or "echo boomers," Generation Y numbers about 60 million people, compared to 72 million baby boomers (born between 1946 and 1964). Generation Y consists mainly of the sons and daughters of baby boomers. While they rival their parents' generation in size, members of the echo boom are much more racially diverse: One in three is not Caucasian. One in four lives in a single-parent household. Three in four have working mothers. Their core values are said to include self-expression, self-fulfillment, creativity, frugality, and public service (Ebenkamp and Barry 2001). Familiar with computers since childhood, members of Generation Y habitually use the Internet to explore sensitive issues they may want to conceal from their parents or friends (Lau 2002).

Market researchers believe that members of Generation Y, growing up in a media-saturated, brand-conscious world, respond to ads differently from their elders. They prefer to encounter ads in different places, such as on the Internet and cable TV. Raised in dual-income and single-parent families, these echo boomers are accustomed to financial responsibility. One in nine high school students has a credit card cosigned by a parent. Most expect to have careers. They are even planning home ownership, according to a 1998 survey of college freshman. "This is a very pragmatic group. At 18 years old, they have five-year plans. They are already looking at how they will be balancing their work/family commitments," said Deanna Tillisch, who directed the survey (quoted in Neuborne and Kerwin 2001).

In North America today, perhaps because of the value our culture bestows on youth, our age statuses are rough, informal, and blurred. The names of our generations tend to be terms that others employ to categorize us rather than labels we use for ourselves. Few people introduce themselves by saying, "Hi, I'm a baby boomer, and I'll be your server tonight." In other societies, however, age and generation are used more formally as principles of social organization—ways of organizing people, giving them a collective consciousness and group identity. In some nonindustrial societies anthropologists have described groups called **sodalities**, which are based on a common age or gender, with all-male sodalities more usual than all-female ones.

Pantribal sodalities are those that extend across the whole society or tribe, spanning several villages. The best examples of pantribal sodalities based on age and gender come from the native societies of the Central Plains of North America and from tropical Africa. Pantribal sodalities are especially likely to develop when there is warfare between tribes but no formal military apparatus. Male sodalities take the place of a standing army. Because such sodalities draw their members from different villages of the same tribe, they can mobilize men in many localities for attack or retaliation against another tribe.

During the 18th and 19th centuries, Indians of the Great Plains of the United States and Canada experienced a rapid growth of pantribal sodalities as their economy came to rely more on bison hunting on horseback. (Horses were reintroduced to North America by the Spanish after the native horse had gone extinct.) Two activities in the horse-bison economy demanded strong leadership: organizing and carrying out raids on enemy camps (to capture horses) and managing the summer bison hunt. Some of the Plains sodalities were age sets of increasing rank. A set was like a generation because it included all the men born during a certain time span. Each set had its distinctive dance, songs, possessions, and privileges. (In our society, boomers and Xers also share such things, but the association is less formally marked.) Among Plains Indians, members of each set would pool their wealth to buy admission to the next higher level (age grade) as they moved through a hierarchy based on age and seniority. Some of these sodalities were warrior associations. Their rituals celebrated militarism, and their leaders organized bison hunting and raiding. Those leaders also arbitrated disputes during the summer, when large numbers of people came together for the hunt.

Raiding of one tribe by another, but in this case for cattle rather than horses, was also common in eastern and southeastern Africa, where pantribal sodalities, including age sets, also developed. Among the Masai of Kenya, men born during the same four-year period were circumcised together and belonged to the same named group, an age set, throughout their lives. The sets moved through grades, the most important of which was the warrior grade. Members of the set wishing to enter the warrior grade were at first discouraged by its current occupants, who eventually would vacate that grade and marry. Members of a set felt a strong allegiance to one another and eventually had sexual rights to each other's wives. Masai women lacked comparable set organization, but they also passed through culturally recognized age grades: initiate, married woman, and postmenopausal woman.

To understand the difference between an age set and an age grade, think of a college class, the class of 2006, for example, and its progress through the university. The age set, or cohort, would be the group of people constituting the class of 2006. The successive college years—first year (freshman), sophomore, junior, and senior—would represent the age grades. The set passes through the grades together, then continues to be known as the class of 2006 even after it graduates.

In some societies, age (usually in combination with gender) also serves as the basis for membership in **secret societies**, which resemble the fraternities and sororities of North American colleges and universities. In certain parts of west and central Africa, the pantribal sodalities are secret societies, made up exclusively of men or women. Like our fraternities and sororities, these associations have secret initiation ceremonies. For example, among the Mende of Sierra Leone, men's and women's secret societies (known as *Poro* and *Sande*, respectively) have been very influential. The men's group, the Poro, trains boys in social conduct, ethics, and religion and supervises political and economic activities. Poro leaders, who play an important role in social control and dispute management, often have more power than village headmen do. *We see then that age and gender are principles that can link people into a single social collectivity and thus create a sense of common identity.*

Let's shift back to contemporary North America. We pass through roughly the same grades as our parents passed and as our children will pass. But there have been shifts in the meaning of the grades and in the cultural expectations associated with them. For example, people in their fifties felt and acted older a generation ago than they do today. Now actresses in their fifties, who would have been "over the hill" in the 1950s, can advertise gym equipment and cosmetics and still be Hollywood sex symbols. Many of Hollywood's leading action heroes are boomers or older (e.g., Harrison Ford).

Our current age, work, and family situations influence the ways in which we view other age groups. Kottak, who has been teaching college since he was 25, began to realize he was aging or getting older when his introductory students started looking like his children. His perception of his own aging strengthened when parents of current students started visiting his class to proclaim themselves his former students. As in the situational negotiation of ethnic identity discussed in Chapter 5, most people probably don't recognize aging by looking in the mirror; they do so situationally and by comparison, gradually perceiving themselves in relation to others who are younger or older.

THE GENERATION GAP

During the 1960s Margaret Mead helped publicize the notion of a *generation gap*. This was the idea that a cultural chasm had opened between American youth and their parents and grandparents. The impetus was the social context surrounding the unpopular Vietnam war, which young Americans resisted, as most of their parents and grandparents had not resisted previous wars, such as the Korean War or the two world wars. In the Vietnam era, young Americans (especially young men) perceived that their lives were being deployed by older people (especially older men) for goals that were not their own and that were not even just. In protesting the war and other social ills, youths used potent symbols, such as flag (and bra) burning, drug consumption, sexual promiscuity, vulgarity, and public confrontation to express resentment toward elders. Steeped in the Civil Rights movement and exposed to mass media as no previous generation had been, young Americans questioned and resisted traditional notions of order, propriety, and obedience. The media, in turn, played a powerful role in spreading images and fueling awareness of protests, opposition, and resistance. The generation gap opened alongside a class chasm, in that less financially privileged and less educated Americans were more likely to support the Vietnam War, and to be sent into it, than were their wealthier compatriots. Social polarization became the order of the day.

Mead's generational chasm was mainly evident in the United States, with echoes in Canada and western Europe. Today's generation gap is worldwide, as trends evident in the United States in the 1960s have achieved global significance. Among the most important is the information and image revolution—the spread of education and the influence of the mass media, particularly television. Nowadays in most parts of the world, members of the current younger generation, like the American baby boomers who came of age in the 1960s and 1970s, are better educated, more media exposed, and more world savvy than their elders. Even for people in very remote areas, the world is radically different from what it was 30 years ago. Third World villagers have never been truly isolated, and most were affected to some degree by colonialism. For generations, centuries, or even millennia in some regions, people in remote areas have encountered government officials and religious proselytizers seeking taxes, tithes, bodies, and souls; but exposure to external people, forces, information, and images has never been greater than it is today.

A proliferating and bewildering array of alien actors and agents now intrudes. Tourism has become the world's number-one industry. Development agents and NGOs entice local people toward their plans, projects, goals, and ideologies. Along with formal educational opportunities, the mass media spread information to rural areas. Development agents and the media preach that work should be for cash rather than mainly for subsistence. Young people feel too educated or too world-exposed to accept traditional jobs in the fishing craft or fields where their elders expected to make their living and where many older people still do labor.

However, today's world has too many young people and too few jobs to meet their expectations. Globally there is an unparalleled generation gap. The elders were raised in the context of ancestral tradition, mainly local experience, and a mainly subsistence economy. Young men and women, by contrast, have grown up in the presence of global forces, agents, images, and information, with opportunities for formal education and expecting eventual cash employment. Since few nations, within their formal economies, provide enough jobs to meet current qualifications and expectations, young people must pursue various alternatives. Worldwide, "informal" economic activities are often illegal and dangerous, with a transnational dimension. Such activities include cattle raiding and rustling (often for eventual sale to foreign markets), trade in arms and drugs, urban hooliganism and gang activities, and banditry. Fairly well educated young people comprise a significant proportion of the migration stream that currently links southern and northern countries. Underemployed and dissatisfied, youths join not only teams, gangs, and raiding parties but also militia, and fundamentalist and terrorist movements. Young men play a disproportionately large role in war and terrorism. Paradoxically, this age/gender-based contrast—this new global generation gap, particularly as it applies to young men—has received little systematic attention from scholars and policymakers. Globally, among men, generational differences may be even sharper than they are among women. The generation gap, and its effects by gender, class, and country, is an important issue demanding further study within the context of global diversity.

AN AGING POPULATION

The population of old people is also growing, especially in North America and western Europe. In 1994, in terms of elderly populations, the United States ranked third (33.2 million) among nations, behind only India (36.3 million) and mainland China (71.1 million). Elderly people, defined as those aged 65 and older, represent one-eighth of the U.S. population. Table 11–1 shows statistics on the elderly population in the United States in 2000.

The oldest old—people aged 85 and over—compose the most rapidly growing elderly age group in the United States. Between 1960 and 1994, their numbers rose 274 percent, compared with just 45 percent for the overall U.S. population. By 2050 the oldest old are projected to number 19 million, or 5 percent of the U.S. population. The health of and care for this rapidly growing elderly population will become pressing issues (U.S. Bureau of the Census 1996b).

The implications of age vary by gender. Men tend to have higher death rates at every age than women do. Figure 11–1 shows the number of men per 100 women by age group in 2000. In the U.S. population under age 20, there were 105 males per 100 females. By age 85, the ratio reverses dramatically, with two women for every man. As a result of this disparity in survival, most elderly men are married, whereas most elderly women are not. Elderly men were much more likely than their female counterparts to be married and living with their spouse (74 percent of men versus 42 percent of women in 1999). Elderly women were more than three times as likely as

TABLE 11–1. Elderly Population of the United States in Millions, 2000

Youngest old (aged 65 to 74)	18.4
Middle old (75 to 84)	12.4
Oldest old (85 or older)	4.2
Elderly total	35.0

Source: Brunner, ed. 2002, p. 121.

elderly men to be widowed (45 percent versus 14 percent in 1999) and thus to live alone (Brunner, ed., 2002, 125).

Compared with other Americans, old people tend to be politically active and economically secure. Politicians are well aware that the elderly are the most reliable of all voters. (It's interesting to speculate about whether this is a cohort effect or an age effect. That is, do older people vote more consistently because their generation has always done so, or is there something about getting old that motivates people to go to the polls?) In constant dollars, the median income for elderly persons tripled between 1957 and 2000. It rose from $6,537 to $19,168 for men and from $3,409 to $10,899 for women. Elderly women had a higher poverty rate (12 percent) than elderly men did (7 percent). (U.S. Census 2000).

Among the elderly, poor health is not as common as might be assumed. In 1992 a striking 75 percent of all noninstitutionalized Americans aged 65 to 74, and 67 percent of those aged 75 and older, considered their health to be good or better (U.S. Census 1995, Statistical Brief, SB 95-8). Despite the prevalent idea (and fear) of the nursing home lurking around the corner, most elderly Americans do live independently or with family members. In fact, the number of elderly Americans living in nursing homes declined from 5.1 percent in 1990 to 4.5 percent in 2000 (U.S. Census 2000). A new autonomy for the elderly, most of whom now live in their own homes with adequate incomes, has a clear economic basis. In general, the elderly have more assets than younger people do. Although 35 percent of the elderly were poor in 1959, that figure had declined to 9.6 percent in 2000. Other segments of the American population were not doing nearly as well as the elderly in terms of overall poverty reduction .

In nonindustrial societies people tend to live with family members until they die. Where do elderly North Americans live? Even if they are not in nursing homes, the elderly, like other segments of the U.S. population, do tend to be more socially isolated from their families than was the case 50 years ago. By 1980, when 5 percent of American old people lived in nursing homes, a much smaller percentage (9 percent) lived with their families than was the case in 1950 (31 percent). The average number of Americans per household has declined steadily from 4.8 in 1900 to 3.4 in 1960, 3.1 in 1970, 2.7 in 1980, and 2.6 in 2000 (*World Almanac and Book of Facts* 1985, 246; U.S. Census 2000). Twenty percent of American households had at least five members in 1970. By 2000 this figure had shrunk to 10 percent.

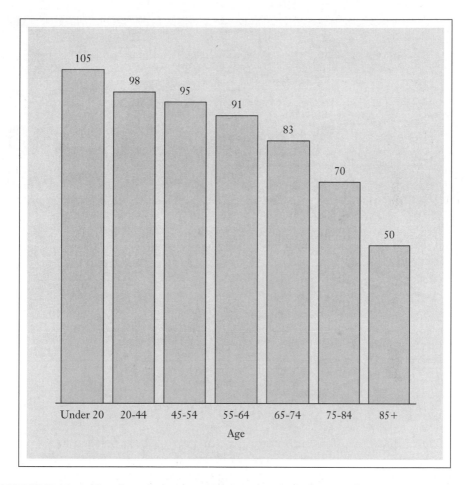

FIGURE 11–1 Number of men per 100 women, United States, by age group, 2000.
Source: U.S. Bureau of the Census. Current Population Survey. March 2000.

Many older people continue to work outside the home. Women compose a growing percentage of the older labor force (55 years and over), rising from 23 percent in 1950 to 44 percent in 1993. One recent trend, especially among men, has been early retirement. In part, earlier retirement has been made possible by rising Social Security payments. Social Security benefits jumped 900 percent between 1950 and 1983, as wages grew 400 percent and prices rose just 300 percent (*Time* 1985). However, there are also signs that some retirees are choosing to reenter the workforce, for varied reasons. Previewing a trend likely to intensify with the aging of the baby boomers, more older people are working part time. Half of American men over 65 worked part time in 1988, versus just a third in 1960 (*New York Times* 1989). Even more of them might be working if Social Security benefits were not taxed above a certain income.

Many older Americans are politically active, economically secure, and determined to ensure their rights. Politicians are well aware that the elderly are the most reliable of all voters. Gladys Lagasse of Tiverton, RI, front center, joins other senior citizens in 1999 in "mass senior action" aimed at universal health care.

THE AGING PROCESS

The aging process offers opportunities for personal expression and collective identity. A woman in her early twenties expresses her young adulthood and educational status by serving in the Peace Corps before pursuing a degree in law. Members of the "Golden Club" shop at their local grocery store on "senior discount day." American children, by virtue of their age, become "preschoolers." Menopausal women, by virtue of their age, construct a support group to help ease a life-course transition. While aging implies physical decline, elders' social engagement continues as long as their minds are healthy.

In colonial times "the powers and privileges of old age were firmly anchored in the society" (Fisher 1978, 58). Veneration of the elderly was due in part to the fact that old age was fairly rare. Given the economic and political structure of early, Puritan North America, wealthy old white men were valued and protected by the state, while poor widows were often marginalized (Fisher 1978). In Chapter 9 we argued that women's status increases relative to their participation in the economy. The value and treatment of the elderly are also linked to their role in production.

Aging is a human universal. The experience and meaning of being old vary, however, according to sex, class, and national or ethnic affiliation. In rural Africa, the elderly, although few in number, tend to be powerful socially and symbolically, as guardians of cultural knowledge. In Hong Kong, physical well-being and productivity decline during the fifties, and being old is associated with inability to work rather than with formal retirement. In Ireland and the United States, senior status is marked at age 65, relative to eligibility for pensions and for full Social Security benefits (Fry 2000).

The well-being of the elderly depends on cultural interpretations of old age and on the social support available to senior citizens. Health-related self-profiles of 252 elderly people in the United States, India, and Congo/Zaire reveal a relationship between biological decline and sociocultural systems of elder care. The American elderly express a denial of death, and value physical and mental health, autonomy, and proactive health behaviors. Congolese elderly accept decline in strength and mobility, expect support by their children, and hope for a good death. Indian elderly fear psychophysical decline, ill health, and dependence. Their concern for a peaceful death finds expression in meditation and other behaviors intended to improve their health (Westerhof et al. 2000).

Gerontological theory and practice must consider the psychological and sociocultural dimensions of aging along with the economic conditions and biomedical issues of the aged. Personal and professional trajectories lead people across state boundaries and oceans, away from hometowns and family. Most North Americans continue to care for their parents by making regular visits, sending money, calling regularly, and including them in family affairs. Elder care is designed to help those who can no longer function as independent adults. In Europe and North America, caregivers include professionals employed by private and government agencies. Paid assistants, including neighbors and friends, also help the elderly with house maintenance, transportation, and shopping. During her field research with elderly Greek people in Chicago, Kozaitis helped her research participants by driving them to various destinations and helping them run errands. She served also as their interpreter during visits to their doctors, the Social Security office, and the local recreational facility for retirees (Kozaitis 1987).

Medications, along with labor-saving and strength-preserving devices, help elderly people who can afford them to live a fuller, more active life. In a market society where goods and services related to elder care can be bought, the wealthier elderly have an easier time than the elderly poor. Elder care also subsumes geriatric care centers, assisted living facilities, continuing care residential communities, and nursing homes—all of which are costly.

Elder care remains a challenge for families and governments. The demographic shift (the baby boom) between the end of World War II and the start of the Vietnam War has produced what Peterson calls the approaching "Gray Dawn" (1999). Increased life expectancies translate into a large retiring population in need of financial security, housing, health, and social well-being. Scholars, local communities, and policymakers urge development of strategic plans to accommodate the "age wave" that a retiring but diverse baby-boom generation in the United States, Japan, France, and Germany is ushering into the 21st century (Villanueva 2000).

Organized efforts to build political unity among the old proliferate—promoting their safety, health, and general well-being. For many retirees, old age offers new opportunities for self-actualization in the form of creative pursuits, new friendships, and exploration of new horizons through travel. A culture constructed by, of, and for the "new aged" is taking root in our society. The saying "Go south, old woman, go south" describes the migration patterns of the elderly to Florida, Arizona, southern New Mexico, and the Rio Grande valley in Texas, where they design and pursue a lifestyle of their own (Rose 1997; *Economist* 2002). In the United States, there is substantial segregation—social and residential—between age groups, compared to African, Asian, and European societies.

INTERGENERATIONAL CONFLICT

In North America and western Europe the cost of supporting an aging population has become a political concern. In the United States this issue will become more volatile by 2011, when the baby boomers start turning 65. People are living longer, and their care has become a personal issue as well as one of policy. Baby boomers, for example, now face a new generational predicament. They are being characterized as the *sandwich generation*. This term describes them as sandwiched between the generations before and after them. Added to child care responsibilities are elder care obligations. In practice, women tend to be especially burdened. As our kids finally get raised, our parents start declining. If that nursing home does indeed lurk around the corner, it will cost more annually than an Ivy League college, with no degree or future at the end. It is likely, however, that society, rather than family, will assume most of the burden of caring for this growing elderly population.

What resources are available for support and care of the elderly? How long will Social Security be kept solvent? Because the answers to these questions remain uncertain, hearsay answers and dire predictions abound. Regularly, we hear these through the mass media, which provide an excellent channel for monitoring social concerns, ideas, and divisions in our society. Young white male workers, in particular, use call-in shows to complain about benefits they perceive as being taken from them and given to other groups, such as Social Security recipients, welfare mothers, women, and minorities. On the other hand, those groups, which are organized politically in such national NGOs as the NAACP and NOW and in more localized (community) organizations (e.g., Haitians in New York), complain that white males still have privileged access to resources.

The allocation of social benefits by age is not just a North American issue. It is even more vexing for western European nations, whose social programs have tended to be more generous than are those of the United States. The German retirement system, for example, was established by Chancellor

Bismarck following the first German unification in 1871. Benefits began by age 65, in an era when the average life expectancy was 45 years, versus over 70 years today. The German retirement age, which until recently was 60 for women and 63 for men, was raised in 1996 to 65 for both.

In the German system current workers directly subsidize retired people. Retirees get 70 percent of the salary they earned during their last few working years. This is like the U.S. system, in that current Social Security payments also fund much of current expenditures, but the German benefits are much more lavish. In the United States a portion of the current worker's salary is placed in a fund for future payment. The supply of future workers to support the older generation is much scarcer in Germany than in the United States. In Germany, Spain, and Italy the average couple has about 1.25 children, versus 2.05 in the United States.

Given Germany's low birthrate, fewer and fewer native-born young people will enter a workforce on which more and more old people will depend for their pensions. In Germany 15.3 percent of the population is 65 or older, versus 12.8 percent in the United States, whose Social Security system pays benefits to 44 million people, of whom 31 million are retirees.

The growing social tension, for many of the same reasons, between old and young is expressed in more extreme form in many European nations, such as Germany, than in the United States. As an official of the Education Ministry in Bonn observed, "We are not talking left/right as the basic social division but young/old" (Cowell 1997, A8). The newspaper *Die Woche* commented that "the prospect of lower pensions at the end of a working life marked by higher contributions is causing many young employees to doubt the validity and justice of the system" (A8).

To change the current system would require greater political mobilization of young voters, either in Germany or the United States, than is true now. Germany's 16 million pensioners are not organized in the same powerful lobby as are the 35 million retirees in the United States, but they are conscientious voters (Cowell 1997).

THE SOCIAL CONSTRUCTION OF CHILDHOOD

Like other aspects of diversity discussed in this book, childhood is socially constructed. Age grades or developmental stages in the life cycle are recognized in all societies, but the names, lengths, perceived attributes, and expected behavior of those stages vary among societies. In any human population, children and adults are biologically different, but cultures vary in their opinions about when childhood (and humanity) begin and end and about what the characteristics of childhood are. Among the Betsileo of Madagascar (Kottak 1980) children acquire their humanity gradually. During infancy they are seen as fragile and not quite human, and they get special treatment designed to enhance the chances of their survival. Parents apply a special paste to babies' heads to ensure that the cranial sutures will close properly. Infants are not praised or complimented, since that might attract the attention of envious ancestors, who might rob the baby for the spirit world. Instead babies get insults. Never does one hear, "What a cute baby!" Instead it's proper to call infants little dogs, anthills, or pieces of shit. If an infant dies, it is excluded from the ancestral tomb and buried in the rice fields. Given survival past infancy, humanity develops gradually and may be marked eventually in a name-changing ceremony.

In his oft-cited book *Centuries of Childhood*, the social historian Philippe Aries (1962) argues that the very concept of childhood was missing in medieval Europe. His analysis of the paintings of that time suggested that children beyond infancy were seen as miniature adults. By the 18th century, Aries argues, the notion of childhood as a distinct stage and sphere of life had developed. The Industrial Revolution, which began around 1750, separated the adult-focused world of work from the home, where nuclear families and children lived. Industrial society constructed childhood as a distinct stage of life, with special attributes and needs (see Stephens 1995).

If childhood did not exist in medieval society, it seems to last forever in our own. The illusion of perpetual youth captures men and women, serving as the basis for thriving cosmetic, clothing, and fitness industries. "Grow up," radio therapists admonish callers who fail to accept adult responsibilities. How long can we go on living with our parents before we finally "get a life"? TV talk shows revel in the infantile behavior of adults. The horde of helping professionals who write books and promote them through the electronic media have propagated the ideas of "adult children" and "the inner child" (Ivy 1995). Marilyn Ivy (1995) quotes from Charles Whitfield's book *Healing the Child Within*: "Since up to 95 percent of families are dysfunctional, we're all adult children either doing our work of recovery or in need of it. Even though our Child Within has gone into hiding, it never dies. When we rescue that frightened, wondrous inner being, we reclaim the power, creativity, and vitality to make life a spiritual adventure" (Ivy 1995, 89). (Or, an anthropologist might suggest, we might call it a little dog, a pesky anthill, or a piece of shit and hope the ancestors would come and remove it, so we could get on with our adult lives. And any social scientist would question the unsupported assertion that 95 percent of families are dysfunctional.)

In some segments of North American society, childhood seems to go on forever. But in other segments and contexts, the adult world increasingly intrudes on childhood. In a larger sense, contemporary North America seems to be witnessing a blurring of the boundaries between childhood and adulthood. As adults are being urged to discover an inner child and to assume identities as adult children, children are being thrust into adulthood. Little bodies are glamorized—dressed up, cosmeticized, and encouraged to emulate teen pop stars and beauty pageant dolls. Neil Postman (1982) laments the role of the mass media in eroding childhood, as advertising and commerce draw kids into the adult world of conspicuous consumption and preprofessional training. As homes are penetrated by television, cable, the VCR, and the Internet, kids have increased access to images of violence, sex, and other adult fare. Formerly privileged information, available only to mature people, is now more generally accessible. In our own society, age-based differences involving knowledge and information appear to be decreasing. But in the rest of the world, as we have seen, a chasm has developed between the old subsistence-oriented, traditional generation and the new media-exposed, cash-oriented, globalized one.

Of course, the expectations, responsibilities, behavior, and experiences associated with being a child vary by social class as well as among cultures. The world's street children, of whom there are millions, including those in such North American cities as Los Angeles and Toronto, habitually fend for themselves, with the help of their age mates more than their parents. The world of street children, who often support themselves by sex work, begging, robbery, and other illegal activities, includes abused substances and bodies. In many Third World societies, children continue to make important contributions to family income. In countries such as Bosnia, Rwanda, Burundi, and Congo, children are perhaps the most powerless victims of war, starvation, and refugee crises. Generally, in Africa and Asia, when kids get AIDS, it is because they have inherited the HIV virus from their parents. People in societies with poor public health and high death rates, especially high infant mortality, tend to have many children, hoping that some will survive.

Our society tells us to offer sensitivity, loving care, and professional help to our real children and to our "inner children." But, remembering that diversity exists within any social category, we should not overlook the children (and adults) who are forced to live underprivileged lives. Those include the children of poverty, of illness, and of social disorder—homeless children; children of the streets; brain-damaged and HIV-infected children; and other children who, before or after birth, have been otherwise abused or victimized.

CHAPTER TWELVE

Bodies, Fitness, and Health

——— BODY POLITICS ———

Like gender, race, and sexual orientation, *health* is socially constructed. So-cieties attribute different meanings and functions to the human body. The most prevalent perception is that the body should be young, healthy, fit, and without defects. So pervasive is the ideal of a sound body that a blemish of any sort triggers a battle for self-esteem.

In a society organized around work, pregnancy becomes a physical dis-order that subjects women to discrimination and low self-esteem. We inter-nalize our society's standard of fitness. We must have "a body that won't quit." Our culture's beauty ideal is supermodel thin. No wonder women get anxious during pregnancy. The pregnant body, which nonindustrial soci-eties view as a sacred vessel, is considered by ours to be compromised. Em-ployers remind us that "disfigurement" during pregnancy lessens capacity, performance, and appearance. The female director of a medical school's fel-lowship program admits to rejecting applications from women: "They get pregnant and don't finish on time." A professional woman seeking a job in a large corporation concealed her "reproductive agenda," fearing rejection as a desirable employee. "Don't tell your advisor; he'll have a fit!" a depart-mental secretary warned a pregnant graduate student.

For many people, a physical ailment becomes some kind of meaningful, life-altering event. For example, regarding cancer as a "disease of repression or inhibited passion" may encourage one to suddenly find meaning in life, indulge in self-expression, get a handle on priorities, and exercise autonomy in new ways. On the other hand, cancer perceived as "debris" or "residue" accumulated during an active life of uninhibited growth and development may encourage one to engage enthusiastically in its treatment regimen. Chemotherapy and radiation take on the form of spring-cleaning, a cleansing and tune-up of the body to ensure efficient functioning and continued self-actualization.

Fitness requires both biochemical treatment and psychosocial management. A man encourages a woman in therapy for breast cancer: "The doctors will do what they can, but we're talking to the man upstairs!" "We're all behind you," someone else chimes in. "We need you; you're too valuable to us," a third asserts. Still another insists, "Big girls just handle it—SNAP!"

Non-Westerners have always known something that medical anthropologists are teaching the industrial West: Health reflects a person's psychological state, or positive attitude. An optimistic mental outlook is itself generated and reinforced by social support. Disorders of the *body* don't exist independently of the *person*. Since persons don't exist independently of society, one's health status is intrinsically both a psychological, private predicament and a social, public concern. In *The Body Silent* (1990) the anthropologist Robert F. Murphy describes his experience with a spinal tumor that resulted in paralysis. He found that his physical deterioration was accompanied by a reduction in his social status and his sense of self. His new profile raised his awareness of our society as one that treats disability as abnormal and the disabled as aliens.

Meeting the special needs of people with disabilities is a challenge for society. Unlike tribal or agrarian societies, in which individuals with any disability were cared for by relatives, "the unfit" in industrial society become a special policy issue. Capitalist, market-based North America has little tolerance or patience for those whose participation is compromised by less than optimum capacity to produce for profit. Our social structure selects out and marginalizes persons with any physical or cognitive limitation from *the pool of the fit*. Such classifications as "the disabled," "the impaired," and "the handicapped" tend to stigmatize individuals by accentuating the disorder and minimizing their humanity.

Kozaitis has worked with young people with sickle-cell anemia, hemophilia, and cancer. She observed a tendency for neighbors, teachers, and classmates to disengage from sick children. But those children themselves were not interested in assuming a new identity as "a patient," as "special," or as "sick." The kids were even less eager to accept a way of life as, in the words of a 16-year-old girl with Hodgkin's disease, "damaged goods." Because of their chronic illness, all the kids spent long periods of time in the hospital as patients. Nonetheless, their self-images as children, teens, and students continued and dominated their conversations and interests. This knowledge led to a treatment plan requiring numerous home and school visits by the social worker to ensure that all interventions were designed with the whole child in mind. The treatment team devised ways for the children to continue to participate in neighborhood and school activities (e.g., through birthday parties and homework) to the extent they were *able*.

Social structures and institutions alienate, marginalize, and often threaten people with disabilities. Supported by our economic and political structure, the media promote the body as a commodity. Bodies are objects to be bought and sold, provided they are young and healthy, with mass aesthetic appeal. American national character prides itself on strength, endurance, and self-reliance. Our predecessors advanced an ethos of rugged individualism and independence. These values still drive us to compete and to conquer, especially in the world of work: "Only the strong survive." The adage "The early bird catches the worm" alerts us that achievement and success, financial and social, require an early start, speed, and competition. This strategy generates a pecking order of later birds who end up with fewer worms. Accepting another American value, "Effort counts," Americans with disabilities may overcompensate by pushing their bodies to meet goals and perform tasks using standards their "abled" counterparts set and reward.

Countering the *social construction of disability*, contemporary civil rights movements by people with disabilities reflect the *cultural construction of fitness*. Educated people who understand the role of agency in creating culture fight to dispel the popular misconception that "disability" means "inferiority." They have forged a civil rights movement that helps them claim their embodiment by encouraging expression of personal interpretations of the body and defining the collective experience of "being different." A person with AIDS explains he always feels "so diseased" in the presence of colleagues at work, but that with other persons with AIDS and with supporters he feels "safe, normal, and protected."

America's mainstream contains various groups of people who use particular conditions as the main criterion of membership around which they create experience and meaning. The formation of cancer support groups; Alcoholics Anonymous (AA) support groups; and communities such as those of the deaf, the blind, and the autistic provide shelter for individuals who find themselves alone and misunderstood. Such people struggle to win a place apart from society's margins as "the disabled" and within its mainstream as "human beings who happen to have a disability." In doing so, they create a "culture of disability." That is, they develop organized conceptions of living that integrate conditions related to an illness or impairment. Collectively they seek to show that societal participation continues despite a physical limitation, that contribution to society includes not-for-profit goods and services, that productivity may be measured as much by quality as by quantity, and that beauty isn't always visually apparent.

Their efforts resist and subvert the social standards of fitness that alienate and exclude them. Such groups promote standards of nondiscriminatory presentation and practice and fair representation of people with disabilities. One of their initiatives focuses on eliminating discriminatory language that devalues and depersonalizes the human being by emphasizing the disability. Such terms include "handicapped," "able-bodied," "physically challenged," "memory impaired," and "differently able." Use of phrases like "people who are deaf," "people with vision impairment," and "people with epilepsy" is preferred. There are no "victims of AIDS," only "persons with AIDS." A person "uses a wheelchair," is not "confined to a wheelchair" or "wheelchair-bound." According to the code of conduct that people with disabilities have established, they are not to be pitied, feared, or ignored. Neither should they be treated as heroic, courageous, or special, but as another way of being normal.

Individual strategies and collective demonstrations of ability in social and occupational arenas alter both public perceptions and structural accommodation of people with particular physical or cognitive limitations. Public policies—for example, the 1990 Americans with Disabilities Act (ADA) and the National Health Law Program (NHeLP)—influence daily operations in business, education, and other occupational settings. Multiple local associations—for instance, the Autism Network, American Disabled for Attendant Programs Today (ADAPT), and Active Voices in Disability (AVID)—serve to "educate ourselves, all levels of government, the general community, and business on disability issues such as accessibility, transportation, employment, home health care, and resources." In today's multicultural society, public opinions and public spaces increasingly accommodate a category of Americans whose difference is the impetus for claiming their common humanity. ☺

CULTURE AND THE BODY

Like our ages, and related to aging, our bodies also make us different. Here we are referring not to the racial and gender differences discussed in previous chapters but to other kinds of contrasts in bodies and their adornment. Among African Americans, for example, variations in skin color are important in personal identity, just as differences in hair and eye color are important among whites. Regardless of race, gender, ethnicity, or sexual orientation, there are fat people, thin people, pretty people, ugly people, short people, tall people, well people, sick people, body builders, and pierced people.

In Chapter 7's discussion of sports success in relation to race, gender, and culture, we considered how culture molds phenotype by promoting certain activities, discouraging others, and setting standards of physical fitness and attractiveness. Bodies—ideal, actual, and normal—vary from culture to culture and within one culture over time. This chapter examines bodies and enhancements to them.

Ideal bodies change from generation to generation and, with the influence of the mass media, even from decade to decade. Old movies make it easy for us to study bodies and clothing over time. Such movie stars of the past as Humphrey Bogart and Barbara Stanwyck wore stylish hats and smoked cigarettes. Contemporary American men and women wear baseball caps and lift weights. When asked how he recognized Americans in the street, one European mentioned lifting (of weights, and its effects on the body) and tennis shoes (an item of dress considered inelegant in Europe, but a mainstay of hard-core American touring).

Ideas about the attractiveness and fitness of bodies also vary in time and space. In today's North America, muscles are in vogue for both men and women. Rosemary Clooney (a popular singer in the 1950s and the aunt of TV/movie star George Clooney) never did push-ups when she sang America's number-one song, as lead singer Gwen Stefani of the rock group No Doubt has done in videos.

If many are more muscular, many Americans are also fatter than the average American man or woman of the same age a generation ago. American women are more likely to be overweight than men are. Women also tend to worry more about being fat than men do and are more likely than men are to suffer from body image eating disorders, such as bulimia and anorexia.

Cultures vary in their emphasis on beauty as well as in their beauty standards. In Brazil feminine beauty is an obsession among the elites. That culture still views women mainly as sex objects and reproducers rather than producers. Brazilian women who can afford to lift sagging faces and bodies do so, not through exercise so much as by means of the surgeon's knife. Plastic surgery has been in vogue for rich, and even middle-class, Brazilian women longer than it has been in the United States, where it is now a spreading industry catering to aging baby boomers of both sexes.

Relevant to the cross-cultural understanding of beauty and the body is the contrast between ascribed and achieved status. Remember that individuals have little control over the ascribed statuses they occupy (e.g., age, gender), which depend on intrinsic qualities, what one is rather than what one does. On the other hand, people have more control over—more to *do* with—the achieved statuses (e.g., student, tennis player) they occupy. Since—in the eyes of American law, if hardly in reality—we start out the same, American culture emphasizes achieved over ascribed status. An American's identity emerges as a result of what he or she does or fails to do. We are supposed to make of our lives and our selves what we will and can. Success comes through achievement—making it or making it over.

In Brazil, by contrast, social identity rests on *being rather than doing*, on what one is from the start, within a family, kin network, and social class. Family position and network membership contribute substantially to self-image, identity, and fortune. How does the contrast of being versus doing apply to beauty? Brazilian culture treats physical attractiveness as an intrinsic attribute. Kids who are identified as beautiful or handsome in early childhood tend to keep that label as part of their self-image through life. Those considered plain or ugly also internalize those labels. Such perceptions usually persist—within a sibling group, for example—regardless of what people look like as adults. They last even into old age, when the "pretty sister" remains just that, regardless of her actual appearance. One might argue that in Brazil the role of plastic surgery is to maintain or restore beauty, whereas in the United States plastic surgery is more often used to create or augment beauty, as with breast implants and penis enlargement. In America most nose jobs are done to correct blemishes that have been there from the start.

In a "doing culture" like that of the United States, we believe we can do something about our appearance, and new technology has fueled this perception. Makeovers have become a national TV obsession. Body image has become an achieved status, over which we believe we have considerable control. When one's body doesn't fit, or no longer fits, our image of what it should be, there are entire industries (e.g., plastic surgery, cosmetics, and fitness centers) waiting to help. A generation ago the best hotels offered pools for lounging and tanning but not lap swimming. Missing then, too, were hotel health clubs, replete with weight machines, StairMasters, and treadmills. Movie stars may have had personal trainers, but young urban professionals did not, as many do today.

The media constantly remind us that we, or some expert, can do something about the way we look and about the ways our bodies (and minds) function. Waiting out there to help us build better bodies, look better, and feel fitter are thousands of products and devices: home gyms, exercise machines, AbSculptors, bun builders. And if hard work or "just minutes a day" can't do it, there are always surgeons standing by, to do penis augmentation, breast enhancement or reduction, and liposuction.

This same tendency to see us in control of our bodies shows up in our habit of assigning blame for illness. When we hear that someone has lung cancer, we immediately ask whether he or she smoked.

Our wish to assign responsibility for misfortune is reminiscent of witchcraft among the Azande of Africa, as described by the anthropologist E. E. Evans-Pritchard (1929/1970, 1937). When a wooden granary collapsed and killed a man seated underneath, the Azande blamed witchcraft for the accident. The Western, "rational" explanation for that event was that destruction by termites caused the structure to fall (plus bad luck for the man seated below). But the Azande ask: Why did it fall when it did? And why did that particular man happen to be the one who was killed? Clearly, someone was using witchcraft to attack a specific other. (To find out the witch's identity, the Azande consult oracles.) For the Azande it is necessary to assign blame for misfortune, and it is witches, discovered through oracles, who get blamed.

Like the Azande, Americans also have ideas about individual responsibility for misfortune, but they don't usually involve malevolent witches. If a third party bears blame, lawyers, judges, and juries (our oracles) are available to conduct our version of the Azande witch-hunt. More often, our value of individual responsibility leads us to blame ourselves or to blame victims for their illnesses. Thus, we tend to blame people with sexually transmitted diseases for their unwise or promiscuous sexual behavior. We are more likely to sympathize with hemophiliacs who have acquired HIV through transfusions than with those who got the virus through sexual activity, particularly homosexual activity. The focus on the power of doing, or achieving,

In a fitness-minded culture, with trainers, instructors, and equipment all around us, we can always do something about our appearance. In today's North America, firm bodies and working out are in vogue—for both men and women. Shown here, an aerobics class in Boston, Massachusetts.

creates an irrational attitude that we can fend off all risks if we just live right (and regulate the activities of others, e.g., smoking, pollution that may damage the environment and endanger public health).

American culture has been called youth-obsessed. The huge baby-boomer generation, known for its narcissism and conspicuous consumption, began turning 50 in 1996. It will surely carry its search for the perfect body, and willingness to pay for it, with it into its fifties and beyond. Plastic surgery and cosmetics will flourish as boomer men and women turn increasingly to face-lifts, liposuction, hair transplants, and other forms of surgical body alteration. Men will go on adding and removing facial hair. Men and women will continue to change their hair length, color, and styles.

In the Terence McNally play *Master Class*, the Maria Callas character admonishes someone in the audience to "get a look," something distinctive that makes a person stand out. The way we dress is part of our look and thus of the body image we project. The beauty and fashion industries are built on our wishes to look good, to dress well, and to fulfill certain images.

Although our own body image may not correspond very closely to what others see, or to what actually is, body types and images do affect our self-confidence and the way we are treated. Certain looks are valued more and others less, and differentially by context. The emaciation of certain models may make them grotesque or ugly outside the context of photography. American society tends to discriminate against people who are fat, small, or ugly. But there is hope. In a fitness-minded culture, with body improvement consultants all around us, we can always do something about our appearance.

Looks, and stereotypes about them, have class implications, thus helping Americans make social distinctions in a culture whose dominant ideology is opposed to class distinctions. What kind of facial hair would you find on a "lowlife sleazeball"? Would he smoke? What brand of cigarette? Old movies remind us that smoking used to be fashionable, with Bette Davis and Humphrey Bogart as incarnations of that image. Although smoking has staged a slight comeback in recent years, its image is decidedly more negative now than it was before the 1960s. Also, cigarette smoking today is something of a class marker. In her study of social class contrasts in American high schools, Penelope Eckert (1989) showed cigarette smoking to be the key identifying symbol of working-class kids (burnouts) versus their middle- and upper-middle-class public school colleagues (jocks). Those today who consider it cool to smoke are likely to belong to a particular social group. (A power image may be associated with cigars.)

Long hair, permed hair, blond hair, and versions of facial hair move in and out of fashion, but at any one time, a fad has class attributes. Besides class, certain groups, such as lesbians and gay men, may be marked by looks, gestures, and mannerisms.

Like our use of language (Chapter 15), our looks, dress, and gestures are means we employ, consciously and unconsciously, to communicate about ourselves. Consider the costumes that mark certain contexts and professions and the implications of dress and body image for the way we are perceived, received, and treated socially. In one study, physicians took more seriously the health complaints of an actress dressed in a business suit and with subtle verbal expression than those of the same woman dressed in gaudy attire and speaking flamboyantly (*New York Times* 1997).

Costumes mark professions. Kottak remembers a colleague, Daniel Moerman, commenting that men in positions of authority (judges, doctors, priests) tend to wear "dresses." Uniforms are badges of certain professions, like law enforcement. Suits are mandatory in many business firms and law offices.

Still, people of every social class wear jeans at least occasionally and in casual contexts. Individuals tend to pick a jeans brand and be loyal to it. Thus, as we engage in mass consumption of the same product, we still express our individuality by affiliation with a brand. (Brand loyalty is a variant, perhaps less intense, of the team loyalty we see in sports.)

Distinct bodies and on-the-field attire are associated with athletic pursuits. What images come to mind when you think of a basketball player, a quarterback, a running back, a golfer, a tennis player? Athletes may be stars in contemporary North America, but there is also discrimination against them. As our culture maintains stereotypes about dumb blondes, bimbos, and twinks, college students also have stereotypes about the off-the-field behavior and abilities of football and basketball players. In an academic setting, team sports bear some stigma among those who do not play. The idea that brains and brawn can't coexist in the same body has diminished somewhat but is still around.

WELL AND SICK BODIES

Bodies may be well, or they may be sick, temporarily or permanently. Ill bodies may become the basis for an identity and thereby enter the arena of identity politics. Robert Murphy (1990) points out that the "sick person" (especially one who is chronically or very ill) is expected to play a *role*. He or she is expected to bear the illness with stoicism and good humor, cooperating and minimizing complaints to caregivers and visitors. Our culture inculcates an attitude that people should be grateful for the health care they receive. Infractions of this attitude, by the militantly disabled, for example, conflict with American views about proper "sick person" comportment.

Some illness behavior is culturally learned; some is physiological. Some cultures encourage people to talk about being sick; others are more stoic. Brazilians have no compunction about publicly discussing their bouts with diarrhea, as an American youth might declare, "I'm wasted, man." But if the ill don't tell us, how do we know when people are unwell? When cats and dogs get sick, their fur droops, and they look unkempt. Are there similar signs with people? Sneezing and coughing fits are distancing mechanisms; people move away from us when we show signs of infection. What does it mean when someone says, "You look tired"? Knowing one has HIV, herpes, asthma, hemophilia, or a heart condition affects body image and feelings about fitness, as does surgery for breast cancer, or even for appendix removal, which may leave a telltale scar.

A permanent physical or health condition can become the basis of an identity, such as a person with a disability. The medical profession may play a role in labeling people with reference to an illness and thus contribute to the internalization of a health condition as part of a person's identity. Physicians and nurses may refer to people by their malady, for example as "diabetics" or "asthmatics." (In Brazil, people with AIDS are called *aideticos*. The American translation would be "aidetics.") The illness becomes an ascribed status, part of what one is, a fact considered paramount in treating the person, socially and medically. According to labeling theory, in society

Today, people with illnesses and disabilities organize politically. Identity politics encompasses illness-based identities, such as "people living with AIDS" and "breast cancer survivors." The group names tend to stress that these are people first, unlike the medical profession, which tends to treat them as "cases." Shown here in 2001, members of an Oregon breast cancer survivors team win their heat in the World Dragon Boat championships.

people are assigned labels with associated roles. Eventually they come to internalize the label as part of their sense of self and to learn and act out the stereotyped behavior that society assigns to the role.

Today, both reflecting and resisting such labels, people with illnesses and disabilities organize politically. Identity politics encompasses illness-based identities, such as people living with AIDS. The group names stress that these are *people* first, unlike the medical profession, which tends to treat them as cases and to use disease-based identity labels (e.g., diabetic). There are also militant organizations of people with disabilities; some advocate wearing the disability like a badge. One group called Let the Children Stare, which advocates pride in disability, has criticized the actor Christopher Reeve for wanting to get better.

There are class-based, age-based, and gender-based differences with respect to health, fitness, and illness. (Women's health issues are the focus of a special section of the *New York Times* regularly published in June.) Wealth and health are correlated; the working rich get better health care than do the working poor. There are diseases of aging. The older one gets, the shorter the future life expectancy. On average, American men don't live as long as American women do. The gap has widened from two to three years in 1900 to more than seven years today (Altman 1997). Men face more dangers, such as accidents and homicide.

There are some striking differences in the causes of death for men and women. Of the top 10 causes of death, accidents rank third for men and sixth for women. AIDS, which ranks seventh among men, is not among the top 10 causes of death for American women. Nor are suicide and homicide, which rank eighth and tenth respectively among men. The two leading causes of death—heart disease and cancer—are the same for men and women. Stroke is third for women and fourth for men (*New York Times* 1997).

Sometimes politics can shroud medical reality. Because of the success of the breast cancer awareness movement, many women erroneously believe that breast cancer is the leading cause of female deaths. Actually, heart attacks kill 10 times more women than breast cancer does. Nor is breast cancer even the leading cause of cancer deaths for women—lung cancer is. Yet, given the political strength of the breast cancer awareness movement, $600 million is spent annually for breast cancer research. This is more than the combined total funding for research on lung, colorectal, and prostate cancer, and Hodgkin's disease (Mansnerus 1997).

Age, gender, ethnicity, and class all affect both our health conditions and the ways we use medical care. Thus, older women don't mind male doctors, but younger women prefer female MDs (Elder 1997). Illustrating increased identity-based specialization are medical practices geared at gay men and fields like elder care and adolescent medicine. Teen girls prefer women doctors, whom they may see in high school clinics, for consultation about STDs, pregnancies, and issues involving sexuality. Today, teen girls are more likely to smoke than teen boys are, and they drink alcohol and use drugs as much as their male counterparts do. Asian-American women smoke and drink less than white women and African-American women do (Feder 1997).

Men are diagnosed more frequently than women for substance abuse, sexual deviance, and out-of-control behavior. Women are diagnosed more often for eating disorders, depression, and anxiety. Although women *attempt* suicide more than men do, men *commit* suicide more often (Stillion and McDowell 1996). Men who accept traditional gender roles, yet feel they aren't fulfilling the male role, often experience psychological distress. Although men need psychotherapy as much as women do, they are less likely to seek help, and they often end therapy prematurely (Kilmartin 2002 294–296). Kilmartin (2000) finds parental conflict and divorce to be especially detrimental to boys' psychological health.

There are also images and stereotypes associated with gender and health. Some examples: Women take pain better than men do. Women get sick more often than men do. Women see doctors more, and make more health care decisions, than men do. A survey showed that women tend to think that doctors take men's health problems more seriously than they do women's health. Better-educated women were especially likely to have this opinion. The issue of whether personal physicians take men's health concerns more seriously than those of women remains open. However, for at least the past 15 years, research on women's-only illnesses has been at least as common as research on men's-only diseases (Elder 1997).

PEOPLE WITH DISABILITIES

The U.S. Bureau of the Census regularly gathers data on disability. Sources include the Survey of Income and Program Participation (SIPP) and the decennial (10-year) census of population. The SIPP is a national household survey in which a group of households is chosen for study annually. The households are interviewed every four months for at least two years. The SIPP includes an extensive set of disability questions, which makes this survey the preferred source for examining most disability issues.

The Americans with Disabilities Act (ADA) of 1990 defines *disability* as a "physical or mental impairment that substantially limits one or more of the major life activities." For people aged 15 and older the SIPP asks about limitations in (1) "functional activities" (seeing, hearing, speaking, lifting and carrying, using stairs, and walking), (2) "activities of daily living" (getting around inside the home, getting into or out of a bed or chair, bathing, dressing, eating, and toileting), and (3) "instrumental activities of daily living" (going outside the home, keeping track of money or bills, preparing meals, doing light housework, and using the telephone). The SIPP also asks about wheelchairs and crutches, canes, and walkers; the presence of conditions related to mental functioning; work disability; and the disability status in children.

The Census Bureau defines "functional disability" as difficulty with, or inability to perform, age-appropriate activities (due to a physical or mental condition). Figure 12–1 shows percentages of each functional disability, and whether severe or not, among Americans aged 15 and older in 1997.

In 1997, 12 percent of Americans aged 25 to 64 had a severe disability, and almost 20 percent had some sort type of disability (McNeil 2001). In 1996 more than half the 29 million disabled Americans aged 21 to 64 were working. The employment rate was lower (one-fourth) for those who were severely disabled. Altogether, the disabled accounted for 14 percent of the employed population (Mergenhagen 1997).

The ADA prohibits discrimination in hiring and requires employers to make reasonable accommodations for disabled workers. Such employees include those who are disabled at the time of hiring and those who become disabled during employment. Whether or not the disability predated their working years, 52 percent of all disabled people aged 21 to 64 had a job in 1997, the same proportion as in 1991. The share of severely disabled people with a job increased from 23 percent to 26 percent over that time period. These shares are much lower than the shares of the nondisabled population aged 21 to 64; of these, 82 percent were working in 1997 (Mergenhagen and Crispell 1997; McNeil 2001).

Passed in 1990, and taking effect in July 1992, the ADA now requires businesses with 15 or more employees to accommodate disabled job applicants. The law does appear to have increased the number of disabled people in the workforce. In so doing, it has helped to bring people with disabilities into the American mainstream. Between 1991 and 1994, the number of

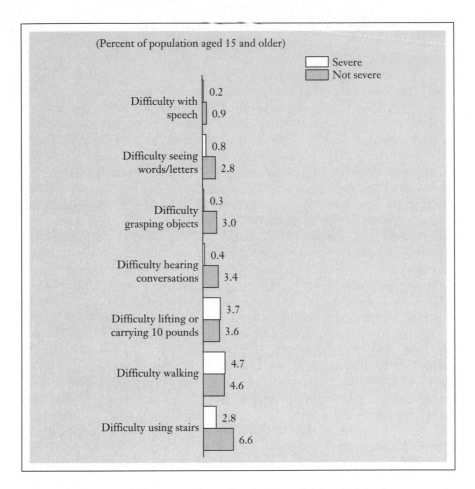

FIGURE 12–1 Disabilities among individuals aged 15 and older by type and severity, 1997.
Source: U.S. Bureau of the Census. 1996 Panel of the Survey of Income and Program Participation. August–November 1997.

disabled Americans in the workforce grew by more than 1.1 million. People with the severest disabilities seem to have benefited most. About 800,000 of those new workers had a severe disability. This means they needed help walking, bathing, shopping, or using the phone (*American Demographics* 1997). Table 12–1 shows the percentage employed of Americans with particular kinds of disabilities. For example, it shows that people with impaired hearing are about twice as likely to work as are people who have trouble walking.

Disabilities, of course, tend to increase with age. Figure 12–2 shows disability presence by age group in the United States in 1997. Some 74 percent of Americans 80 and older had disabilities, compared to about 8 percent of Americans aged 15 and younger.

TABLE 12–1. Kinds of Disabilities and Employment (persons age 21–64)

Disability	Percent employed*
Difficulty hearing	64.4
Difficulty seeing	43.7
Mental disability	41.3
Difficulty walking	33.5

*Persons may have more than one type of disability.
Source: U.S. Bureau of the Census, 1997.

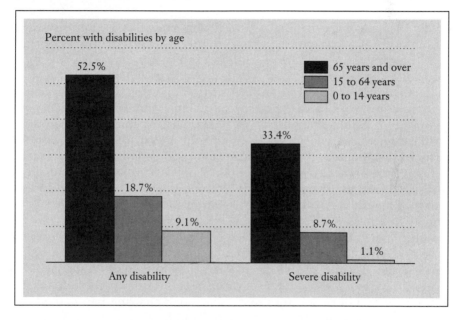

FIGURE 12–2 Disabilities and age, October 1994–January 1995.
Source: U.S. Bureau of the Census, 1997.

MENTAL HEALTH

Mental disorders are certified as such in the fourth edition of the *Diagnostic and Statistical Manual of Mental Disorders* (DSM-IV), the 886-page clinical "bible" published by the American Psychiatric Association. Therapists routinely consult the DSM to identify a set of behaviors as a mental illness. More than 300 conditions are now certified as mental disorders (Sharkey 1997).

Critics contend that the DSM-IV "medicalizes" behavior once considered traceable to character flaws. Many disorders have powerful lobbies in the therapeutic and political worlds, because of the DSM's influence on health care spending. Codes in the DSM-IV are used to bill for mental health care and third-party insurance payment (Sharkey 1997).

In 2002 Americans were spending $1 trillion annually on health care. The mental health industry lobbies to require insurers and HMOs to cover treatment for mental disorders and the cost of psychotropic medications (see Kirk and Kutchins 1998). According to Herb Kutchins (quoted in Sharkey 1997), 18 years ago, the DSM-IV listed only 106 mental disorders. In the mid-nineteenth century, the federal government recognized only one: idiocy/insanity.

HEALTH AND HEALING IN CYBERSPACE

People increasingly use the Internet for health care information, clinical advice, and psychological counseling and support. According to a 1999 Harris Poll, 74 percent of an estimated 97 million Internet users had visited one or more health-related websites, of which more than 20,000 exist. They were seeking medical information, online support groups, consultations, and chats moderated by health experts (Coile 2000). Internet-delivered health care technologies are changing clinical practices as they enhance patient-provider interactions (Lewis and Behana 2001). Providers can collect data directly from patients and offer clinical suggestions. This strategy especially benefits patients who are homebound, live in rural areas, or have difficulty establishing rapport with providers. "Online disease management and tele-health initiatives may be the 'next frontier' in Internet e-health" (Lewis and Behana 2001, 246).

Diabetes mellitus, for instance, is a chronic illness that requires lifestyle changes and strict self-care. Internet technology now offers information and education outside the clinical setting. One study identified 47,365 visits over a 21-month period to three Internet discussion groups about diabetes. Seventy-nine percent of the visitors said that online chatting had helped them cope with diabetes (Zrebiec and Jacobson 2001).

An online survey of 10,069 patients with 35 separate chronic illnesses found that those who spent the most time seeking health information online described themselves as being sicker than did respondents who spent less time. Habitual users of the Internet for health information often described themselves as skeptical about, and dissatisfied with their access to, health care; many lacked health insurance. Women spent more time seeking help online than men did (Millard and Fintak 2002). A "digital divide" continues to limit access to the Internet by geographically isolated and low-income groups. Although Internet use has increased by 50 percent among economically disadvantaged Americans, this population still represents only 9.7 percent of Internet users.

Online *mental* health groups include autonomous self-help groups as well as support groups led by mental health professionals (Hsiung 2000). In either case members can help each other in a nonjudgmental setting. One study found that support groups run by therapists benefit from the therapists' professional training, which helps maintain a well-run group and a support-ive environment (Hsiung 2000).

According to Harvey Blume (1997), the impact of the Internet on autis-tics in particular may one day be compared to the spread of sign language among the deaf. By filtering out the sensory overload that impedes face-to-face communication among autistics, the Internet opens new opportunities for exchange.

"Independent Living" is a group of e-mail forums created by and for autistics. Topics include jobs; hobbies; "sexuality and being different"; and the issue of how to relate to people whom autistics consider neurologically typical" (NT) and whom they call NTs. According to Blume, "autistics are constituting themselves as a new immigrant group online" (1997). Seeking to blend in, to pass, they are studying the ways of the NT natives. For exam-ple, one online discussion was about figuring out when NTs make eye con-tact during conversation.

Although online autistics wish to adapt to an NT-dominated world, they also seek to preserve their own customs and identity. They have proposed a new social contract, which emphasizes *neurological pluralism*—the idea that NT is only one, and not necessarily the best, of many neurological configu-rations (Blume 1997). In the past, psychologists erroneously blamed autism on bad parenting, and especially on the "cold touch" of the "refrigerator mother." As a more accurate (but probably still incomplete) explanation, the advocates of neurological pluralism might prefer to say, "It's the wiring, stu-pid" (Blume 1997).

According to Sharkey (1997), to be listed in the DSM, a disorder needs voluminous field research indicating that it exists as a set of pathological symptoms among a significant number of people. Also necessary are a lobby of therapists and press publicity. (Coverage on TV talk shows also helps.) DSM conditions are more likely to be added than removed. One exception is homosexuality, which was listed as a mental disorder until 1980. "Jury-duty disorder" was defined in 1996 by the *Bulletin of the Academy of Psychiatry and the Law* and may eventually be included in the DSM. This refers to a condition reported by people who have such problems as sexual problems, heart palpitations, phobic reactions, depression, and anorexia after stressful jury duty. One recent candidate for DSM inclusion is "road rage" (Sharkey 1997).

According to the Survey of Income and Program Participation (SIPP), 14.3 million Americans had a mental disability in 1997. Over 1 million Americans (1.4 million) had mental retardation, and 1.9 million had Alzheimer's, senility, or dementia. The number with a learning disability was 3.5 million, and about the same number had some other mental or emotional condition (e.g., depression, anxiety, stress management prob-lems) (McNeil 2001). The National Institute of Mental Health estimates that one-third of the U.S. population has a clinical mental disorder in any given year. The institute also predicts that more than half of us will experience such a clinical condition during our lifetimes.

CHAPTER THIRTEEN

Class

CULTURE AND CLASS

Lip-synching Sheryl Crow's song "Every Day Is a Winding Road," a nine-year-old boy stops and wonders: "How can a vending machine repairman be high on intellectualism? It doesn't make sense. He's not like a professor or something." What constitutes *class* in today's world? Do occupation and education determine class? How useful is class in understanding our own multicultural society?

Stratification is global. Social and economic inequities stratify a world system defined by economic returns and political alliances. Billions of people have unequal access to life chances. The world is marked by strong disparities in income and living standards among and within nations. Most people now live under economic conditions over which they have little control.

However, besides wealth and power, other kinds of resources have been discovered in the global village. The Information Revolution and the multicultural movement have heightened our awareness of and appreciation for different cultures and the people who create them. Although certain societies may be less wealthy or "progressive" than others are, they are still legitimate as designs for living. They may be respected for their belief structures, their health care systems, their courting and mating rituals, or their recreational outlets.

We no longer value nations exclusively by their degree of technological development or their gross national product (GNP). As relevant as a people's economic and political position in the international hierarchy is its wealth in tradition, custom, and ritual. Such social capital and cultural riches sustain a group and distinguish it among societies and nations, including our own. We no longer equate human value and quality of life solely with technological and economic advance.

Despite being "developed" nations, the United States and Canada have not eliminated social inequality—disparities in income, power, and prestige. The creed of equal opportunity and efforts by civil rights activists to enhance access to education and employment for all have not eroded the hierarchy of ranked categories of people. Ours is a class-based society, the by-product of industrialism and capitalism.

Class, or socioeconomic status (SES), permeates our social behavior and thought. Income and education correlate with job security and satisfaction, family size, political attitudes, and cultural values. Poverty is associated with a short life expectancy. Wealth correlates with elite education. Middle-class people tend to favor small families. Sexism and homophobia are more likely among people of moderate to restricted means.

Such classifications as upper-upper class, lower-middle class, and working class help us understand the **differential access** to **strategic resources** and the cultural variation and stratification that result from it. People who share certain characteristics, for example, income and education, tend to pursue similar lifestyles. But in today's multicultural society, classes tend to be more internally varied than they are unified in opposition to other classes (as Weber, rather than Marx, would have predicted). An open class system favors the mobility of members of many identity groups, be these class-, ethnicity-, nationality-, or sex-based.

An open class system rewards those who believe in and conform to the meritocratic ethic. Such people work hard. If at first they don't succeed, they try, try again. Among the high achievers are some people who succeed through a fierce determination to compensate for having had a lower class status at birth. Symptomatic of an open class system in a multicultural society is a hierarchy of heterogeneous classes, ranked segments of the population representing significant sociocultural variation within each class. The Cuban assistant professor, the African-American nurse, the Irish Catholic priest, the Greek building contractor, and the Haitian bank teller all identify as middle-class. And based on income range, they are indeed middle-class.

However, a closer examination of their lifestyles reveals significant variation in how they interpret and spend their salaries to support different ways of life. Moreover, one need only pay attention to the lifestyles of middle- and upper-class Americans to realize that *working class* does not describe only blue-collar occupations (lower-prestige work involving manual labor). For most Americans, upward mobility also implies working—longer, more intensive schedules, the rewards of which aren't always commensurate with the time and labor invested.

Upward mobility doesn't always extinguish the "hidden injuries of class" (Sennett and Cobb 1972/1993). In an interview about his book, *All Over but the Shoutin'*, Pulitzer Prize–winning *New York Times* journalist Rick Bragg (1997) admits to having a chip on his shoulder: "ugly memories of people who considered themselves a class above us. I use it as a weapon." Bragg's childhood was plagued by poverty. Lingering "resentment and condescension" drove him to "prod forward," all the way to "the most prestigious college in America." His candidacy for the Nieman Fellowship at Harvard, "the most prestigious fellowship in the country" (which he was awarded), did little to diminish his *imposter complex*. His doubts were expressed by his "raining sweat" during his interview for the fellowship. Privately he had reflected that he "had about as much business at Harvard as a hog in a cocktail dress."

In the United States the effects of classism on individual psyches do not appear to translate into lower-class consciousness, despite Marx's predictions. Class, as a basis of collective identity, has always been the construction mainly of social scientists and activists. Today, the primacy of culture overrides class as the banner for organized reform movements. Of course, all the culture-coded movements for human rights, including the black movement, the women's movement, and the people-with-disabilities movement, are class-based at the core. They are rooted in economic and political disparities. Given the prominence we now grant culture in North America and throughout the world, it remains the most promising back entrance to security and legitimacy for more, if not all, members of society's peripheries. ☺

CLASS IN AMERICA

Socioeconomic classes represent another aspect of diversity affecting North American identities, lifestyles, and life chances. An interesting part of being different in the United States is the fact of class contrasts, coupled with a simultaneous unwillingness to discuss them.

We deny the benefits of a higher-class background when we tell and accept stories suggesting we can all rise from humble roots, as in the Horatio Alger rags-to-riches tales. Our work ethic suggests that anyone can succeed as a self-made man or woman if he or she works hard enough. Denying class, we see signs of class in images and behavior, as in the bodies and dress habits mentioned in the last chapter.

Consider "people" familiar to millions of Americans, the characters on some of our most popular sitcoms. Would you accept the following class-based ranking of sitcom casts from highest to lowest: *Frasier*, *Seinfeld*, *Friends*, *Roseanne*, and *Married with Children*? If so, we are agreeing on elements of a tacit American class structure.

Although Americans don't like to talk about class, we do routinely use labels that are related to class: yuppies (young urban professionals, who are educated people with disposable incomes). Other terms for class include rich, status, highfalutin', middle class, white collar, blue collar, working poor, urban poor, the homeless, welfare mothers, rednecks (adding a southern regional component), and underclass.

Mass education and increased employment have modified the American class structure. Following the Great Depression, which began in 1929, living standards have risen for most Americans. When W. Lloyd Warner and his associates did their classic social research in a New England town they called Yankee City during the 1930s, they found a class structure that differed substantially from today's American class structure (see Warner and Lunt 1941, Warner 1963). With educational opportunities more limited and a much smaller inventory of professions for people to aspire to, the elite and middle class were much smaller than they are now.

The post–World War II American economy emphasized heavy goods manufacture, with a unionized blue-collar workforce. Men with high school educations and union jobs could support their households and even think of sending their children to college. More recently in the United States there has been a shift away from such a manufacturing economy toward one based on the provision of services and the processing of information. In the new high-tech economy education has become more important in landing a good job. No longer can the average high school graduate hope to earn enough to support a family. Typically today, both partners in a marriage work outside the home. When they are well-educated professionals their combined income permits a life of relative luxury, if not of leisure.

Since the 1970s—accelerating in the 1980s and 1990s—the gap between most Americans and the very well off (i.e., the top quintile or 20 percent of Americans) has widened. Consider a 1997 study by the Center on Budget and Policy Priorities, a research group in Washington, D.C. Comparing U.S. Census Bureau data on family incomes in the mid-1980s and the mid-1990s, the study found the gap between the wealthiest 20 percent of American families and the poorest 20 percent to have increased in 37 states, representing 87 percent of the U.S. population (Perez-Pena 1997). Lower-paid workers have been hurt by the loss of low-skilled jobs in manufacturing and construction and a related decline in unionization.

According to U.S. Census data from 1967 to 2000 the top (richest) fifth, or quintile, of American households increased their share of national income by 13.5 percent, while all other quintiles fell. The percentage share of the lowest fifth fell most dramatically—17.6 percent. Thus, in 2000 the highest quintile of households got 49.7 percent of all national income, while the share of the lowest fifth was 3.6. Comparable figures in 1967 had been 43.8 and 4.0. The 2000 ratio was 14:1, versus 11:1 in 1967. In other words, the richest fifth of American households, with a mean annual income of $141,621, is now 14 times wealthier than the poorest fifth, with a mean annual income of $10,188 (U.S. Census 2000).

FORMS OF SOCIOECONOMIC STRATIFICATION

The class structures of contemporary North America are variations on a more general theme of socioeconomic **stratification**, which the anthropologist Morton Fried discussed in his classic article "On the Evolution of Social Stratification and the State" (1960). Socioeconomic stratification is not a cultural universal; it arose with the earliest states (or civilizations, a near synonym), which first appeared in Mesopotamia (currently Iran and Iraq) some 6,000 years ago. A few thousand years later states also arose in two parts of the western hemisphere—Mesoamerica (Mexico, Guatemala, Belize) and the central Andes (Peru and Bolivia).

The presence of socioeconomic stratification is a defining feature of the state. That is, all states—and only states—have some kind of class system. In ancient states, for the first time in human history, there were contrasts in wealth, power, and prestige between entire groups (social strata or classes) of men and women. Each **stratum** included people of both sexes and all ages. The **superordinate** (the higher or elite) stratum had privileged access to valued resources. Access to resources by members of the **subordinate** (lower or underprivileged) stratum was limited by the privileged group.

In states, the elites control much of the means of production, for example, land, herds, water, capital, farms, factories, Microsoft, Time Warner, and the *New York Times*. Because of elite ownership, ordinary people lack free access to resources. Those born at the bottom of the **stratified** hierarchy have reduced chances of social mobility.

How does social stratification in modern nations compare with that in ancient states? The hereditary rulers and elites of ancient states and empires, like the feudal nobility that ruled Europe before 1500, viewed the state as their property (conferred by gods, tradition, or war), to control and do with as they pleased (Shannon 1989). The most basic distinction in ancient states was between those who controlled the state machinery and those who did not. With industrialization, however, the main differentiating factor became ownership of the means of production.

Industrial Stratification

The social theorists Max Weber and Karl Marx both focused on the stratification systems associated with industrial economies. The socioeconomic effects of the **Industrial Revolution**, which first occurred in England around 1750, were mixed. National income and living standards rose, but prosperity was uneven. From his observations in England and his analysis of 19th-century industrial capitalism, Marx (Marx and Engels 1848/1976) viewed socioeconomic stratification as a sharp and simple division between two opposed classes: the bourgeoisie (capitalists) and the proletariat (propertyless workers). The bourgeoisie traced its origins to overseas ventures and the rise of world capitalism, which had transformed the social structure of northwestern Europe, creating a wealthy commercial class.

The **bourgeoisie** were the owners of the factories, mines, large farms, and other means of production. The **working class**, or **proletariat**, was made up of people who had to sell their labor to survive. With industrialization, subsistence production declined, the possibility of unemployment increased, and urban migration became more common. The bourgeoisie came to stand between workers and the means of production.

Faulting Marx for an overly simple and exclusively economic view of stratification, Weber (1922/1968) defined three related dimensions of social stratification: wealth (economic status), power (political status), and prestige (social status). Economic status, or **wealth**, encompassed material assets, including income, land, and other types of property. **Power**, the ability to exercise one's will over others—to do what one wants—is the basis of political status. **Prestige**—the basis of social status—refers to esteem, respect, or approval for acts, deeds, or qualities considered exemplary. Prestige, or "cultural capital" (Bourdieu 1984), provides people with a sense of worth and respect, which they may often convert into economic advantage.

Having one of the three does not entail having the others, but wealth, power, and prestige do tend to be associated. Again disputing Marx, Weber also argued that social solidarity based on ethnicity, religion, race, nationality, and other attributes often took priority over class (social identity based on economic status).

Class consciousness (recognition of collective interests and personal identification with one's economic group) was a vital part of Marx's view of class. He saw bourgeoisie and proletariat as groups with radically opposed interests. Marx viewed classes as powerful collective forces that could mobilize to influence the course of history. He postulated that workers would develop organizations to protect their interests and increase their share of industrial profits. And so they did. During the nineteenth century, trade unions and socialist parties emerged to express a rising anticapitalist mass spirit. By 1900, many governments had factory legislation, social-welfare programs, and rising mass living standards.

Today's world maintains the distinction between owners and nonowners, but the class division of capitalists and workers is now worldwide. But modern class systems are not simple and dichotomous. They include a middle class of skilled and professional workers. Gerhard Lenski (1966) argues that social equality tends to increase in advanced industrial societies. The growth of the middle class softens the polarization between owners and workers. Intermediate occupations proliferate, creating opportunities for social mobility. The stratification system grows more complex (Giddens 1973). However, in some contemporary nations, such as Brazil, the middle class may be shrinking as the rich get richer; and the poor, poorer. Some commentators even see evidence for an increasingly bifurcated class system, with a widening gap between the richest and the poorest, in the United States.

Poverty and Homelessness

Poverty persists in North America, although the poverty rate had been declining prior to 2001. Recession leads to a rise in the poverty rate; economic recovery and expansion increase employment and reduce poverty. The U.S. poverty rate ambled up from a record low of 11.1 in 1973, to 11.4 percent in 1978, 12.8 percent in 1989, 13.5 percent in 1990, and 13.8 percent in 1995. In that period the number of poor Americans rose from 24.5 million to 36.4

TABLE 13–1. Incomes and Poverty in the United States, 1990 versus 2000

	1990	2000
Median family money income	$35,353	$42,148
In constant 2000 dollars	$41,223	$42,148
Persons below poverty level (millions)	33.6	31.1
Pecentage of all persons	13.5%	11.3%

Source: U.S. Bureau of the Census, 2001.

TABLE 13–2. Groups Matching or Setting New All-Time High Median Household Income, 2000

Characteristic	2000 Median Household Income	Status
Blacks	$30,439	New all-time high
Hispanics	33,447	New all-time high
Non-Hispanic whites	45,904	Matches all-time high
Asians and Pacific Islanders	55,521	Matches all-time high
All households	42,148	Matches all-time high

Source: U.S. Bureau of the Census, 2001.

million (*Statistical Abstract of the United States* 1991, 1996). The direction of the poverty rate turned in the late 1990s, falling from 11.8 percent in 1999 to 11.3 percent in 2000, the lowest rate in 21 years, as the poor population declined to 31.1 million. (See Table 13–1.)

As shown in Table 13–2, the rise in prosperity in the late 1990s was distributed across all social groups. Median household income rose to, or matched, the all-time high for African Americans, Hispanics, non-Hispanic whites, Asian and Pacific Islanders, and indeed for all American households.

The late 1990s posed quite a contrast with the 1980s, when 70 percent of the rise in family income in the United States between 1977 and 1989 went to the top 1 percent of the population (Nasar 1992a, 1992b). The top 5 percent got 24 percent of total national income in 1989, up from 18 percent in 1977. The share of national income received by the bottom 60 percent declined from 34 to 29 percent in the same period (Nasar 1992a, 1992b). Despite the good news of the late 1990s, a new recession began in late 2000 and became a matter of serious policy concern in 2001, especially after September 11. A recovery seemed likely but uncertain in 2002. Where are the economy and the poverty rate headed as you read this?

Homelessness is an extreme form of downward mobility, which may follow job loss, layoffs, or situations in which women and children flee from domestic abuse. Our work ethic suggests that anyone can succeed as a self-made man or woman if he or she works hard enough, and we tend to look down on those who obviously haven't succeeded. Part of being different in the United State is class contrasts, coupled with unwillingness to discuss them. Denying class, we see signs of class in images, behavior, bodies, and dress.

Much of the poverty in industrial nations is caused by unemployment. The ongoing North American economic shift from manufacturing to services and information processing demands a better-educated and more skillful workforce. Although overall unemployment has been dropping, poorly educated people find it especially hard to make a living in the new economy. In the United States and throughout the world, members of the **underclass** (the abjectly poor) lack jobs, adequate food, medical care, even shelter.

Homelessness is an extreme form of downward mobility, which may follow job loss, layoffs, or situations in which women and children flee from domestic abuse. The causes of homelessness are varied—psychological, economic, and social. They include inability to pay rent, eviction, sale of urban real estate to developers, and mental illness. In Washington, New York, and San Francisco, the urban poor sleep in cardboard cartons and at train stations, on sidewalks, and near warm-air gratings. The homeless are the hunters and gatherers of modern society. They feed themselves by begging, scavenging, and raiding garbage (particularly that of restaurants) for food.

The most extreme socioeconomic contrasts within the world capitalist economy today are between the wealthiest people in the richest nations and the poorest people in the less-developed countries. However, as the gap between richest and poorest widens in North America, the social distance between the underclasses of the developed and the underdeveloped countries shrinks. The road to Bangladesh passes close to Washington's Pennsylvania Avenue.

Closed Class Systems

In nation-states, socioeconomic inequalities tend to persist across the generations. The extent to which they do or do not is a measure of the openness of the class system, the ease of social mobility it permits. With respect to such openness, stratification has taken many forms, including caste, slavery, and class systems.

Caste systems are closed, hereditary forms of stratification, often dictated by religion. Social rank is ascribed at birth, so people are locked into their parents' social position. The world's best-known caste system is associated with Hinduism in traditional India, Pakistan, and Sri Lanka. Another castelike system, apartheid, plagued South Africa until recently. Blacks, whites, and Asians had their own separate (and unequal) neighborhoods, schools, laws, and punishments. Slavery, in which people are treated as property, is the most extreme and coercive form of legalized inequality.

DOMINATION, HEGEMONY, AND RESISTANCE

Such systems of domination—cultural, socioeconomic, political, or religious—always have their more muted aspects along with their public dimensions. In studying apparent cultural domination, or actual political domination, we must pay careful attention to what lies beneath the surface of evident, public behavior. In public the oppressed may seem to accept their own domination, but they always question it offstage. James Scott (1990) uses the term **public transcript** to describe the open, public interactions between dominators and oppressed. The public transcript is the outer shell of power relations. Scott uses **hidden transcript** to describe the critique of power that goes on offstage, where the power holders can't see it— for example, in the slave quarters of the old American South.

In public the oppressed and the elites observe the etiquette of power relations. The dominants act like haughty masters; subordinates are humble and defer. Antonio Gramsci (1971) developed the concept of **hegemony** for a stratified social order in which subordinates comply with domination by internalizing its values and accepting its "naturalness" (this is the way things were meant to be). According to Pierre Bourdieu (1977, 164) every social order tries to make its own arbitrariness seem natural, including its oppression. All hegemonic ideologies offer explanations about why the existing order is in everyone's best interest. Often promises are made, such as,

"Things will get better if you're patient." Gramsci and others use the idea of hegemony to explain why people conform even without coercion, why they knuckle under when they don't really have to.

Hegemony, the internalization of a dominant ideology, is one way to curb resistance. Another way is to let subordinates know they will eventually gain power—as young people usually foresee when they let their elders dominate them. Another way of curbing resistance is to separate or isolate subordinates and supervise them closely. According to Michel Foucault (1979), describing control over prisoners, solitude (as in solitary confinement) is an effective way to induce submission.

Often, situations that seem to be hegemonic do have active resistance, but it is individual and disguised rather than collective and defiant. Scott (1985) uses Malay peasants, among whom he did fieldwork, to illustrate small-scale acts of resistance, which he calls "weapons of the weak." The Malay peasants used an indirect strategy to resist an Islamic tithe (religious tax). The goods, usually rice, that peasants were expected to give went to the provincial capital. In theory, the tithe would come back as charity, but it never did. Peasants didn't resist the tithe by rioting, demonstrating, or protesting. Instead they used a "nibbling" strategy, based on small acts of resistance. For example, they failed to declare their land, or they lied about the amount they farmed. They underpaid or delivered rice paddy contaminated with water, rocks, or mud, to add weight. Because of this resistance, only 15 percent of what was due was actually paid (Scott 1990, p. 89).

Subordinates also use various strategies to protest or resist *publicly*, but again, often in disguised form. Discontent may be expressed in public rituals and language, including metaphors, euphemisms, and folk tales. For example, trickster tales (like the Brer Rabbit stories told by slaves in the southern United States) celebrate the wiles of the weak as they triumph over the strong.

Resistance is most likely to be expressed openly when the oppressed are allowed to assemble. The hidden transcript may become apparent on such occasions. In such contexts, people see their dreams and anger shared by others with whom they haven't been in direct contact. The oppressed may draw courage from the crowd, from its visual and emotional impact and its anonymity. Sensing danger, the elites discourage such gatherings. They try to limit and control holidays, funerals, dances, festivals, and other occasions that might unite the oppressed. Thus, in the southern United States, gatherings of five or more slaves were forbidden unless a white person was present.

Factors that impede the formation of communities—for example, geographic or cultural separateness—also work to curb resistance. Thus, U.S. plantation owners sought slaves with diverse African ethnic and linguistic backgrounds. But divisiveness can be overcome. Despite the measures used to separate them, the slaves resisted. They developed their own tales, popular culture, linguistic codes, and religious vision. The masters taught portions of the Bible that stressed compliance. But the slaves preferred the story of Moses, the promised land, and deliverance. Key in the slaves' religious beliefs was the idea of a reversal in the conditions of whites and

Because of its costumed anonymity, Carnival is an excellent arena for expressing normally suppressed speech. This is vividly symbolized by these Carnival headdresses in Trinidad. Is there anything like Carnival in your society?

blacks. According to Scott (1990), it's always easy to visualize a reversal of the existing distribution of status and rewards. People can always imagine an end to oppressive conditions. Slaves also resisted directly, through sabotage and flight. In many parts of the western hemisphere, slaves fled and established free communities in remote and isolated areas (Price 1973).

Hidden transcripts tend to be expressed at certain times (festivals and Carnivals) and places (e.g., markets). Because of its costumed anonymity and its ritual structure (reversal), **Carnival** (a pre-Lenten festival comparable to Mardi Gras in Louisiana, popular in Brazil and in certain Mediterranean and Caribbean societies) is an excellent arena for exposing normally suppressed speech and aggression—antihegemonic discourse. (**Discourse** includes talk, speeches, gestures, and actions.) Carnivals, which are public rituals of reversal, celebrate freedom through immodesty, dancing, gluttony, and sexuality (DaMatta 1991). Carnival may begin as a playful outlet for frustrations built up during the year. Over time it may evolve into a powerful annual critique of domination and a threat to the established order (Gilmore 1987). (Recognizing that ceremonial license could turn into political defiance, the Spanish dictator Francisco Franco banned Carnival.)

In medieval Europe, according to Mikhail Bakhtin (1984), the market was the main place where the dominant ideology was questioned. The anonymity of the crowd put people on an equal footing. The deference used with lords and clergy didn't apply to the marketplace. Later in Europe, the hidden transcript also went public in pubs, taverns, inns, cabarets, beer cellars, and gin mills. These locales helped breed a resistant popular culture—in games, songs, gambling, blasphemy, and disorder—that was at odds with the official culture. People met in an atmosphere of freedom encouraged by alcohol. Church and state alike condemned such settings as subversive.

CLASS AND VALUES ACROSS CULTURES

Vertical mobility is an upward or downward change in a person's social status, a rise or fall in life. A truly open class system would facilitate mobility, with individual achievement and personal merit determining rank. Social status would be achieved through personal effort. Things would actually work the way they are supposed to work in American ideology. Ascribed statuses (family background, ethnicity, gender, religion) would decline in importance.

Compared with ancient states, modern industrial nations do tend to have more open class systems. In modern economies, wealth is based to some extent on income—earnings from wages and salaries. Economists contrast such a return on labor with interest, dividends, and rent, which are returns on property or capital.

Class tends to be more marked in wealth than in income. For example, in the mid-1980s the bottom fifth of American households got about 5 percent of total national income, compared with about 45 percent for the top fifth. However, when we consider wealth rather than income, the contrast was much more extreme: 1 percent of American families held one-third of the nation's wealth (Light, Keller, and Calhoun 1994).

Many social and cultural differences between the United States and other countries, including Brazil, flow from patterns of socioeconomic stratification, the allocation and distribution of wealth, prestige, and power. Although the distribution of income in the United States is not as even as in Japan or the Netherlands, it is much more so than in Brazil. Latin nations with strongly hierarchical systems of vested wealth and power tend to resist competition and change. Such values, found in more open societies, such as the United States and Canada, work in opposition to established privileges. Brazilian society, for example, is self-consciously hierarchical. American society is self-consciously democratic. This doesn't mean that the United States lacks socioeconomic contrasts and social classes; but Brazilian poverty is much more extreme than poverty in the United States. The most affluent 20 percent of American households average 14 times the income of the poorest fifth. The analogous multiple is more than 30 in Brazil.

Comparing resource distribution, Brazil has a much wider gap between richest and poorest, and Brazilians are much more class conscious than Americans are. Most Americans, regardless of income, consider themselves to be middle class, and most are. As has been stated, Americans have trouble dealing with, even recognizing, class differences. Like good Weberians (followers of Max Weber), U.S. citizens prefer to make social distinctions in terms of factors other than class, such as region, ethnicity, religion, race, or occupation. With their ideology of equality, Americans feel uneasy using such labels as lower class, working class, or upper class. We are reluctant to acknowledge a role for class background because we believe that ours is an open society in which capable people can rise through their own efforts and hard work. Self-sufficiency and individual achievement are such powerful American values that we resent, and often deny, that class background *does* affect chances for success. As our culture reconstructs its history, we forget that many of our "self-made men" came from wealthy families.

The United States has a pervasive, although idealized, egalitarian ethos that is notably absent in Brazil. Our Constitution tells us that all men (and, by extension, women) are created equal. Although it is well known that in practice U.S. justice is neither blind nor equal for the rich and the poor, there is supposed to be equality before the law. But in Brazil all is hierarchy. The penal code authorizes privileged treatment for certain classes of citizens, such as people with university degrees.

Brazilians' social identities are based in large part on class background and family connections, which Brazilians see nothing wrong with using for all they're worth. Parents, in-laws, and extended kin are all tapped for entries to desired settings and positions. Family position and network membership contribute substantially to individual fortune. All social life is hierarchical. No one doubts that rank confers advantages in myriad contexts and encounters in everyday social life. High-status Brazilians don't stand patiently on line as Americans do. Important people expect their business to be attended to immediately, and social inferiors yield. Rules don't apply uniformly, but differentially, according to social class. The final resort in any conversation is, "Do you know who you're talking to?" (DaMatta 1991). The American opposite, reflecting our democratic and egalitarian ethos, is, "Who do you think you are?"

The contrast is one of doing (United States) versus being (Brazil).* In the United States identity emerges as a result of what one does. In Brazil one's social identity arises from what one is. A person is a strand in a web of social connections, originating in the extended family, which has an established place in the stratified hierarchy of the region and nation. In such a consciously hierarchical society, prestige, power, and privilege rest on the extent and influence of the personal network.

Most Americans, by contrast, would probably argue that what someone does (achieves) is more important than his or her family, class background,

---

*Long ago, Sir Henry Sumner Maine, in *Ancient Law* (1861/1963), his well-known treatise on the evolution of law and society, characterized the transition from primitive to modern society as the movement from status to contract. This parallels the distinction between being (status) and doing (contract). A related opposition is that of ascribed to achieved status.

or personal connections—in the long run, at least. American culture sees reason for pride in excellence in any line of work. "I may be just a plumber, but I'm a good plumber," is a much likelier American than Brazilian statement.

Class-based diversity is evident in the mainstream media. For example, the work ethic influences media portrayals. Unemployed people, rich or poor, are suspect in American culture and are rare among TV heroes. The lazy rich man, who in the United States is a "playboy" or "ne'er-do-well," in Brazil (in life and the media) can enjoy gracefully what family status or fortune was generous enough to provide. Americans believe personal worth and moral value come through work, but Brazilian culture has had a "gentleman complex" for centuries (see Wagley 1963). Brazilians who can afford to hire others should not do manual work. Menial jobs should be done by menials, millions of whom are available. The "do-it-yourselfer" or "home handyman" valued by North American culture would only take jobs away from millions of lower-class people in Brazil.

Portrayals of Class in the Mainstream Media

For several years, George Gerbner and his associates at the University of Pennsylvania's Annenberg School of Communication have been studying television's content and effects in relation to Americans' images of social reality (see Gerbner 1988). They have compared answers to certain questions with televiewing habits. In so doing they have detected a cultivation effect: The more time people spend watching TV, the more they view the real world as being like the world on television. When we consider the nature and impact of television in other cultures, we see that it is not simply television as a medium, but specific TV content (which varies among nations) that does the cultivating. The social worlds encapsulated in television programs are constructed not just artistically and technically but culturally, within the societies in which they are imagined, written, performed, and produced.

Ideas about prestige, or cultural capital (Bourdieu 1984), are both reflected in and influenced by media portrayals. For example, a bias against low-status occupations and lower-class characters is common to Brazilian and American television. In both countries TV characters tend to have higher-status occupations than do people in real life (see DeFleur 1964; Glennon and Butch 1979, 1982). (This shapes the belief, according to the cultivation hypothesis, that high-status jobs are more common than they really are.) In the real-life workforce in the United States in 1984, 51 percent of women held clerical and service jobs. But 75 percent of the TV women introduced that year were professionals (National Commission on Working Women 1984). In Brazil the most popular TV programs are *telenovelas*, daily programs with a continuous story line, which, although shown at night, are often compared to American daytime soap operas. Telenovela characters typically seek status mobility; they attempt to rise in life by manipulating personal network ties—strategic kin connections, friendships, romances, or marriages.

Television tends to dote on people who can afford to live, or aspire to, glamorous lives. Telenovelas, which dominate prime time in Brazil as in much of Latin America, always have a rich family to illustrate, and encourage, conspicuous consumption. One set of characters must be able to afford all the products that sponsor the show. Consumers are shown the rewards that come at the top. However, particular cultures stress different routes to success and different values about work. Research in Brazil confirms a contrast with the American cultural notion that work is valuable in itself, not just because money is needed. When asked if they would go on working having won the lottery, most Brazilians, unlike most Americans, said no. Indolent playboys are rare, and not admirable, American TV characters, but glamorous Brazilian characters often don't work if they are independently wealthy.

Reflecting their respective societies, class contrasts are much more evident on Brazilian than American television. Brazilian TV characters discuss class identities openly. To rise in life, *subir na vida*, is one of the most common telenovela expressions. Most telenovelas are modern-day Cinderella stories. A girl or boy from a lower-status family falls in love with and eventually marries someone from a richer family. The interclass friendships and romances shown on Brazilian television link members of classes A (upper), B (middle), and sometimes C (upper working). Only occasionally is there a romance between a working-class character and someone from the upper or upper-middle class. Even rarer in entertainment programming are class D Brazilians (lower working, unemployed poor), with their impoverished, untelegenic lifestyles. Even the fantasy world of the telenovela recognizes that such people have virtually no chance to rise in life by marrying someone from the elite group.

Obvious class contrasts are less developed in American productions. Recent exceptions include the 1997 movies *Titanic* and *Good Will Hunting*. Both films recall Brazilian telenovela themes. Each features a romance between a poor boy and a girl from a wealthier family. *Titanic's* Jack Dawson uses charm, verbal skills, courage, and talent (as an artist) to win his Rose. Rose fumes about the constraints and responsibilities imposed on her by her class status, while Jack celebrates the freedom, independence, and adventure inherent in his own. The hero of *Good Will Hunting* is an orphaned genius who works as a janitor; his love interest is a Harvard student. Will Hunting attracts her with his intelligence and charm, while lying about his family background. His friends are ridiculed by Harvard students because of their lack of the knowledge and skills that come from being raised in privileged families.

Typically on Brazilian TV, such class-mismatched couples eventually marry. The talented young man usually gets a job through his wealthy father-in-law. By contrast, and true to American ideology, most American tales with similar themes have the hero make it on his own, through work, education, or some kind of self-growth. The expectation is for social status to rise through individual achievement.

In a culture in which self-reliance is a dominant value (Hsu 1975), Americans disapprove when people use marriage or kin ties to gain money, position, or status. Relatives who work in the same business, like the children of famous people who follow their parents' profession, must prove themselves and make it on their own. This, of course, is in the ideal culture. Relatives often do help each other professionally, though much more covertly in the United States than in Brazil. If young Americans are to succeed in a family business, we expect them to work as hard as they would in any other firm.

The themes of work and achievement always emerge in interviews with people who have followed in a parent's profession. The interviewer invariably asks if famous parentage was a help or a liability. The usual answer is that the relationship helped at first, but was more of a hindrance later, because the child's achievements were constantly compared with those of the successful parent. The newcomers had to work hard to convince others that they could make it on their own. Success achieved merely through family connections, without hard work, is taboo in American ideology.

Although prestige occupations, which can best support and exemplify conspicuous consumption, dominate both American and Brazilian television, actual occupations differ. Prestige occupations in the United States are in medicine, law, science, engineering, and the top ranks of business and industry. Brazilians also respect successful businessmen, engineers, and architects and accord high status to successful actors and entertainers. However, professors and writers have more prestige in Brazil than they do in North America. They outrank all but the most famous physicians (e.g., plastic surgeons and cardiac surgeons), who themselves become celebrities. Detectives and police officers have much less prestige in Brazil and are much rarer on Brazilian than American TV.

In both Brazil and the United States, the proportion of certain occupations and social classes on television contrasts markedly with reality. Not only are physicians, attorneys, and other professionals much more common among American TV characters than in real life, TV characters also include a much higher percentage of cops and robbers than there are in the American population.

Again, a prominent cultural difference produces a contrast between American and Brazilian TV content. Neither in Brazil nor the United States is police work a prestige occupation. However, Brazilians give law enforcement officers less respect, and much less TV coverage, than Americans do. This cultural difference has to do with regard for law and the derivative prestige that goes to those who uphold and enforce it.

Brazilian anthropologist Roberto DaMatta, who has spent several years in the United States, has explained why Brazilians have so little confidence in the police. Americans tend to perceive police officers as figures who uphold the law. Brazilians, on the other hand, see the police as similar to politicians. They view these figures as having little actual respect for the law, as using government and legally constituted power for their own advantage. According to DaMatta, (personal communication), "Whenever you do something wrong in your country the police seem to be there to stop you. But in Brazil the police usually stop you when you're not doing anything wrong" (to try to extract a bribe).

Attorneys and law enforcement officers are also so much more common on American than Brazilian television because laws are rules designed to regulate behavior in *public*. Public and work scenes and relationships between nonrelatives are common on American television, whereas domestic settings and family relationships dominate Brazilian TV.

Social class is another important reason police officers are so rare on Brazilian television. The matter of class also explains why state intrusion on the family is so much less characteristic of (middle-class and above) Brazilian society, televised or real, than of the contemporary United States. The social network of virtually every middle-class Brazilian includes lawyers and other protectors of private rights. Brazilian police officers, who usually have no more than lower-middle-class status, are reluctant to interfere in the private affairs of their social "betters" or even to regulate their public behavior.

In these varied examples, then, we see ways in which a culture's characteristic class relations and ideas about proper avenues of status mobility influence and are influenced by the mass media. We also see that analysis of media content can inform us about social relations and the status system and values of the society that creates that content.

DIVERSITY WITHIN SOCIAL CATEGORIES

Racial, ethnic, and class labels can conceal considerable diversity. There are ways of being different within the social categories—such as black, white, or poor—and we hear about them every day. For example, differentiation within America's black population dates back to the era of enslavement. Those with lighter skin color worked as house servants rather than as field workers. This status distinction continued through Reconstruction. Early in the 20th-century, upward mobility distinguished prosperous urban blacks from their poorer rural counterparts (Frazier 1957). Many African Americans still accord higher status to the "light-skin black."

Following the civil rights movement of the 1960s, the "new black middle class" consisted of teachers, social workers, nurses, small business owners, and managers (Landry 1987). Some of these positions reflected affirmative action policies; most were concentrated in the public sector of the American economy. Northern African Americans shared class markers with northern whites, which further differentiated them from southern blacks (Hogan and Featherman 1977). One aspect of stratification among African Americans has been called the "neocolonial model." This is the idea that African-American professionals negotiate and maintain their own privileged status while perpetuating a disadvantaged, largely black, underclass. Countering neocolonialist tendencies, an active, intellectual, Afrocentric elite works for the advancement of all black people. The Afrocentric movement was launched in the late 1960s and early 1970s to promote black economic equality. Its agenda now seeks to foster the political freedom and cultural integrity of diasporic Africans as a people with a past and a future that override enslavement.

Discrepancies in access to information, networks, skills, and employment continue both between and within racial and ethnic groups. Our economy includes "racialized jobs," such as migrant agricultural work. Low-skilled jobs, such as janitorial work in hotels, restaurants, hospitals, and universities, tend to be held by minorities.

Intersections of class and culture are especially illuminating in understanding the position of the poor, regardless of their "race" or ethnicity. Historically, and cross-culturally, the poor have been classified as functionally and morally inferior to their more prosperous counterparts. Distorted images of the poor prevail in our assumptions about "the welfare class." Diversity among the poor contradicts the popular tendency to see welfare recipients as a "kind of people" with a fixed socioeconomic profile and set of values. Many welfare recipients have previously worked and are participating in the welfare system for a brief period following a crisis. Most welfare recipients actively seek to rejoin the formal labor force (Monroe and Tiller 2001).

A study of 84 welfare-reliant rural women, 80 percent of whom were African Americans, revealed that they prized work, but they were limited by the bleak rural labor market. Having internalized the American work ethic, these women wished for the tangible and symbolic benefits of paid employment. Excluded from the formal labor force, and aware of those peers who "abuse the system," these women hoped to return to, or to acquire, work for pay. Meanwhile,

> they engage in informal labor, resource exchanges, and value-added activities to stretch their meager resources. They engage in just about any tactic or strategy—whatever it takes—to survive, keep their children together, fed, housed, and clothed. And they are involved in the daily care of their families, just like many other American mothers. (Monroe and Tiller 2001, 827)

How do we judge these activities by welfare mothers? If by "work" we mean paid labor, do we stigmatize middle-class women who are "stay-at-home moms"? How about upper-class women who volunteer their time to various social causes, or engage in leisure and recreational activities with their peers, all without earning wages or a salary?

How much attention do we pay to diversity among whites? Stereotypes about poor Southern whites have fueled the idea of a "white trash culture," characterized:

> as backward or excessive to the norm, from the darker aspects of racial politics and the Ku Klux Klan, feuding, incest, and the cult of the Rebel, to country music, faith-healing and snake-handling, and the phenomenon of Elvis veneration . . . of violence and excess, of hysterical gorging and

indulging in food, drink, and drugs, and of living life large and in mythic
terms in a Southern culture rife with cults and worship of the dead and the
lost, from fundamentalist Christian sects to the adoration of the Confederate cause. (Sweeney 2001, 144)

White trash culture, regardless of its marginality, is linked to mainstream
white America. It is not a creation of a racial or ethnic minority. These
Americans defy the category "other" by virtue of their whiteness and their
native birth.

The experience of poor rural whites as different from, and less than, the
societal norm may be as painful and destructive as the experience of poor
urban blacks. Both groups are victims of a classism that marginalizes and
subordinates the poor, whatever their color. According to Sweeney, "White
Trash is an aesthetic of ultimate marginalization" (2001, 144). In the words
of another social critic, to call someone "white trash" is "the last racist thing
you can say and get away with" (quoted in Sweeny 2001, 144).

Class, race, and culture are inextricably linked in the lives of poor Americans. Because people of color are disproportionately poor, the "disentan-
glement" of poverty and race must precede analysis and planned change
(Johnson 2000). History, social organization, and family structure distinguish one poor community from another. Consider a comparative study of
poor people belonging to three different groups: African Americans,
Hmong, and whites. Hmong Americans share an ethnic status and background as a tribal people who live in remote mountain villages throughout
China, Laos, Thailand, and Vietnam. For centuries, Hmong have suffered
persecution by many groups, while fiercely defending their ethnic heritage.
Hmong in the United States have been criticized as unwilling to assimilate.

African Americans, Hmong Americans, and Euro-Americans living below the poverty line experience being poor according to historical and cultural factors that distinguish them, despite their shared class status. In
education, Euro-Americans have had access to public education since the
early 1800s. African Americans were the victims of a separate but unequal
school system in the American South. As first-generation immigrants,
Hmong Americans have been formally schooled. In family and household
organization, one-parent, female-headed households are common among
African Americans, as compared to multigenerational families living in a
single household among Hmong Americans, and nuclear families of four
(two parents and two children) among Euro-Americans. In geographic location, largely urban black communities contrast with Hmong communities
in mainly white small towns and small cities, and poor Euro-Americans in
largely rural homogeneous white communities. Although the poor may
share an economic status, social analysts and service providers need to recognize that poverty encompasses diverse groups, each with its own history
and culture (Johnson 2000).

CHAPTER FOURTEEN

Where We Live

─────────── It's Not Just a Zip Code; It's a Lifestyle ───────────

The link between space, place, and lifestyle translates into perceptions of identity—our own, and that of others. For North Americans today, "home" has varied meanings. We continue to designate and identify with a specific geographic location, typically the place where we spent our formative years. "I'm a Texan to the bone," explains a middle-aged woman who has lived in four other states and has been educated abroad. Some of us speak of a "chosen home," the place to which we move for higher education, a better career, or a more suitable lifestyle. The working-class kid from Ohio turned Wall Street executive distinguishes himself as a "New Yorker," a label denoting not only location, but also social status and lifestyle.

Where we live influences how we live. An agrarian way of life and value system distinguish rural communities from urban and industrial segments of the population. Greeks differentiate between islanders and mainlanders, Athenians and villagers, locals and expatriates. In Greece one's *ascribed* status is inextricably linked with his or her place of birth, irrespective of *achieved* social standing. For example, a village-born, internationally educated top surgeon at the most prestigious hospital in Athens carries with him a childhood identity as a peasant—a self-image his Athenian wife rejects, and his city-born colleagues never let him forget.

The stigma that some Americans associate with being "southern" represents a rejection of rural culture—associated with living off the land, close-knit relations, and conservative values. Poor rural southerners must contend with cultural standards imposed by a national urban elite. Values of the dominant culture, such as cosmopolitanism, wealth, and formal education, tend to marginalize the rural poor. An illustrious academic record and star status at Yale's law school did not protect a young woman who grew up in the Tennessee hills from having to justify her roots to herself, and to the legal establishment in New York City, where she is now a successful attorney.

Industrialization brought rural people into a global subculture—as people different from, and considered inferior to, a dominant, urbanized, global culture. The southern gentry, and beneficiaries of an industrial economy, may be as prejudiced against their region's rural poor as are the Yankees. In many countries peasants are perceived as backward, simpleminded, old fashioned, and parochial. In Guatemala, urbanites consider mountain people to be uncouth and wild. Stereotypes distort group images and are used to justify discrimination against those who live outside industrial regions.

Urban living quarters, such as ghettos, barrios, and ethnic enclaves, accommodate specific segments of the population for whom integration may or may not be an option. Earlier waves of immigrants settled in ghettos and barrios chiefly because property was affordable and they could live with "people like us." Such neighborhoods served as temporary settlements until individuals earned enough money to "move on up" to more integrated, middle-class neighborhoods, usually in the suburbs. More recently, ethnic and gay enclaves, such as Little Brazil in New York and San Francisco's Castro district, respectively, provide residents a potentially long-term, integrated, multiclass, and relatively self-sufficient sociocultural milieu with its own local infrastructure.

The unpredictability of the labor market, the search for job advancement, and the core value of upward mobility drive most North Americans to pursue a new home several times during a lifetime. A common question urbanites ask one another is, "Where are you from?" Of course, the assumption is that one is "not from here." Answering the question typically leads people to mention numerous residences—where I was born, where my parents moved, where my dad was transferred, where my wife got a job, and where my son or daughter lives. Consider the middle-class child who, by his seventh birthday, had lived in six different neighborhoods, four cities, two states, and two countries, because his parents have maintained a dual-career family.

Consider the following reflection by a Jewish woman who was born and raised in the United States but now lives and works in Israel: "What I find amazingly touching is that I've managed to make a circle of friends ranging from their late 20s to their 60s—native-born Israelis as well as those, like me, who came from somewhere else. However, very few if any of them are originally from the USA. In fact, the same is true of my friends in the USA! *Diasporean reality is the only one I know and find comforting*" (our emphasis).

Most North Americans live where they can afford to, not where they choose to. Immigrants settle in enclaves where housing is affordable and

The poor, immigrants, and minorities often live in areas where toxins are concentrated. Environmental activists have been fighting for cleaner, healthier neighborhoods since the early 1980s. Shown here, residents of a poor area near Detroit's Henry Ford Hospital demand the shutdown of a polluting incinerator.

public transportation is accessible. Workers live where they can earn a living. During the 1950s immigrants from southeastern Europe settled in cities with steel mills. Adults with young children left clean, rural communities to live in industrial neighborhoods. One such community in Detroit was so near a factory that its residents had to contend with constant soot on their bodies, furniture, and carpets.

Like most resources, desirable space is distributed inequitably. Research shows a correlation between class, race, and the likelihood of exposure to environmental hazards. The poor, immigrants, and minorities often live in areas where toxins are concentrated. The bumper sticker "It's not just a zip code, it's a lifestyle" may have been created by people who are socioeconomically privileged and proud of their neighborhood, but it also describes much less appealing locations to which the poor are subjected.

To their rescue comes the environmental justice movement. Environmentalists have fought for cleaner, healthier neighborhoods for more than a decade. Today, an increasing number of political activists include minority group members seeking justice and equity in living conditions. They work to protect vulnerable communities from exposure to threats linked to hazardous facilities. Human agency, a key determinant of social change in a multicultural society, is evident once again. ☺

REGIONAL DIVERSITY

North Americans live in communities of various sizes: cities, suburbs, towns, and rural areas. We are geographically mobile, following the job market, but planes, phones, and the computer help us maintain our social networks as we move. Phone lines give us access to people and to the information and contacts available through cyberspace, which is worldwide in scope. The links provided by modern systems of transportation and communication and by the national economy have reduced somewhat the role of regional contrasts in promoting diversity among us. Because Americans move a lot and are exposed to the same media, Atlantans and New Yorkers are not as different as they once were.

But regional diversity does persist. Table 14–1 lists the regions of the United States. It shows that the South and West are increasing, while the Northeast and Midwest are decreasing, their share of the American population.

Diversity in the regions and settlement types we live in is correlated with our exposure to other kinds of diversity, such as that based on race, ethnicity, and class. We have seen that ethnic diversity is increasing in North America as a whole, but some states (e.g., Texas, California) and cities (New York, Los Angeles, Toronto) are much more ethnically diverse than others are. Steven Holmes (1997) describes a new American population movement in which white residents of some states are moving from ethnically diverse metropolitan areas, such as Los Angeles and New York, to smaller towns and rural areas to escape urban gangs, crimes, and pollution. This movement reverses a decade-long decline in the rural U.S. population. According to the U.S. Census Bureau, from 1990 through 1995, rural counties had a net influx of more than 1.6 million people. Almost all of this was from domestic migration. During the 1980s, by contrast, rural counties lost 1.4 million people (Holmes 1997).

The current trend has been likened to an earlier "white flight" from inner cities to suburbs. As the metropolitan areas, including their suburbs, have become more ethnically mixed, whites are now moving to rural areas and small towns. Supporting the trend has been the decline of concentrated urban industry. The owners and employees of small businesses have less

TABLE 14–1. Population of the United States by Region

	1990	2000
Northeast	20.4%	19.0%
Midwest	24.0	22.9
South	34.4	35.6
West	21.2	22.5

Source: U.S. Bureau of the Census.

need to be concentrated in the same area than do those of large businesses, plants, and factories. Given modern transportation and communication, it is easier than ever to conduct business from nonmetropolitan areas. Among the target states of this new white flight are Colorado, Utah, Missouri, Idaho, Kansas, Montana, and Nevada.

Current population shifts may be creating a kind of racial and ethnic polarization. A few states, mainly along the East and West Coasts, are becoming more heterogeneous, while other regions, such as the Rocky Mountain states, the upper Midwest, and New England remain overwhelmingly white. "While there is increasing diversity, it is not happening all over America," according to the demographer William Frey. "It's happening in California, Texas, New York and Florida" (quoted in Holmes 1997).

North American diversity has, and will continue to have, a clear regional aspect. Assume that present trends of immigration and high birthrates among immigrants continue. By the year 2025, in only four states (Texas, California, New Mexico, and Hawaii) will (non-Hispanic) whites compose less than half the population. "Parts of the country are just not being affected by any of this immigration," according to Frey. "They see it on TV or in the newspaper, but it won't touch them" (quoted in Holmes 1997).

GEOGRAPHIC MOBILITY

Americans move around a lot. Consider the authors. Kottak was born and raised in Atlanta, now lives in Michigan, and wrote sections of this book in South Carolina. Kozaitis moved from Greece to Michigan and now lives in Atlanta.

Because of cultural background, historical experience, economic necessity, and media reinforcement, Americans are mobile, exploratory people. Our fondness for mobility and for wide-open spaces is not characteristic of all cultures. Brazilians, for instance, tend to prefer densely packed cities and constant human contact. The pursuit of the frontier has given us (non-Native) Americans a history replete with travel and encounters with strangers. Growing up in the United States still entails separation from those who raised us. Issues of venturing out, breaking with home (breaking away from family and, perhaps, from class background), and creating ties with strangers have been critically important in American history. It is no wonder then that so many American creations, from literature to the mass media, express these themes—our willingness "to boldly go where no one has gone before."

Costs of migrating include loss of kin support and of contact with friends, and disruption of children's schooling. Benefits of migration may include better opportunities for social integration, a safer environment, or a more pleasant climate. However, the primary reason to migrate is to increase earnings (Borjas 1994). A flexible and unregulated North American labor market with substantial geographic mobility results in lower unemployment and higher

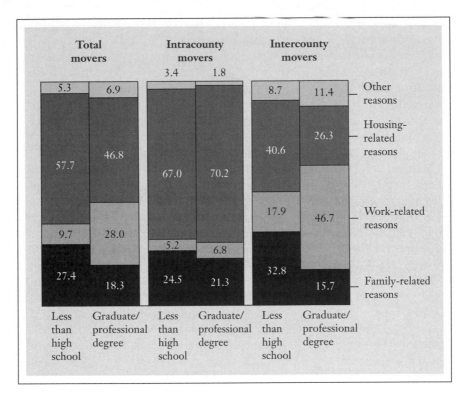

FIGURE 14–1 Reason for moving by educational status and type of move, March 1999–2000. (Percent distribution of movers within the United States, age 18 and older)
Source: U.S. Bureau of the Census, "Why People Move: Exploring the March 2000 Current Population Survey," p. 6.

labor force participation. Our economy encourages flexibility in hiring and firing practices, and ongoing changes in conditions of work, types of jobs, and job descriptions. Accordingly, and compared to other technologically and economically advanced societies, the United States has a more mobile workforce.

A recent study of the effects of geographic mobility on male workers supported "the human-capital hypothesis of migration": long-term financial benefits of moving exceed any temporary costs. According to Rodgers and Rodgers, "moving has a significant, positive effect on earnings" (2000, 124). Six years after moving, the earnings of migrants had increased about 20 percent over what they would have been without the move. The financial benefits were greatest for men younger than 40 years old and with household incomes below $50,000 (Rodgers and Rodgers 2000, 124–129).

College graduates are more likely to move than are those without a college education. According to the National Longitudinal Survey of Youth, five years after graduating from college, 30 percent of graduates move out of the state where they went to college. Figure 14–1 shows reasons for moving ac-

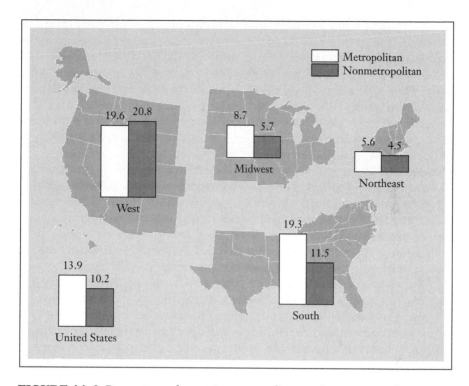

FIGURE 14–2 Percentage change in metropolitan and nonmetropolitan populations by region, 1990–2000.
Source: U.S. Bureau of the Census, Population Profile of the United States: 2000 (Internet Release), 2002, p. 2-1.

cording to educational status and type of move—whether within the same county (intracounty) or from one county to another (intercounty). Considering intercounty moves, college graduates and those with professional degrees are much more likely to move for work-related reasons than are less educated people. Figure 14–1 also shows that in all other categories (excepting intercounty moves by educated people), most moves are for housing-related reasons. This is true for about 70 percent of people who move to a different residence within the same county (U.S. Bureau of the Census, 2002, "Why People Move," p. 6, Figure 2). What was the reason for your last move?

From 1979 to 1991 the southern and western regions of the United States gained the most migrants. Other sections of the country maintained or lost population. Pull factors of interstate migration included stronger economies, lower unemployment, higher earnings, and lower housing costs (Kodrzycki 2001). From 1990 to 2000, the populations of the West and the South increased by 20 and 17 percent, respectively. The midwestern population grew by 8 percent, and the northeastern growth rate was slowest—at 6 percent. Figure 14–2 shows changes in metropolitan and nonmetropolitan populations by region in the United States between 1990 and 2000. Overall and in every region but the West, metropolitan populations grew faster than nonmetropolitan ones. Using material from earlier in the chapter, how might you explain why the trend was different in the West?

Chances are you are reading this book not at home but in a college dorm or library. You are away from home, and eventually you plan to have a place of your own. You may even be residing out of state; you may seek a summer job there rather than where you came from. When you are graduated you may be willing to look for the best job available, no matter what its distance from your hometown.

Think of all the songs that extol independence and individuality expressed through mobility. "I've traveled each and every byway; and more, much more than this, I did it my way." "It's my life; I'll live it wherever and however I want." Primed to travel if necessary to make it on their own, Americans are predestined commuters.

There are many forms of commuting. For some it's a matter of daily physical commuting via mass transit or automobile. Some married couples, residing duolocally (maintaining separate residences near their different workplaces), see each other on weekends or during leaves or vacations from their jobs. Business travelers and tourists have fueled the growth of hotels as homes away from homes. But it has become much easier than it used to be to maintain contact with home, by phone or electronically, even as we move. Modem jacks are ubiquitous and have become a necessity, for business travelers and all others who have come to depend on "connectedness" through cyberspace.

Kottak can transport the notebook computer on which he is currently writing (at home, as it happens) anywhere he goes. With a phone line and access to a server he can wander at will through cyberspace and check his e-mail most places he ever is physically. Via e-mail and phone he can maintain his ties with his son in northern Mozambique and his daughter in Atlanta. During times of little activity, Kottak even chairs his anthropology department from afar via e-mail, phone, and fax. The futurists were right: The virtual office has arrived. Such constant long-distance communication was impossible a decade ago.

Social scientists disagree about the effects of cyberspace-based (virtual) communication on face-to-face social life. Some contend that advanced information technology (AIT) is promoting the decline of face-to-face social relations. But in industrial society, the trend toward impersonality is much older. Social scientists have long linked a decline of face-to-face interactions to *urbanization*. In several books, the anthropologist Robert Redfield (1941) contrasted rural communities, whose daily social relations are on a personal basis, with cities, where impersonality, including constant interaction with strangers, characterizes many aspects of life.

In many ways the world of cyberspace is like New York City—filled with impersonality, anonymity, and strangers. The city never sleeps, but its denizens do sleep, wake up, and work in different spaces, having little to do with their residential neighbors. In work space they interact with their co-workers, and they get together with family, friends, and others who share their interests in varied settings. Despite certain rather utopian visions of the potential role of virtual networks in integrating physical communities (Kling 1996), it is doubtful that AIT will play much of a role in strengthening whole local communities—towns and cities. Rather, it is likely that AIT will be used mainly to facilitate communication among affinity groups (family, friends) and identity-based groups (people with common identities, experiences, or interests, especially involving work). AIT will be used especially for immediate communication within groups of co-workers and members of common organizations. Its main role, however, will be to establish and maintain links between physically dispersed people who have much, and come to have more, in common, such as family members residing in different places.

AIT links people in different regions, even nations, in a common communication network. As it is the favored language in commerce, English has become the key language of international cyberspace. In this way AIT may be promoting linguistic uniformity, even as it reinforces other kinds of diversity, for example, affinity groups based on special interests. To see what we mean, examine the variously titled chat rooms on AOL or MSN.

Despite mobility and communication, regional differences (and regional stereotypes, which, like ethnic stereotypes, are often negative) still exist and have social significance in Canada and the United States. American national prejudice against southern accents has surely affected public evaluations of presidents Jimmy Carter and Bill Clinton. Because southern speech continues to be stigmatized, southerners who move outside the South usually modify their speech to fit national norms or to meet new local standards. With speech closer to national norms, northerners who are transplanted to Atlanta are more linguistically secure than Atlantans in New York. Northerners feel less need to trade in their speech for a more favored dialect.

Regional differences are linked not only to speech but also to religion, race, and ethnicity. In Chapter 8, on religious diversity, we considered regional contrasts in religious affiliations and participation. The South has traditionally been a region of Protestantism and religious conservatism, whereas Boston and New York are, respectively, more Catholic and more Jewish than the rest of the country. Those who are different by virtue of religion have faced persecution in certain areas of the United States. Best known in the South, the Ku Klux Klan (which originated in Michigan) has attacked Catholics and Jews as well as blacks. But today Islamic mosques have joined Protestant churches, Roman Catholic chapels, and Jewish synagogues in many states and Canadian provinces. For members of all those religions, this spread of their houses of worship makes it easier to maintain their participation even as they move and travel.

Regions are adapting to globalization. For instance, there are now Chinese restaurants, and Chinese immigrants, all over the United States and

Canada. With the growth of the larger communities (e.g., virtual communities and self-conscious, politically organized diasporas) being forged through advanced information technology, transnational migration, and other globalizing trends, regional difference per se may become less important.

On the other hand, especially when strongly correlated with ethnic or racial contrasts, regional differences may continue to divide us. Earlier in this chapter we discussed white flight to such states as Colorado, Utah, Missouri, Idaho, Kansas, Montana, and Nevada. These states are much less racially and ethnically diverse than the rest of the United States. Robert D. Kaplan (1994) speculates that regional or ethnic identities may eventually disrupt the United States and Canada. The more prominent role of regionalism in Canada than in the United States is suggested by the results of the Canadian elections of June 2, 1997. The Liberal party, which won the election, was the only one of Canada's five main political parties with national, rather than merely regional, success. The Liberals took 38 percent of the vote and won seats in the House of Commons in every province but Nova Scotia. The four other parties winning seats were all regionally based—the Reform party in the West, the Bloc Québécois in Quebec, and the New Democrats and Progressive Conservatives in the East.

Compared with the United States, Canada appears to be more split by region, language, and culture (English-speaking Canada versus Quebec) as well as by political orientation. The Reform party and New Democrats are right- and left-wing, respectively (DePalma 1997). The Bloc Québécois fields candidates only in the province of Quebec. The Reform party, based in the West, is opposed to any special recognition of Quebec and Canada's French heritage.

Despite its 1997 success, the Liberal majority won fewer seats than it had in the previous election. Voters reacted to Prime Minister Jean Chretien's cuts in government services, including the nation's social welfare blanket, to reduce the national deficit. Cost cutting and reduction of government services were also issues in Germany and other European Economic Community (EEC) nations as those countries attempted to meet deficit reduction goals in preparation for a shift to a common European currency—the euro.

Canada features a major linguistic contrast associated with region, pitting French-speaking Quebec against the rest of the country, where mainly English is spoken. In the United States one is more likely to hear Spanish in California, Florida, New Mexico, New York, and Texas than in other states. California, the scene of so much immigration, particularly from Asia, has more linguistic diversity than other states have.

In terms of English dialects or accents, some regions of the United States have traditionally been more linguistically marked than others. We all have stereotypes about accents found in the South, New York City, and New England, especially the Boston area. No one thought much about how Minnesotans and North Dakotans talked until the movie *Fargo* helped correct the erroneous belief that midwesterners don't have accents. (Jeez, Hon, how could anyone think that!)

In Los Angeles (shown here), as in Atlanta, Detroit, and Washington, downtown residential areas tend to be marked racially and ethnically. The populations of such downtowns are much more varied during the (work)day than at night. In these typical American metro centers, much of the daytime urban population is car dependent and commutes from outlying areas.

CITIES AND URBANITES

In contemporary North America, a few true cities, such as New York, San Francisco, Montreal, and Toronto, recall such European cities as Amsterdam, London, Paris, Berlin, and Rome. Known as the city that doesn't sleep, New York is the truest American city. All kinds of people (men, women, old, young, gay, straight, drunk, sober, addicted, drug-free, of all races and ethnic groups) use its urban space 24 hours a day. Many other cities shut down at night, except for marginal groups, such as the homeless.

In much of North America, many people commute by car from suburbs to work in cities. In Atlanta, Detroit, Los Angeles, and Washington, downtown residential areas tend to be marked racially and ethnically. The populations of such downtowns are much more varied during the workday than at night.

In these typical American metro centers, much of the daytime urban population is car dependent and commutes from outlying areas.

Millions of Americans and Canadians commute daily, working in the
city while keeping and educating their children in the suburbs. Inner cities,
suburbs, and rural areas vary markedly in what we might call their *diversity
index*. This contrast has political implications. Downtown residents tend to
vote for Democrats, whereas suburbanites and small-town dwellers tend to
prefer Republicans. Cities are known not only for their ethnic mix but for
their ethnic clashes, of which the most extreme (given the diversity of ethnic
groups and intensity of passions) was probably the Los Angeles riots of
1992.

Small towns, at the other extreme, are known for various expressions of
homogeneity, such as racial/ethnic uniformity, conformity, reduced privacy,
constant public scrutiny, restricted lifestyle choices, and political and social
conservatism. For generations, social scientists have used face-to-face social
relations to contrast small towns with the more impersonal ties that characterize cities. We have mentioned a resurgence of small-town and rural life
in the 1990s, but the decline of the small town has been celebrated in books,
TV shows, and movies such as *The Last Picture Show*. Even though small-
town life may be reviving today, it is vastly different from how it was one or
two generations ago. Televisions, videos, and mall cinemas seemed to have
doomed downtown movie houses, but there may be a resurgence of small-
town-center life as more affluent people move in. Modern communication
systems allow small-town residents and businesses to be as much a part of
the World Wide Web as urbanites are.

Urban anthropology is the anthropological study of cities. Particularly
since the 1950s, anthropologists have systematically investigated urban issues, problems, social organization, and lifestyles in North America and
abroad. For example, from ethnography in a small city in the American
Midwest, anthropologist Carol Stack discovered that close-knit networks
can exist in urban settings. Her book *All Our Kin* (1975) shows the strength
of expanded family networks and of close-knit, kin-based relationships
among urban African Americans. Ethnographers have influenced social policy by showing that strong kin ties exist in city neighborhoods whose social
organization is often considered fragmented or pathological.

Social scientists have long recognized that in rural communities social
relations are typically on a face-to-face basis, but impersonality is more
characteristic of urban life. Part of being different is liking to live in different kinds of places. Many of us have settlement orientations just as we have
sexual orientations. Some people hate New York; some think it's a nice place
to visit; and many can't imagine living anywhere else. Arriving in the city,
migrants from small towns may discover their "little town blues are drifting
away." Many people like cities precisely because of the impersonality and
anonymity they offer. Lots of Americans enjoy living in, or at least visiting,
places where nobody (rather than everyone) knows your name. To some
extent, the anonymity of urban life can be replicated in cyberspace, where

we can, more or less privately, craft new identities and chart personal paths in search of new images and information.

Cities themselves tend to be more diverse than smaller places are, and many of the groups discussed so far in this book tend to be overrepresented in cities. (That is, members of such groups are more likely to live in cities than in other places, and their demographic percentages are higher in cities than they are in the nation as a whole.) The ethnic and racial diversity of New York, Los Angeles, Chicago, San Francisco, and Toronto are well known. Such cities tend to be politically liberal, have a higher percentage of Catholics, Jews, Muslims, Hindus, and Buddhists than smaller communities do, and also to have larger and more concentrated gay and lesbian populations. Atlanta, Los Angeles, New York, San Francisco–Oakland, and Toronto all have recognized gay and lesbian districts.

Differing in income, household organization, and ethnic affiliation, neighborhoods influence their residents' quality of life and their opportunities for upward mobility. In low-income neighborhoods, recreational and learning opportunities for children are limited. Parents save money to buy a house "in a good neighborhood," with "a good school," typically meaning a middle- or upper-middle-class neighborhood.

The market fuels patterns of housing inequities and "location inequalities" (Alba, Logan, and Stults 2000, 589). Immigrants cluster in inner-city enclaves near other low-income minorities. Acculturation and upward mobility may offer a "ticket out" of the barrio, ghetto, or ethnic enclave—and into more integrated, higher-income neighborhoods. One study of ethnic groups in five metropolitan areas found non-Hispanic whites to be the most "locationally advantaged." Most disadvantaged were African Americans, with Asians and Latinos falling in between (Logan et al. 1996).

Waves of immigration in the 1990s increased the diversity of neighborhoods in the United States and Canada. Settlement patterns of racially and ethnically defined groups vary according to their economic stability, and tolerance by the dominant group of individuals in their neighborhoods who are deemed to be different (Alba et al. 2000).

REGION AND THE INCOME GAP

Table 14–2 suggests some interesting relations between regions, urban settings, and socioeconomic stratification. Table 14–2 is based on a 1997 study by the Center on Budget and Policy Priorities, a research group in Washington, D.C. It displays data on average family incomes (1994–1996) for the bottom and top fifths of the population of each state and the ratio of the latter to the former. Notice that the income gap between the richest and the poorest was largest in New York State. (The gap was even larger in the District of Columbia, which is not included in Table 14–2.) In 1994–1996, the richest 20 percent of New York State families earned an average of $132,390

TABLE 14–2. Average Family Income (1994–1996), for the Bottom and Top Fifths of the Population of Each State and the Ratio of the Latter to the Former

	Average Income of Families with Children		
	Bottom Fifth	Top Fifth	Ratio
1. New York	$6,787	$132,390	19.5
2. Louisiana	6,430	102,339	15.9
3. New Mexico	6,408	91,741	14.3
4. Arizona	7,273	103,392	14.2
5. Connecticut	10,415	147,594	14.2
6. California	9,033	127,719	14.1
7. Florida	7,705	107,811	14.0
8. Kentucky	7,364	99,210	13.5
9. Alabama	7,531	99,062	13.2
10. W. Virginia	6,439	84,479	13.1
11. Tennessee	8,156	106,966	13.1
12. Texas	8,642	113,149	13.1
13. Mississippi	6,257	80,980	12.9
14. Michigan	9,257	117,107	12.7
15. Oklahoma	7,483	94,380	12.6
16. Massachusetts	10,694	132,962	12.4
17. Georgia	9,978	123,837	12.4
18. Illinois	10,002	123,233	12.3
19. Ohio	9,346	111,894	12.0
20. S. Carolina	8,146	96,712	11.9
21. Pennsylvania	10,512	124,537	11.8
22. N. Carolina	9,363	107,490	11.5
23. Rhode Island	9,914	111,015	11.2
24. Washington	10,116	112,501	11.1
25. Maryland	13,346	147,971	11.1
26. Virginia	10,816	116,202	10.7
27. Kansas	10,790	110,341	10.2
28. Oregon	9,627	97,589	10.1
29. New Jersey	14,211	143,010	10.1
30. Indiana	11,115	110,876	10.0
31. Montana	9,051	89,902	9.9
32. S. Dakota	9,474	93,822	9.9
33. Idaho	10,721	104,725	9.8
34. Delaware	12,041	116,965	9.7
35. Arkansas	8,995	83,434	9.3
36. Colorado	14,326	131,368	9.2
37. Hawaii	12,735	116,060	9.1
38. Missouri	11,090	100,837	9.1
39. Alaska	14,868	129,025	8.7
40. Wyoming	11,174	94,845	8.5
41. Minnesota	14,655	120,344	8.2
42. Nebraska	12,546	102,992	8.2

TABLE 14–2. (Continued)

43. Maine	11,275	92,457	8.2
44. New Hampshire	14,299	116,018	8.1
45. Nevada	12,276	98,693	8.0
46. Iowa	13,148	104,253	7.9
47. Wisconsin	13,398	103,551	7.7
48. Vermont	13,107	97,898	7.5
49. N. Dakota	12,424	91,041	7.3
50. Utah	15,709	110,938	7.1
Total U.S.	9,254	117,499	12.7

Source: From Richard Perez-Pena "Study Shows New York has Greatest Income Gap." *New York Times*, December 17, 1997, p. A14. © 1997 by the New York Times Co. Reprinted by permission.

a year, but the poorest 20 percent averaged $6,787. This ratio, 19.5 to 1, was well above the national average of 12.7 (14.0 to 1 in 2000).

The data in Table 14–2 suggest that ethnically heterogeneous states, especially those with large cities, tend to have wider gaps in income than do more homogeneous states. Examples of the former include New York, New Mexico, Arizona, Connecticut, California, Florida, and Texas (all in the top 12 with the most skewed incomes). Consider the bottom 10, all of them states in which the gap between richest and poorest was less than half of New York's gap. They are, from 50th up: Utah, North Dakota, Vermont, Wisconsin, Iowa, Nevada, New Hampshire, Maine, Nebraska, and Minnesota. These states lack the ethnic and racial diversity that characterizes most of the top 10.

States such as New York, California, and Texas all have large populations of immigrants, who tend to accept lower wages for unskilled labor than do native-born Americans. These states also have high-tech industries and large concentrations of well-educated professionals, working in services and information processing. Widening the family income gap are their higher salaries and tendency to choose domestic partners with similar professions. In states like New York, the decline in manufacturing jobs (from 1.5 million in 1978 to 925,000 in 1997) and union benefits has also contributed to the gap (Perez-Pena 1997). We have seen in this chapter that diversity in the regions and settlement types we live in is correlated with our exposure to other kinds of diversity, such as that based on race, ethnicity, and class.

URBAN ETHNIC GROUPS, POVERTY, AND CRIME

Kin-modeled, ethnic, and voluntary associations help reduce the stress of urban life on migrants. In North American cities such groups even play a role in organizing crime. Francis Ianni (1977) has studied criminal organizations among African Americans and Hispanics. He views organized crime as a long-established feature of American economic life, a response to poverty and differential power. Ianni sees criminal organizations as representing one end of an economic continuum, with legitimate businesses at the other end. That is, illegitimate businesses often differ from legitimate ones only in degree. Poor neighborhoods and regions *are* likely to have more informal economic activities, including crime, because of their lack of formal economic opportunities. As the mass media cover the news, they reinforce the perceived link between poor neighborhoods and crime, ignoring or downplaying the incidence of white-collar crime in more affluent environments.

Like most white Americans, most African Americans and Hispanics, even those who face severe poverty, don't become criminals. Historically, however, some ethnic group members have used crime as a route to financial and psychological security. Crime tends to blossom when legitimate economic opportunities dry up. In nonstate societies people derive their subsistence from land, livestock, and natural resources. Everyone who wants to work can do so. Only states have joblessness.

Crime is also a creation of state organization. By definition, a crime is an illegal act, and only states have legal codes. According to Ianni (1977), poverty and powerlessness, rather than ethnic background, cause crime. After all, in American history successive ethnic groups with very different cultural backgrounds, but facing similar conditions of poverty, have used crime to better themselves economically.

Ianni (1977) found that several types of personal relations introduced African-American and Hispanic criminals to each other and to crime. Links between adult criminals often grow out of childhood friendships or membership in a gang. Commonly, however, boys begin their careers in crime as apprentices to older men. Established criminals, who become role models, recruit boys for criminal ventures. Links established in prison also lead to later criminal association. Women occasionally join criminal groups through male friends or husbands.

Once people are committed to crime, their common activity holds the networks together. Networks link crime partners, employers and employees, and buyers and sellers of goods and services. Social solidarity, an esprit de corps, cements criminal networks. The stronger this spirit is, the more successful the ventures in crime tend to be. One kind of criminal association is the entrepreneurial organization, which Ianni compares to a legitimate business. Consisting of a head and the head's agents in illegality, it has a code of rules designed to protect itself and its activities. The rules stress secrecy (don't tell the police or nonmembers), honesty (don't cheat on members), and competence.

Ianni (1977) discusses the ethnic succession of crime in American cities. Segments of Italian, Cuban, Puerto Rican, African-American, and other ethnic groups have all used crime to escape poverty and powerlessness. However, the criminal networks of these groups have differed. Kinship is one of the most obvious differences. Kinship has played a stronger role in organizing Italian-American and Cuban-American criminals than it has in organizing African-American and Puerto Rican criminals.

Modern North American cities have many kinds of kin-based ethnic associations. Another (noncriminal) example comes from Los Angeles, which has the largest Samoan immigrant community (at least 12,000 people) in the United States. Samoans in Los Angeles draw on their traditional system of *matai* (respect for elders) to deal with modern urban problems. For example, in 1992 a white policeman shot and killed two unarmed Samoan brothers. When a judge dismissed charges against the officer, local leaders used the matai system to calm angry youths (who have formed gangs, like other ethnic groups in the Los Angeles area). Clan leaders and elders organized a well-attended community meeting, in which they urged young members to be patient. Los Angeles Samoans aren't just traditionalists; they also use the American judicial system. They brought a civil case against the officer in question and pressed the U. S. Justice Department to initiate a civil rights case in the matter (Mydans 1992b).

THE AMERICAN PERIPHERY

Poverty in North America has rural as well as urban expressions. Job scarcity in rural areas is a prime reason for rural-urban migration. In a comparative study of two counties at opposite ends of Tennessee, Thomas Collins (1989) reviews the effects of industrialization on poverty and unemployment in these rural areas. Hill County, with an Appalachian white population, is on the Cumberland Plateau in eastern Tennessee. Delta County, predominantly African American, is 60 miles from Memphis in western Tennessee's lower Mississippi region. Both counties once had economies based on agriculture and timber, but jobs in those sectors declined sharply with the advent of mechanization. Both counties have unemployment rates more than twice that of Tennessee as a whole. More than a third of the people in each county live below the poverty level. Given very restricted job opportunities, the best-educated local youths have migrated to northern cities for three generations.

To increase jobs, local officials and business leaders have tried to attract industries from outside. Their efforts exemplify a more general rural southern strategy, which began during the 1950s, of courting industry by advertising a good business climate, meaning low rents, cheap utilities, and a nonunion labor pool. However, few firms are attracted to an impoverished and poorly educated workforce. All the industries that have come to such areas have very limited market power and a narrow profit margin. Such firms survive by offering low wages and minimal benefits, with frequent layoffs. These industries tend to emphasize traditional female skills such as sewing, and they mostly attract women.

The garment industry, which is highly mobile, is Hill County's main employer. The knowledge that a garment plant can be moved to another site very rapidly tends to reduce employee demands. Management can be as arbitrary and authoritarian as it wishes. The unemployment rate and low educational level ensure that many women will accept sewing jobs for a bit more than the minimum wage.

In neither county has new industry brought many jobs for men, who have a higher unemployment rate than do women (as do blacks, compared to whites). Collins (1989) found that many men in Hill County had never been permanently employed; they had just done temporary jobs, always for cash.

The effects of industrialization in Delta County have been similar. That county's recruitment efforts have likewise attracted only marginal industries. The largest is a bicycle seat and toy manufacturer, which employs 60 percent women. Three other large plants, which make clothing and auto seat covers, employ 95 percent women. Egg production was once significant in Delta County but folded when the market for eggs fell in response to rising national concern over the effects of cholesterol.

In both counties the men, ignored by industrialization, maintain an informal economy. They sell and trade used goods through personal networks. They take casual jobs, such as operating farm equipment on a daily or seasonal basis. Collins found that maintaining an automobile was the most important and prestigious contribution these men made to their families. Neither county had public transportation; Hill County even lacked school buses. Families need cars to get women to work and kids to school. The men who kept an old car running longest got special respect.

Collins (1989) found that the limited opportunities for men to do well at work created a feeling of lowered self-worth, which expressed itself in physical violence. The rate of domestic violence in Hill County exceeded the state average. Spousal abuse arose from men's demands to control women's paychecks. (Men regard the cash they earn themselves as their own, to spend on male activities.)

One important difference between the two counties involved labor unions, which were more developed in Delta County. At the time of the study, there was just one unionized plant in Delta County, but recent campaigns for unionization at two other factories had failed in close votes. In the rural South, attitudes toward workers' rights tend to correlate with race. Rural southern whites, such as those in Tennessee's Hill County, usually don't vote for unions when they have a chance to do so. African Americans are more likely to challenge management about pay and work rules. Local blacks tend to view their work situation in terms of black against white, rather than from a position of working-class solidarity. They are attracted to unions because they see only whites in managerial positions and resent differential advancement of white factory workers. One manager told Collins that "once the workforce of a plant becomes more than one-third black, you can expect to have union representation within a year" (Collins 1989, 10). Considering the probability of unionization, Japanese businesses don't build their plants in the primarily African-American counties of the lower Mississippi. Tennessee's Japanese factories cluster in the "whiter" eastern and central parts of the state.

Poverty pockets in the rural South (and other areas) should not be viewed as pristine survivors from a more rural past but as influenced by larger trends, including the expansion of industry and world capitalism. Through mechanization, industrialization, and other changes promoted by larger systems, local people have been deprived of land and jobs. After years of industrial development, a third of the people of Hill and Delta counties remain below the poverty level. Emigration of educated and talented people continues as local opportunities shrink. Collins (1989) concluded that rural poverty will not be reduced by attracting additional marginal industries, because such firms lack the market power to improve wages and benefits. Different development schemes are needed for these counties and the rural South generally.

CHAPTER FIFTEEN

Speech

REGIONAL AND CLASS-BASED SPEECH

Depending on where they live, North Americans have certain stereotypes about how people in other regions, and nations, talk. Some stereotypes, spread by the mass media, are more generalized than others. Most Americans think they can imitate a southern accent. They also have nationwide stereotypes about speech in New York City (the pronunciation of *coffee*, for example) and Boston ("I pahked the kah in Hahvahd Yahd").

Many Americans also believe that midwesterners don't have accents. This belief stems from the fact that midwestern dialects don't have many stigmatized linguistic variants—speech patterns that people in other regions recognize and look down on, such as *r*-lessness and *dem, dese,* and *dere* (instead of *them, these,* and *there*).

Actually, regional patterns influence the way all Americans speak. Midwesterners do have detectable accents. College students from out of state easily recognize that their in-state classmates speak differently. In-state students, however, have difficulty hearing their own speech peculiarities because they are accustomed to them and view them as normal.

In Detroit-area high schools, sociolinguist Penelope Eckert, as described in her book *Jocks and Burnouts* (1989), studied variation in speech correlated with high school social categories. Eckert's study revealed links between speech and social status, the local high school manifestation of a larger and underlying American social class system. Social variation showed up most clearly in the division of the high school population into two main categories—jocks and burnouts.

Along with teachers, administrators, and parents (particularly jock parents), jocks helped maintain the school's formal and traditional social structure. They participated more in athletics, student government, and organized school-based activities. In contrast, burnouts (a social label derived from their tendency to smoke cigarettes) had their main social networks in their neighborhoods. They took school social structure less seriously.

A comparable split exists in many American public high schools, although the specific names of the two categories vary from place to place. Jocks have also been called preppies or tweeds, and burnouts have been called freaks, greasers, hoods, and rednecks. No matter what the opposed groups have been called in different regions and at different times, the social division always correlates with linguistic differences. Many adult speech habits are set when people are teens, as adolescents copy the speech of people they like and admire. Because jocks and burnouts move in different social systems, they come to talk differently.

The first step in a sociolinguistic study is to determine which speech forms vary. In New York City, the pronunciation of *r* varies systematically with social class and thus can be used in studies of sociolinguistic variation. However, this feature doesn't vary much among midwesterners, most of whom are adamant *r* pronouncers. However, vowel pronunciation does vary considerably among midwesterners and can be used in a sociolinguistic study.

Far from having no accents, midwesterners, even in the same high school, demonstrate sociolinguistic variation. Furthermore, dialect differences in Michigan are immediately obvious to people from other parts of the country. One of the best examples of variable vowel pronunciation is the /e/ phoneme, which occurs in words like *ten, rent, French, section, lecture, effect, best,* and *test.* In southeastern Michigan there are four different ways of pronouncing this phoneme. Speakers of black English and immigrants from Appalachia often pronounce *ten* as "tin," just as southerners habitually do. Some Michiganders say "ten," the correct pronunciation in standard English. However, two other pronunciations are more common. Instead of "ten," many Michiganders say "tan" or "tun" (as though they were using the word *ton,* a unit of weight).

Kottak's Michigan students often astound him with their pronunciations. One day he met one of his Michigan-raised teaching assistants in the hall. She was deliriously happy. When Kottak asked why, she replied, "I've just had the best suction."

"What?" Kottak queried.

"I've just had a wonderful suction," she repeated.

"What?" He still wasn't understanding.

She finally spoke more precisely. "I've just had the best saction." She considered this a clearer pronunciation of the word *section.*

Another TA once complimented Kottak, "You luctured to great effuct today." After an exam a student lamented that she hadn't been able to do her "bust on the tust." Once Kottak lectured about uniformity in fast-food restaurant chains. One of his students had just vacationed in Hawaii, where, she told him, hamburger prices were higher than they were on the mainland. It was, she said, because of the runt. Who, Kottak wondered, was this runt? The very puny owner of Honolulu's McDonald's franchise? Perhaps he advertised on television, "Come have a hamburger with the runt." Eventually Kottak figured out that she was talking about the high cost of *rent* on those densely packed islands. ☺

LINGUISTIC RELATIVISM

Just as there are no documented differences in brain complexity among contemporary human populations, no one has ever shown the *intrinsic* superiority of any language or dialect over another. The doctrine of **linguistic relativism** recognizes all known languages and dialects as effective means of communication. This doctrine contradicts popular beliefs and stereotypes. Many French people, for example, believe theirs is the only appropriate language for civilized conversation (and they are eager to ban foreign word *contamination* from their mass media). Many British and North Americans assert the superiority of English as a commercial language. (It *is* true that the vocabularies of particular languages do grow and develop as they are used repeatedly in particular contexts. However, any language used in a given context can undergo such a process of growth and differentiation, sometimes by borrowing foreign terms, sometimes by elaborating its own.)

Claims of intrinsic *linguistic* superiority are actually based on *cultural* rather than linguistic developments. The use of language in particular contexts reflects world politics and economics rather than inherent properties of the language itself. In creating and imposing a nation-state, and thereafter a world empire, the French spread their culture through their language. They asserted to the provinces they attached and the people they conquered that they were engaged in a civilizing mission. They came to equate the French language with civilization itself.

The contemporary use and distribution of a language reflect factors other than features of the language itself. One language spoken in China has more native speakers than English does not because it is a better language but because the population that speaks it has multiplied as a result of nonlinguistic factors. English is the native language of British people, North Americans, Australians, New Zealanders, and many South Africans because of English colonization and conquest. The success of this colonization and conquest had nothing to do with the language itself. Weapons, ships, commerce, and sociopolitical organization played decisive roles.

Between 2,000 and 3,000 years ago a western African (proto-Bantu) population lived in a small area of what is now Nigeria and Cameroon. Today the linguistic descendants of the proto-Bantu language cover most of central and southern Africa. Speakers of Bantu did not expand because their languages were superior as means of communication. Rather, they grew, prospered, and spread because they developed a highly competitive cultural adaptation based on iron tools and weapons and very productive food crops.

No language or dialect can confer, by virtue of its purely linguistic qualities, a differential advantage on its speakers. Only the social evaluation of its speakers and, by extension, of the language itself can do this. Languages are flexible and constantly changing systems. They easily admit and adopt new items and new terms. Speakers modify old forms, borrow foreign words, and create entirely new expressions. This process is so usual and constant that some nations, such as France, maintain agencies to safeguard the purity of the standard language and discourage its contamination by foreign words.

SOCIOLINGUISTICS: THE STUDY
OF LINGUISTIC DIVERSITY

Actually, no language is a homogeneous system in which everyone speaks just as everyone else does. One reason for variation is geography, as in regional dialects and accents. The field of **sociolinguistics** investigates language in its social context, examining relationships between social and linguistic variation. Examples of linguistic variation associated with social divisions include the bilingualism of ethnic groups and speech patterns associated with particular social classes. To show that linguistic features correlate systematically with social, economic, and regional differences, the social attributes of speakers must be measured and related to speech (Labov 1972a).

As an illustration of the linguistic diversity encountered in all nation-states, consider contemporary North America. Besides English and French, Canada includes the languages of its First Nations (Native Americans) and many immigrants. Mexicans speak Indian languages as well as Spanish. In the United States, reflecting ethnic diversity, millions of Americans learn first languages other than English. Spanish is the most common. Most of these people eventually become bilingual, adding English as a second language. In many multilingual (including colonized) nations, people use two languages on different occasions—one in the home, for example, and the other on the job or in public.

Whether bilingual or not, we all vary our speech in different contexts; that is, we engage in **style shifts.** In certain parts of Europe, people regularly switch dialects. This phenomenon, known as **diglossia**, applies to "high" and "low" variants of the same language, for example, German and Flemish (spoken in Belgium). People use the high variant at universities and in writing, professions, and the mass media. They use the low variant for ordinary conversation with family members and friends.

Just as social situations influence speech, so do geographical, cultural, and socioeconomic differences. Many dialects coexist in the United States

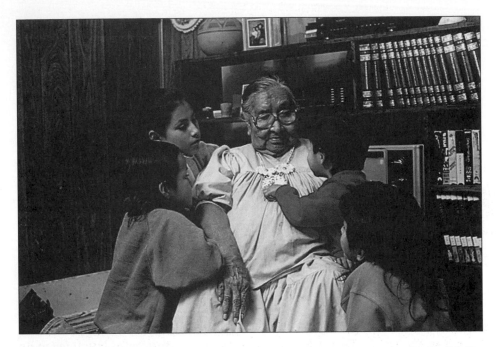

Reflecting cultural and ethnic diversity, millions of Americans learn first languages other than English. Yet global linguistic richness is being reduced as people abandon their native languages for dominant and national languages. Shown here, an Apache woman transmits her ancestral language and culture to her grandchildren in Whiteriver, Arizona.

and Canada with Standard (American or Canadian) English (SE). SE itself is a dialect that differs, say, from BBC English, which is the preferred dialect in Great Britain. All dialects are effective as systems of communication, which is the main job of language. Our tendency to think of particular dialects as better or worse than others is a social rather than a linguistic judgment. We rank certain speech patterns because we recognize that they are used by groups that we also rank. People who say *dese, dem,* and *dere* instead of *these, them,* and *there* communicate perfectly well with anyone who recognizes that the *d* sound systematically replaces the *th* sound in their speech. However, this form of speech has become stigmatized, an indicator of low social rank. We call it, like the use of *ain't,* "uneducated speech." The use of *dem, dese,* and *dere* is one of many phonological differences that Americans recognize and look down on.

Gender Speech Contrasts

Women's speech tends to be more similar to the standard dialect than men's is. Consider the data in Table 15–1, gathered in Detroit. In all social classes, but particularly in the working class, men were more apt to use double negatives (e.g., "I don't want none"). Women are more careful about "uneducated

TABLE 15–1. Multiple Negation ("I Don't Want None")

According to Gender and Class (In percentages)

	Upper-Middle Class	Lower-Middle Class	Upper-Working Class	Lower-Working Class
Male	6.3	32.4	40.0	90.1
Female	0.0	1.4	35.6	58.9

Source: From *Sociolinguistics: An Introduction to Language and Society* by Peter Trudgill (London: Pelican Books, 1974, revised edition 1983), p. 85. Reproduced by permission of Penguin Books Ltd.

speech." This trend shows up in both the United States and England. Men may adopt working-class speech because they associate it with hard labor and thus with masculinity. Perhaps women pay more attention to the mass media, where standard dialects tend to be employed. Also, women may compensate for the socioeconomic barriers they have faced by copying the linguistic norms of upper-status groups.

According to Robin Lakoff (1975) and Deborah Tannen (1990), the use of certain types of words and expressions has reflected women's lesser power in American society. For example, "Oh dear," "Oh fudge," and "Goodness!" are less forceful than "Hell," "Damn," and many stronger expressions. Men's customary use of forceful words reflects their traditional public power and presence. Watch the lips of a disgruntled athlete in a televised competition, such as a football game. What's the likelihood he's saying "Phooey on you"? Men can't normally use certain "women's words" (*adorable, charming, sweet, cute, lovely, divine*) without raising doubts about their masculinity.

In certain domains, such as sports and color terminology, men and women have different sorts of vocabularies. Men typically know more terms related to sports, make more distinctions among them (e.g., runs versus points), and try to use the terms more precisely than women do. Correspondingly, influenced more by the fashion and cosmetics industries than men are, women use more color terms and attempt to use them more specifically than men do. Thus, to make this point when lecturing on sociolinguistics, Kottak brings an off-purple shirt to class. Holding it up, he first asks women to say aloud what color the shirt is. The women rarely answer with a uniform voice, as they try to distinguish the actual shade (mauve, lavender, wisteria, or some other purplish hue). He then asks the men, who consistently answer as one, "Purple." Rare is the man who on the spur of the moment can imagine the difference between fuchsia and magenta.

Another gender contrast noted by Lakoff (1975), which she links to linguistic insecurity, is women's greater tendency to end a declarative sentence with the intonation of a question? The gender difference even shows up in cyberspace communication. Using expletives or beginning a message with the salutation "Dude" suggests male identity. And female use of cyberspace sometimes shows some of the sociolinguistic insecurity that has been noted in other contexts (Lakoff 1975; Tannen 1990). From postings we have read we suspect that women are more likely to end their messages with disclaimers, such as "But that's just my opinion," whereas men choose the more emphatic IMHO (in my humble opinion) to express the same sentiment.

Language is our principal means of communicating, but it isn't the only one we use. We communicate whenever we transmit information about ourselves to others and receive such information from them. Our facial expressions, bodily stances, gestures, and movements, even if unconscious, convey information and are part of our communication styles. Deborah Tannen (1990, 1993) discusses differences in the communication styles of American men and women, and her comments go beyond language. She notes that girls and women tend to look directly at each other when they talk, whereas boys and men do not. Males are more likely to look straight ahead rather than to turn and make eye contact with someone, especially another man, seated beside them. Also, in conversational groups, men tend to relax and sprawl out. Women may adopt a similar relaxed posture in all-female groups, but when they are with men they tend to draw in their limbs and adopt a tighter stance.

Tannen (1990, 1993) uses the terms "rapport" and "report" to contrast women's and men's overall linguistic styles. Women, says Tannen, typically use language and the body movements that accompany it to build rapport, social connections with others. Men, on the other hand, tend to make reports, reciting information that serves to establish a place for themselves in a hierarchy, as they also attempt to determine the relative ranks of their conversation mates.

Interestingly, the rise of a service economy may be helping to mainstream feminine speech styles. In a study of telephone call-center operators in Great Britain, Cameron (2000) found a particular speech style to be the norm in customer service settings. This speech style emphasized affect, caring, empathy, accommodation, and sincerity—characteristics associated with the speech of women. Men working in customer service settings were also trained to use this communication style. Cameron notes that "the commodification of language in contemporary service workplaces is also in some sense the commodification of a quasi-feminine service persona" (2000, 324).

Stratification and Symbolic Domination

We use and evaluate speech—and language changes—in the context of extralinguistic forces—social, political, and economic. Mainstream Americans evaluate the speech of low-status groups negatively, calling it uneducated. This is not because these ways of speaking are bad in themselves but because they have come to symbolize low status. Consider variation in the pronunciation of *r*. In some parts of the United States *r* is regularly pronounced, and in other (*r*-less) areas it is not. Originally, American *r*-less speech was modeled on the fashionable speech of England. Because of its prestige, *r*-lessness was adopted in many areas and continues as the norm around Boston and in the South.

Language may be our main way of communicating, but it isn't the only one we use. Our facial expressions, bodily stances, gestures, and movements, even if unconscious, convey information and are part of our communication styles. What differences do you notice among these telemarketers? Do you think those differences are linked specifically to gender?

New Yorkers sought prestige by dropping their *r*'s in the 19th century, after having pronounced them in the 18th. However, contemporary New Yorkers are going back to the 18th-century pattern of pronouncing *r*'s. What matters, and what governs linguistic change, is not the reverberation of a good strong midwestern *r*, but social evaluation, whether *r*'s happen to be in or out.

Studies of *r* pronunciation in New York City have clarified the social mechanisms of phonological change. William Labov (1972b) focused on whether *r* was pronounced after vowels in such words as *car, floor, card,* and *fourth*. To get data on how this linguistic variation correlated with social class, he used a series of rapid encounters with employees in three New York City department stores, each of whose prices and locations attracted a different socioeconomic group. Saks Fifth Avenue (68 encounters) catered to the upper-middle-class, Macy's (125) attracted middle-class shoppers, and S. Klein's (71) had predominantly lower-middle-class and working-class customers. The class origins of salespeople in those stores tended to reflect those of their respective clients.

Having already determined that a certain department was on the fourth floor, Labov approached ground-floor salespeople and asked where that department was. After the salesperson had answered, "Fourth floor," Labov repeated his "Where?" in order to get a second response. The second reply was more formal and emphatic, the salesperson presumably thinking that Labov hadn't heard or understood the first answer. For each salesperson, therefore, Labov had two samples of *r* pronunciation in two words.

He calculated the percentages of workers who pronounced *r* at least once during the interview. These were 62 percent at Saks, 51 percent at Macy's, but only 20 percent at S. Klein's. Labov also found that personnel on upper floors, where he asked, "What floor is this?" (and where more expensive items were sold), pronounced *r* more often than ground-floor salespeople did.

In Labov's study, *r* pronunciation was clearly associated with prestige. Certainly the job interviewers who had hired the salespeople never actually counted *r*'s before offering employment. However, they did use speech evaluations to make judgments about how effective certain people would be in selling particular kinds of merchandise. In other words, they practiced sociolinguistic discrimination, using linguistic features in deciding who got certain jobs.

In stratified societies, our speech habits help determine our access to employment, material resources, and positions of power and prestige. Because of this, "proper language" itself becomes a strategic resource—and a path to wealth, fame, and power (Gal 1989). Illustrating this, many ethnographers have described the importance of verbal skill and oratory in local-level politics (Bloch 1975). A "great communicator," Ronald Reagan, dominated American society in the 1980s as a two-term president. Another twice-elected president, Bill Clinton, despite his southern accent, was known for his verbal skills in certain contexts (e.g., televised debates and town-hall meetings). Communications flaws may have helped doom the presidencies of Gerald Ford, Jimmy Carter, and George H. W. Bush ("Couldn't do that; wouldn't be prudent").

The French anthropologist Pierre Bourdieu views linguistic practices as *symbolic capital* that properly trained people may convert into economic and social capital. The value of a dialect—its standing in a "linguistic market"—depends on the extent to which it provides access to desired positions in the labor market. In turn, this reflects its legitimation by formal institutions—the educational establishment, state, church, and prestige media. In stratified societies, where there is always differential control of prestige speech, even people who don't use the prestige dialect accept its authority and correctness, its "symbolic domination" (Bourdieu 1982, 1984). Thus, linguistic forms, which lack power in themselves, take on the power of the groups and relations they symbolize. The education system, however (defending its own worth), denies this, misrepresenting prestige speech as being inherently better. The linguistic insecurity of lower-class and minority speakers is a result of this symbolic domination.

Research indicates that Americans can infer race and class from speech patterns (accents, grammar, and diction). Americans may use such information to discriminate. Real estate and rental agents, who may discriminate against people of color on sight, also ascribe to prospective tenants a race or class category on the phone and discriminate accordingly. Phone tag and voice mail provide the means for "racial screening," protecting the racist landlord from any discomfort or inconvenience that would arise in a face-to-face rejection (Massey and Lundy 2001, 454–455). Telephone audit studies provide one measure of racial discrimination in urban housing markets. One such study of 79 rental units in Philadelphia showed that rental agents do systematically discriminate against African-American callers on the basis of speech. Researchers called rental agents to inquire about apartments listed in the local papers, using one of three linguistic styles: white middle-class English, black accented English, and Black English Vernacular.

Speech marks race, class, and gender, and speech influenced a caller's likelihood of reaching a rental agent and of obtaining a rental unit. Compared to whites, African Americans were less likely to get through and speak to a rental agent, less likely to be told of a unit's availability, more likely to pay application fees, and more likely to be questioned about their credit history. The findings indicate that the combination of being black and female limits access to housing even more. The callers who were black, female, and lower-income (signified by speaking BEV) were the most disadvantaged in securing housing (Massey and Lundy 2001, 467).

Black English Vernacular (BEV), a.k.a. "Ebonics"

No one pays much attention when someone says "runt" instead of "rent"—an example of linguistic variation given at the start of this chapter. But some nonstandard speech carries more of a stigma. Sometimes stigmatized speech is linked to region, class, or educational background; sometimes it is associated with ethnicity or "race."

A national debate involving language, race, and education was triggered by a vote on December 18, 1996, by the Oakland, California, school board. The board unanimously declared that many black students did not speak standard English but instead spoke a distinct language called "ebonics" (from "ebony" and "phonics"), with roots in western African languages. The poet Maya Angelou, the Reverend Jesse Jackson, and spokespersons for the Clinton administration soon disputed this claim. Indeed, professional linguists do regard ebonics as a dialect of English rather than a separate language. Linguists call ebonics Black English Vernacular (BEV) or African-American English Vernacular (AAEV).

Some saw the Oakland resolution as a ploy designed to permit the school district to increase its access to federal funds available for bilingual programs for Hispanic and Asian students. According to federal law, BEV is not a separate language eligible for Title 7 funds. Funds for bilingual education (itself a controversial issue, especially in California politics) have been available to support the educations of immigrant students (Golden 1997). Some educators have argued that similar support should be available to blacks. If ebonics were accepted as a foreign language, teachers could receive merit pay for studying BEV and for using their knowledge of it in their lessons (Applebome 1996).

Early in 1997, responding to the widespread negative reaction to its original resolution, the Oakland educational task force proposed a new resolution. This one required only the recognition of language differences among black students, in order to improve their proficiency in English. School officials emphasized that they had never intended to teach black students in ebonics. They had just sought to employ some of the same tools used with students brought up speaking a foreign language to help black students improve their English-language skills. The Oakland school board planned to expand its 10-year-old pilot program for black students, which taught the phonetic and grammatical differences between Standard English and what the students spoke outside the classroom (Golden 1997).

While recognizing ebonics as a dialect of American English rather than as a separate language, most linguists see nothing wrong with the Oakland schools' goal of understanding the speech patterns of black students and respecting that speech while teaching standard English. Indeed, this is policy and teaching strategy in many American school districts. The Linguistic Society of America (LSA) considers ebonics or Black English Vernacular to be "systematic and rule-governed" (Applebome 1997).

BEV is not an ungrammatical hodgepodge but a complex linguistic system with its own rules, which linguists have described. The phonology and syntax of BEV are similar to those of southern dialects. This reflects generations of contact between southern whites and blacks, with mutual influence on each other's speech patterns. Many features that distinguish BEV from Standard English (SE) also show up in southern white speech, but less often than in BEV.

Linguists disagree about exactly how BEV originated (Rickford 1999). Smitherman (1986) calls it an Africanized form of English reflecting both an African heritage and the conditions of servitude in America. She notes certain structural similarities between West African languages and BEV. Their African linguistic backgrounds no doubt influenced how early African Americans learned English. Did they restructure English to fit African linguistic patterns? Or did they quickly learn English from whites, with little continuing influence from the African linguistic heritage? Another possibility is that English was fused with African languages to form a pidgin or Creole language in Africa or the Caribbean. This Creole might then have been brought to the American colonies by the many slaves who were imported from the Caribbean during the 17th and 18th centuries (Rickford 1999; Rickford and Rickford 2000).

Origins aside, there are phonological and grammatical differences between ebonics and SE. One phonological difference is that BEV speakers are less likely to pronounce *r* than SE speakers are. Actually, many SE speakers don't pronounce *r*'s that come right before a consonant (ca*r*d) or at the end of a word (ca*r*). But SE speakers do usually pronounce an *r* that comes right before a vowel, either at the end of a word (fou*r* o'clock) or within a word (Carol). BEV speakers, by contrast, are much more likely to omit such intervocalic (between vowels) r's. The result is that speakers of the two dialects have different *homonyms* (words that sound the same but have different meanings). BEV speakers who don't pronounce intervocalic r's have the following homonyms: Carol/Cal; Paris/pass. BEV's phonological rules also dictate that certain word-final consonants, such as t's, d's and the s in *he's*, be dropped.

Observing these phonological rules, BEV speakers pronounce certain words differently from SE pronunciation. Particularly in the elementary school context, where the furor over ebonics has raged, the homonyms of BEV-speaking students typically differ from those of their SE-speaking teachers. To evaluate reading accuracy, teachers should determine whether students are recognizing the different meanings of such BEV homonyms as *passed, past,* and *pass.* Teachers need to make sure students understand what they are reading, which is probably more important than whether they are pronouncing words correctly according to the SE norm.

Phonological rules may lead BEV speakers to omit *ed* as a past-tense marker and *s* as a marker of plurality. However, other speech contexts demonstrate that BEV speakers do understand the difference between past and present verbs, and between singular and plural nouns. Confirming this are irregular verbs (e.g., *tell, told*) and irregular plurals (e.g., *child, children*), in which BEV works the same as SE.

The phonological contrasts between BEV and SE speakers often have grammatical consequences. One of these is **copula deletion,** which means the absence of SE forms of the copula—the verb *to be.* For example, SE and BEV may contrast as follows:

SE	SE Contraction	BEV
You are tired	You're tired	You tired
He is tired	He's tired	He tired
We are tired	We're tired	We tired
They are tired	They're tired	They tired

In its deletion of the present tense of the verb *to be,* BEV is similar to many languages, including Russian, Hungarian, and Hebrew. BEV's copula deletion is simply a grammatical result of its phonological rules. Notice that BEV deletes the copula where SE has contractions. BEV's phonological rules dictate that r's (as in *you're, we're,* and *they're*) and word-final s's (as in *he's*) be dropped. However, BEV speakers do pronounce *m,* so that the BEV first-person singular is "I'm tired," just as in SE. Thus, when BEV omits the copula, it merely carries contraction one step further, as a result of its phonological rules.

BEV, like SE, is a rule-governed dialect. SE is not superior to BEV as a linguistic system, but it does happen to be the prestige dialect—the one used in the mass media, in writing, and in most public and professional contexts.

SE is the dialect that has the most "symbolic capital." In areas of Germany where there is diglossia, speakers of Plattdeusch (Low German) learn the High German dialect to communicate appropriately in the national context. Similarly, upwardly mobile BEV-speaking students learn SE.

Note that most of the speech forms we use every day are not learned from remote experience (such as the mass media) but within our own personal social networks, particularly from peers. Speech responds to primary influences—real people who make a difference in your life, such as supervisors, co-workers, and classmates. Urban ghetto existence tends to isolate blacks from whites. Many black children have never talked to white children before entering school. Despite the use of SE on radio and television, American dialect variance is actually growing, not just between blacks and whites but also between whites in different cities. Dialect divergence may have the effect of "locking" blacks out of "important networks that lead to jobs, housing, and basic rights and privileges" (J. Williams 1985, 10).

Although BEV is diverging from SE, the dialects are still close. This means that teachers in multiethnic classrooms should know something about the phonology and grammar of both dialects if they are to teach successfully. Schoolteachers should be able to help BEV-speaking students learn SE by showing them exactly how the standard dialect differs in phonology and syntax from BEV.

Many Americans who spoke regional and ethnic dialects as children have learned to shift their linguistic styles. Since BEV is a bit more different from SE than other American English dialects are, mastery of the prestige dialect requires more effort. If learning and teaching SE are to be goals of blacks and whites within our educational system, school personnel need linguistic knowledge and sensitivity. Otherwise, as Labov notes, "We're in danger of forming a permanent underclass [of ghetto blacks]" (Quoted in J. Williams, 1985, 10).

EDUCATION AND LINGUISTIC DIVERSITY

Knowledge of linguistic differences is important in a multicultural society whose populace grows up speaking many languages and dialects. Because linguistic differences may affect children's schoolwork and teachers' evaluations, many schools of education now require courses in sociolinguistics. Also, sociolinguists and cultural anthropologists have worked side by side in education research, for example, in a study of Puerto Rican seventh graders in the urban Midwest (Hill-Burnett 1978). Researching in classrooms, neighborhoods, and homes, anthropologists discovered several misconceptions by teachers. For example, the teachers had mistakenly assumed that Puerto Rican parents valued education less than other parents did. In-depth interviews revealed that the Puerto Rican parents valued it more.

Researchers also found that certain practices were preventing Hispanics from being adequately educated. For example, the teachers' union and the Board of Education had agreed to teach English as a foreign language. However, they had not provided bilingual teachers to work with Spanish-speaking students. The school started assigning all students (including non-Hispanics) with low reading scores and behavior problems to the English-as-a-foreign-language classroom.

This educational disaster brought together a teacher who spoke no Spanish, children who barely spoke English, and a group of English-speaking students with reading and behavior problems. The Spanish speakers fell further behind not just in reading but in all subjects. They could at least have kept up in the other subjects if a Spanish speaker had been teaching them science, social studies, and math until they were ready for English-language instruction in those areas.

The researchers also found that Anglo-Americans and Hispanics reacted differently to humor and teasing. Many Hispanic youths believed that teachers' kidding comments went too far. They heard the remarks as insults and slurs rather than as jokes. The Hispanics who adapted most successfully were those who had learned the general American norm about kidding, so that teachers' attempts at humor didn't damage their self-esteem.

A dramatic illustration of the relevance of sociolinguistics to education comes from Ann Arbor, Michigan. In 1979 the parents of several black students at the predominantly white Dr. Martin Luther King, Jr., Elementary School sued the Board of Education. They claimed their children faced linguistic discrimination in the classroom. The children, who lived in a neighborhood housing project, spoke BEV at home. At school, most had encountered problems with their class work. Some had been labeled learning-impaired and placed in remedial reading courses. (Consider the embarrassment that children may suffer and the potential impact on self-image of such labeling.)

The African-American parents and their attorney contended that their children had no intrinsic learning disabilities but simply did not understand everything their teachers said. Nor did their teachers always understand them. The lawyer argued that because BEV and SE are so similar, teachers often misinterpreted a child's correct pronunciation (in BEV) of an SE word as a reading error. The children's attorney recruited several linguists to testify on their behalf. The school board, by contrast, could not find a single qualified linguist to support its argument that there was no linguistic discrimination.

The judge ruled in favor of the children and ordered the following solution: Teachers at the King School had to attend a full-year course designed to improve their knowledge of nonstandard dialects, particularly BEV. The judge did not advocate that the teachers learn to speak BEV or that the children be allowed to do their assignments in BEV. Nor did he find BEV to be a foreign language, as some of the champions of ebonics claim it to be. In the Ann Arbor case, the school's goal remained to teach the children to use SE, the standard dialect, correctly. Before this could be accomplished, however, teachers and students alike had to learn how to recognize the differences between these similar dialects. At the end of the year most of the teachers interviewed in the local newspaper said the course had helped them.

Awareness programs focusing on linguistic, cultural, and ethnic diversity require unusual sensitivity. One program intended to enhance teachers' appreciation of cultural differences led instead to ethnic stereotyping (Kleinfeld 1975). Specifically, Native American students did not welcome teachers' frequent comments about their Indian heritage. The students felt set apart from their classmates and saw this attention to their ethnicity as patronizing and demeaning.

In a diverse, multicultural society, teachers (and citizens in general) do need to be sensitive to and knowledgeable about linguistic and cultural differences, and children need to be protected so that their ethnic or linguistic background isn't used against them.

 CHAPTER SIXTEEN

Family Background

"We Are Family"

A woman who is fully qualified to compete in the national labor force limits her job search to the local market because of "family obligations." "My husband and kids are here," she insists. Her "family" consists of the man she has lived with for five years, but who is legally married to another woman, the mother of his two children, whom the woman being quoted considers to be her own.

Two men identify themselves as "domestic partners" and have "a home life" that includes the children of one from a former marriage.

A legally married heterosexual couple and their biological children share a "household."

"We have a commuter marriage," claim a "dual-career couple." The two spouses reside in different states, and "We get together most weekends," they say.

A 50-year old man lives with his widowed mother, the "only family" he has ever known.

Which of these scenarios represents *the* American family? Reflect on this question. Construct what you think is a national standard or a popular conception of the *American* family. What sources have influenced your answer?

Now reflect on your own experience. How many variants of the "American family" can you identify? Do these types of family match a cultural ideal? What criteria do you use to define your "family"? Whom do you include in it?

The pursuit of "better opportunities" fosters personal independence, which in turn leads people to detach from local ties in search of survival or self-fulfillment. Economic mobility separates individuals from their family of origin. It also disrupts romantic attachments and breaks many marriages. To accommodate particular economic, political, and psychological needs, people pursue a number, and a variety, of "relationships." For many people, marriage has become nothing more than "a trial-and-error relationship," rather than "the ultimate relationship." Monogamy persists as the ideal form of North American marriage. However, given the high rate of divorce and remarriage, **consecutive (a.k.a. serial) monogamy** more accurately describes the pattern for many Americans.

The decline of a marriage imperative in North America fuels the diversity of civil statuses. Adults may seek to "grow old together" with another person, not in law but in friendship. Such arrangements as "living together," "long-distance relationships," and "long-term companions" are undeniably familiar. A heterosexual unmarried couple have "been together" 15 years. The "partners" live in different cities; communicate by phone and e-mail; are "sexually exclusive"; and share weekends, holidays, two cats, and "material resources." When asked about how they define this relationship, the woman replied, "As a marriage of sorts." Other kinds of households that now characterize our cultural mainstream include "being single," " having a roommate," and "sharing a house with a group of people." These domestic arrangements may be temporary or periodic, but they are common and legitimate.

Cross-cultural studies of kinship show that biology is not a prerequisite to "family." In our society individuals form strong attachments, loyalties, and interdependencies with persons to whom they are not "blood related," but "spirit related." Along with "blood families" and "families-in-law," many North Americans cultivate *fictive kinship* ties (reciprocal provision of goods and services, including affection, companionship, and shared values, between nonbiologically, nonlegally, but socially related individuals). Some speak of work colleagues as "family," introduce a close friend as being "like a brother to me," and demonstrate affection and responsibility toward "surrogate parents." Every year an elderly widow brings Christmas cookies to her "neighbor family." A twice-divorced writer looks forward to professional conferences so he can visit with "the extended family I never had."

Fictive kinship relations may coexist with biological ties, or may substitute for absent biological ties. People aren't always joking when they speak of their "dysfunctional families." It is common for mainstream North Americans to admit they "haven't seen [their] parents in more than a year," "haven't spoken with [a] sister in months," "don't know all [their] aunts and uncles," or "don't like" their family. Nonetheless, "Blood is thicker than water." Loyalty to our blood relatives remains strong despite how we feel about them. Yet members of industrial urban societies cannot live by blood alone. Survival and well-being often depend more on soul ties than on blood ties.

Estrangement from one's biological family, by force, necessity, or choice, rarely turns individuals into absolute loners. To bond and to belong is a basic human need. When our "natural family" isn't available or adequate in meeting our needs, we construct a **family of affiliation**—psychological ties with people we love and can count on for emotional, social, and material support. In her study of gay and lesbian kinship, Kath Weston (1991) discovered that individuals linked themselves with "chosen families." Friends, lovers, and children form supportive networks that prove comforting for individuals and useful in meeting affective and basic needs.

Familial attachment is both a universal value and a practice. In North America, kinship takes many forms. "Family values" reflect the experience and aspirations of diverse categories of Americans, not only those who ascribe to the heterosexual nuclear family. Domestic organization and civil status are frequently matters not of choice but of adjustment. Contemporary economic conditions, including upward and downward mobility, threaten family ties. Most Americans struggle to create and maintain a healthy, gratifying, and predictable family life, often in the face of adversity. Adaptations to poverty, psychological development, social disfranchisement, marital exploitation, and spouse abuse result in particular domestic arrangements, not "alternative" types of families.

The educated elite, and other financially secure professionals, express "personal preferences" in what constitutes "adulthood" and socially approved civil statuses. Disparaging labels such as "spinster," "confirmed bachelor,"

When our "natural family" isn't available, or is inadequate in meeting our needs, we construct a family of affiliation—psychological ties with people we love and can count on for emotional, social, and material support. Here three close friends celebrate the 50th birthday of the woman seated at the center. Who belongs to your family of affiliation?

and "divorcée," which once were accepted usage, have been replaced by more legitimate classifications, such as "career woman," "feminist," "single," and "domestic partner." A multicultural society acknowledges and accommodates diversity in kinship organization. We are careful to ask that a child's parent *or guardian* sign a report card. We aren't supposed to question a child whose last name is different from his father's. We may welcome a woman and her female date at the Christmas party, or honor an unwed mother and her kids at a Cub Scout meeting.

However, politeness toward people who don't conform to our sense of what is "proper" may not translate into actions that ensure their economic security and social integration. Access to strategic resources, such as legal protection, housing, employment, and insurance remains inequitable for many poor families, gays and lesbians, single-parent households, orphaned or neglected children, and long-term companions, regardless of sexual orientation. Families and civil statuses that may differ from our conception of what is "normal" or "legitimate" require greater understanding and appreciation for their nature and the factors that determine their existence. The American family is not dying; it is changing. ☉

CHANGING NORTH AMERICAN FAMILIES

In the present chapter, we consider contrasting family backgrounds and experience as ways of establishing our individual and social identities and thus making us different. Part of your identity reflects the kind of home you grew up in and your family of orientation. What did you think of your family as you were growing up? Was it like or unlike the families of your friends? Did you think it was an abnormal or a normal family? Were you ashamed of it? What kind of family was it—a nuclear family (parents and kids residing together), a single-parent family (one parent and kids), a blended family (including a parent, a stepparent, one or more children, or stepchildren), or perhaps a matrifocal extended family (mother, mother's mother, and people related mainly through female links)? If your parents got divorced, how did that affect your image of your family? Was one (or were both) of your parents gay?

Recent decades have produced significant changes in North American households and families. The U.S. Census Bureau defines a *household* as an individual or group living in a housing unit. A *family* consists of two or more people, one of whom is the householder (household head), living together, who are related by birth, marriage, or adoption. Among households, the proportion consisting of two parents with kids is smaller than ever. Childless couples, single-parent families, and people living alone are increasingly common. As Ken Bryson observes, "the increasing diversity of household types continues to challenge our efforts to measure and describe American society," and "the 'typical' household is an illusion" (Bryson 1996). Table 16–1

TABLE 16–1. Changes in Family and Household Organization in the United States, 1970 versus 2000.

	1970	2000
Married couples with children	40%	24%
Number of people per household	3.1	2.6
Family households	81%	69%
Households with five or more people	21%	10%
People living alone	17%	26%
Number of single-mother families	3 million	12 million
Number of single-father families	393,000	2 million
Households that included own children under 18	45%	33%

Source: From data in Fields 2001.

summarizes several changes in family and household organization in the United States from 1970 to 2000.

ALL SORTS OF FAMILIES

The family as an institution is a social universal. Humans in all societies belong to kinship groups. Marriage, a publicly and legally sanctioned relationship, is the most important basis for the formation of kinship in North America. Familial bonds regulate who should have sex with whom, who can bear and raise children with whom, and who can depend on whom for goods and services. The ideology of romantic love and sexual exclusivity associated with marriage in contemporary North America also regulates social and emotional intimacy. In our society "falling in love" is a prerequisite to marriage, and sexual jealousy threatens many marital relationships. Most North Americans are suspicious of extramarital, especially heterosexual, friendships, and consider adultery "grounds for divorce."

Although all human societies have kin groups, marriage, and families, anthropologists have documented considerable variation in systems of kinship and marriage among cultures (and over time in the same culture). Among societies, as is also true within the United States and Canada today, it is difficult to single out a statistically "normal" or modal pattern of household organization. Is the "normal" North American household a nuclear family, a couple, or an individual? A global, cross-cultural view reveals many kinds of kin groups, including nuclear and extended families, as well as descent groups such as clans. Among human societies, nuclear family organization is widespread but not universal. In some societies, nuclear families are rare or nonexistent. In others, the nuclear family exists but lacks a special role in social life. Other social units—most notably descent groups (e.g., clans) and extended families—assume most of the functions elsewhere associated with the nuclear family (e.g., raising children).

Cross-cultural study has revealed myriad alternatives to nuclear family organization. For example, in certain Caribbean societies, many women head households with no permanently resident husband-father. We call such units "matrifocal" families or households because the mother (mater) is the household head.

An even stronger contrast with American-type "marriage and family" comes from the Trans-Fly region of Papua New Guinea, which is the homeland of several homosexual tribes. Here, although men must marry, they prefer homosexual acts to heterosexual coitus with their wives. Members of Trans-Fly group, the Etoro, are so disapproving of heterosexual intercourse that it is actually banned for more than 200 days per year (Kelly 1976). Men of the neighboring Marind-anim tribe (Van Baal 1966) also prefer homosexuality. During Van Baal's study, their birthrate was so low that, in order to reproduce their population, the Marind-anim had to raid neighboring tribes. Many children who grew up to be Marind-anim had been captured in such raids. Within the realm of cultural diversity documented by anthropology, there are, we see vividly, a series of alternatives to North American images of "marriage and the family."

As an association, "family" takes multiple forms cross-culturally and within our own society. In the United States, "home and hearth" have a variety of meanings and functions. Most children are born and raised in a family, but the composition of this unit includes various combinations of child-parenting relationships. Examples include extended, nuclear, foster, adoptive, single-parent, gay, and blended families. Children are not always raised by their biological parents, and adults may be rearing children to whom they are not related by blood, or by law. Many children become accustomed to living in "mom's house" or "dad's house." One child, who has grown up from birth in a household composed of his biological parents, a sibling, and a grandmother, confuses museum and theater clerks when he steps up to the ticket counter to announce "Two children, three parents, please!"

In North America, the nuclear family, despite the social reality of changing and varied kinship patterns, remains the cultural ideal. Many Americans look down on other family arrangements. One example is adoptive families, which are often the target of prejudice and stigmatization. According to Wegar, adoptive families constitute "an alternative kinship model in North American culture," but one that many Americans consider to be "second best and suspect" (2000, 363). In one study, people who had been raised in an adoptive home were generally positive about their own upbringing, but thought that society looked down on adoptive families. The perception of a stigma attached to adoption motivated adoptees to search for their biological mothers (March 1995, 658). Within the variety of American families, adoption illustrates "the social nature of kinship," a form of family "that

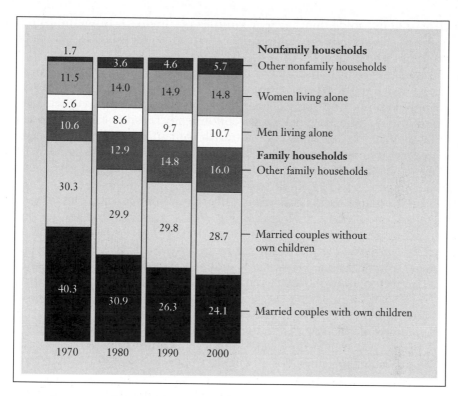

FIGURE 16–1 Households by type: selected years, 1970–2000. (Percent distribution)
Source: Fields 2001.

supports and even celebrates the human ability to feel and create kinship bonds beyond the confines of blood relations" (Wegar 2000, 367).

Anthropologists distinguish between the family of orientation (the family in which one is born and grows up) and the family of procreation (formed when one marries and has children). From the individual's point of view, the critical relationships are with parents and siblings in the family of orientation and with spouse and children in the family of procreation. The family of orientation plays an important role in enculturation and thus in identity formation. Less than 3 percent of the U.S. population now farms, so that most people are not tied to the land. Selling our labor on the market, we often move to places where jobs are available. Born into a family of orientation, we leave home for work or college, and the break with parents is under way. Eventually most Americans marry and start a family of procreation.

Although the nuclear family remains a cultural ideal for many Americans, Table 16–1 and Figure 16–1 show that nuclear families composed just 24 percent of American households in 2000, down from 40 percent in 1970. People living alone now account for a larger percentage (26 percent) of

American households than nuclear families do. Living arrangements other than the nuclear family now outnumber the traditional American household more than three to one.

North American household composition has changed for several reasons. We leave home to work, often in a different community. Women increasingly join the workforce. This usually removes them from their family of orientation, while also making it economically feasible for them to delay marriage. Also, job demands compete with romantic attachments. The median age at first marriage for American women jumped from age 20 in 1955 to over age 25 in 2000 (Saluter 1996; Fields 2001). The comparable ages for men were ages 23 and 27 (Fields 2001).

Economic and social conditions directly influence the roles men and women assume. Today, an increasingly diverse and flexible services-and-information labor market selects more for talent than for gender. Increased participation by women in the labor force offers more choices to women *and* men. Women who are financially independent and, correspondingly, socially connected, may choose to marry, to delay marriage, or to remain single. The increasing divorce rate in recent decades is related to women's ability to support themselves financially.

Female employment outside the home also liberates men, who may exercise more choice in professional pursuits and lifestyle. While marriage benefits men categorically, not all genetic males are suited for matrimony, any more than all genetic females are. Men today are freer to choose or reject the obligations and pressure associated with being "the breadwinner," whose earnings must support dependents. Free from the gender-linked duty "to support a family," men may choose careers that hold more personal appeal to them regardless of the "potential earning power," a symbol of social manhood. Men may choose to remain "single," or to participate in an egalitarian marriage or a domestic partnership. Others may become "dependents" themselves by assuming such roles as "househusband."

In the context of these choices, the U.S. divorce rate has risen, with the number of divorced Americans more than quadrupling from 4.3 million in 1970 to over 19 million in 2000 (Lugaila 1999). Single-parent families increased from fewer than 4 million in 1970 to 12 million in 2000. Kids in fatherless homes tripled from 8 percent in 1960 to 26 percent in 2000. The percentage in motherless homes increased from 1 percent in 1960 to 5 percent in 2000. Only 56 percent of American men were currently married in 2000, compared to 65 percent in 1970. The comparable figures for women were 52 percent in 2000 versus 60 percent in 1970 (Fields 2001).

Cherlin (1992) did a study of changing patterns of American marriage, divorce, and remarriage, using four generations of American women, the first born between 1908 and 1912, the last born in 1970. Although there was little change in the first marriage rate across the generations, the likelihood of divorce changed strikingly. Likelihood for the first generation was 22 percent, versus its double, 44 percent, for women born in 1970. The chance of remarriage and redivorce also increased across the generations. The likelihood of a

TABLE 16–2. Household and Family Size in the United States and Canada, 1975 versus 2000

	1975	2000
Average family size		
United States	3.4	3.2
Canada	3.5	3.1
Average household size		
United States	2.9	2.6
Canada	2.9	2.6

Sources: Fields 2001; U.S. Bureau of the Census; *Statistical Abstract of the United States, 2000;* and Statistics Canada, 1991.

second divorce was 2 percent for the oldest generation, versus 16 percent for women born in 1970 (see also Simpson 1998).

In contemporary Western societies, we maintain the idea that romantic love is necessary for a good marriage. When romance fails, so may the marriage; or it may not fail, if other features of the marriage are strong. Economic ties and obligations to kids, along with other factors, such as concern about public opinion, or simple inertia, may keep marriages intact after sex, romance, and/or companionship fade. Also, even in modern societies, royalty, leaders, and other elites may have political marriages similar to arranged marriages.

Table 16–2 documents comparable changes in family and household size in the United States and Canada between 1975 and 2000. Those figures confirm a general trend toward smaller families and smaller living units in North America (see also Hansen and Garey 1998). This trend is also detectable in western Europe and other industrial nations.

The entire range of kin attachments is narrower for North Americans, particularly those in the middle class, than it is for nonindustrial peoples. Although we recognize ties to our grandparents, uncles, aunts, and cousins, we have less contact with, and depend less on, those relatives than people in other cultures do. This becomes apparent when we answer a few questions: Do we know exactly how we are related to all our cousins? How much do we know about our ancestors, such as their full names and where they lived? How many of the people with whom we associate regularly are our relatives?

The figures showing smaller families, increased divorce, and more and more people living alone suggest that life may be growing increasingly lonely for many North Americans. To be sure, we live socially through friendship, work, clubs, sports, religion, and organized group activities. However, the isolation from kin that these figures suggest is unprecedented in human history. Because primates (monkeys, apes, and humans) are intensely social creatures, many observers of contemporary society see the decline of kinship as unfortunate and wonder whether these trends are harming our mental health.

FAMILY AND WORK

To maintain the lifestyle of contemporary consumers, men, women, and teenagers need cash employment. Work stresses family ties. For example, job demands compete with child care—and child care is an expensive proposition in itself; it costs more than $100,000 to raise an American child to age 18. Accordingly, nuclear families have shrunk, and more couples now raise one child than two children. "Beaver Cleaver" families, consisting of children, a working father, and a homemaker mother, now make up fewer than 10 percent of all households.

Child care is itself commercialized. Organized child care facilities accounted for 30 percent of all child care arrangements in 1993 (Casper 1996). In fall 1993, about 10 million American children under age five needed child care while their mothers worked. Of those kids, almost half (48 percent) were cared for primarily by relatives—grandparents or fathers. Child care arrangements varied according to the economic, regional, and ethnic characteristics of households. Children in families receiving public assistance were more likely to be cared for by relatives than other children were (57 percent versus 46 percent). Relatives provided 60 percent of all child care for preschoolers in poor families versus 46 percent in nonpoor families. Families in the South were most likely to choose organized child care

More than a third of all child care in the United States takes place in organized child care centers. More than 10 million American children under age five, including infants such as those shown here, now use child care while their parents work. What are the costs and benefits of such day care arrangements?

facilities, and least likely to choose relatives as primary care providers for their preschoolers. Families in the Northeast were the most likely to call on relatives to care for preschoolers. African-American (50 percent) and His-panic (57 percent) children were more likely to be cared for by relatives than were non-Hispanic white children (45 percent).

MEDIA AND THE FAMILY

The media help inform us about what's in and what's out (including child-rearing expectations, family types and relations, work roles, and living arrangements). Media portrayals are texts, which can be read as lessons in cultural change. For example, changing North American household organi-zation, as documented above, has been reflected in the mass media. During the 1950s and the early 1960s such television sitcoms as *The Adventures of Ozzie and Harriet* and *Leave It to Beaver* portrayed "traditional" nuclear fam-ilies. The incidence of "blended families" (kin units formed when parents re-marry and bring their children into a new household) has risen, as represented in programs like *The Brady Bunch*. Three-quarters of divorced Americans remarry (*Ann Arbor News* 1989). Television programs and other media presentations now routinely feature coresident "roommates," "friends," unmarried couples, "singles," and unrelated retirees, as well as hired male housekeepers, working mothers, and even "two dads."

Because the popularity of television programs tends to reflect their cul-tural fit, media content illustrates changing values and institutions. Con-trasts in media content across time periods and across cultures can be keys to perceiving and understanding cultural differences. Changes in lifestyles are reflected by the media, which in turn help promote further modifi-cations in values concerning kinship, marriage, and living arrangements (Kottak 1990b).

There is, for example, a striking contrast between American and Brazil-ian cultures, reflected in TV content, involving the meaning and the role of the family. North American adults usually define their families as consist-ing of spouse and children. However, when Brazilian adults speak of their *família*, they normally mean their parents, siblings, aunts, uncles, grand-parents, and cousins. Brazilian adults may include their children as *família*, but they often exclude their husbands or wives who have their own *família*.

Especially for the middle class, Brazilians have less geographical mobil-ity than people in the United States have. Ongoing relationships between parents and their *adult* children, and among extended family members, are more significant in Brazil in real life, and Brazilian TV content reflects that social reality. Because contemporary Americans tend to lack an extended family support system, marriage and children assume tremendous impor-tance. Marriage provides theme, context, stability, conflict, and dramatic tension for many American TV programs and other "texts." U.S. culture's overwhelming emphasis on marital and parental responsibilities—in real life and the media—places severe strains on American marriages. Many social issues addressed by American media reflect this emphasis.

Surprisingly, marriages are at least as unstable in Brazilian TV programs as in American prime-time series, even though divorce (which used to be against the law there) is much less common in Brazil. Marital instability in the media reflects a Brazilian social reality that accords relatively less value to the family of procreation (spouse and children) and more to the family of orientation (parents and siblings). On Brazilian TV, the marital tie often yields to the continuing link between adult characters and their parents, siblings, and extended kin.

TV reflects the real-life fact that a Brazilian's social world is more exclusively familial than an American's is. In U.S. TV, by comparison, we can also detect a characteristically American theme—leaving home and living with strangers, who eventually become "friends." North Americans live with strangers more and more, even at home. Many central themes of American television, films, and literature revolve around problems that arise in dealing with strangers, people who are different from ourselves. (To provide an understanding of such differences is the goal of this book.) This focus on differences and strangeness is true of all our genres, including adventure, suspense, fantasy, and science fiction. In Brazil the preoccupation with the stranger is missing, and popular genres are different. Brazilian television shows people almost always interacting with their families and friends, rarely with such aliens as unrelated roommates, police officers, lawyers, extraterrestrials, pets, wild animals, or mass murderers.

Mainstream American cultural traditions prepare and goad us to leave home and family, seeking autonomy and "independence"—life among strangers in faraway places. American historical themes that are frequently celebrated by literature and the mass media include pioneer spirit and wide-open spaces. Americans need space for solitude. We are much more private people than Brazilians—or than Samoans, whom Margaret Mead described as living in a "civilization which suspects privacy" (1961, 219). Such cultural preferences are rooted in experience. It is hard to be alone, ever, on a tropical island, or in a torrid and densely packed city, such as Rio de Janeiro, where windows and doors are almost always open.

Also illustrating the importance of the stranger in American life is the constant intervention in personal and family matters by hospitals, lawyers, courts, social workers, physicians, and other "experts." This intrusion supplies fodder for countless television programs and films. On Brazilian TV, in contrast, such experts are conspicuous by their absence.

A more subtle contrast in television content between cultures is in the frequency of domestic versus public settings. Prime-time Brazilian programs are usually set in a family home. Family settings also are popular on American TV (from Cleavers through Bradies and Huxtables to Simpsons). Furthermore, many American programs (e.g., *Friends* and *Seinfeld*) mold their unrelated characters into a quasi-family. However, it is evident to anyone who has watched TV regularly in both the United States and Brazil that American TV much more often depicts its characters in public and work settings. This reflects, among other things, both the North American "work ethic" and the larger real percentage of Americans employed outside the home.

THE CULT OF CHILDHOOD "SUCCESS"

As we have seen, the American economy has shifted from an industrial manufacturing economy focusing on heavy-goods production toward a postindustrial economy based on the provision of services and information. Today, countries with cheaper labor can produce cars, steel, and other heavy goods less expensively than the United States can; but the American workforce excels at services. Despite its inadequacies, our public mass education system has no rival when it comes to training millions of people for service and information-oriented jobs, from salesclerk to computer operator. Schools, the media, high-tech machines, sports, and games all conspire to prepare our children to join the army of 21st-century information processors. The other dimension of the information-processing, services-oriented economy is human services (e.g., health care and education).

Economic transformations have social implications, including changes in child-rearing expectations, goals, and practices. Middle-class parents are increasingly sensitive to the need to raise children prepared to succeed in the high-tech world. In the services and information society, the experts and the media (which help spread the opinions of the experts) have worked to enlarge our culture's definitions of child welfare and achievement. Before World War II, parents could do an adequate job by providing responsible care, love, food, and shelter. By the 1950s, parents had added an increasing array of consumer goods to "the necessities of life." By the 1980s—and continuing today—possessions were no longer enough. The ideals of a trauma-less childhood and childhood fulfillment were emerging as parental obsessions. It was no accident that hundreds of thousands of newly trained professionals were now available to help or treat any child who showed the smallest sign of harm or frailty. Ironically, the cultural definition of child welfare and the psychological burden of parenthood expanded just as the mushrooming two-gender workforce made it increasingly difficult to satisfy even the traditional parental responsibilities—to provide attention, loving care, material well-being, and an adequate supply of consumer goods.

To meet today's expanded definition of proper child rearing, "good" parents need not just money, but also time, energy, good health, patience, and psychological sensitivity. For two parents with full-time, eight-hour-a-day jobs outside the home, it is an almost impossible task. No wonder family size has fallen. No wonder we feel guilty, our mental health suffers, and we resort to surrogates and experts. We need help in managing the responsibilities of modern life, including those of parenting.

North American networks of close personal ties are restricted compared to those of other societies. The average number of Americans per household has declined steadily from 4.8 in 1900 to 2.6 in 2000. Modern families confront numerous problems that are dissipated within larger kin networks in other cultures. Obligations and expectations vis-à-vis spouses and children overshadow all others (e.g., to parents or siblings) in our kinship system. When people are expected to manage many stresses and strains in a competitive, achievement-oriented society, tensions mount. Because marriage and children are so important, stresses are particularly evident in these relationships.

Along with the rising cost of raising children, another reason for smaller family size is increasing extradomestic employment. More and more women work outside the home. Fewer than one-third of mothers had paying jobs in 1960, versus more than two-thirds today. The demands of work outside the home reduce the parental time and energy needed for large families. More and more Americans live in small families consisting of at least one parent and a small number of children. The fewer children parents have, the more they invest in each child. One study showed that children's expenses take 30 percent of the budget in one-child households, 40 to 45 percent in two-child families, and 50 percent in three-child households (*World Almanac and Book of Facts* 1985). The more children, the less each child gets.

More and more Americans are striving to raise children capable of succeeding in an even higher-tech future. Each year, the college degree increases its clout as the key to professional success. A study by Peter Francese (1995) showed the average income of a college graduate to be more than twice that of a high school graduate with no college degree. (The difference had been just 18 percent in the 1970s.) Also, college-educated households tend to have two high earners. It cost $145,320 to raise a child through age 18 in the United States in 1995, versus $129,900 in 1960 (in inflation-adjusted 1995 dollars—$25,230 unadjusted)—or 12 percent more. Most middle-class parents will also have to spend money on at least one college education—at a cost that can easily exceed $100,000. Child-rearing and educational costs are among the economic considerations that lead Americans to limit family size.

In their attempts to raise a "successful" child, parents may take special steps from infancy on. In some cases, a child is registered at a series of in-demand schools soon after birth. Eventually, evenings and weekends fill up with a string of lessons, team practices, pot-luck dinners, competitions, and performances. Middle-class parents tend to believe they must nurture not only the intellectual and mental but also the athletic and musical talents of their progeny (for, it is believed, "extracurricular" activities help with admission to college). Imagine a family with two children, both taking weekly piano lessons, one also studying flute, the other trumpet. The monthly bill could exceed $200, plus the cost of purchasing instruments. Add hockey, gymnastics, skiing, ballet, or tennis lessons, and the investment leaps. To meet these expenses, both parents will almost surely be working outside the home.

"Successful" children have sound minds in sound bodies. Sound minds are stimulated, we believe, by computers, which cost hundreds of dollars to buy and equip. Sound bodies come from workouts—swimming, running, and sports with more expensive equipment needs. All these activities demand investments of time, energy, and money. Someone has to be available to drive kids to lessons, practices, and performances. After-school activities often necessitate two cars, including the increasingly common minivan. If no "soccer mom" or dad is immediately available, someone may have to be hired as a babysitter or transporter.

Besides all this, of course, the sound minds and bodies of "honor roll students" should not be endangered or abused. The cult of childhood "success" and "fulfillment" provides the cultural weft for a whole range of contemporary issues, ranging from the drive for "excellence" in education, at one extreme, to public concern about substance abuse, teen crime and suicide, and child molestation, at the other. Forced by employment demands to entrust their young to others, parents expect responsible and "caring" attention from well-trained professionals.

Assuming that "successful" children survive their years in day-care centers and nursery schools, the next step is a "quality" education in a private school, or an enriched curriculum in public schools. Through the pressure of middle-class parents, many elementary schools have formally recognized the "gifted" child. Such kids are set apart from their peers and placed on the road to professional success. In middle school they take advanced and enriched classes. In high school come accelerated and advanced placement courses. Science and math are emphasized, for they provide skills considered necessary in an increasingly high-tech society—skills that are basic to the best jobs in information processing and complex data analysis.

Some children, however, are labeled "learning-impaired" or only "average achievers." Knowledgeable specialists, such as social workers, psychologists, and school administrators, tend to believe that less successful kids often come from "broken homes" with divorced or single parents, or from "dysfunctional" families. "Troubled" children may suffer from an array of behavior problems, such as "acting out" or "hyperactivity." If the diagnosis is in doubt, many school systems now employ psychologists to provide an appropriate label.

According to some experts, one reason children from broken homes have behavioral and adjustment problems is their lack of appropriate "role models" of both sexes. However, there is a more powerful explanation. The characteristics of individuals aside, social problems have, first and foremost, a socioeconomic basis. To be sure, kids with adjustment problems often come from single-parent families. More significant than any absent role model, perhaps, is the reduction not just in money but in parental time that is almost inevitable when there is just one parent to give the child attention, and to ensure that he or she participates in the numerous activities in which our culture expects "successful" children to engage.

Math, science, computers, and software are the strategic resources of a high-tech, information-rich society, which rests on the most sophisticated means of data collection, storage, retrieval, and analysis ever invented. We are training our "successful" children for careers that demand skills in math, science, and information processing. They must be comfortable with numbers and on friendly terms with computers. Kids must learn to manage time and money, because "time is money," and both are measured in numbers. As the services-and-information economy develops further, this will be increasingly true. Already, we have at our fingertips instantaneous solutions to problems that once took days to solve, or that were insoluble. We stand in the middle of a maze of numbers that define us. To familiar addresses and phone numbers have been added zip and area codes. We are defined by salary, tax bracket, grade-point average, college board scores, driver's license, and Social Security number. We carry a dozen credit and registration cards, all computer processed. North Americans have serial numbers for all the appliances we have ever bought. No longer does a "name, rank and serial number" suffice to identify us.

KINSHIP AND CLASS

Most of the people we see every day are either nonrelatives or members of our immediate family. Although we recognize ties to grandparents, uncles, aunts, and cousins, we have less contact with, and depend less on, those relatives than people in other societies do. However, patterns of interaction with kin vary by class. Thus, Carol Stack's (1975) study of welfare-dependent families in a ghetto area of a small midwestern city showed that sharing with nonnuclear relatives is an important strategy the urban poor use to adapt to poverty. In the American lower class, the incidence of expanded family households (those that include nonnuclear relatives) is greater than it is in the middle class. The higher proportion of expanded family households in certain American ethnic groups and classes has been explained as an adaptation to poverty (Stack 1975). Unable to survive economically as nuclear family units, relatives band together in an expanded household and pool their resources.

Poverty causes kinship values and attitudes to diverge from middle-class norms. Thus, when Americans raised in poverty achieve financial success, they often feel obligated to provide substantial financial assistance to less fortunate relatives. Upper-class households, living in bigger homes supported by greater wealth, may also diverge from the nuclear family norm, for they can afford to lodge and feed extended family, guests, and servants.

One "marriage-and-family" issue, illustrating diversity within the United States, receives frequent media attention. This is "the problem of the black family"—the problematic status of which, from the anthropologist's perspective, originates in the general American cultural preference for marriage and the nuclear family. The "problem" is that half the African-American babies born in the United States have unmarried mothers. In 1995, single parents accounted for almost two-thirds (65 percent) of all African-American family groups, compared to 35 percent among Hispanics and 25 percent among non-Hispanic whites (Saluter 1995).

Government has played a key role in creating "the problem of the black family." Welfare policies that deny benefits to households with able-bodied male residents have fostered the pattern of unwed mothers and female-headed households. Just how serious are these problems? What does the view of such families as problematic tell us about American culture? For Americans, despite social reality, the *ideal* family continues to be a married couple and their children. American culture tends still to favor this kind of family and to be biased against others. Even anthropologists sometimes fall into the trap, teaching a course entitled "Marriage and the Family" rather than the more neutral "Kinship and Social Organization."

However, a cross-cultural perspective makes it evident (although American culture tends to deny it) that families can exist without marital ties. Unmarried Brazilians, for example, easily see the ethnocentrism in the American viewpoint. Adult Brazilians certainly believe they have families (parents, siblings, aunts, nephews, cousins, etc.), even if they lack spouses. In the United States, too, there can be families without marriage. Although many Americans don't realize it, strong kin ties exist among unmarried African Americans, as anthropologist Carol Stack (1975) showed in her classic field study of black family structure. Stack demonstrated that although "Beaver Cleaver" families were less common among poverty-level blacks than among middle-class whites, urban blacks still maintained very strong kin ties. Even when fathers lived elsewhere, children often visited their fathers and paternal kin. Furthermore, children saw their extended kin—grandparents, uncles, aunts, great-aunts and uncles, and cousins—more often than their white middle-class counterparts did.

Confirming Stack's findings are comprehensive statistical surveys done by the Institute for Social Research at the University of Michigan. This research has shown that families and churches are very important sources of emotional support and sustenance for African-Americans. Twenty percent of the black households surveyed were extended families. Sixty percent of the respondents saw, phoned, or wrote to relatives outside their own households at least once a week. Ninety-two percent had attended a church regularly since age 18 (*Ann Arbor Observer*, 1985). Indeed, compared to blacks, many American whites are more cut off from their kin, living alone or in nuclear family houses in suburban neighborhoods.

Many Americans think, erroneously, of the category "single-parent household" as referring only to a mother and her kids. For various reasons, the number of single-parent homes headed by fathers is also on the rise. For example, a father may gain custody of a child because his former wife is pursuing a demanding career (Garasky and Meyer 1996). According to Hamer and Marchioro (2002), a growing number of poor, black, urban fathers are assuming primary care for their children despite economic difficulties. Their study of working-class, low-income, mostly unmarried, African-American fathers in an impoverished midwestern city suggested that many of these men had become single parents by default—for one of three main reasons: First, the mother expressed no interest in caring for the child. Second, a child welfare worker contacted the father after removing the child from the mother's care. Third, the child expressed a preference for living with the father. Parenthood is especially difficult for men with low levels of education, poor access to health care and housing, and inflexible work schedules. To compensate for limited socioeconomic resources, poor, single fathers rely on biological and fictive kin to help provide a home for their children, and to build a kind of family that their circumstances permit.

FAMILY DIVERSITY

Most of us recognize that family background is one reason we differ. A newly married couple (or a same-sex couple) may have to negotiate not only differences related to religious or ethnic backgrounds but also specific family traditions, customs, and expectations. Psychologists, sociologists, and anthropologists continue to study the ways in which family experiences influence adult personality, security, identity, and behavior. Are people ashamed of their family backgrounds because they deviate from perceived cultural norms? Do men raised by women get along better with women than do men raised by men, or by a married couple? How does a girl form a female identity if she is raised by a man? What is the relation between a parent's sexual orientation and a child's identity formation? Are African Americans closer to extended family kin than white Americans are? Some of these questions have been addressed in the chapters on race, gender, and sexual orientation. In the present chapter, the focus has been specifically on changing cultural expectations about family organization, and on contrasting family backgrounds as ways of establishing our individual and social identities and thus making us different.

CHAPTER SEVENTEEN

Conclusion

OF TRUTH OR CONSEQUENCES

A nine-year-old, apparently white, boy enjoys a stroll in downtown Atlanta with his parents. Father and son have taken mommy away from her computer for an hour or so to share food and fun while listening to the jazz band that entertains the lunch crowd at Woodruff Park.

Stepping out of a favorite Chinese restaurant, the boy studies his surroundings and asks loudly, without warning, "Mommy, why does it seem that there are no black people living in our neighborhood? It seems there are tons and tons of white people where we live. But there are no black people there!" (He assumes his family to be white, which is debatable.)

His mother, the social studies queen, as he calls her, replies, taking full advantage of a teaching moment. Mommy's break turns automatically into work of the kind that is worth doing—thoughtful, leisurely, hopefully accurate, and responsible conversations with youth about social conditions, the causes behind them, and the prospects for improving them.

We ask you, gentle reader. Beyond your own, private thoughts on the subject raised, how would you answer this precocious little boy if he were your brother, nephew, or son? Would your answer be different if you were speaking with a child from your neighborhood? How might your response vary if you were a schoolteacher forced to reply to a pupil on his way to building a social consciousness?

In what ways might your conversation be shaped if you and this little boy were seated near and among a majority of African Americans, who were by this time amused and intrigued? Would you have an answer for this child at all? Is there a code of etiquette on which you could rely to get you through this? If so, begin to identify its origins, rules, content, function, and the justification for its existence.

Decorum is a cultural universal. Among North American rules of etiquette are two that we tend to follow, but with variation in consistency: (1) protection of youth from realities of adulthood and (2) discretion in what we reveal in public about our private beliefs, especially our politics.

Politeness is a way of acting that we deem necessary and desirable. A polite society has and shows good taste. Its citizens are polished, refined, and proper. They know what to say, to whom, how much, and how.

Most of us maintain, to varied degrees, courtesy, tact, and civility in public. We learn forms, manners, and ceremonies that convention establishes as acceptable or required in social relations, in professional interactions, or in official life. Right? When an elderly person gets on a bus that is fully occupied, a younger one automatically offers his seat to her. Or does he? When one meets a woman in a wheelchair struggling to open the door to a restroom, one offers to open it for her. Or does one? A young child or adolescent enters a room full of adults engaged in conversation, waits for a cue of welcome, and proceeds to greet each guest with a handshake and some version of, "Pleased to meet you." Is that right? Or are young Americans more likely to walk right by without a glance, barge in and start talking to a parent, or simply grunt and stand around?

Propriety, that is, being proper, appropriate, or fitting, assumes knowledge of, and conformity to, an accepted set of standards for proper manners. Suitable taste in behavior, speech, dress, and style is achieved easily in small-scale, relatively homogeneous societies, such as a mountain village in Spain. The same is true in closed class or caste-based social groups (e.g., the British elite) and within some tradition-bound ethnic or religious groups in complex stratified societies (e.g., nomadic Gypsies in Greece and Orthodox Jews in the United States).

However, conformity to a single, national code of conduct is virtually impossible in the United States or Canada. To follow the *Amy Vanderbilt Complete Book of Etiquette: A Guide to Contemporary Living*, or *Miss Manners' Guide to Excruciatingly Correct Behavior*, one runs the risk of offending or alienating many North Americans. A society of millions cannot hope to have a unified code of normative ethics—universal understanding and practice of what is socially good or bad, right or wrong, proper or improper, just or unjust. The prospect for this, even if desirable, is not an option in a multicultural society like our own. What's an American to do? Try anyway.

Political correctness (PC) was developed in the early 1980s by academics and other members of the cultural elite. It forms a set of rules, standards, and patterns of behavior that its agents deem correct and just in achieving equity, equality, and harmony in a multicultural society. PC has, without a doubt, protected many from embarrassing situations, helped others to accomplish social goals, and encouraged communication between some groups and individuals in contexts where avoidance or conflict might prevail.

To its creators PC may be a hopeful guide to postmodern living, an etiquette for a multicultural society. Yet PC is based more on assumptions and biased views about what is correct and implicitly just than on mass agreement, or critical decisions, about social conduct. Like all systems of etiquette, PC is the product of a few, who design and define what is proper for all. A recommendation to a faculty member by the administration of a university to place a "safe space" sign, symbolic of Gay Pride, on his or her office door is not only naive but PI (politically incorrect). Where do the rest of the students, faculty, and staff go to be safe? Moreover, why should a school require safe space stickers to protect its personnel?

Most North Americans are not privy to the new glossary of PC terms, body language, or styles of interaction that proponents of PC manage with relative ease. But this is only part of the problem. The more serious risk is that PC discourages Americans from talking at all, or honestly, about important issues confronting us today. Because of PC, many people fear talking about homelessness, social welfare policy, intergroup marriages, alcoholism, admissions tests, unemployment, the failure of schools, out-of-wedlock children, AIDS, Social Security, affirmative action, or college curricula. To attempt a conversation in public on these topics is for most people like walking on eggshells. It is safer, perceptibly, to say nothing, and just get along.

The truth hurts, sometimes. More often, it liberates. In either case, it has consequences. PC is not always accurate or responsible. It seems to us that mere politeness, and especially an unfounded or assumed set of standards for social conduct, is not enough to encourage communication or peace between individuals and groups in our society. Honest conversations between people of all cultural orientations and ages, sprinkled with more questions than answers, guided by contemplation and a good deal of listening, is a better way of reaching understanding in a highly complicated, diverse, and rapidly changing society.

The boy in Woodruff Park had the right idea, and his mother followed his cue. In doing so, she taught him something about the human condition, and he taught her to take the time to answer. Political correctness is an admirable and ambitious ideal. For it to become reality requires time, leisure (always the prerequisite to critical thinking), and generosity. Are we North Americans prepared to put action where our rhetoric is? ☻

USING CULTURE TO BUILD HUMANITY

East is East, and West is West, and never the twain shall meet. In his poem "The Ballad of East and West," Rudyard Kipling asserts that Western culture will always be separate and different from the East. A look at contemporary North America contradicts Kipling. In the United States and Canada, East and West, and all the rest, don't just meet. They blend into a social mosaic that defies clear cultural categories and fixed boundaries. Human diversity and multiculturalism are defining features of mainstream North America. They denote both a culturally diverse population and the central role that culture plays in organizing social and political life.

People have always relied on culture in adapting to environmental, economic, and political stresses. However, not all individuals, and certainly not all groups, have been conscious of this adaptive capacity. Today culture has become a key concept and a strategic resource, which validates, empowers, and mobilizes groups to claim their humanity.

Urban Gypsies in Greece distinguish themselves from poor, nomadic Gypsies by showing their *politismo* (civilization) and *anthropia* (humanity). Markers of humanity include property, jobs, proficiency in spoken Greek, and participation in public education, the military, and the Greek Orthodox Church. Such indicators have earned these urban Gypsies prosperity and autonomy, both prerequisites for their ultimate goal—preserving their own social organization (Kozaitis 1997).

In the 1960s and 1970s, American minority groups spoke of black, yellow, and red power. That emphasis on the physical (skin color) has shifted today to the cultural. African Americans expose their kids to the intellectual, artistic, and scientific contributions of their ancestors. Many families now celebrate Kwanzaa (observation of seven principles for building family, community, and culture) and Juneteenth, the National Negro Day, which represents the end of slavery and continuing struggle for freedom. Native North Americans stress continuity with their cultural origins, traditional customs and values, to enhance a sense of identity.

Education is a dominant force in our multicultural society. Kids are taught to recognize customs, places, and cultural markers (e.g., flags) of all kinds of people in the world. In many places the social studies curricula of primary and secondary schools resemble introductory college courses in cultural anthropology. Historical and cultural aspects of mainstream North America are compared and contrasted with those of other regions of the world. The annual Christmas play is replaced by a multicultural pageant of winter holidays. In many schools Halloween is no longer observed because it offends the cultural sensibilities of some parents and school personnel.

Compared with a generation ago, higher education includes a larger and more culturally diverse faculty and student body. Women and African Americans have influenced educational and curricular content. Asian, Latino, and, more recently, gay and lesbian studies are now part of a liberal arts education. These influences challenge the old underrepresentation of minorities in higher education.

Courses in social sciences and the humanities may teach as much about other cultures, traditions, and intellectual models as they do the canons associated with European history and scholarship. North American academic culture is being de-Europeanized. It has been multiculturalized to suit the needs, interests, and values of those who rule it, and consume it, today. Attention to difference, otherness, and equity creates an image of the Eurocentric perspective as just another other. A recent trend on college campuses known as "whiteness studies" illustrates this shift.

Through the media and the increased representation of minorities in the American mainstream, masses of people have learned that culture

The multicultural model, of increasing prominence in our schools, recognizes the multiplicity of American cultures. Multiculturalism recognizes that America includes people of differing community, ethnic, and cultural histories, different points of view, and degrees of empowerment. Such a perspective spurs studies of specific ethnic and other kinds of traditions.

counts. Multiculturalism is the organization and coexistence of a variety of cultural systems in a single nation-state. People actively imbue social statuses such as ethnicity, race, sex, age, and gender with meaning and value. This strategy has enhanced economic security and social and political legitimacy for millions of Americans.

Affinity groups, organized according to lived experience, cognitive ties, and political interests, are themselves diverse and stratified. Consider Queer Nation, a politically constructed category that includes gay men, lesbians, bisexuals, and transgendered persons. The leaders of Queer Nation advance a sense of peoplehood, of solidarity and power in numbers. This ideology enhances internal cohesion and promotes political legitimacy. However, gay men and lesbians are themselves diverse in terms of class, age, ethnicity, and race. Further cultural divisions exist between, say, the gay leather community and the community of "pretty boys." Lesbians share certain aesthetic, political, and intellectual interests that distinguish them from gay men. Yet among lesbians, too, there are cultural divisions, such as that between "butches" and "lipstick lesbians."

Culture has always eased human adaptation. Today we see an emphasis on cultural content—particular patterned activities, knowledge, and beliefs—as the basis of a safe and gratifying collective identity and existence. A person with a disability gains protection and respect by joining a political group of people with disabilities. Homosexually identified persons find comfort as members of the gay community.

The human rights movement has spurred many cultural factions. For example, nativist sentiments (e.g., white supremacy) have emerged among some white Americans with no special allegiance to any particular ethnic group. All human rights movements, including the men's movement and the white movement, are more expressions of affinity than of exclusion. Often the wish to belong is erroneously interpreted as a will to separate. Instead, identity politics expresses the voices of fragmented Americans seeking psychological refuge, a home to call their own. Culture is the means by which this home is constructed.

Multiculturalism is not an appendage of North American society; rather, it is intrinsic to society's core. The struggle to define, defend, and advance a cultural front at the local level is a symptom of social neglect or abuse at the national and international levels. When formal institutions and policies fail to meet their needs, citizens invent informal institutions, standards, and values to protect themselves and to create meaningful ways of life. The varied culture-based identities, statuses, and movements generate multiculturalism, a new ethos that characterizes North American social organization. It is now a key feature of our national character.

FROM CIVIL RIGHTS TO HUMAN RIGHTS

Social differentiation within a nation-state includes functional groups, such as professional associations and political parties. Groups are also organized on the basis of culture—distinctive rituals, ceremonies, artifacts, and values. Some cultural segments identify themselves as nations (self-conscious ethnic groups) in order to differentiate their collective sentiments, activities, and goals from those of the state (a territorial unit).

The Civil Rights movement of the 1950s and 1960s sought to end segregation in public accommodations and facilities and to promote equal access to jobs, housing, and education. Out of the organized efforts for Civil Rights emerged a worldwide initiative to ensure Human Rights. Multiculturalism, the master movement of the 1980s and 1990s, advances the interests and needs of many and diverse groups, including people of color, women, and the poor, by emphasizing equal access to resources and cultural value.

International migration has altered the demographic and cultural landscapes of Europe and North America. Immigrants strive to adapt to state requirements, public racism, and backlash that would reject cultural diversity in the name of national unity. The emphasis on peoplehood, on culture as a basis of identity, has become a global phenomenon. As a form of collective action, peoplehood is adaptive in the modern world, where psychosocial insecurity reigns and cultural integrity is threatened. Cultural nationalism is a progressive political movement. Cultural nationalists are those who strive to construct autonomous and coherent communities fit to compete in the contemporary world system.

In North America, the elites of minority groups have organized human rights movements to benefit their members. Leaders work to create a sense of peoplehood and cultural content that transcends internal divisions. For example, the Afrocentric movement is the product of the African-American intelligentsia. (Afrocentrism celebrates the cultural contributions of Africans and the peoples, such as African Americans and Afro-Brazilians, of the African diaspora.) The majority of African Americans know little about Afrocentrism and are much more preoccupied with jobs, housing, and education than with the roots of African-American culture or with developing a contesting voice.

Groups that now use culture to claim economic, political, and symbolic legitimacy are found in nation-states throughout the world. In Africa, the Americas, and Papua New Guinea, indigenous peoples struggle for cultural survival. In Europe, immigrants organize to combat new forms of racism. In North America, social movements by ethnic, racial, and sexual minorities, people with disabilities, and the elderly seek legal recognition and protection.

Traditionally, state-building has been the project of economic, political, and intellectual elites, who have neglected minority rights. This process has been challenged by mobilizing agents and social movements seeking representation, integration, and self-determination. Increasingly evident human diversity has fueled identity politics and affinity-group formation. People need coherent and stable communities to belong to.

The new social movements express resistance to statist ideology and unequal treatment. Minorities have faced prejudice and discrimination in states with assimilationist agendas. Proponents of modernization and innovation have sometimes viewed traditional, or native, culture as a hindrance to progress and have subjugated **ethnic minorities.** Ethnocide is the process by which such groups are denied the opportunity to reproduce socially and culturally and to meet their own material, psychosocial, and spiritual needs. A review of UNESCO documents shows that cultural policies, including those concerned with education and language, tend to fit the interests of national and international entities rather than those of ethnic or subnational groups.

A group-based approach to social and economic security encourages minorities to claim resources, to practice native forms of social life, and to maintain a self-determined relation with the state. Regional and ethnic movements in Europe, Asia, and Africa have challenged the nation-state as the controlling body within a bordered territory. States increasingly acknowledge pressures by minorities seeking human rights and security. Cultural mobilization is aided by policies of certain contemporary states, which offer formal protection of linguistic, educational, and cultural diversity.

Globally, the collective human rights movement has mobilized and legitimized diversity. It has also gained the attention of regional and international agencies, such as UNESCO, the Organization of American States, the Organization of African Unity, the European Economic Community, and the European Court of Human Rights. All those entities address ethnic rights in their particular fields and regions. In response to pressures from historically underrepresented groups, state ideologies and the policies of formal institutions (e.g., academia) are increasingly directed at the formal education and cultural survival of subaltern groups. The political underpinnings of cultural identity in today's world are remarkable.

HUMAN AGENCY AS A PRIME MOVER
OF SOCIAL REFORM

For more than a century, anthropologists have written about the collective human ability to invent rules, create standards, and establish norms. Unfortunately, the fund of information that anthropologists and other social scientists have produced is accessible only to those who can afford it and to those few who can make sense of it. The knowledge of the human experiences, struggles, and accomplishments on which social science is based remains chiefly the property of an academic elite. Social researchers must do more to share their findings and insights with the public.

Students are too often oblivious to the cultural and social critiques that the arts, humanities, and sciences have contributed over the centuries. Today's students are frustrated when they can't understand a reading assignment because it is filled with jargon, and "doesn't mean anything" to them. Students complain, often justifiably, that readings are boring or irrelevant. If students are excluded from the knowledge that social research produces, how can we expect them to make a difference? Content that is necessary to understand and improve the human condition, as Margaret Mead reminded us in her many works, must be especially accessible if we hope to narrow the gap between knowledge and action.

In contemporary North America, formal education dominates as a socializing force. Rates of literacy are higher than ever, and global communication prevails. But we still hear people explain social phenomena naively as "that's just the way things are." Notions of inequity as natural and inevitable persist in our social institutions, including education, the economy, and government. Racism, classism, anti-Semitism, ageism, and other forms of prejudice and discrimination continue. A conventional elite stresses tradition (e.g., traditional values) as right and good in social life. Yet, given the demographic profile, nature, and culture of contemporary North America, we question both the justification and plausibility of such an absolute social ethic.

The initiative to create, or resist, culture depends on knowing that all humans possess the capacity of *agency*—the ability to make and remake culture. Elites have always known about human agency. Access by a few to this knowledge, and to the resources, strategies, and connections needed to construct social reality or truth, has distinguished and stratified human groups throughout history. Today more and more people are learning that agency is an equal opportunity good and are acting on this knowledge. Consequently, the quality of life for individuals and groups improves. The cultural web of a large, complex society, like our own, changes to embrace and validate more, and different, ways of life.

Contemporary humans face the perennial challenge of managing the relation between individual interests and the collective good. The dilemma is complicated further when it involves managing the relation between diverse group interests and societal harmony. Such is the predicament of North Americans today. Anthropology, the study of humanity across time and space, teaches us that the key to this dilemma is the creative capacity of humans, by manipulating culture, to adapt to change. Since our origins as hunters and gatherers, through farming, herding, trade, industrialization, and the information age, humans have adapted *culturally* in order to survive and reproduce *socially*. What are the mechanisms of social and cultural change?

Alterations in subsistence strategies, people's means of meeting basic needs and obtaining other necessities, always affect the structure and quality of life. Also critical to social change is the role of government. Forms of social control, from gossip and leveling mechanisms to centralized power, contribute significantly to societal organization. The limits that formal institutions, such as government and religion, set on the productivity, creativity, and destiny of individuals continue to influence social and cultural life.

Throughout history, humans have adapted according to the following mechanisms of change. *Innovation* is the discovery of something new. Convergence describes the development of similar traits, institutions, or patterns of behavior as a result of living in similar environments and innovating in parallel ways. Cultural loss is the abandonment of a cultural pattern that proves useless or maladaptive in a new context. *Diffusion* refers to borrowing and integrating cultural traits from another society. *Acculturation* is the exchange of cultural features that results when groups have continuous firsthand contact. *Modernization* refers to changes that small-scale, technologically simple communities adopt from, or have imposed by, modern industrial societies. *Imperialism* is a pattern of political subordination in which a dominant society exploits subjugated populations to extract economic and political advantages.

To understand social organization and change in North America, we must certainly consider these mechanisms. In addition, colonialism, the slave trade, several wars, and labor migration and immigration have altered

Multiculturalism pervades the worlds of work, travel, recreation, politics, public service, and personal relations. In August 2000, commuters enter a tunnel at the Los Angeles Amtrak-Metrolink Union Station, where artist Richard Wyatt's mural illustrates California's diversity. According to the 2000 census, non-Hispanic whites are now a minority in that state for the first time since 1860. What is a non-Hispanic white?

our society. Contemporary American culture expresses a particular trajectory of change and adaptation by a diverse population in a particular region of earth during the modern age, a particular point in the time line of humanity.

Contemporary Americans and Canadians live in the presence of cultural diversity, multiple traits, customs, rituals, and beliefs, and multiculturalism, the development and organization of many culturally identified groups that constitute society. Multiculturalism constitutes a way of life and an ethos that supports and reinforces it.

Discussed previously are several processes or mechanisms of social change. But what of human consciousness? What role might ordinary people play in changing society? Our analysis shows human agency to be a prime mover of social reform. To be sure, human consciousness and goal-oriented action are not new. Social institutions and cultural standards don't appear from nowhere. Historically, social construction (the making and framing of society) has been the property and privilege of political and economic elites. More recently, as we have discussed, cultural elites have been competing successfully with economic and political elites in building our society.

Of course, as Eric Wolf (1982) shows in his influential book *Europe and the People without History,* all kinds of people participate in the making of societies and cultures, whether or not they know it, consent consciously, or are given credit for it. Agency is intrinsic to being human. It needs only to be activated and expressed. This book has emphasized the role of elite agency in transforming our own society culturally and politically, especially in the last 40 years. Led by elites, the Civil Rights movement spawned many human rights movements, which have liberated millions of people to claim their human nature and culture.

What about *popular* agency? To what extent will ordinary people take charge of social and cultural construction and contribute to their own and the general well-being? We think that the master movement of multiculturalism is poised to accommodate not just elites but also masses of people eager to improve the quality of human life. Among the environmentalists, for example, are thousands of parents, teachers, and children who recycle, car pool, and clean up neighborhoods and creeks. Feminists include men and women who raise their kids to appreciate sexual differences but also to honor gender similarities. Classroom moms, Cub Scout dads, and professional peers come from a variety of ethnic, racial, and class backgrounds. They share and transmit customs, ideas, and beliefs that we integrate into our own ways of life. From daily cultural exchange with others we learn to be more aware, thoughtful, and appreciative of human diversity and unity.

One factor inhibiting conscious popular agency is a sense of despair and helplessness—that the world is coming to an end, that our society is in trouble, and that nothing can be done. The idea that ordinary people, as individuals and in groups, cannot improve the human condition is based on a misguided notion of scale. Problems are seen as too big to solve. But socially responsible agency can occur on multiple scales. Would-be social agents can work and make a difference in a wide variety of settings, as different as one's own household, the local shelter for homeless people, and the writing and production of screenplays. Strategies of popular participation may vary from direct hands-on social work (e.g., volunteering at a clinic for AIDS patients) to writing child welfare policy.

The elites and other participants in the various human rights movements have taught us that choosing a cause, a scale, a forum, and a strategy can and does make a difference. Moreover, the master movement works for goals that accord with the findings of anthropological research. Most anthropologists would agree that key ingredients of a congenial, gratifying way of human life include community, identity, ritual, meaning, autonomy, reciprocity, responsibility, and participation. In a way, today's mobilizing agents are engaged in organized efforts to reconstitute the small-scale society.

As the world contracts, and the North American mainstream expands, the importance of paying attention to local life becomes greater. A multicultural society favors small-scale sociocultural organization and encourages popular agency. As global economics and politics challenge human lives and lifestyles, the greater the need, and apparently the inclination, to ennoble the local. The cultural construction of locally defined political causes, communities of experience, soul groups, fictive kinship, and cognitive ties reflects the eternal search by humans for meaning, solidarity, and belonging.

Multiculturalism, as a master movement, is increasingly materializing this need into social reality. A multicultural society fosters democracy, empowers people to define and design meaningful ways of life, and encourages popular agency. Human potential may be maximized not for the profit it may generate for the few, but for the quality of life it may ensure for the many. As students and teachers of the human condition, our responsibility is to reinforce this social current. As citizens of a multicultural society, our duty is to set the example of a more enlightened and liberating humanity. Organizers of the master movement have prepared the groundwork for the rest of us.

Glossary

acculturation: The exchange of cultural features that results when groups come into continuous firsthand contact; the original cultural patterns of either or both groups may be altered, but the groups remain distinct.

achieved status: Social status that comes through talents, actions, efforts, activities, and accomplishments rather than ascription.

affinity groups: Common-interest groups, including families, kin networks, neighborhoods, local communities, political parties, religious affiliations, professional organizations, and groups organized by common culture and cognitive ties.

Afrocentric: Orientation of many African Americans, emphasizing Africa as a cultural center.

agape: Humanitarianism, or love for humanity; as contrasted with *eros* and *philia.*

age grades: In the individual's life cycle, the various age phases or categories, such as infancy, childhood, adolescence, the college years, young adulthood, middle age, and old age.

age sets: Groups uniting all men or women (usually men) born during a certain time span; these groups control property and often have political and military functions.

ageism: Prejudice and discrimination against the elderly.

agency: The active role of individuals in making and remaking culture.

androgyny: Similarities (e.g., in dress, adornment, or body features) between males and females.

antiracists: Those who reject ideas and practices based on presumed innate superiority and inferiority of groups; antiracist strategies include refusal to behave according to one's prescribed racial category and participation in activities to combat racism.

ascribed status: Social status (e.g., race or gender) that people have little or no choice about occupying.

asexuality: Indifference toward, or lack of attraction to, either sex.

assimilation: The merging of groups and their traditions within a society that endorses a single common culture. The process of change that a minority group may experience when it moves to a country where another culture dominates; the minority is incorporated into the dominant culture to the point that it no longer exists as a separate cultural unit.

attitudinal discrimination: Discrimination against members of a group because of prejudice toward that group.

berdaches: Among the Crow Indians, members of a third gender, for whom certain ritual duties were reserved.

biological determinism: Viewing human behavior and social organization as biologically determined.

bisexuality: A person's habitual sexual attraction to, and sexual activities with, persons of both sexes.

Black English Vernacular (BEV): The rule-governed dialect spoken by American black youth, especially in inner city areas; also spoken in rural areas and used in the casual, intimate speech of many adults; also known as *ebonics*.

bourgeoisie: One of Marx's opposed classes; owners of the means of production (factories, mines, large farms, and other sources of subsistence).

capital: Wealth or resources invested in business, with the intent of producing a profit.

Carnival: A pre-Lenten festival comparable to Mardi Gras in Louisiana, popular in Brazil and in certain Mediterranean and Caribbean societies; features costumed anonymity and a ritual structure of reversal.

class consciousness: Recognition of collective interests and personal identification with one's economic group, particularly the proletariat; basic to Marx's view of class.

cognitive ties: Social links based on common knowledge and perceptions of reality, on what people know, or on what they think they know.

colonialism: The political, social, economic, and cultural domination of a territory and its people by a foreign power for an extended time.

communitas: Intense community spirit, a feeling of great social solidarity, equality, and togetherness; characteristic of people experiencing liminality together.

complex societies: Nations that are large and populous, with social stratification and central governments.

consecutive (a.k.a. serial) monogamy: Divorce and remarriage, rather than being married to multiple spouses at the same time (*polygamy*).

copula deletion: Absence of the verb *to be;* featured in BEV and in diverse languages, including Hebrew and Russian.

core values: Key, basic, or central values that integrate a culture and help distinguish it from others.

cultural anthropology: Or *sociocultural anthropology;* the field that describes, interprets, and explains similarities and differences among societies and cultures.

cultural colonialism: Internal domination by one group and its culture/ideology over others, such as Russian domination in the former Soviet Union.

cultural determinism: Viewing human behavior and social organization as determined mainly by cultural and environmental factors. Cultural determinists focus on variation rather than universals and stress learning and the role of culture in human adaptation.

cultural relativism: The position that the values and standards of cultures differ and deserve respect. Extreme relativism argues that cultures should be judged solely by their own standards.

cultural rights: Certain rights that are vested not in individuals but in identifiable groups, such as religious and ethnic minorities and indigenous societies.

culture: Traditions and customs that govern behavior and beliefs; distinctly human; transmitted through learning.

culture pattern: A coherent set of interrelated culture traits; customs and beliefs that are connected, so that if one changes, the others also change.

culture shock: Disturbed feelings that often arise when one has contact with an unfamiliar culture—either in North America or, more usually, abroad. It is a feeling of alienation, of being without some of the most ordinary and basic cues of one's culture of origin.

culture trait: An individual item in a culture, such as a particular belief, tool, or practice.

culturelets: In a multicultural society, multiple centers, each based on specialized cultural identity, pride, and knowledge, within the nation-state.

descent: Rule assigning social identity on the basis of some aspect of one's ancestry.

diaspora: The offspring of an area who have spread to many lands.

differential access: Unequal access to resources; basic attribute of chiefdoms and states. Superordinates have favored access to such resources, while the access of subordinates is limited by superordinates.

diffusion: Borrowing between cultures either directly or through intermediaries.

diglossia: The existence of high (formal) and low (familial) dialects of a single language, such as German.

discourse: Talk, speeches, gestures, and actions.

discrimination: Policies and practices that harm a group and its members.

domestic: Within or pertaining to the home.

domestic-public dichotomy: Contrast between women's role in the home and men's role in public life, with a corresponding social devaluation of women's work and worth.

ebonics: Another name for Black English Vernacular; derived from *ebony* and *phonics*.

ecocide: Destruction of local ecosystems.

education: The acquisition of formal knowledge, normally in a place called a school; tends to be found in nation-states; exposes certain, not all, people in a society to a body of formal knowledge or lore (as contrasted with *enculturation*, which applies to everyone).

enculturation: The social process by which culture is learned and transmitted across the generations.

environmental racism: The systematic use of institutionally based power by a majority group to make policy decisions that create disproportionate environmental hazards in minority communities.

environmentalists: See *nurturists*.

eros: Sexual love; the most critical gauge of sexual orientation is one's erotic experiences.

ethnic expulsion: A policy aimed at removing groups who are culturally different from a country.

ethnic group: Group distinguished by cultural similarities (shared among members of that group) and differences (between that group and others); ethnic group members share beliefs, values, habits, customs, and norms, and a common language, religion, history, geography, kinship, or race.

ethnic minorities: Indigenous peoples who have moved to urban areas.

ethnicity: Identification with, and feeling part of, an ethnic group, and exclusion from certain other groups because of this affiliation.

ethnocentrism: The tendency to view one's own culture as best and to judge the behavior and beliefs of culturally different people by one's own standards.

ethnocide: Destruction by a dominant group of the cultures of an ethnic group.

ethnography: The firsthand, field-based study of a particular culture; usually entails spending a year or more in the field, living with natives and learning about their customs.

Etoro: A Papua New Guinea culture in which males are culturally trained to prefer homosexuality.

explanatory approach: The approach to human biological diversity that strives to discover the causes of specific human biological differences.

family of affiliation: Refers to psychological ties with people one loves and can count on for emotional, social, and material support; especially useful when an individual's natural family isn't available or adequate in meeting his or her needs.

family of orientation: The nuclear family in which one is born and grows up.

family of procreation: A nuclear family established when one marries and has children.

fictive kinship: Reciprocal provision of goods and services, including affection, companionship, and shared values, between nonbiologically, nonlegally, but socially related individuals; often with the fiction of kinship ties, for example, honorary aunts and uncles.

First World: The democratic West—traditionally conceived in opposition to *Second World*, ruled by communism.

forced assimilation: Use of force by a dominant group to compel a minority to adopt the dominant culture—for example, penalizing or banning the language and customs of an ethnic group.

gay: Or *lesbian;* stands for *a way of life* by persons who desire, and have sex with, persons of the same sex (men in this case); as contrasted with *homosexual.*

gender roles: The tasks and activities that a culture assigns to each sex.

gender stereotypes: Oversimplified but strongly held ideas about the characteristics of males and females.

gender stratification: Unequal distribution of rewards (socially valued resources, power, prestige, and personal freedom) between men and women, reflecting their different positions in a social hierarchy.

generalities: Culture patterns or traits that exist in some but not all societies.

genocide: The deliberate elimination of a group; for example, through mass murder, warfare, or introduced diseases.

geriatrics: The medical specialty focusing on diseases and disabilities associated with aging and on treatment of the elderly.

gerontology: The study of aging and especially of older people.

globalization: The accelerating interdependence of nations in a world system linked economically and through mass media and modern transportation systems.

hegemonic reading (of a "text"): The reading or meaning that the creators intended, or the one the elites consider to be the intended or correct meaning.

hegemony: As used by Antonio Gramsci, a stratified social order in which subordinates comply with domination by internalizing its values and accepting its naturalness.

heteromorphic: Varied in shape or appearance.

heterosexuality: A person's habitual sexual attraction to, and sexual activities with, persons of the opposite sex.

hidden transcript: As used by James Scott, the critique of power by the oppressed that goes on offstage (in private) where the power holders can't see it.

hijras: In India, a third gender composed of biological males who have undergone an operation to have their genitals removed; they exaggerate female dress codes and decorum, have certain ritual duties, and work as prostitutes.

holistic: Interested in the whole of the human condition: past, present, and future; biology, society, language, and culture; holism is a key attribute of anthropology.

homonyms: Words that sound the same but have different meanings; for example, *bare* and *bear.*

homosexual: A term used to describe sexual desire and activity between persons of the same sex.

homosexuality: A person's habitual sexual attraction to, and sexual activities with, persons of the same sex.

human rights: A doctrine that invokes a realm of justice and morality beyond and superior to particular countries, cultures, and religions. Human rights, usually seen as vested in individuals, would include the right to speak freely, to hold religious beliefs without persecution, and not to be enslaved.

humanities: The fields that study art, narratives, music, dance, and other forms of creative expression.

hypervitaminosis D: A nutritional disorder caused by too much vitamin D; calcium deposits build up in the body's soft tissues and the kidneys may eventually fail.

hypodescent: A rule that automatically places the children of a union or mating between members of different socioeconomic groups in the less-privileged group.

ideal culture: What people say they should do and what they say they do; contrasted with *real culture.*

ideational solidarity: Social integration through relations, bonds, and loyalties based on common knowledge.

identity: A psychosocial and political orientation that individuals internalize and that is shared by people united by a common status or experience.

identity politics: Sociopolitical identities based on the perception of sharing a common culture, language, religion, or race, rather than citizenship in a nation-state, which may contain diverse social groups.

income: Earnings from wages and salaries.

independent invention: The process by which humans innovate, creatively finding solutions to old and new problems; an important mechanism of cultural change.

indigenized: Modified to fit the local culture.

Industrial Revolution: The historical transformation (in Europe, after 1750) of traditional into modern societies through industrialization of the economy.

institutional discrimination: Programs, policies, and arrangements that deny equal rights and opportunities to, or differentially harm, members of particular groups.

intellectual property rights (IPR): A society's cultural base—its core beliefs and principles. IPR is claimed as a group right—a cultural right, allowing indigenous groups to control who may know and use their collective knowledge and its applications.

international culture: Cultural traditions that extend beyond national boundaries.

Iroquois: A confederation of indigenous societies in New York State; matrilineal, with communal longhouses and a prominent political, religious, and economic role for women.

!Kung: A group of San ("Bushmen") foragers of southern Africa; the exclamation point indicates a click sound in the San language.

lesbian: Or *gay;* stands for *a way of life* by persons who desire, and have sex with, persons of the same sex (women in this case); as contrasted with *homosexual.*

leveling mechanisms: Customs and social actions that operate to reduce differences in wealth and thus to bring standouts in line with community norms.

libido: The sex drive.

liminality: The critically important marginal or in-between phase of a rite of passage.

linguistic relativism: The notion that all languages and dialects are equally effective as systems of communication.

majority group: A superordinate, dominant, or controlling group in a social/political hierarchy.

matriarchy: A society ruled by women; unknown to ethnography.

matrifocal: Mother-centered; often refers to a household with no resident husband-father.

matrilineal descent: A unilineal descent rule in which people join the mother's group automatically at birth and stay members throughout life.

matrilocality: Customary residence with the wife's relatives after marriage, so that children grow up in their mother's community.

matrons: Senior women, as among the Iroquois.

melanin: A chemical substance manufactured in cells in the epidermis, or outer skin layer; the melanin cells of darker-skinned people produce more and larger granules of melanin than do those of lighter-skinned people.

minority groups: Subordinate groups in a social/political hierarchy, with inferior power and less secure access to resources than majority groups have.

mobilizing agents: Politically active individuals and community organizers, including elite members of minority groups, who are often artists and intellectuals with access to major social institutions, especially education and the media.

monogamous: Having only one sexual partner or mate at a time.

multiculturalism: The view of cultural diversity in a country as something good and desirable; a multicultural society socializes individuals not only into the dominant (national) culture but also into an ethnic culture.

nation: Once a synonym for *ethnic group*, designating a single culture sharing a language, religion, history, territory, ancestry, and kinship; now usually a synonym for *state* or *nation-state*.

nation-state: An autonomous political entity; a country, such as the United States or Canada.

national culture: Cultural experiences, beliefs, learned behavior patterns, and values shared by citizens of the same nation.

nationalities: Ethnic groups that once had, or wish to have or regain, autonomous political status (their own countries).

native anthropologist: An anthropologist who studies his or her own culture, such as an American working in the United States or a Canadian in Canada.

natural selection: The process by which nature selects the forms most fit to survive and reproduce in a given environment, such as the tropics.

naturists: Those who argue that human behavior and social organization are biologically determined.

négritude: African identity; developed by African intellectuals in Francophone (French-speaking) western Africa.

neolocality: A postmarital residence rule or custom by which a married couple chooses a new place to live rather than residing with or near the parents of either spouse.

nongovernmental organizations (NGOs): Organized interest or affinity groups with local (e.g., a bowling league), state (e.g., a Michigan lawyers' group), regional (e.g., Sons of Dixie), national (e.g., Young Americans for Freedom), or international (e.g., Save the Children) memberships.

nuclear family: Kinship group consisting of parents and children.

nurturists: Those who link behavior and social organization to environmental factors. Nurturists focus on variation rather than universals and stress learning and the role of culture in human adaptation.

pantribal sodalities: Nonkin-based groups that exist throughout a tribe, spanning several villages.

particularities: Distinctive or unique culture traits, patterns, or integrations.

patrilineal descent: A unilineal descent rule by which people join the father's group automatically at birth and stay members throughout life.

patrilineal-patrilocal complex: An interrelated constellation of patrilineality, patrilocality, warfare, and male supremacy.

patrilocality: Customary residence with the husband's relatives after marriage.

phenotype: An organism's evident traits; its manifest biology—anatomy and physiology.

philia: Friendship, the most enduring form of love; born out of higher faculties, as contrasted with *eros* and *agape.*

plural society: According to Frederik Barth, a society that features ethnic contrasts, ecological specialization of its ethnic groups, and the economic interdependence of those groups.

pluralism: The view that ethnic and racial difference should be allowed to thrive, so long as such diversity does not threaten dominant values and norms.

Polynesia: A triangle of South Pacific islands formed by Hawaii to the north, Easter Island to the east, and New Zealand to the southwest.

postmodern: In its most general sense, describes the blurring and breakdown of established canons (rules, standards), categories, distinctions, and boundaries.

postmodernism: A style and movement in architecture that succeeded modernism. Compared with modernism, postmodernism is less geometric, less functional, less austere, more playful, and more willing to include elements from diverse times and cultures; *postmodern* now describes comparable developments in music, literature, and visual art.

postmodernity: The condition of a world in flux, with people on the move, in which established groups, boundaries, identities, contrasts, and standards are reaching out and breaking down.

power: The ability to exercise one's will over others—to do what one wants; the basis of political status.

prejudice: Devaluing (looking down on) a group because of its assumed behavior, values, capabilities, or attributes.

prestige: Esteem, respect, or approval for acts, deeds, or qualities considered exemplary.

proletariat: See *working class.*

public transcript: As used by James Scott, the open, public interactions between dominators and oppressed; the outer shell of power relations.

race: An ethnic group assumed to have a biological basis.

racial classification: A now-rejected approach to the study of human biological diversity, which seeks to assign human beings to categories based on assumed common ancestry.

racism: Discrimination against an ethnic group assumed to have a biological basis.

real culture: Actual behavior as observed by the anthropologist; contrasted with *ideal culture.*

refugees: People who have been forced (involuntary refugees) or who have chosen (voluntary refugees) to flee a country to escape persecution or war.

religion: Belief and ritual concerned with supernatural beings, powers, and forces.

rickets: A nutritional disorder caused by a shortage of vitamin D, so that calcium is imperfectly absorbed in the intestines; causes softening and deformation of the bones.

rites of passage: Culturally defined activities associated with the transition from one place or stage of life to another.

rituals: Behaviors that are formal, stylized, repetitive, and stereotyped, performed earnestly as social acts; rituals are held at set times and places and have liturgical orders.

role: A set of expected (culturally proper) behaviors, attitudes, rights, and obligations attached to a particular status.

science: A systematic field of study that aims, through experiment, observation, and deduction, to produce reliable explanations of phenomena with reference to the material and physical world.

Second World: The Warsaw Pact nations, including the former Soviet Union, the Socialist and once-Socialist countries of eastern Europe and Asia.

secret societies: Sodalities, usually all-male or all-female, with secret initiation ceremonies.

serial monogamy: Marriage of a given individual to several spouses, but not at the same time.

sexual dimorphism: Marked differences in male and female biology besides the contrasts in breasts and genitals.

sexual fit: Combines physical traits with psychosocial sensibilities; this fit, that is, a particular set of characteristics that activates one's libido, reappears in different potential partners during one's life span.

sexual orientation: The patterned way in which a person views and expresses the sexual component of his or her personality; a person's habitual sexual attraction to, and activities with, persons of the opposite sex (*heterosexuality*), the same sex (*homosexuality*), or both sexes (*bisexuality*). *Asexuality* refers to indifference toward, or lack of attraction to, either sex.

social races: Groups assumed to have a biological basis but actually perceived and defined in a social context, by a particular culture rather than by scientific criteria.

society: In social science terminology, organized life in groups. In the United States, *society* has acquired an additional and more restrictive meaning: the "proper" organization of individuals and groups, with people in assigned stations, or places, in the social order.

sociocultural anthropology: Or simply *cultural anthropology;* the field that describes, interprets, and explains similarities and differences among societies and cultures.

sociolinguistics: Study of relationships between social and linguistic variation; study of language (performance) in its social context.

sodalities: See *pantribal sodalities*.

state (nation-state): A complex sociopolitical system that administers a territory and populace with substantial contrasts in occupation, wealth, prestige, and power. An independent, centrally organized political unit, a government.

status: Any position that determines where someone fits in society; may be ascribed or achieved.

stereotypes: Fixed ideas, often unfavorable, about what members of a group are like.

strategic resources: Things necessary for life, such as food and space.

stratification: A characteristic of a system with socioeconomic strata; see *stratum*.

stratified: Class-structured; stratified societies have marked differences in wealth, prestige, and power between social classes.

stratum: One of two or more groups that contrast in regard to social status and access to strategic resources. Each stratum includes people of both sexes and all ages.

style shifts: Variations in speech in different contexts.

subaltern: Lower in rank, subordinate, traditionally lacking an influential role in decision making.

subcultures: The diverse cultural patterns and traditions associated with different groups in the same nation; subcultures (a problematic term) may originate in ethnicity, class, region, or religion.

subordinate: The lower, or underprivileged, group in a stratified system.

superordinate: The upper, or privileged, group in a stratified system.

symbol: Something, verbal or nonverbal, that arbitrarily and by convention stands for something else, with which it has no necessary or natural connection.

text: Something that is creatively "read," interpreted, and assigned meaning by each person who receives it; includes any media-borne image, such as Carnival.

Third World: The less-developed countries (LDCs).

tropics: A geographic zone extending some 23 degrees north and south of the equator, between the Tropic of Cancer and the Tropic of Capricorn.

underclass: The abjectly poor, in North America and throughout the world; people who lack jobs, adequate food, medical care, even shelter.

universals: Traits that exist in every culture.

variables: Attributes (e.g., sex, age, height, weight) that differ from one person or case to the next.

vernacular: Ordinary, casual speech.

wealth: All a person's material assets, including income, land, and other types of property; the basis of economic status.

working class: Or *proletariat;* those who must sell their labor to survive; the antithesis of the bourgeoisie in Marx's class analysis.

Bibliography

ABELMANN, N., AND J. LIE
1995   *Blue Dreams: Korean Americans and the Los Angeles Riots.* Cambridge: Harvard University Press.

ABELOVE, H., M. A. BARALE, AND D. M. HALPERIN, EDS.
1993   *The Lesbian and Gay Studies Reader.* New York: Routledge.

ADHERENTS.COM
2001   Major Religions of the World Ranked by Number of Adherents. http://www.adherents.com/Religions_By_Adherents/html.

ALBA, R. D., J. R. LOGAN, AND B. J. STULTS
2000   The Changing Neighborhood Contexts of the Immigrant Metropolis. *Social Forces* 79(2): 587–621.

ALDRED, L.
2000   Plastic Shamans and Astroturf Sun Dances. *American Indian Quarterly* 24(3): 329–352.

ALTMAN, L. K.
1997   Is the Longer Life the Healthier One? *New York Times,* June 22, http://www.nytimes.com.

AMADIUME, I.
1987   *Male Daughters, Female Husbands.* Atlantic Highlands, NJ: Zed.

AMERICAN ALMANAC
1994–   *Statistical Abstract of the United*
1995   *States,* 114th ed. Austin, TX: Reference Press.

1996–   *Statistical Abstract of the United*
1997   *States,* 116th ed. Austin, TX: Reference Press.

AMERICAN DEMOGRAPHICS
1996   The Mother Market. October, http://www.demographics.com/publications.
1997   The Disability Act Is Working—Forecast. January, http://www.demographics.com/publications.

ANDERSON, B.
1991   *Imagined Communities: Reflections on the Origin and Spread of Nationalism,* rev. ed. London: Verso.

ANN ARBOR NEWS
1985   Testimony of Linda Tarr-Whelan of the National Education Association to the House Committee on Science, Research, and Technology; quoted in Karen Grassmuck, Local Educators Join Push for a Computer in Every Classroom. February 10, p. A11.
1989   Census Shows Big Change in Families. September 5, p. C2.

ANN ARBOR OBSERVER
1985   Surveys of Black Americans: Most Feel Oppressed. May, pp. 42–43.

AOKI, M. Y., AND M. B. DARDESS, EDS.
1981   *As the Japanese See It: Past and Present.* Honolulu: University Press of Hawaii.

B

APPADURAI, A.
1990   Disjuncture and Difference in the Global Cultural Economy. *Public Culture* 2(2): 1–24.
1991   Global Ethnoscapes: Notes and Queries for a Transnational Anthropology. In *Recapturing Anthropology: Working in the Present*, R. G. Fox, ed., pp. 191–210. Santa Fe: School of American Research Advanced Seminar Series.

APPIAH, K. A.
1990   Racisms. In *Anatomy of Racism*, D. T. Goldberg, ed., pp. 3–17. Minneapolis: University of Minnesota Press.

APPLEBOME, P.
1996   English Unique to Blacks Is Officially Recognized. *New York Times*, December 20, http://www.nytimes.com.
1997   Dispute over Ebonics Reflects a Volatile Mix. *New York Times*, March 1, http://www.nytimes.com.

ARENS, W.
1981   Professional Football: An American Symbol and Ritual. In *The American Dimension: Cultural Myths and Social Realities*, 2nd ed., W. Arens and S. B. Montague, eds., pp. 1–10. Sherman Oaks, CA: Alfred.

ARIES, P.
1962   *Centuries of Childhood*. Trans. R. Baldick. London: Jonathan Cape.

ASANTE, M. K.
1987   *The Afrocentric Idea*. Philadelphia: Temple University Press.
1988   *Afrocentricity*. Trenton, NJ: African World Press.

A.V.I.D. NEWS
1997   A.V.I.D. Active Voices in Disabilities. May 5, p. 1. http://www/acun.com/avid.

BAKHTIN, M.
1984   *Rabelais and His World*. Trans. H. Iswolksy. Bloomington, IN: Indiana University Press.

BARLETT, P. F.
1993   *American Dreams, Rural Realities: Family Farms in Crisis*. Chapel Hill: University of North Carolina Press.

BARRET, R. L., AND B. E. ROBINSON
1990   *Gay Fathers*. Lexington, MA: Lexington Books.

BARRINGER, F.
1992   New Census Data Show More Children Living in Poverty. *New York Times*, May 29, pp. A1, A12, A13.

BARTH, F.
1968   (orig. 1958) Ecologic Relations of Ethnic Groups in Swat, North Pakistan. In *Man in Adaptation: The Cultural Present*, Y. Cohen, ed., pp. 324–31. Chicago: Aldine.
1969   *Ethnic Groups and Boundaries: The Social Organization of Cultural Difference*. London: Allyn and Unwin.

BEHAR, R., AND D. A. GORDON, EDS.
1995   *Women Writing Culture*. Berkeley: University of California Press.

BELL, W.
1981   Neocolonialism. In *Encyclopedia of Sociology*, p. 193. Guilford, CT: DPG Publishing.

BELLAH, R. N., ED.
1978   Religious Evolution. In *Reader in Comparative Religion: An Anthropological Approach*, 4th ed., W. A. Lessa and E. Z. Vogt, eds., pp. 36–50. New York: Harper and Row.

BENEDICT, B.
1970   Pluralism and Stratification. In *Essays in Comparative Social Stratification*, L. Plotnicov and A. Tuden, eds., pp. 29–41. Pittsburgh: University of Pittsburgh Press.

BENEDICT, R.
1940   *Race, Science and Politics*. New York: Modern Age Books.

BHARDWAJ, S. M.
1998   Non-Hajj Pilgrimage in Is-
        lam: A Neglected Dimension of
        Religious Circulation. *Journal
        of Cultural Geography* 17(2):
        69–87.
BLOCH, M., ED.
1975   *Political Language and Oratory
        in Traditional Societies.* London:
        Academic.
BLUM, H. F.
1961   Does the Melanin Pigment of
        Human Skin Have Adaptive
        Value? *Quarterly Review of Biol-
        ogy* 36: 50–63.
BLUME, H.
1997   Autistics Are Communicating in
        Cyberspace. *New York Times,*
        June 30, http://www.nytimes.
        com.
BOAS, F.
1966   (orig. 1940) *Race, Language, and
        Culture.* New York: Free Press.
BONVILLAN, N.
1995   *Women and Men: Cultural Con-
        structions of Gender.* Englewood
        Cliffs, NJ: Prentice Hall.
BORJAS, G. J.
1994   The Economics of Immigration.
        Journal of Economic Literature
        32: 1667–1717.
BOSERUP, E.
1970   *Women's Role in Economic De-
        velopment.* London: Allen and
        Unwin.
BOURDIEU, P.
1977   *Outline of a Theory of Practice.*
        Trans. R. Nice. Cambridge:
        Cambridge University Press.
1982   *Ce Que Parler Veut Dire.* Paris:
        Fayard.
1984   *Distinction: A Social Critique of
        the Judgment of Taste.* Trans. R.
        Nice. Cambridge, MA: Harvard
        University Press.
BOURQUE, S. C., AND K. B. WARREN
1987   Technology, Gender and Devel-
        opment. *Daedalus* 116(4):
        173–197.

BOZETT, F. W.
1989   Gay Fathers: A Review of the
        Literature. *Journal of Homosex-
        uality* 18: 137–162.
BRAGG, R.
1997   *All Over but the Shoutin'.* New
        York: Pantheon.
BRONFENBRENNER, U.
1975   Nature with Nurture: A Reinter-
        pretation of the Evidence. In
        Race and IQ, A. Montagu, ed.,
        pp. 114–144. New York: Oxford
        University Press.
BRONNER, E.
1997   Colleges Look for Answers to
        Racial Gaps in Tests. *New York
        Times,* November 8, pp. A1, A8
        (national ed.); also http://www.
        nytimes.com.
BROOKE, J.
2000   A Commercial Makes Canadian
        Self-Esteem Bubble to the Sur-
        face, May 29, http://www.ny-
        times.com.
BROWN, J. K.
1975   Iroquois Women: An Ethnohis-
        toric Note. In *Toward an An-
        thropology of Women,* R. Reiter,
        ed., pp. 235–251. New York:
        Monthly Review Press.
BROWNING, F.
1994   *The Culture of Desire: Paradox
        and Perversity in Gay Lives Today.*
        New York: Random House.
BRUMFIEL, E. M.
1980   Specialization, Market Ex-
        change, and the Aztec State: A
        View from Huexotla. *Current
        Anthropology* 21(4): 459–478.
BRUNNER, B., ED.
2002   *Time Almanac 2002, with Infor-
        mation Please.*
BRYANT, B., AND P. MOHAI
1991   Race, Class, and Environmental
        Quality in the Detroit Area. In
        *Environmental Racism: Issues
        and Dilemmas,* eds. Bryant and
        Mohai. Ann Arbor: University of
        Michigan Office of Minority
        Affairs.

BRYSON, K.
1996   Household and Family Charac-
        teristics: March 1995. P20-488,
        November 26. U.S. Department
        of Commerce, Bureau of Cen-
        sus, Public Information Office,
        CB96–195.
BURNS, J. F.
1997   Bosnian Strife Cuts Old Bridges
        of Trust. *New York Times*, May
        22, pp. A1, A6.
BUTLER, R. N.
1975   *Why Survive? Being Old in Amer-
        ica.* New York: Harper and Row.
BUVINIC, M.
1995   The Feminization of Poverty?
        Research and Policy Needs.
        In *Reducing Poverty Through
        Labour Market Policies.* Geneva:
        International Institute for
        Labour Studies.
CALLENDER, C., AND L. KOCHEMS.
1983   The North-American Berdache.
        Current Anthropology 24:
        443–470.
CAMERON, D.
2000   Styling the Worker: Gender and
        the Commodification of Lan-
        guage in the Globalized Service
        Economy. *Journal of Sociolin-
        guistics* 4(3): 323–347.
CARNEIRO, R. L.
1970   A Theory of the Origin of the
        State. *Science* 69: 733–738.
CARVER, T.
1995   *Gender Is Not a Synonym for
        Women.* Boulder, CO: Lynne
        Reinner.
CASPER, L.
1996   Who's Minding Our Preschool-
        ers? P70-53, April 24. U.S. De-
        partment of Commerce, Bureau
        of Census, Public Information
        Office, CB96-61.
CASTELLI, J.
1984   Twelve Rules for Mixing Reli-
        gion and Politics. People for the
        American Way, 2000 M Street
        NW, Suite 400, Washington,
        DC, 20036, pfaw@pfaw.org.

CHERLIN, A. J.
1992   *Marriage, Divorce, Remarriage.*
        Cambridge, MA: Harvard Uni-
        versity Press.
CLIFFORD, J.
1988   *The Predicament of Culture:
        Twentieth-Century Ethnography,
        Literature and Art.* Cambridge,
        MA: Harvard University Press.
COILE, R. C.
2000   The Digital Transformation of
        Health Care. *Physician Execu-
        tive* 26: 8–14.
COLLINS, L. V.
1996   Facts from the Census Bureau
        for Black History Month. Mem-
        orandum for Reporters, Edi-
        tors, News Directors, February
        5. Washington: Department of
        Commerce, Bureau of Census,
        Public Information Office.
COLLINS, T. W.
1989   Rural Economic Development
        in Two Tennessee Counties: A
        Racial Dimension. Paper pre-
        sented at the annual meetings of
        the American Anthropological
        Association, Washington, DC.
CONNELL, R. W.
1995   *Masculinities.* Berkeley: Univer-
        sity of California Press.
CONNOR, W.
1972   Nation-Building or Nation De-
        stroying. *World Politics* 24(3):
        319–355.
COOLEY, C. H.
1909   *Social Organization.* New York:
        Scribner.
COWELL, A.
1997   It's Young vs. Old in Germany
        as the Welfare State Fails. *New
        York Times*, June 4, pp. A1, A8
        (national ed.).
CRISPELL, D.
1994   Child Care Choices Don't Match
        Mom's Wishes. *American Demo-
        graphics*, July, http://www.de-
        mographics.com/publications.

DaMatta, R.
1991 *Carnivals, Rogues, and Heroes: An Interpretation of the Brazilian Dilemma.* Trans. J. Drury. Notre Dame, IN: University of Notre Dame Press.

D'Andrade, R.
1984 Cultural Meaning Systems. In *Culture Theory: Essays on Mind, Self, and Emotion,* eds. R. A. Shweder and R. A. Levine, pp. 88–119. Cambridge, England: Cambridge University Press.

Davis, D. L., and R. G. Whitten
1987 The Cross-Cultural Study of Human Sexuality. *Annual Review of Anthropology* 16: 69–98.

Davis, K., M. Leijenaar, and J. Oldersma, eds.
1991 *The Gender of Power.* Newbury Park, CA: Sage.

Deal, T. E., and K. Peterson
1999 *Shaping School Culture: The Heart of Leadership.* San Francisco: Jossey-Bass.

DeFleur, M.
1964 Occupational Roles as Portrayed on Television. *Public Opinion Quarterly* 28: 57–74.

Degler, C.
1970 *Neither Black nor White: Slavery and Race Relations in Brazil and the United States.* New York: Macmillan.

DePalma, A.
1997 Canadian Leader Keeps Majority but Loses Strength. *New York Times,* June 4, p. A3 (national ed.).

Despres, L., ed.
1975 *Ethnicity and Resource Competition.* The Hague: Mouton.

De Vos, G. A., and H. Wagatsuma
1966 *Japan's Invisible Race: Caste in Culture and Personality.* Berkeley: University of California Press.

De Vos, G. A., W. O. Wetherall, and K. Stearman
1983 *Japan's Minorities: Burakumin, Koreans, Ainu and Okinawans.*

Report no. 3. London: Minority Rights Group.

De Waal, F. B. M.
1997 *Bonobo: The Forgotten Ape.* Berkeley: University of California Press.

Diagnostic and Statistical Manual of Mental Disorders: DSM-IV.
1994 Washington, D.C.: American Psychiatric Association.

Di Leonardo, M., ed.
1990 *Toward a New Anthropology of Gender.* Berkeley: University of California Press.

Divale, W. T., and M. Harris
1976 Population, Warfare, and the Male Supremacist Complex. *American Anthropologist* 78: 521–538.

Draper, P.
1975 !Kung Women: Contrasts in Sexual Egalitarianism in Foraging and Sedentary Contexts. In *Toward an Anthropology of Women,* R. Reiter, ed., pp. 77–109. New York: Monthly Review Press.

Durkheim, É.
1961 (orig. 1912) *The Elementary Forms of the Religious Life.* New York: Collier Books.

Ebenkamp, B., and C. G. Barry
2001 Transitional Meditation. *Brandweek* 42(21): 24–27.

Eckert, P.
1989 *Jocks and Burnouts: Social Categories and Identity in the High School.* New York: Teachers College Press, Columbia University.

Economist
2002 On the Road to Heliopolis. 362(5256): 28–30.

Elder, J.
1997 Poll Finds Women Are the Health-Savvier Sex, and the Warier. *New York Times,* June 22, http://www.nytimes.com.

Elliott, S.
1997 Gay-Oriented Ads Hit Mainstream Media. *New York Times,*

June 30, http://www.nytimes.com.

EMBER, M., AND C. R. EMBER
1997   Science in Anthropology. In *The Teaching of Anthropology: Problems, Issues, Decisions*, C. P. Kottak, J. J. White, R. H. Furlow, and P. C. Rice, eds., pp. 29–33. Mountain View, CA: Mayfield.

ENGLAND, P.
1992   *Comparable Worth: Theories and Evidence*. New York: Aldine.

ENGSTROM, J. D.
2001   Industry and Immigration in Dalton, Georgia. In *Latino Workers in the Contemporary South*, eds. A. D. Murphy, C. Blanchard, and J. A. Hill, pp. 43–56. Athens: University of Georgia Press.

ERRINGTON, F., AND D. GEWERTZ
1987   *Cultural Alternatives and a Feminist Anthropology: An Analysis of Culturally Constructed Gender Interests in Papua–New Guinea*. New York: Cambridge University Press.

ESCOBAR, A.
1994   Welcome to Cyberia: Notes on the Anthropology of Cyberculture. *Current Anthropology* 35(3): 211–231.

EVANS-PRITCHARD, E. E.
1937   *Oracles and Magic among the Azande*. Oxford: Clarendon Press.
1970   (orig.1929) Witchcraft amongst the Azande. In *Witchcraft and Sorcery*, M. Marwick, ed. Baltimore: Penguin.
1970   Sexual Inversion among the Azande. *American Anthropologist* 72: 1428–1433.

FADERMAN, L.
1991   *Odd Girls and Twilight Lovers: A History of Lesbian Life in Twentieth-Century America*. New York: Columbia University Press.

FARNSWORTH, C. H.
1992   Canada to Divide Its Northern Land. *New York Times*, May 6, p. A7.

FEATHERSTONE, M., ED.
1990   *Global Culture: Globalization, Nationalism and Modernity*. Newbury Park, CA: Sage.

FEDER, B. J.
1997   Girls Light Up, while Women Struggle to Quit. *New York Times*, June 22, http://www.nytimes.com.

FIELDS, J.
2001   *Current Population Reports: America's Families and Living Arrangements, 2000*. U.S. Census Bureau. P20-537, June. http://www.census.gov.

FIRESTONE, D.
2001   U of Georgia Cannot Use Race in Admission Policy, Court Rules. *New York Times*, August 28, http://www.nytimes.com.

FISHER, D. H.
1978   *Growing Old in America*. Oxford, England: Oxford University Press.

FISHER-THOMPSON, J.
2002   http://usinfo.state.gov/regional/af/ttrade/a1021601.htm.

FISKE, J.
1989   *Understanding Popular Culture*. Boston: Unwin Hyman.

FORD, C. S., AND F. A. BEACH
1951   *Patterns of Sexual Behavior*. New York: Harper Torchbooks.

FOST, D.
1991   American Indians in the 1990s. *American Demographics* 13(12): 26–34.

FOUCAULT, M.
1978   *The History of Sexuality, Volume I: An Introduction*. Trans. R. Hurley. New York: Pantheon.
1979   *Discipline and Punish: The Birth of the Prison*. Trans. A. Sheridan. New York: Vintage Books, University Press.

FRANCESE, P.
1995   America at Mid-Decade. *American Demographics*. February, http://www.demographics.com/publications.

FRAZIER, E. F.
1957   *Black Bourgeoisie*. Glencoe, IL: Free Press.

FREEMAN, M.
1994   (revision of Castelli 1984) Twelve Rules for Mixing Religion and Politics. People for the American Way, 2000 M Street NW, Suite 400, Washington, DC, 20036, pfaw@pfaw.org.

FRIED, M.
1960   On the Evolution of Social Stratification and the State. In *Culture and History*, S. Diamond, ed., pp. 713–731. New York: Columbia University Press.

FRIEDL, E.
1975   *Women and Men: An Anthropologist's View*. New York: Holt, Rinehart and Winston.

FRIESEN, G.
2001   The Evolving Meanings of Region in Canada. *Canadian Historical Review* 82(3): 530–545.

FRY, C.
2000   Culture, Age, and Subjective Well-Being. *Journal of Family Issues* 21(6): 751–777.

FURNIVALL, J. S.
1944   *Netherlands India: A Study of Plural Economy*. New York: Macmillan.

GAL, S.
1989   Language and Political Economy. *Annual Review of Anthropology* 18: 345–367.

GARASKY, S., AND D. R. MEYER
1996   Reconsidering the Increase in Father-Only Families, *Demography* 33: 385–394.

GEERTZ, C.
1963   The Integrative Revolution: Primordial Sentiments and Civil Politics in the New States. In *Old Societies and New States: The Quest for Modernity in Asia and Africa*, C. Geertz, ed., pp. 107–113. New York: Free Press.
1973   *The Interpretation of Cultures*. New York: Basic Books.

GEIGER, J. H.
2001   Racial Stereotyping and Medicine: The Need for Cultural Competence. *Canadian Medical Association Journal*, 164(12): 1699.

GERBNER, G.
1988   *Violence and Terror in the Mass Media*. Paris: UNESCO.

GIDDENS, A.
1973   *The Class Structure of the Advanced Societies*. New York: Cambridge University Press.

GILMORE, D.
1987   *Aggression and Community: Paradoxes of Andalusian Culture*. New Haven: Yale University Press.
1990   *Manhood in the Making: Cultural Concepts of Masculinity*. New Haven: Yale University Press.

GIUFFO, J.
2001   Smoke Gets in Your Eyes. *Columbia Journalism Review* 40(3): 14–17.

GIULIANI, R. W.
2001   "We Have Met the Worst of Humanity with the Best of Humanity," September 11 Tribute Introduction. *One Nation: America Remembers September 11, 2001*. Life Books. http://www.life.com/Life/lifebooks/911/intro.html.

GLENNON, L. M., AND R. J. BUTSCH
1979   The Devaluation of Working Class Lifestyle in Television's Family Series, 1947–1977. Paper presented at the meeting of the Popular Culture Association.
1982   The Family as Portrayed on Television: 1946–1978. In *Television and Behavior: Ten Years of Scientific Progress and Implica-*

tions for the Eighties, v. 2, Technical Reviews, D. Pearl, L. Bouthilet, and J. Lazar, eds., pp. 246–271. Rockville, MD: National Institute of Mental Health.

GOLDBERG, S. T., AND E. BURT
2002   Trend Spotting. *Kiplinger's Personal Finance Magazine* 56(2): 34–39.

GOLDEN, T.
1997   Oakland Revamps Plan to Teach Black English. *New York Times*, January 14, http://www.nytimes.com.

GORDON, A. A.
1996   *Transforming Capitalism and Patriarchy: Gender and Development in Africa.* Boulder, CO: Lynne Reinner.

GRAMSCI, A.
1971   *Selections from the Prison Notebooks.* Eds. and trans. Q. Hoare and G. N. Smith. London: Wishart.

GRASMUCK, S., AND P. PESSAR
1991   *Between Two Islands: Dominican International Migration.* Berkeley: University of California Press.

GREAVES, T. C.
1995   Problems Facing Anthropologists: Cultural Rights and Ethnography. *General Anthropology* 1(2): 1, 3–6.

GREEN, J. W.
1982   *Cultural Awareness in the Human Services.* Englewood, Cliffs, NJ: Prentice Hall, Inc.

GRIFFIN, P. B., AND A. ESTIOKO-GRIFFIN, EDS.
1985   *The Agta of Northern Luzon: Recent Studies.* Cebu City, Philippines: University of San Carlos.

GUNTER, B.
1986   *Television and Sex Role Stereotyping.* London: John Libbey.

GUTNER, T.
2002   A Balancing Act for Generation X Women. *Business Week* 3766: 82.

HACKING, I.
1991   The Making and Molding of Child Abuse. *Critical Inquiry* 17(2): 253–288.

HAMER, J., AND K. MARCHIORO
2002   Becoming Custodial Dads: Exploring Parenting among Low Income and Working-Class African American Fathers. *Journal of Marriage and Family* 64: 116–129.

HANSEN, K. V., AND A. I. GAREY, EDS.
1998   *Families in the U.S.: Kinship and Domestic Politics.* Philadelphia: Temple University Press.

HARRIS, M.
1964   *Patterns of Race in the Americas.* New York: Walker.
1970   Referential Ambiguity in the Calculus of Brazilian Racial Identity. *Southwestern Journal of Anthropology* 26(1): 1–14.
1979   *Cultural Materialism: The Struggle for a Science of Culture.* New York: Random House.

HARRIS, M., AND C. P. KOTTAK
1963   The Structural Significance of Brazilian Racial Categories. *Sociologia* 25: 203–209.

HARVEY, K.
1996   Online for the Ancestors: The Importance of Anthropological Sensibility in Information Superhighway Design. *Social Science Computing Review* 14(1): 65–68.

HAY, A.
2001   What If There Were a Mass Anti-Globalization Movement? *World Link* Sep/Oct: 76–78.

HERDT, G.
1981   *Guardians of the Flutes.* New York: McGraw-Hill.
1987   *Sambia: Ritual and Gender in New Guinea.* New York: Harcourt Brace.
1997   *Same Sex Different Cultures: Exploring Gay & Lesbian Lives.* Boulder, CO: Westview Press.

HERDT, G., ED.
1984   *Ritualized Homosexuality in Melanesia.* Berkeley, CA: University of California Press.
1992   *Gay Culture in America. Essays from the Field.* Boston: Beacon Press.
HERRNSTEIN, R. J.
1971   I.Q. *The Atlantic* 228(3): 43–64.
HERRNSTEIN, R .J., AND C. MURRAY
1994   *The Bell Curve: Intelligence and Class Structure in American Life.* New York: Free Press.
HILL-BURNETT, J.
1978   Developing Anthropological Knowledge through Application. In *Applied Anthropology in America*, E. M. Eddy and W. L. Partridge, eds., pp. 112–128. New York: Columbia University Press.
HOGAN, D. P., AND D. L. FEATHERMAN
1977   Racial Stratification and Socioeconomic Change in the American North and South. *American Journal of Sociology* 83: 100–126.
HOLMES, S. A.
1997   Many Whites Leaving Suburbs for Rural Areas. *New York Times* October 19, http://www.nytimes.com.
HSIUNG, R. C.
2000   The Best of Both Worlds: An Online Self-Help Group Hosted by a Mental Health Professional. *CyberPsychology and Behavior* 3(6): 935–950.
HSU, F. L. K.
1975   American Core Values and National Character. In *The Nacirema: Readings on American Culture*, J. P. Spradley and M. A. Rynkiewich, eds., pp. 378–394. Boston: Little, Brown.
HUBBARD, L. R.
1997   *Scientology: The Fundamentals of Thought.* Los Angeles: Bridge.

HUTSON, S. R.
2000   The RAVE: Spiritual Healing in Modern Western Subcultures. *Anthropological Quarterly* 73(1): 35–49.
HYMAN, H. H.
1942   *The Psychology of Status.* New York: Columbia University, Archive of Psychology no. 269.
IANNI, F.
1977   New Mafia: Black, Hispanic and Italian Styles. In *Readings in Anthropology*, pp. 66–78. Guilford, CT: Dushkin.
IVY, M.
1995   Have You Seen Me? Recovering the Inner Child in Late Twentieth-Century America. In *Children and the Politics of Culture*, S. K. Stephens, ed., pp. 79–104. Princeton, NJ: Princeton University Press.
JACOBY, R., AND N. GLAUBERMAN, EDS.
1995   *The Bell Curve Debate: History, Documents, Opinions.* New York: Times Books.
JAMESON, F.
1984   Postmodernism, or the Cultural Logic of Late Capitalism. *New Left Review* 146: 53–93.
1988   *The Ideologies of Theory: Essays 1971–1986.* Minneapolis: University of Minnesota Press.
JENSEN, A.
1969   How Much Can We Boost I.Q. and Scholastic Achievement? *Harvard Educational Review* 29: 1–123.
JOHNSON, D.
2000   Disentangling Poverty and Race. *Applied Developmental Science* 4(1) 55–67.
JOHNSTON, W. B.
1994   Global Work Force 2000: The New World Labor Market. In *Differences That Work: Organizational Excellence through Diversity*, M. C. Gentile, ed., pp. 3–26. Boston: Harvard Business School Publishing Corporation.

JOSEPHY, A. M., JR.
1982   *Now that the Buffalo's Gone: A Study of Today's American Indians.* New York: Alfred A. Knopf.

KANTOR, P.
1996   Domestic Violence against Women: A Global Issue. http://metalab.unc.edu/ucis/pubs/Carolina_Papers/Abuse/figure1.html.

KAPLAN, R. D.
1994   The Coming Anarchy: How Scarcity, Crime, Overpopulation, and Disease Are Rapidly Destroying the Social Fabric of Our Planet. *Atlantic Monthly* February: 44–76.

KELLY, R. C.
1976   Witchcraft and Sexual Relations: An Exploration in the Social and Semantic Implications of the Structure of Belief. In *Man and Woman in the New Guinea Highlands,* P. Brown and G. Buchbinder, eds., pp. 36–53. Special publication, no. 8. Washington, DC: American Anthropological Association.

KENT, S.
1992   The Current Forager Controversy: Real versus Ideal Views of Hunter-Gatherers. *Man* 27: 45–70.

KILMARTIN, C. T.
2000   *The Masculine Self.* New York: McGraw-Hill.

KIMMEL, M. S. AND M. KAUFMAN
1993   The New Men's Movement: Retreat and Regression with America's Weekend Warriors. *Feminist Issues* 13(2): 3–16.

KIMMEL, M. S., AND M. A. MESSNER, EDS.
1995   *Men's Lives,* 3rd ed. Needham Heights, MA: Allyn and Bacon.

KING, A. D., ED.
1991   *Culture, Globalization, and the World-System: Contemporary Conditions for the Representation of Identity.* Binghamton, NY: State University of New York.

KINSEY, A. C., W. B. POMEROY, AND C. E. MARTIN
1948   *Sexual Behavior in the Human Male.* Philadelphia: W. B. Saunders.

KINSEY, A. C., W. B. POMEROY, P. H. GEBHARD, AND C. E. MARTIN.
1953   *Sexual Behavior in the Human Female.* Philadelphia: Saunders.

KIRK, S. A., AND H. KUTCHINS
1998   *Making Us Crazy: DSM—the Psychiatric Bible and the Creation of Mental Disorders.* New York: Free Press.

KLEIN, M.
1997   Disabled and Working—Kaleidoscope. *American Demographics,* May, http://www.demographics.com/publications.

KLEINFELD, J.
1975   Positive Stereotyping: The Cultural Relativist in the Classroom. *Human Organization* 34: 269–274.

KLINEBERG, O.
1951   Race and Psychology. *In The Race Question in Modern Science.* Paris: UNESCO.

KLING, R.
1996   Synergies and Competition between Life in Cyberspace and Face-to-Face Communities. *Social Science Computing Review* 14(1): 50–54.

KLUCKHOHN, C.
1944   *Mirror for Man: A Survey of Human Behavior and Social Attitudes.* Greenwich, CT: Fawcett.

KODRZYCKI, Y. K.
2001   Migration of Recent College Graduates: Evidence from the National Longitudinal Survey of Youth. *New England Economic Review* (January–February): 13–34.

KOTTAK, C. P.
1980   *The Past in the Present: History, Ecology, and Social Organization in Highland Madagascar.*

Ann Arbor: University of Michigan Press.

1990a   Culture and "Economic Development." *American Anthropologist* 93(3): 723–731.

1990b   *Prime-Time Society: An Anthropological Analysis of Television and Culture.* Belmont, CA: Wadsworth.

1992   *Assault on Paradise: Social Change in a Brazilian Village,* 2nd ed. New York: McGraw-Hill.

1997   *Anthropology: The Exploration of Human Diversity,* 7th ed. New York: McGraw-Hill.

1999   *Assault on Paradise: Social Change in a Brazilian Village,* 3rd ed. New York: McGraw-Hill.

KOTTAK, C. P., ED.

1982   *Researching American Culture: A Guide for Student Anthropologists.* Ann Arbor: University of Michigan Press.

KOZAITIS, K. A.

1987   Being Old and Greek in America. In *Ethnic Dimensions of Aging,* D. E. Gelfand and C. M. Barresi, eds., pp. 179–185. New York: Springer Publishing Company.

1993   Conscious Adaptation: Change in Perpetuity among the Roma of Athens, Greece. Ph.D. Dissertation, University of Michigan.

1997   Foreigners among Foreigners: Social Organization among the Roma of Athens, Greece. *Urban Anthropology and Studies of Cultural Systems and World Economic Development* 26(2): 165–199.

2000   Anthropological Influence on Urban Educational Reform. *Practicing Anthropology* 22(4): 37–44.

KREILKAMP A., ED.

1994   *Crone Chronicles: A Journal of Conscious Aging.* Summer Solstice, Autumn Equinox.

KRETCHMER, N.

1975   (orig. 1972) Lactose and Lactase. In *Biological Anthropology, Readings from Scientific American,* S. H. Katz, ed., pp. 310–318. San Francisco: W. H. Freeman.

LABOV, W.

1972a   *Language in the Inner City: Studies in the Black English Vernacular.* Philadelphia: University of Pennsylvania Press.

1972b   *Sociolinguistic Patterns.* Philadelphia: University of Pennsylvania Press.

LAGUERRE, M.

1984   *American Odyssey: Haitians in New York.* Ithaca, NY: Cornell University Press.

LAKOFF, R.

1975   *Language and Woman's Place.* New York: Harper and Row.

LANDRY, B.

1987   *The New Black Middle Class.* Berkeley: University of California Press.

LASSITER, L. E.

1998   *The Power of Kiowa Song: A Collaborative Ethnography.* Tucson: University of Arizona Press.

LAU, D.

2002   Generation Y Looks to Net for Health Information. *Library Journal* 127(1): 4–6.

LEMERT, C., ED.

1993   *Social Theory: The Multicultural and Classic Readings.* Boulder, CO: Westview Press.

LENSKI, G.

1966   *Power and Privilege: A Theory of Social Stratification.* New York: McGraw-Hill.

LENSKI, G., J. LENSKI, AND P. NOLAN

1991   *Human Society: An Introduction to Macrosociology,* 6th ed. New York: McGraw-Hill.

LEWIS, D., AND K. BEHANA
2001   The Internet as a Resource for Consumer Healthcare. *Disease Management and Health Outcomes* 9(5): 241–247.

LICHTER, D. R.
1989   Race, Employment Hardship, and Inequality in the American Nonmetropolitan South. *American Sociological Review* 54(3): 436–446.

LIGHT, D., S. KELLER, AND C. CALHOUN
1994   *Sociology,* 6th ed. New York: McGraw-Hill.
1997   *Sociology,* 7th ed. New York: McGraw-Hill.

LINDENBAUM, S.
1972   Sorcerers, Ghosts, and Polluting Women: An Analysis of Religious Belief and Population Control. *Ethnology* 11: 241–253.

LINTON, R.
1943   Nativistic Movements. *American Anthropologist* 45: 230–240.

LOGAN, J., R. ALBA, T. MCNULTY, AND B. FISHER
1996   Making a Place in the Metropolis: Residential Assimilation and Segregation in City and Suburb. *Demography* 33: 443–453.

LONG, J. D.
1998   North America: Decline and Fall of World Religions, 1990–2025. http://www.gem-werc.org/mmrc/mmrc9805.htm.

LOOMIS, W. F.
1967   Skin-Pigmented Regulation of Vitamin-D Biosynthesis in Man. *Science* 157: 501–506.

LOSEE, J.
1997   Older Women in the United States in the 1990s: The Emergence of the Crone. Honors thesis, Department of Anthropology, University of Maryland, College Park, Maryland.

LUGAILA, T.
1999   Married Adults Still in the Majority, Census Bureau Reports. http://www.census.gov/Press-Release/www/1999/cb99-03.html.

MCKINLEY, J.
1996   Board's Decision on Black English Stirs Debate. *New York Times,* December 21, http://www.nytimes.com.

MCNEIL, J.
2001   Americans with Disabilities, Household Economic Studies, 1997. *Current Population Reports.* Washington, DC: U.S. Census Bureau, P70–73. http://www.census.gov.

MAINE, H. S.
1963   (orig. 1861) *Ancient Law,* 10th ed. Boston: Beacon.

MANSNERUS, L.
1997   More Research, More Profits, More Conflict. *New York Times,* June 22, http://www.nytimes.com.

MAR, M. E.
1997   Secondary Colors: The Multiracial Option. *Harvard Magazine,* May–June: 19–20.

MARCH, K.
1995   Perception of Adoption as Social Stigma: Motivation for Search and Reunion. *Journal of Marriage and Family* 57: 653–660.

MARCINIAK, E.
2001   Racism Isn't What It Used to Be. *Commonweal* 128(11): 12–14.

MARCUS, G. E., AND M. M. J. FISCHER
1986   *Anthropology as Cultural Critique: An Experimental Moment in the Human Sciences.* Chicago: University of Chicago Press.

MARCUS, R., AND K. E. JOHN
1986   In the Voice of Public Opinion, Lawyers Rank Low. *Washington Post National Weekly Edition,* September 1, p. 14.

MARGOLIS, M.
1984   *Mothers and Such: American Views of Women and How They Changed.* Berkeley: University of California Press.

1994   *Little Brazil: An Ethnography of Brazilian Immigrants in New York City.* Princeton: Princeton University Press.

2000   *True to Her Nature: Changing Advice to American Women.* Prospect Heights, IL: Waveland.

MARTIN, K., AND B. VOORHIES
1975   *Female of the Species.* New York: Columbia University Press.

MARTIN, P., AND E. MIDGLEY
1994   Immigration to the United States: Journey to an Uncertain Destination. *Population Bulletin* 49(3): 1–47.

MARX, K., AND F. ENGELS
1976   (orig. 1848) *Communist Manifesto.* New York: Pantheon.

MASSEY, D. S., AND G. LUNDY
2001   Use of Black English and Racial Discrimination in Urban Housing Markets: New Methods and Findings. *Urban Affairs Review* 36(4): 452–469.

MEAD, M.
1950   (orig. 1935) *Sex and Temperament in Three Primitive Societies.* New York: New American Library.

1961   (orig. 1928) *Coming of Age in Samoa.* New York: Morrow Quill.

MELYMUKA, K.
2001   The Growing Gay Workforce. *Computerworld* 35(30): 34–36.

MERGENHAGEN, P.
1997   Enabling Disabled Workers. *American Demographics*, July, http://www.demographics.com/publications.

MERGENHAGEN, P., AND D. CRISPELL
1997   Who's Disabled?—Sidebar to Enabling Disabled Workers. *American Demographics*, July, http://www.demographics.com/publications.

MICHAEL, T. R., J. H. GAGNON, E. O. LAUMANN, AND G. B. KOLATA
1994   *Sex in America: A Definitive Survey.* Boston: Little, Brown.

MICHAELS, E.
1986   Aboriginal Content. Paper presented at the meeting of the Australian Screen Studies Association, Sydney, December.

MIDDLETON, J.
1967   Introduction. In *Myth and Cosmos: Readings in Mythology and Symbolism*, J. Middleton, ed., pp. ix–xi. Garden City, NY: Natural History Press.

MICROSOFT ENCARTA ENCYCLOPEDIA
2002   Articles on Hajj and Mecca. http://encarta.msn.com/find/Concise.asp?z=1&pg=2&ti=76157917&cid=16#p16. http://encarta.msn.com/find/concise.asp?z=1&pg=2&ti=761577367.

MIGRATION NEWS
2000   Elections 2000. 7(12, December). http://migration.ucdavis.edu/mn/archive_mn/dec_2000-01mn.html.

MILLARD, R. W., AND P. A. FINTAK
2002   Use of the Internet by Patients with Chronic Illness. *Disease Management and Health Outcomes* 10(3): 187–194.

MILLER, B. D.
1997   *The Endangered Sex: Neglect of Female Children in Rural North India.* New York: Oxford University Press.

MILLER, B. D., ED.
1993   *Sex and Gender Hierarchies.* New York: Cambridge University Press.

MILLER, R.
2000   Does Anybody Love the IMF or World Bank? *Business Week* 3678: 46–48.

MOERMAN, M.
1965   Ethnic Identification in a Complex Civilization: Who Are the Lue? *American Anthropologist* 67(5, Part I): 1215–1230.

MOHR, R. D.
1988   *Gays/Justice: A Study of Ethics, Society, and Law.* New York: Columbia University Press.

MONROE, P. A., AND V. V. TILLER
2001   Commitment to Work among Welfare-Reliant Women. *Journal of Marriage and Family* 63: 816–828.

MONTAGU, A.
1962   The Concept of Race. *American Anthropologist* 64:919–928.
1963   *Race, Science, and Humanity.* New York: Van Nostrand.
1964   *Man's Most Dangerous Myth: The Fallacy of Race.* New York: Meridian Books.

MONTAGUE, S., AND R. MORAIS
1981   Football Games and Rock Concerts: The Ritual Enactment. In *The American Dimension: Cultural Myths and Social Realities,* 2nd ed., W. Arens and S. B. Montague, eds., pp. 33–52. Sherman Oaks, CA: Alfred.

MORGEN, S., ED.
1989   *Gender and Anthropology: Critical Reviews for Research and Teaching.* Washington, DC: American Anthropological Association.

MUKHOPADHYAY, C., AND P. HIGGINS
1988   Anthropological Studies of Women's Status Revisited: 1977–1987. *Annual Review of Anthropology* 17: 461–495.

MURPHY, R. F.
1990   *The Body Silent.* New York: W. W. Norton.

MURRAY, S. O., AND W. ROSCOE, EDS.
1998   *Boy-Wives and Female Husbands: Studies in African Homosexualities.* New York: St. Martin's.

MYDANS, S.
1992a   Criticism Grows over Aliens Seized during Riots. *New York Times,* May 29, p. A8.
1992b   Judge Dismisses Case in Shooting by Officer. *New York Times,* June 4, p. A8.

NANDA, S.
1990   *Neither Man nor Woman: The Hijras of India.* Belmont, CA: Wadsworth.

NASAR, S.
1992a   Federal Report Gives New Data on Gains by Richest in 80s; Concentration of Assets; Top 1% Had Greater Net Worth than Bottom 90% of U.S. Households by 1989. *New York Times,* April 21, p. A1.
1992b   However You Slice the Data, the Richest Did Get Richer. *New York Times,* May 11, p. C1.

NASH, J., AND H. SAFA, EDS.
1986   *Women and Change in Latin America.* South Hadley, MA: Bergin and Garvey.

NASH, M.
1989   *The Cauldron of Ethnicity in the Modern World.* Chicago: University of Chicago Press.

NATIONAL ASSOCIATION OF SOCIAL WORKERS (NASW) NEWS
1985   Editorial Note. October, p. 4.

NATIONAL COMMISSION ON WORKING WOMEN
1984   Study Shows Increase in Women, and Their Authority, on TV. Report of the National Commission on Working Women. *Ann Arbor News,* December 23, p. F10.

NEUBORNE, E., AND K. KERWIN
1999   Generation Y: Today's Teens— the Biggest Bulge since the Boomers—May Force Marketers to Toss Their Old Tricks. *Business Week.* http://www.business week.com/1999/99_07/b3616001 .htm.

NEVID, J. S., AND S. A. RATHUS
1995   *Human Sexuality in a World of Diversity,* 2d ed. Needham Heights, MA: Allyn and Bacon.

New York Times
1989   More Retirees on the Job, September 7, p. 20.
1992   Alexandria Journal: TV Program for Somalis is a Rare Unifying Force. December 18, 1992, http://www.nytimes.com/archives.

1997   Special section, *Women's Health,*
        June 22. http://www.nytimes.
        com.
2001   Friday, September 14. http:/
        www.nytimes.com2001/09/14/
        national/141SLA.html?ex=1001
        491750&ei=1&en=6e114f39f.
NEWMAN, M.
1992   Riots Bring Attention to Grow-
        ing Hispanic Presence in South-
        Central Area. *New York Times,*
        May 11, p. A10.
NEWMAN, K.
1988   *Falling from Grace: The Experi-
        ence of Downward Mobility in
        the American Middle Class.* New
        York: Free Press.
NEWTON, E.
2000   *Margaret Mead Made Me Gay.*
        Durham, NC: Duke University.
NIELSSON, G. P.
1985   States and Nation-Groups: A
        Global Taxonomy. In *New Na-
        tionalisms of the Developed
        World,* E. A. Tiryakian and R.
        Rogowski, eds., pp. 27–56.
        Boston: Allen and Unwin.
NUSSBAUM, M., AND J. GLOVER, EDS.
1995   *Women, Culture, and Develop-
        ment: A Study of Human Capa-
        bilities.* New York: Oxford
        University Press.
OJITO, M.
1997   Connecticut Puerto Ricans Find
        Pride and a Voice. *New York
        Times,* June 18, http//www.ny
        times.com.
ONG, A.
1989   Center, Periphery, and Hierar-
        chy: Gender in Southeast Asia.
        In *Gender and Anthropology:
        Critical Reviews for Research
        and Teaching,* S. Morgen, ed.,
        pp. 294–312. Washington,
        DC: American Anthropological
        Association.
ONTARIO CONSULTANTS ON RELIGIOUS
TOLERANCE
1996   Religious Access Dispute Re-
        solved. Internet Mailing List,

        April 12, http://www.religious-
        tolerance.org/news_694.htm.
1997   Swiss Cult Promotes Cloning.
        http://www.religious-tolerance.
        org/news_697.htm.
2002   Religions of the World: Num-
        bers of Adherents; Rates of
        Growth. http://www.religious-
        tolerance.org/worldrel.htm.
PARRENAS. R. S.
2001   *Signs. Journal of Women in
        Culture and Society* 26(4):
        1128–1154.
PATTERSON, C. J.
1992   Children of Lesbian and Gay
        Parents. *Child Development* 63:
        1025–1042.
PEAR, R.
1997   Report Says Immigration Is
        Beneficial to the U.S. *New York
        Times,* May 18, http://www.
        nytimes.com.
PEEBLES, S.
1985   Preschool: A Headstart toward
        Academic Success? *Ann Arbor
        News,* May 5, p. H4.
PELETZ, M.
1988   *A Share of the Harvest: Kinship,
        Property, and Social History
        among the Malays of Rembau.*
        Berkeley: University of Califor-
        nia Press.
PEPLAU, L. A., ED.
1999   *Gender, Culture, and Ethnicity:
        Current Research about Women
        and Men.* Mountain View, CA:
        Mayfield.
PEREZ-PENA, R.
1997   Study Shows New York Has
        Greatest Income Gap. *New York
        Times,* December 17, p. A14 (na-
        tional ed.).
PETERSON, P. G.
1999   *Gray Dawn: How the Coming
        Age Wave Will Transform Amer-
        ica—and the World.* New York:
        Times Books/Random House.
POSTMAN, N.
1982   *The Disappearance of Childhood.*
        New York: Delacorte.

PRICE, R., ED.
1973 *Maroon Societies*. New York: Anchor Press/Doubleday.

PSYCHOLOGY TODAY
1985 Abstract of report presented to the 1984 annual meeting of the American Sociological Association by D. P. Mueller and A. H. Wilder. February, p. 15.

RAPPAPORT, R. A.
1974 Obvious Aspects of Ritual. *Cambridge Anthropology* 2: 2–60.

RATHUS, S. A., J. S. NEVID, AND J. FICHNER-RATHUS
2000 *Human Sexuality in a World of Diversity*, 4th ed. Boston: Allyn and Bacon.

REDFIELD, R.
1941 *The Folk Culture of Yucatan*. Chicago: University of Chicago Press.

REDFIELD, R., R. LINTON, AND M. HERSKOVITS
1936 Memorandum on the Study of Acculturation. *American Anthropologist* 38: 149–152.

RICKFORD, J. R.
1997 Suite for Ebony and Phonics. http:www.stanford.edu/~rickford/papers/SuiteFor EbonyAndPhonics.html. (Also published in *Discover* magazine, December 1997.)
1999 *African American Vernacular English: Features, Evolution, Educational Implications*. Malden, MA: Blackwell.

RICKFORD, J. R., AND R. J. RICKFORD
2000 *Spoken Soul: The Story of Black English*. New York: Wiley.

RICOEUR, P.
1971 The Model of the Text: Meaningful Action Considered as a Text. *Social Research* 38: 529–562.

ROBERTSON, J.
1992 Koreans in Japan. Paper presented at the University of Michigan Department of Anthropology, Martin Luther King Jr. Day Panel, January. Ann Arbor: University of Michigan Department of Anthropology (unpublished).

RODGERS, J. R., AND J. L. RODGERS
2000 The Effects of Geographic Mobility on Male Labor-Force Participants in the United States. *Journal of Labor Research* 21(1): 117–132.

ROGERS, E. M.
1995 (orig. 1962) *Diffusion of Innovations*. New York: Free Press.

ROSALDO, M. Z.
1980a *Knowledge and Passion: Notions of Self and Social Life*. Stanford, CA: Stanford University Press.
1980b The Use and Abuse of Anthropology: Reflections on Feminism and Cross-Cultural Understanding. *Signs* 5(3): 389–417.

ROSE, S.
1997 We're All Going Hollywood. *Money* 26(10): 107.

ROUSE, R.
1991 Mexican Migration and the Social Space of Postmodernism. *Diaspora* 1(1): 8–23.

RUSHTON, J. P.
1995 *Race, Evolution and Behavior*. New Brunswick, NJ: Transaction Books.

RUSSELL, J. W.
1994 *After the Fifth Sun: Class and Race in North America*. Upper Saddle River, NJ: Prentice-Hall.

RYAN, S.
1990 *Ethnic Conflict and International Relations*. Brookfield, MA: Dartmouth.
1995 *Ethnic Conflict and International Relations*, 2nd ed. Brookfield, MA: Dartmouth.

SACHS, C. E.
1996 *Gendered Fields: Rural Women, Agriculture, and Environment*. Boulder, CO: Westview.

SALUTER, A.
1995 Household and Family Characteristics: March 1994. P20-483,

press release, October 16. Single-Parent Growth Rate Stabilized; 2-Parent Family Growth Renewed, Census Bureau Reports. U.S. Department of Commerce, Bureau of Census, Public Information Office, CB95-186.

1996 Marital Status and Living Arrangements: March 1994. P20-484, press release, March 13. U.S. Department of Commerce, Bureau of Census, Public Information Office, CB96-33. http://www.census.gov/prod/www/titles.html#popspec.

SANDAY, P. R.
1974 Female Status in the Public Domain. In *Woman, Culture, and Society,* M. Z. Rosaldo and L. Lamphere, eds., pp. 189–206. Stanford, CA: Stanford University Press.

SANDOR, G.
1994 College Pays Off, but Who's Going to Pay for It? *American Demographics,* February, http://www.demographics.com/publications.

SCHIEFFELIN, E.
1976 *The Sorrow of the Lonely and the Burning of the Dancers.* New York: St. Martin's.

SCOTT, J. C.
1985 *Weapons of the Weak.* New Haven: Yale University Press.
1990 *Domination and the Arts of Resistance.* New Haven: Yale University Press.

SENNETT, R., AND J. COBB
1993 (orig. 1972) *The Hidden Injuries of Class.* New York: Norton.

SHANKLIN, E.
1995 *Anthropology and Race.* Belmont, CA: Wadsworth.

SHANNON, T. R.
1989 *An Introduction to the World System Perspective.* Boulder, CO: Westview.

SHAPIRO, J. P.
1993 *No Pity: People with Disabilities Forging a New Civil Rights Movement.* New York: Times Books.

SHARKEY, J.
1997 You're Not Bad, You're Sick. It's in the Book. *New York Times,* September 28, sect. 4, pp. 1, 5.

SILVERSTEIN, L. B.
2000 Fathering Is a Feminist Issue. *Psychology of Women Quarterly* 20(1): 3–37.

SIMPLICIO, J. S. C.
2001 A Lesson on Racial Differences. *Journal of Instructional Psychology* 28(2): 108–110.

SIMPSON, B.
1998 *Changing Families: An Ethnographic Approach to Divorce and Separation.* New York: Berg.

SMITH, M. G.
1965 *The Plural Society in the British West Indies.* Berkeley: University of California Press.

SMITHERMAN, G.
1986 *Talkin and Testyfyin: The Language of Black America.* Detroit: Wayne State University Press.

SNOWDEN, F. M., JR.
1970 *Blacks in Antiquity: Ethiopians in the Greco-Roman Experience.* Cambridge, MA: Belknap Press of Harvard University Press.
1983 *Before Color Prejudice: The Ancient View of Blacks.* Cambridge, MA: Harvard University Press.
1992 Whither Afrocentrism? *Georgetown* 24(1): 7–8.
1995 Europe's Oldest Chapter in the History of Black White Relations. In *Racism and Anti-Racism in World Perspective,* B. P. Bowser, ed., pp. 3–26. Thousand Oaks, CA: Sage.

SOLWAY, J., AND R. LEE
1990   Foragers, Genuine and Spurious: Situating the Kalahari San in History (with CA treatment). *Current Anthropology* 31(2): 109–146.

STACK, C. B.
1975   *All Our Kin: Strategies for Survival in a Black Community.* New York: Harper Torchbooks.

STATISTICAL ABSTRACT OF THE UNITED STATES
1991   111th ed. Washington: U.S. Bureau of the Census, U.S. Government Printing Office.
1996   116th ed. Washington: U.S. Bureau of the Census, U.S. Government Printing Office.
1999   119th ed. Washington: U.S. Bureau of the Census, U.S. Government Printing Office.
2000   120th ed. Washington: U.S. Bureau of the Census, U.S. Government Printing Office.
2001   121st ed. Washington: U.S. Bureau of the Census, U.S. Government Printing Office.

STATISTICS CANADA
1991   Catalogue no. 91-213, http//www.StatCan.CA/english/Pgdb/People/Famili.htm#fam.
2001   1996 Census. Nation Tables. http://www.StatCan.Ca/english/census96/nation.htm.

STAUB, S.
1989   *Yemenis in New York City: The Folklore of Ethnicity.* Philadelphia: Balch Institute Press.

STEELE, C. M.
1997   A Threat in the Air: How Stereotypes Shape Intellectual Identity and Performance. *American Psychologist*, June, pp. 613–629.

STEINFELS, P.
1997   Beliefs: Cloning, as Seen by Buddhists and Humanists. *New York Times*, July 12, http://www.nytimes.com.

STEINHAUER, J.
1997   Hispanic Dollars Flow as Stores Redo Merchandise Mix. *New York Times*, July 2, http://www.nytimes.com.

STEPHENS, S. K., ED.
1995   *Children and the Politics of Culture.* Princeton, NJ: Princeton University Press.

STEVENS, W. K.
1992   Humanity Confronts Its Handiwork: An Altered Planet. *New York Times*, May 5, pp. B5–B7.

STILLION, J. M., AND E. E. MCDOWELL
1996   *Suicide across the Life Span.* Washington, DC: Taylor and Francis.

STOLER, A.
1977   Class Structure and Female Autonomy in Rural Java. *Signs* 3: 74–89.

STRATHERN, M.
1988   *The Gender of the Gift: Problems with Women and Problems with Society in Melanesia.* Berkeley: University of California Press.

SWEENEY, G.
2001   The Trashing of White Trash: *Natural Born Killers* and the Appropriation of the White Aesthetic. *Quarterly Review of Film and Video* 18(2): 143–155.

SWIFT, M.
1963   Men and Women in Malay Society. In *Women in the New Asia,* B. Ward, ed., pp. 268–286. Paris: UNESCO.

TAKAKI, R.
1993   *A Different Mirror: A History of Multicultural America.* Boston: Little, Brown.

TANNEN, D.
1990   *You Just Don't Understand: Women and Men in Conversation.* New York: Ballantine.

TANNEN, D., ED.
1993   *Gender and Conversational Interaction.* New York: Oxford University Press.

TANNER, N.
1974   Matrifocality in Indonesia and Africa and among Black Americans. In *Women, Culture, and Society*, M. Z. Rosaldo and L. Lamphere, eds., pp. 129–156. Stanford, CA: Stanford University Press.

TIME
1985   New Look at the Elderly: A White House Report Seeks to Dispel Some Myths. February 18, p. 81.

TONER, R.
1992   Los Angeles Riots Are a Warning, Americans Fear. *New York Times*, May 11, pp. A1, A11.

TREPAGNIER, B.
2001   Deconstructing Categories: The Exposure of Silent Racism. *Symbolic Interaction* 24(2) 141–164.

TRUDGILL, P.
1983   (orig. 1974) *Sociolinguistics: An Introduction to Language and Society*. New York: Penguin.

TURNER, T.
1993   Anthropology and Multiculturalism: What Is Anthropology that Multiculturalists Should Be Mindful of It? *Cultural Anthropology* 8(4): 411–429.

TURNER, V. W.
1974   (orig. 1969) *The Ritual Process. Structure and Anti-Structure*. Harmondsworth, England: Penguin.
1995   (orig. 1969). *The Ritual Process: Structure and Anti-Structure*. New York: Aldine de Gruyter.

TYLOR, E. B.
1958   (orig. 1871) *Primitive Culture*. New York: Harper Torchbooks.

U.S. BUREAU OF THE CENSUS
1995   http://www.census.gov/hhes/poverty/pov95/povest1.html.
1996a   Education Attainment in the United States: March 1995. Current Population Reports, Series P-20, No. 489. Washington, DC: U.S. Government Printing Office.
1996b   Income Summary Measures for Families in the United States: 1947-1995. Suitland, MD: Census Bureau.
1996c   Census Bureau Releases 1995 Tabulations on the Marital Status and Living Arrangements of Americans, December 4, 1996, CB96-200, http://www.census.gov/prod/www/titles.html/popspec.
1997   Census Brief: Disabilities Affect One-Fifth of All Americans, Proportion Could Increase in Coming Decades. http://www.census.gov/prod/3/97pubs/cenbr975.pdf.
1998   http://www.census.gov/hhes/www/disable.html.
2000a   Money Income in the United States: 2000. http://www.census.gov.
2000b   Current Population Survey, March, p. 6, Figure 2.
2001   Nation's Household Income Stable in 2000, Poverty Rate Virtually Equals Record Low, Census Bureau Reports. http://www.census.gov/Press-Release/www/2001/cb01-158.html.
2002a   Why People Move: Exploring the March 2000 Current Population Survey. http://www.census.gov/prod/2001pubs/p23-204.pdf
2002b   The Population Profile of the United States: 2000. Internet release. http://www.census.gov/population/www/pop-profile/profile2000.html.

VAN BAAL, J.
1966   *Dema, Description and Analysis of Marindanim Culture (South New Guinea)*. The Hague: M. Nijhoff.

VILLANUEVA, A. B.
2000   Review Essay: Population Aging and Retirement Issues

in the Next Millennium. *Social Science Journal* 37(2): 321–325.

WAGLEY, C. W.

1963   *An Introduction to Brazil.* New York: Columbia University Press.

1968   (orig. 1959) The Concept of Social Race in the Americas. In *The Latin American Tradition*, C. Wagley, ed., pp. 155–174. New York: Columbia University Press.

WALLACE, A. F. C.

1956   Revitalization Movements. *American Anthropologist* 58: 264–281.

1966   *Religion: An Anthropological View.* New York: McGraw-Hill.

WARD, M. C.

1996   *A World Full of Women.* Needham Heights, MA: Allyn and Bacon.

WARNER, W. L.

1963   *Yankee City*, abridged ed. New Haven: Yale University Press.

WARNER, W. L., AND P. S. LUNT

1941   *The Social Life of a Modern Community.* New Haven: Yale University Press.

WATSON, P.

1972   Can Racial Discrimination Affect IQ? In *Race and Intelligence: The Fallacies behind the Race-IQ Controversy*, K. Richardson and D. Spears, eds., pp. 56–67. Baltimore: Penguin.

WEBER, M.

1958   (orig. 1920) *The Protestant Ethic and the Spirit of Capitalism.* New York: Scribner's.

1968   (orig. 1922) *Economy and Society*, trans. E. Fischoff et al. New York: Bedminster Press.

WEBSTER'S NEW WORLD ENCYCLOPEDIA

1993   College ed. New York: Prentice Hall.

WEEKS, J.

1991   Sexual Identification Is a Strange Thing. In *Social Theory: The Multicultural and Classic Readings*, C. Lemert, ed., pp. 633–637. Boulder, CO: Westview Press.

WEGAR, K.

2000   Adoption, Family Ideology, and Social Stigma: Bias in Community Attitudes, Adoption Research, and Practice. *Family Relations* 49: 363–370.

WEINBERG, D. H.

1996   Press briefing on 1995 Income, Poverty, and Health Insurance Estimates Housing and Household Economic Statistics Division, U.S. Bureau of the Census, September 26.

WEST, C.

1993   *Race Matters.* Boston: Beacon Press.

WESTERHOF, G., M. W. KATZKO, F. DITTMANN-KOHLI, AND B. HAYSLIP

2000   Life Contexts and Health-Related Selves in Old Age. *Journal of Aging Studies* 15(2): 105–127.

WESTON, K.

1991   *Families We Choose: Lesbians, Gays, Kinship.* New York: Columbia University Press.

WHITE, L. A.

1949/   *The Science of Culture.* New
1969   York: Farrar, Strauss.

1959   *The Evolution of Culture: The Development of Civilization to the Fall of Rome.* New York: McGraw-Hill.

WILLIAMS, B.

1989   A Class Act: Anthropology and the Race to Nation across Ethnic Terrain. *Annual Review of Anthropology* 18: 401–444.

WILLIAMS, J.

1985   What They Say, Home? English Dialects Are Adding to Racial Misunderstandings. *Washington Post National Weekly Edition*, May 6, p. 10.

WILLIAMS, W., AND S. CECI
1997   Are Americans Becoming More or Less Alike? *American Psychologist*, November, pp. 1226–1235.

WILMSEN, E. N.
1989   *Land Filled with Flies: A Political Economy of the Kalahari*. Chicago: University of Chicago Press.

WILMSEN, E. N., AND P. MCALLISTER, EDS.
1996   *The Politics of Difference: Ethnic Premises in a World of Power*. Chicago: University of Chicago Press.

WILSON, W. J.
1984   The Black Underclass. *The Wilson Quarterly* 8: 88–99.

WINTER, R.
2001   Jesus Christ Known to 11% of World's Population. *Religion Today*, January 25. http://news.crosswalk.com/religion/item.

WOLF, E. R.
1982   *Europe and the People without History*. Berkeley: University of California Press.

WORLD ALMANAC AND BOOK OF FACTS
1985   New York: Newspaper Enterprise Association.
1992   New York: Newspaper Enterprise Association.

YETMAN, N.
1991   *Majority and Minority: The Dynamics of Race and Ethnicity in American Life*, 5th ed. Boston: Allyn and Bacon.
1997a   Swiss Cult Promotes Cloning. News Services, June 9, http://www.religious-tolerance.org.
1997b   Southern Baptist Convention vs. Disney Co. News Services, CNN News, June 16 and 18, http://www.religious-tolerance.org.
1997c   Disney Wars. News Services, July 11, http://www.religious-tolerance.org.

ZREBIEC, J. F. AND A. M. JACOBSON
2001   What Attracts Patients with Diabetes to an Internet Support Group? A 21-Month Longitudinal Website Study. *Diabetic Medicine* 18: 154–158.

Photo Credits

Index